Blue Pelican Java

by Charles E. Cook

Version 3.0.5c

"Blue Pelican Java," by Charles E. Cook. ISBN 1-58939-758-4.

Published 2005 by Virtualbookworm.com Publishing Inc., P.O. Box 9949, College Station, Tx 77842, US.

Manufactured in the United States of America.

Preface

You will find this book to be somewhat unusual. Most computer science texts will begin with a section on the history of computers and then with a flurry of definitions that are just "so many words" to the average student. My approach with Blue Pelican Java is to first give the student some experience upon which to hang the definitions that come later, and consequently, make them more meaningful.

This book does have a history section in Appendix S and plenty of definitions later when the student is ready for them. If you will look at Lesson 1, you will see that we go right to work and write a program the very first day. The student will not understand several things about that first program, yet he can immediately make the computer do something useful. This work ethic is typical of the remainder of the book. Rest assured, that full understanding comes in time. Abraham Lincoln himself subscribed to this philosophy when he said, "Stop petting the mule, and load the wagon."

The usual practice in most Java textbooks of introducing classes and objects alongside the fundamental concepts of primitive variable types, loops, decision structures, etc. is deferred until the student has a firm grasp of the fundamentals. Thus, the student is not overwhelmed by **simultaneous** introduction of OOPs (Object Oriented Programming) and the fundamentals. Once introduced, (Lesson 15), OOPs is heavily emphasized for the remainder of the book.

I fully realize that there are those who disagree with this idea of deferring the introduction of OOPs, and from their own point of view, they are right. In most cases they teach only the very highest achieving, mature students. In those cases, I agree that it is acceptable to begin with OOPs; however, for the average student and especially the younger high school students, I feel that they need to understand the fundamentals first.

Upon first examination of this book it may not appear to be very "robust" in that there is not great depth for some of the topics. Actually the depth **is** there,… in the Appendix. The Appendix for this book is unusually large. Here is why the book is organized this way:

- The lessons are kept purposely short so as to hold down the intimidation factor. As a result, the lessons should look "doable" to the students.
- The in-depth material is placed in the Appendices, and references to the Appendices are made in the lessons. As an example, in Lesson 18 the *split* method is introduced. The *split* method uses regular expressions that are briefly discussed there; however, the in-depth presentation of regular expressions is placed in Appendix AC.

Unfortunately this book does not introduce any graphics or windows programming. The 57 lessons in this book can be covered in one school year, but just barely. To prepare students for the AP test (and contests) there is only time to cover the essentials presented in this book. A second Blue Pelican Java book is planned that will cover those other important topics. Check http://www.bluepelicanjava.com for the availability of the new book, updates on this book, and an inexpensive way to purchase hard-cover books.

I am often asked **how to use this book**. "Which lessons are really important and which can be skipped?" The answer is simple:

- **Start on Lesson 1.**
- **Proceed at a reasonable rate.** (See Appendix P for a time-line.)
- **Don't skip anything** (except for, perhaps Lesson 23, Lesson 48 and Lesson 54)
- **Give a simple, confidence-building quiz on each lesson.** Quizzes and keys are provided in the Answer Book (available at www.bluepelicanjava.com).
- **Make sure the students do the provided exercises and projects.**
- **Give tests at regular intervals.** Tests and keys are provided in the Answer Book.

In this book you will also notice another part of my philosophy of teaching and educational material in general…**Keep it simple**… I try to keep things as simple and uncluttered as possible. For example, you will find specific examples in greater numbers than long-winded explanations in this book. You won't find many pictures and sidebars and lots of little colored side notes scattered about. Some of that type format does contain some useful information; however, I feel that it is largely distracting. Apparently more and more people are coming around to my way of thinking on this, and here is why I think so. Recall that just a few years ago that nearly all web pages looked like cobbled together ransom notes with just a profusion of colors, links, and tidbits scattered all over the page. Take a look at professional web pages today. They typically have a very neat, clean appearance…often with just a plain white background and with plenty of space between the various elements. This is good. Simple is better.

Since this textbook has a strong emphasis on preparation for the AP test and competition (computer science contests), special "contest type" problems are provided at the end of most lessons. I realize that most students will not compete and some may not even take the AP exam; however, the material is not wasted on them. Those "contest type" problems are good for the average student too, as long as they are not overwhelmed with too many problems at one sitting. Hopefully, I have just the optimum number of these type problems on each lesson and students won't be burned-out by too much of a good thing.

Finally, we come to the reason for the choice of Blue Pelican Java as a name for this book. One of the early (and free) java IDE's available for students was BlueJ and it was the first my students used. I always thought BlueJ was an elegant name and had expressed a desire to a colleague to continue the tradition by naming the book after some other blue-colored bird. He jokingly suggested Blue Pelican, not really being serious about naming a book after this rather ungainly, clunky bird. For the lack of an existing name for the book during development, it continued to be called Blue Pelican. If you call something by a particular name long enough, that's its name, and so the name stuck.

I truly hope Blue Pelican Java is useful to you and that you find the experience of learning to program a rewarding one. Just remember, few things worthwhile are acquired without some sacrifice. The "sacrifice" here will be the time you invest in creating programs and trying the code suggested in these pages.

Charles E. Cook

Table of Contents

Golden Nuggets of Wisdom are short learning/review activities. In the six weeks preceding an AP exam, contest, or other major evaluation, study one of these each day. Follow up with a quiz (provided in the Teacher's Test/Answer Book) on that topic the next day.

Lesson 1…..Hello World

Program Skeleton:

Enter the following program skeleton, compile (prepare it to run), and then run (execute). Your instructor may have you give it a specific project name; otherwise, call the project *Lesson1*.

If you do not know how to enter and execute a program, ask your instructor, or use the appendices in this book for two of the more popular programming environments. See Appendix N for the BlueJ environment and Appendix O for the JCreator environment.

```
public class Tester
{
	public static void main(String args[])
	{

	}
}
```

At this point don't worry about what any of this means. It's just something we must do every time. Soon we will learn the meaning of all of this. For now it's just the skeleton that we need for a program.

Adding some meaningful code:

Now, let's add some meaningful code inside the *main* method. (Notice this word, **method**. We will constantly refer to **methods** throughout this course.) We will also add a **remark**.

```
public class Tester //We could put any name here besides Tester
{
	public static void main(String args[])
	{
		System.out.println("Hello world");
	}
}
```

Remarks:

Notice the rem (remark) above that starts with //. You can put remarks anywhere in the program without it affecting program operation. Remarks are also called comments or notes.

Printing:

System.out.println("Hello world"); is how we get the computer to printout something. Notice the trailing semicolon. Most lines of code are required to end in a semicolon.

Now try putting in some other things in the *println* parenthesis above. Each time recompile and run the program:

1. "Peter Piper picked a peck of pickled peppers."
2. "I like computer science."

3. 25/5
4. 4 / 7.0445902
5. 13 * 159.56

Two *printlns* for the price of one:

Next, modify your program so that the *main* method looks as follows:

```
public static void main(String args[])
{
        System.out.println("Hello world");
        System.out.println("Hello again");
}
```

Run this and note that it prints :

```
Hello world
Hello again
```

Printing "Sideways":

Now remove the *ln* from the first *println* as follows:

```
public static void main(String args[])
{
        System.out.print("Hello world");
        System.out.println("Hello again");
}
```

Run this and note that it prints:

```
Hello worldHello again
```

Here are the rules concerning *println* and *print*:

- *System.out.println()* completes printing on the current line and pulls the print position down to the next line where any subsequent printing continues.
- *System.out.print()* prints on the current line and stops there. Any subsequent printing continues from that point.

An in-depth look at rems:

Let's take a further look at rems. Consider the following program (class) in which we wish to document ourselves as the programmer, the date of creation, and our school:

```
public class Tester
{
        //Programmer: Kosmo Kramer
        //Date created: Sept 34, 1492
        //School: Charles Manson High School; Berkley, Ca

        public static void main(String args[])
        {
                System.out.println("Hello again");
        }
}
```

Block rems:

It can get a little tedious putting the double slash rem-indicator in front of each line, especially if we have quite a few remark lines. In this case we can "block rem" all the comment lines as follows:

```
public class Tester
{
        /*Programmer: Kosmo Kramer
        Date created: Sept 34, 1492
        School: Charles Manson Junior High; Berkley, Ca*/

        public static void main(String args[])
        {
                System.out.println("Hello again");
        }
}
```

Notice we use /* to indicate the start of the block and */ for the end. **Everything** between these two symbols is considered to be a remark and will be ignored by the computer when compiling and running.

Project… From Me To You

Create a new project called *FromMeToYou* having a *Tester* class with the following content. Also include remarks above *public class Tester* that identifies you as the author along with the date of creation of this program:

```
//Author: Charles Cook
//Date created: Mar 22, 2005
public class Tester
{
   public static void main(String args[])
   {
       …
   }
}
```

Supply code in the place of … that will produce the following printout:

```
From: Bill Smith
Address: Dell Computer, Bldg 13
Date: April 12, 2005

To: Jack Jones

Message: Help! I'm trapped inside a computer!
```

Lesson 2…..Variable Types (*String*, *int*, *double*)

Three variable types:

(A good way to learn the following points is to modify the code of the "Hello World" program according to the suggestions below.)

1. ***String***….used to store things in quotes….like "Hello world"

   Sample code:

```
public static void main(String args[])
{
        String s = "Hello cruel world";
        System.out.println(s);
}
```

2. ***int*** ….used to store integers (positive or negative)

   Sample code:

```
public static void main(String args[])
{
        int age = 59;
        System.out.println(age);
}
```

3. ***double*** ….used to store "floating point" numbers (decimal fractions). *double* means "double precision".

   Sample code:

```
public static void main(String args[])
{
        double d = -137.8036;
        System.out.println(d);

        d = 1.45667E23;  //Scientific notation…means 1.45667 X 10^23
}
```

Declaring and initializing:

When we say something like

```
double x = 1.6;
```

we are really doing **two** things at once. We are **declaring** *x* to be of type *double* **and** we are **initializing** *x* to the value of 1.6. All this can also be done in **two** lines of code (as shown below) instead of one if desired:

```
double x;  //this declares x to be of type double
x = 1.6;  //this initializes x to a value of 1.6
```

What's legal and what's not:

```
int arws = 47.4;  //illegal, won't compile since a decimal number cannot "fit" into an
                  //integer variable.
double d = 103; //legal…same as saying the decimal number 103.0
```

Rules for variable names:

Variable names must begin with a letter and cannot contain spaces. The only "punctuation" character permissible inside the name is "_". Variable names cannot be one of the reserved words (key words…see Appendix A) that are part of the Java language.

Legal names	**Illegal names**
Agro	139
D	139Abc
d31	fast One
hoppergee	class
hopper_gee	slow.Sally
largeArea	double
goldNugget	gold;Nugget
	hopper-gee

Variable naming conventions:

It is traditional (although not a hard and fast rule) for variable names to start with a lower case letter. If a variable name consists of multiple words, combine them in one of two ways:

bigValue… jam everything together. First word begins with a small letter and subsequent words begin with a capital.

big_value… separate words with an underscore.

Exercise on Lesson 2

1. What are the three main types of variables used in Java and what are they used to store?

2. What type of variable would you use to store your name?

3. What type of variable would you use to store the square root of 2?

4. What type of variable would you use to store your age?

5. Write a single line of code that will create a double precision variable called *p* and store $1.921 \text{ X } 10^{-16}$ in it.

6. Write a single line of code that will create an integer variable called *i* and store 407 in it.

7. Write a single line of code that will create a *String* variable called *my_name* and store your name in it.

8. Write a line of code that will **declare** the variable *count* to be of type *int*. Don't initialize.

9. Write a line of code that **initializes** the double precision variable *bankBalance* to 136.05. Assume this variable has already been declared.

10. Which of the following are legal variable names?
    scooter13 139_scooter homer-5 ;mary public doubled double ab c

11. Which of the following is the most acceptable way of naming a variable. Multiple answers are possible.
    a. GroovyDude
    b. GROOVYDUDE
    c. groovyDude
    d. Groovydude
    e. groovy_dude
    f. groovydude

12. Comment on the legality of the following two lines of code.

```
double dist = 1003;
int alt = 1493.86;
```

Lesson 3…..Simple *String* Operations

In this lesson we will learn just a few of the things we can do with *String*s.

Concatenation:

First and foremost is **concatenation.** We use the plus sign, +, to do this. For example:

```
String mm = "Hello";
String nx = "good buddy";
String c = mm + nx;
System.out.println(c);  //prints Hellogood buddy…notice no space between o & g
```

The above code could also have been done in the following way:

```
String mm = "Hello";
String nx = "good buddy";
System.out.println(mm + "  " + nx);  //prints Hello good buddy…notice the space
```

We could also do it this way:

```
System.out.println("Hello" + "  good buddy");  // prints Hello good buddy
```

The *length* method:

Use the ***length( )*** method to find the number of characters in a *String*:

```
String theName = "Donald Duck";
int len = theName.length( );
System.out.println(len);  //prints 11…notice the space gets counted
```

Right now we don't see much value in this length thing…just wait!

A piece of a *String (substring)*:

We can pick out a piece of a *String*…**substring**

```
String myPet = "Sparky the dog";
String smallPart = myPet.substring(4);
System.out.println(smallPart);  //prints ky the dog
```

Why do we get this result? The various characters in a *String* are numbered starting on the left with 0. These numbers are called **indices**. (Notice the spaces are numbered too.)

S p a r k y   t h e   d o g… so now we see that the 'k' has **index** 4 and we go from
0 1 2 3 4 5 6 7 8 9 10 11 12 13 k all the way to the end of the string to get "ky the dog".

A more useful form of *substring*:

But wait! There's another way to use ***substring***

```
String myPet = "Sparky the dog";
String smallPart = myPet.substring(4, 12);
System.out.println(smallPart);  //prints ky the d
```

How do we get ***ky the d***? Start at *k*, the 4th index, as before. Go out to the 12th index, 'o' in this case and pull back one notch. That means the last letter is *d*.

Conversion between lower and upper case:

toLowerCase converts all characters to lower case (small letters)

String bismark = "Dude, where's MY car?"
System.out.println(bismark.toLowerCase( )); // prints **dude, where's my car?**

toUpperCase converts all characters to upper case (capital letters)

System.out.println("Dude, where's My car?".toUpperCase( ));
//prints **DUDE, WHERE'S MY CAR?**

Note: *length*, *substring*, *toLowerCase*, and *toUpperCase* are all **methods** of the *String* class. There are other methods we will learn later.

Concatenating a *String* and a numeric:

It is possible to concatenate a *String* with a numeric variable as follows:

int x = 27;
String s = "Was haben wir gemacht?"; //German for "What have we done?"
String combo = s + " " + x;
System.out.println(combo); //prints **Was haben wir gemacht? 27**

Escape sequences:

How do we force a **quote** character (") to printout…. or, to be part of a *String*. Use the **escape sequence**, \", to print the following (note escape sequences always start with the \ character…see Appendix B for more on escape sequences):

```
What "is" the right way?
```

String s = "What \"is\" the right way?";
System.out.println(s); //prints **What "is" the right way?**

Another **escape sequence**, \n, will create a **new line** (also called **line break**) as shown below:

String s = "Here is one line\nand here is another.";
System.out.println(s);

Prints the following:

```
Here is one line
and here is another.
```

The **escape sequence**, \\, will allow us to print a backslash within our *String*. Otherwise, if we try to insert just a single \ it will be interpreted as the beginning of an escape sequence.

System.out.println("Path = c:\\nerd_file.doc");

Prints the following:

```
Path = c:\nerd_file.doc
```

The **escape sequence**, \t, will allow us to "tab" over. The following code tabs twice.
System.out.println("Name:\t\tAddress:");

Prints the following:

```
Name:           Address:
```

Exercise on Lesson 3

1. Write code in which a *String* variable *s* contains "The number of rabbits is". An integer variable *argh* has a value of 129. Concatenate these variables into a *String* called *report*. Then print *report*. The printout should yield:
   ```
   The number of rabbits is 129.
   ```
   Note that we want a period to print after the 9.

2. What is the output of *System.out.println(p.toUpperCase( ));* if p = "Groovy Dude"?

3. Write code that will assign the value of "Computer Science is for nerds" to the *String* variable *g*. Then have it print this *String* with nothing but "small" letters.

4. What will be the value of *c*?
   ```
   String c;
   String m = "The Gettysburg Address";
   c = m.substring(4);
   ```

5. What will be the value *c*?
   ```
   String b = "Four score and seven years ago,";
   c = b.substring(7, 12);
   ```

6. What is the value of *count*?
   ```
   int count;
   String s = "Surface tension";
   count = s.length( );
   ```

7. Write code that will look at the number of characters in *String m = "Look here!";* and then print
   ```
   "Look here!" has 10 characters.
   ```
   Use the *length()* method to print the 10 ….you must also force the two quotes to print.

8. How would you print the following?
   ```
   All "good" men should come to the aid of their country.
   ```

9. Write code that will produce the following printout using only a single *println()*.

```
Hello
Hello again
```

10. Write code that will produce the following printout.

```
A backslash looks like this \, …right?
```

11. What is output by the following?

```
String pq = "Eddie Haskel";
int  hm = pq.length( );
String ed = pq.substring(hm - 4);
System.out.println(ed);
```

12. Which character is at the 5th index in the String "Herman Munster"?

Project… Name that Celebrity

Create a new project called *NameThatCelebrity* in which only partially recognizable names of celebrities are to be produced. In a real implementation of this game, the idea is for a contestant to be able to guess the real name of the celebrity after the first two and last three letters are dropped from the name. We have been given the task of testing the feasibility of this idea by producing the following printout:

```
Allan Alda>>>lan A
John Wayne>>>hn Wa
Gregory Peck>>>egory P
```

Begin your code within the *main* method as follows:

```
String s1 = "Allan Alda";
String s2 = "John Wayne";
String s3 = "Gregory Peck";
```

Apply the *length* and *substring* methods to these *Strings* to produce the above printout.

Lesson 4.....Using Numeric Variables

The assignment operator:

The assignment operator is the standard equal sign (**=**) and is used to "assign" a value to a variable.

```
int i = 3;  // Ok,…assign the value 3 to i.
```
Notice the direction of data flow.

```
3 = i; // Illegal! Data never flows this way!
```

```
double p;
double j = 47.2;
p = j;  // assign the value of j to p. Both p and j are now equal to 47.2
```

Multiple declarations:

It is possible to declare several variables on one line:

```
double d, mud, puma;  //the variables are only declared
double x = 31.2, m = 37.09, zu, p = 43.917;  //x, m, & p declared and initialized
                                              // zu is just declared
```

Fundamental arithmetic operations:

The basic arithmetic operation are +, -, * (multiplication), / (division), and % (modulus).

Modulus is the strange one. For example, System.out.println(5%3); will print 2. This is because when 5 is divided by 3, the **remainder** is 2. **Modulus gives the remainder.** Modulus also handles negatives. The answer to *a%b* always has the same sign as *a*. The sign of *b* is ignored.

PEMDAS:

The algebra rule, PEMDAS, applies to computer computations as well. (PEMDAS stands for the order in which numeric operations are done. P = parenthesis, E = exponents, M = multiply, D = divide, A = add, S = subtract. Actually, M and D have equal precedence, as do A and S. For equal precedence operation, proceed from left to right. A mnemonic for PEMDAS is, "Please excuse my dear Aunt Sally"… See Appendix H for the precedence of all operators.)

```
System.out.println(5 + 3 * 4 –7);  //10
System.out.println(8 – 5*6 / 3 + (5 –6) * 3); //-5
```

Not the same as in Algebra:

An unusual assignment….consider the following:

```
count = count +3;  //this is illegal in algebra; however, in computer science it
                   //means the new count equals the old count + 3.
```

```
int count =15;
count = count + 3;
```

```
System.out.println(count); //18
```

Increment and Decrement:

The increment operator is ++, and it means to add one. The decrement operator is --, and it means to subtract one:

```
x++;  means the same as        x = x +1;
x--;  means the same as        x = x – 1;
x++   is the same as   ++x     (the ++ can be on either side of x)
x--   is the same as   --x     (the -- can be on either side of x)
```

```
int y = 3;
y++;
System.out.println(y); //4
```

Compound operators:

	Syntax Example		Simplified meaning
a.	+=		
	x += 3;	→	x = x + 3;
b.	-=		
	x -= y - 2;	→	x = x – (y - 2);
c.	*=		
	z*= 46;	→	z = z * 46;
d.	/=		
	p/= x-z;	→	p = p / (x-z);
e.	%=		
	j%= 2	→	j = j%2;

Code Examples

```
int g = 409;
g += 5;
System.out.println(g); //414

double d = 20.3;
double m =10.0;
m*=d –1;
System.out.println(m); //193
```

The whole truth:

Actually, the full truth was not told above concerning *x++*. It does not always have the same effect as does *++x*. Likewise, x-- does not always have the same effect as does --x.

x++ increments *x* **after** it is used in the statement.
++x increments *x* **before** it is used in the statement.

Similarly,

x-- decrements *x* **after** it is used in the statement.
--x decrements *x* **before** it is used in the statement.

Code Examples

```
int q = 78;
int p = 2 + q++;
System.out.println("p = " + p + ", q = " + q); //p = 80, q = 79

int q = 78;
int p = ++q + 2;
System.out.println("p = " + p + ", q = " + q); //p = 81, q = 79
```

Integer division truncation:

When dividing two integers, the fractional part is truncated (thrown away) as illustrated by the following:

```
int x = 5;
int y = 2;
System.out.println(x / y);  //Both x and y are integers so the "real" answer of 2.5
                            //has the fractional part thrown away to give 2
```

Exercise on Lesson 4

Unless otherwise directed in the following problems, state what is printed. Some of these problems may have incorrect syntax and in those cases you should answer that the code would not compile.

1.
```
int h = 103;
int p =5;
System.out.println(++h + p);
System.out.println(h);
```

2. Give three code examples of how to increment the integer *j* by 1.

3.
```
double def;
double f = 1992.37;
def = f;
System.out.println(def);
```

4. Write a **single** line of code that will print the integer variable *zulu* and **then** decrement its value by 1.

5. int a = 100;
   int b = 200;
   b/=a;
   System.out.println(b + 1);

6. Write a **single** line of code that uses the compound operator, -=, to subtract *p-30* from the integer value *v* and store the result back in *v*.

7. Write a single line of code that does the same thing as #6 but without using - =.

8. int p = 40;
   int q = 4;
   System.out.println(2 + 8 * q / 2 - p);

9. int sd = 12;
   int x = 4;
   System.out.println(sd%(++x));
   System.out.println(x);

10. int g;
    3 = g;
    System.out.println(++g*79);
    What is the result?

11. On a single line of code declare *m*, *b*, and *f* to be *double* and on that same line initialize them all to be 3.14.

12. On a single line of code declare *x*, *y*, and *z* all to be of integer type.

13. int m = 36;
    int j = 5;
    m = m / j; // new m is old m divided by j
    System.out.println(m);
    What's printed?

14. System.out.println(3/4 + 5*2/33 –3 +8*3);
    What's printed?

15. What is the assignment operator?

16. Write a statement that stores the remainder of dividing the variable *i* by *j* in a variable named *k*.

17. int j = 2;
    System.out.println(7%3 + j++ + (j – 2));

18. Show three different ways to decrement the variable *j*.

Project… Cheating on Your Arithmetic Assignment

Create a new project called *ArithmeticAssignment* with a class called *Tester* that will calculate and print the results of the following arithmetic problems:

79 + 3 * (4 + 82 –68) – 7 +19

(179 +21 +10) / 7 + 181

10389 * 56 * 11 + 2246

The printout should look like the following:

```
79 + 3 * (4 + 82 - 68) -7 + 19  =  145

(179 + 21 + 10) / 7 + 181 =   211

10389 * 56 * 11 + 2246  =  6401870
```

Lesson 5.....Mixed Data Types, Casting, and Constants

So far we have looked mostly at simple cases in which all the numbers involved in a calculation were either **all** integers or **all** *doubles*. Here, we will see what happens when we **mix** these types in calculations.

Java doesn't like to lose data:

Here is an important principle to remember: Java **will not** normally store information in a variable if in doing so it would **lose** information. Consider the following two examples:

1. An example of when we would **lose** information:

   ```
   double d = 29.78;
   int  i = d;  //won't compile since i is an integer and it would have to chop-off
                // the .78 and store just 29 in i....thus, it would lose information.
   ```

   There is a way to make the above code work. We can **force** compilation and therefore result in 29.78 being "stored" in *i* as follows (actually, just 29 is stored since *i* can only hold integers):

   ```
   int i = (int)d;  //(int) "casts" d as an integer... It converts d to integer form.
   ```

2. An example of when we would **not** lose information:

   ```
   int j = 105;
   double d = j; //legal, because no information is lost in storing 105 in the
                 // double variable d.
   ```

The most precise:

In a math operation involving **two different data types**, the result is given in terms of the **more precise** of those two types...as in the following example:

```
int i = 4;
double d = 3;
double ans = i/d;  //ans will be 1.33333333333333...the result is double precision
```

20 + 5 * 6.0 returns a d*ouble*. The 6.0 might look like an integer to us, but because it's written with a decimal point, it is considered to be a floating point number...a *double*.

Some challenging examples:

What does   3 + 5.0/2 + 5 * 2 – 3   return? **12.5**

What does   3.0 + 5/2 + 5 * 2 – 3   return? **12.0**

What does   (int)(3.0 + 4)/(1 + 4.0) * 2 – 3   return? **-.2**

Don't be fooled:

Consider the following two examples that are very similar...but have different answers:

```
double d = (double)5/4;  //same as 5.0 / 4...(double) only applies to the 5
System.out.println(d);  //1.25

int j = 5;
int k = 4;
double d = (double)(j / k); //(j / k) is in its own little "world" and performs
                            //integer division yielding 1 which is then cast as
                            //a double, 1.0
System.out.println(d);  //1.0
```

Constants:

Constants follow all the rules of variables; however, once initialized, they **cannot be changed**. Use the keyword ***final*** to indicate a constant. Conventionally, constant names have all capital letters. The rules for legal constant names are the same as for variable names. Following is an example of a constant:

```
final double PI = 3.14159;
```

The following illustrates that constants can't be changed:

```
final double PI = 3.14159;
PI = 3.7789;  //illegal
```

Constants must be initialized at the time they are declared.

```
final double PI;  //illegal,...must be initialized right here on this line
PI = 3.14159;
```

Constants can also be of type *String* or *int*.

```
final String NAME= "Pewee Herman";
final int LunchCount = 122;
```

Project… Mixed Results

Create a new project called *MixedResults* with a class called *Tester*. Within the *main* method of *Tester* you will eventually printout the result of the following problems. However, you should first calculate by hand what you expect the answers to be. For example, in the parenthesis of the first problem, you should realize that strictly integer arithmetic is taking place that results in a value of 0 for the parenthesis.

```
double d1 = 37.9;  //Initialize these variables at the top of your program
double d2 = 1004.128;
int i1 = 12;
int i2 =  18;

    Problem 1:  57.2 * (i1 / i2) +1
    Problem 2:  57.2 * ( (double)i1 / i2 ) + 1
    Problem 3:  15 – i1 * ( d1 * 3) + 4
    Problem 4:  15 – i1 * (int)( d1 * 3) + 4
    Problem 5:  15 – i1 * ( (int)d1 * 3) + 4
```

Your printout should look like the following:

```
Problem 1: 1.0
Problem 2: 39.13333333333333
Problem 3: -1345.39999999999
Problem 4: -1337
Problem 5: -1313
```

Exercise on Lesson 5

Unless otherwise instructed in the following problems, state what gets printed.

1. Write code that will create a constant *E* that's equal to 2.718.

2. Write the simplest type constant that sets the number of students, *NUM_STUDENTS*, to 236.

3. What's wrong with the following code in the *main* method?
   final double Area;
   Area = 203.49;

4. int cnt = 27.2;
   System.out.println(cnt);
   What's printed?

5. double d = 78.1;
   int fg = (int)d;
   System.out.println(fg);
   What's printed?

6. Is *double f4 = 22;* legal?

7. The following code stores a 20 in the variable *j*:
   double j = 61/3;
   What small change can you make to this single line of code to make it print the "real" answer to the division?

8. System.out.println((double)(90/9));

9. System.out.println(4 + 6.0/4 + 5 * 3 – 3);

10.
```
int p = 3;
double d = 10.3;
int j = (int)5.9;
System.out.println(p + p * d – 3 * j);
```

11.
```
int p = 3;
double d = 10.3;
int j = (int)5.9;
System.out.println(p + p * (int)d – 3 * j);
```

The following code applies to 12 – 15:

```
int dividend = 12, divisor = 4, quotient = 0, remainder = 0;
int dividend2 = 13, divisor2 = 3, quotient2 = 0, remainder2 = 0;
quotient = dividend/divisor;
remainder = dividend % divisor;
quotient2 = dividend2 / divisor2;
remainder2 = dividend2 % divisor2;
```

12. System.out.println(quotient);

13. System.out.println(remainder);

14. System.out.println(quotient2);

15. System.out.println(remainder2);

16. Write a line of code in which you divide the double precision number *d* by an integer variable called *i*. Type cast the *double* so that strictly integer division is done. Store the result in *j*, an integer.

17. Suppose we have a line of code that says

```
final String M = "ugg";
```

Later in the same program, would it be permissible to say the following?

```
M = "wow";
```

Lesson 6…..Methods of the *Math* Class

One of the most useful methods of the *Math* class is *sqrt()* …which means square root. For example, if we want to take the square root of 17 and store the result in *p* do the following:

```
double p = Math.sqrt(17);
```

Notice that we must store the result in a *double*…. *p* in this case. We must store in a *double* since square roots usually don't come out even.

Signature of a method:
Below we will give the description of some methods of the *Math* class… along with the signatures of the method. First, however, let's explain the meaning of signature. Consider the signature of the *sqrt()* method:

```
        double sqrt( double x )
          |      |       |
type returned   method name   type of parameter we send to the method
```

Method	Signature	Description
abs	int abs(int x)	Returns the absolute value of x
abs	double abs(double x)	Returns the absolute value of x
pow	double pow(double b, double e)	Returns b raised to the e power
sqrt	double sqrt(double x)	Returns the square root of x
ceil	double ceil(double x)	Returns next highest whole number from x
floor	double floor(double x)	Returns next lowest whole number from x
min	double min(double a, double b)	Returns the smaller of a and b
max	double max(double a, double b)	Returns the larger of a and b
min	int min(int a, int b)	Returns the smaller of a and b
max	int max(int a, int b)	Returns the larger of a and b
random	double random( )	Returns a random double (range $0 \leq r < 1$)
round	long round(double x)	Returns x rounded to nearest whole number
PI	double PI	Returns 3.14159625…..

Now, we offer examples of each (most of these you can do on a calculator for verification):

1. double d = -379.22;
   System.out.println(Math.abs(d)); //**379.22**

2. double b = 42.01;
   double e = 3.728;
   System.out.println (Math.pow(b, e)); //**1126831.027**

3. double d = 2034.56;
   System.out.println(Math.sqrt(d)); //**45.10609715**

4. double d = 982.47;
   System.out.println(Math.ceil(d)); //**983.0**

   double d = -982.47;
   System.out.println(Math.ceil(d)); //**-982.0**

5. double d = 982.47;
   System.out.println(Math.floor(d)); //**982.0**

   double d = -982.47;
   System.out.println(Math.floor(d)); //**-983.0**

6. double d = 7.89;
   System.out.println(Math.log(d)); //**2.065596135** ...log is base e.

7. double x = 2038.5;
   double y = -8999.0;
   System.out.println(Math.min(x,y)); //**-8999.0**

8. double x = 2038.5;
   double y = -8999.0;
   System.out.println(Math.max(x,y)); //**2038.5**

9. double x = 148.2;
   System.out.println(Math.round(x)); //**148**

   double x = 148.7;
   System.out.println(Math.round(x)); //**149**

   double x = -148.2;
   System.out.println(Math.round(x)); //**-148**

   double x = -148.7;
   System.out.println(Math.round(x)); //**-149**

10. System.out.println(Math.PI); //**3.14159625...**

Advanced *Math* methods:
Below are some additional *Math* methods that advanced math students will find useful:

Method	Signature	Description
log	double log(double x)	Returns log base e of x
sin	double sin(double a)	Returns the sine of angle a... a is in rad
cos	double cos(double a)	Returns the cosine of angle a... a is in rad
tan	double tan(double a)	Returns the tangent of angle a... a is in rad
asin	double asin(double x)	Returns arcsine of x...in range -PI/2 to PI/2
acos	double acos(double x)	Returns arccosine of x...in range 0 to PI
atan	double atan(double x)	Returns arctan of x. in range -PI/2 to PI/2
toDegrees	double toDegrees(double angRad)	Converts radians into degrees
toRadians	double toRadians(double angDeg)	Converts degrees into radians

Exercise on Lesson 6

1. Write code that will take the square root of *x* and store the result in *y*.

2. Write code that will multiply the value of the integer *j* times the absolute value of the integer *m* and then store the result in the integer *k*;

3. Is the following legal? If not, what would you do to make it legal?
   int k = Math.abs(-127.5);

4. Write a statement that will print the result of $2^{1.5}$.

5. System.out.println(Math.ceil(-157.2));

6. System.out.println(Math.floor(-157.2));

7. System.out.println(Math.ceil(157.2));

8. System.out.println(Math.floor(157.2));

9. System.out.println(Math.round(-157.2));

10. System.out.println(Math.ceil(-157.7));

11. System.out.println(Math.ceil(157));

12. System.out.println(Math.ceil(157.7));

13. Write a statement that will print the natural log of 18…. same as ln(18) on a calculator.

14. Write a line of code that multiplies *double p* times π and stores the result in *b*.

Project… Compute This

Create a new project called *ComputeThis* having a class called *Tester*. The *main* method of *Tester* should calculate the value of the following formulas and present the answers as shown.

$d1 = 3\pi\sin(187°) + |\cos(122°)|$ …Remember that the arguments of sin and cos must be in radians.

$d2 = (14.72)^{3.801} + \ln 72$ …ln means log base e

The output of your code should appear as follows:

```
d1  =  -0.618672251701355

d2  =  27496.99609375
```

Verify these answers with a calculator.

Lesson 7…. Input from the Keyboard

We will consider how to input from the keyboard the three data types…. *int*, *double*, and *String*.

Inputting an integer:

Use the *nextInt* method to input an **integer** from the keyboard:

```
import java.io.*;  //see Note 1 below
import java.util.*;
public class Tester
{
    public static void main( String args[] )
    {
        Scanner kbReader = new Scanner(System.in); //see Note 2
        System.out.print("Enter your integer here. "); //enter 3,001
        int i = kbReader.nextInt( );
        System.out.println(3*i);  //prints 9003
    }
}
```

Inputting a *double*:

Use the *nextDouble* method to input a ***double*** from the keyboard:

```
import java.io.*;
import java.util.*;
public class Tester
{
    public static void main( String args[] )
    {
        Scanner kbReader = new Scanner(System.in);
        System.out.print("Enter your decimal number here. "); //1,000.5
        double d = kbReader.nextDouble( );
        System.out.println( 3*d );  //prints 1001.5
    }
}
```

Inputting a *String*:

Use the *next* method to input a ***String*** from the keyboard:

```
import java.io.*;
import java.util.*;
public class Tester
{
    public static void main( String args[] )
    {
        Scanner kbReader = new Scanner(System.in);
        System.out.print("Enter your String here. "); //Enter One Two
        String s = kbReader.next( ); //inputs up to first white space
        System.out.println( "This is first part of the String,… " + s);
        s = kbReader.next( );
        System.out.println( "This is next part of the String,… " + s);
    }
}
```

Output would be as shown below:

```
Enter your String here. One Two
This is first part of the String,... One
This is next part of the String,... Two
```

Multiple inputs:

In a similar way *nextInt()* and *nextDouble()* can be used multiple times to parse data input from the keyboard. For example, if **34 88 192 18** is input from the keyboard, then *nextInt()* can be applied 4 times to access these four integers separated by white space.

Inputting a line of text:

Inputting a ***String*** from the keyboard using *nextLine()*:

```
import java.io.*;
import java.util.*;
public class Tester
{
        public static void main( String args[] )
        {
                Scanner kbReader = new Scanner(System.in);
                System.out.print("Enter your String here. "); //Enter One Two
                String s= kbReader.nextLine( );
                System.out.println( "This is my string,... " + s);
        }
}
```

Output would be as shown below:

```
Enter your String here. One Two
This is my string,... One Two
```

Note 1:

We must **import** two classes,….*java.io.* and java.util.** that provide methods for inputting integers, doubles, and Strings. See Appendix I for more on the meaning of "importing".

Note 2:

In the above three examples we used the following code:

```
Scanner kbReader = new Scanner(System.in);
```

It simply creates the keyboard reader **object** (we arbitrarily named it *kbReader*) that provides access to the *nextInt()*, *nextDouble()*, *next()*, and *nextLine()* methods. For now just accept the necessity of all this…it will all be explained later.

The *Scanner* class used here to create our keyboard reader object only applies to1.5.0_xx or higher versions of Java. For older versions, see Appendix M for an alternate way to obtain keyboard input.

Project... Going in Circles

The area of a circle is given by:

$$area = \pi (r^2)$$

Now, suppose we know the area and wish to find r. Solving for r from this equation yields:

$$r = \sqrt{(area / \pi)}$$

Write a program (project and class both named *RadiusOfCircle*) that uses *sqrt( )* and *PI* from the *Math* class to solve for the radius of a circle. Use keyboard input to specify the area (provide for the possibility of area being a decimal fraction).

Write out your solution by hand and then enter it into the computer and run. Before inputting the area, put a prompt on the screen like this.

What is the area? _ ...(the underscore indicates the cursor waiting for input)

Present your answer like this:

```
Radius of your circle is 139.4.
```

Project... What's My Name?

From the keyboard enter your first and then your last name, each with its own prompt. Store each in a separate *String* and then concatenate them together to show your full name. Call both the project and the class *FullName*. When your program is finished running, the output should appear similar to that below:

```
What is your first name? Cosmo
What is your last name? Kramer
Your full name is Cosmo Kramer.
```

Lesson 8…The boolean Type and boolean Operators

Back in Lesson 2 we looked at three fundamental variable types… *int*, *double*, and *String*. Here, we look at another very important type…..***boolean***. This type has only two possible values… ***true*** or ***false***.

Only two values:

Let's look at some statements that could come out either *true* or *false*. Suppose we know that x = 3 and also that y = 97. What could we say about the truth (or falseness) of the following statements?

((x <10) AND (y = 97)) Both parts are *true* so the **whole** thing is *true*.

((x <10) AND (y = -3)) First part is *true*, second part is *false*, **whole** thing *false*

((x <10) OR (y = 97)) If either part is *true* (both are) the **whole** thing is *true*.

((x <10) OR (y = -3)) If either part is *true* (first part is) the **whole** thing *true*.

Correct syntax:

In the above examples there are three things we must change in order to have correct Java syntax:

1. To compare two quantities…such as (y = 97) above we must instead do it this way:

   (y = = 97)….recall that a single "=" is the assignment operator.

   Similarly, read y != 97 as "y is not equal to 97".

2. In Java we don't use the word "and" to indicate an **AND** operation as above. We use "**&&**" instead……..((x <10) && (y = = 97))

3. In Java we don't use the word "or" to indicate an **OR** operation as above. We use "||" instead……..((x <10) | | (y = = 97))

Truth tables:

Here are truth tables that show how && and || work for various combinations of *a* and *b*:

a	b	(a && b)
false	false	false
false	true	false
true	false	false
true	true	true

Table 8-1 **AND-ing**

a	b	(a || b)
false	false	false
false	true	true
true	false	true
true	true	true

Table 8-2 **OR-ing**

Negation (not) operator:

Another operator we need to know about is the **not** operator (!). It is officially called the negation operator. What does it mean if we say **not true** (!true)? … **false**, of course.

1. System.out.println(!true); //false
2. System.out.println(!false); //true
3. System.out.println(!(3 < 5)); //false
4. System.out.println(!(1 = = 0)); //true

Creation of *booleans*:

Create *boolean* variables as shown in the following two examples:

```
boolean b = true;
boolean z = ( (p < j) && (x != c) );
```

Use the following code for example 1 – 10 below:

```
int x =79, y = 46, z = -3;
double d = 13.89, jj = 40.0;
boolean b = true, c = false;
```

1. System.out.println(true && false); //false
2. System.out.println(true && !false); //true
3. System.out.println(c | | (d > 0)); //true
4. System.out.println(!b || c); //false
5. System.out.println((x >102) && true); //false
6. System.out.println((jj = = 1) | | false); //false
7. System.out.println((jj = = 40) && !false); //true
8. System.out.println(x != 3); //true
9. System.out.println(!(x!=3)); //false
10. System.out.println(!!true); //true

Operator precedence:

Consider a problem like:

```
System.out.println( (true && false) | | ( (true && true) | | false ) );
```

We can tell what parts we should do first because of the grouping by parenthesis. However, what if we had a different problem like this?

```
System.out.println( false && true || true);
```

Which part should we do first? The answers are different for the two different ways it could be done. There is a precedence (order) for the operators we are studying in this lesson (see Appendix H for a complete listing of operator precedence). The order is:

! **= =** **!=** **&&** **||**

Example 1

System.out.println(true || false && false); //**true**

Do the false && false part **first** to get a result of false.
Now do true || false to get a final result of true.

Example 2

```
System.out.println( true && false || false); //false
```

Do the true && false part first to get a result of false.
Now do false || false to get a final result of false.

Using a search engine:

You can use your knowledge of Booleans on the Internet. Go to your favorite search engine and type in something like,

“Java script” and “Bill Gates”

and you will find only references that contain **both** these items.

On the other hand, enter something like,

“Java script” or “Bill Gates”

and you will be overwhelmed with the number of responses since you will get references that contain **either** of these items.

You should be aware that the various search engines have their own rules for the syntax of such Boolean searches.

Now that we have learned to write a little code, it’s time to turn to another part of our Computer Science education. Computers haven’t always been as they are today. Computers of just a few years ago were primitive by today’s standards. Would you guess that the computers that your children will use someday would make our computers look primitive? Take a few minutes now to review a short history of computers in Appendix S.

Exercise for Lesson 8

In problems1 – 5 assume the following:

```
int z = 23, x = -109;
double c = 2345.19, v = 157.03;
boolean a = false, s = true;
```

1. ```
   boolean gus = (x > 0) && (c = = v);
   System.out.println(!gus);
   ```

2. ```
   System.out.println(a | | s);
   ```

3. ```
   System.out.println( ( (-1 * x) > 0) && !a );
   ```

4. ```
   boolean r = z = =x;
   System.out.println( r | | false );
   ```

5. System.out.println(z!=x);

6. Fill in the following charts.

a	b	(!a && b)
false	false	
false	true	
true	false	
true	true	

a	b	(a || !b)
false	false	
false	true	
true	false	
true	true	

7. Assume *b*, *p*, and *q* are *booleans*. Write code that will assign to *b* the result of **AND-ing** *p* and *q*.

8. Assign to the *boolean* variable *w* the result of **OR-ing** the following two things:
   A test to see if *x* is positive: A test to see if *y* equals *z*:

9. What are the two possible values of a *boolean* variable?

10. Write a test that will return a true if *a* is not equal to *b*. Assume *a* and *b* are integers. Store the result in *boolean kDog*.

11. Write the answer to #10 another way.

12. What is the Java operator for boolean **AND-ing**?

13. What is the Java operator for boolean **OR-ing**?

14. System.out.println((true && false) || ((true && true) || false));

15. System.out.println(true && true || false);

16. System.out.println(true || true && false);

17. System.out.println(false || true && false);

18. System.out.println(false && true || false);

Lesson 9….The *if* Statement

Now that we understand *boolean* quantities, let's put them to use in an *if* statement, one of Java's most useful "decision-making" commands. Consider the following code:

Example 1:

```
//Get a grade from the keyboard
Scanner kbReader = new Scanner(System.in);
System.out.print("What is your grade? ");
int myGrade = kbReader.nextInt( );

//Make a decision based on the value of the grade you entered
if (myGrade >= 70)
{
        //Execute code here if the test above is true
        System.out.println("Congratulations, you passed.");
}
else
{
        //Execute code here if the test above is false
        System.out.println("Better luck next time.");
}
```

Leave off the *else*:

We do not necessarily always need the ***else*** part. Consider the following code without an *else*.

Example 2:

```
Scanner kbReader = new Scanner(System.in);
System.out.print("What state do you live in? ");
String state = kbReader.nextLine( ); //get state from keyboard

System.out.print("What is the price? ");
double purchasePrice = kbReader.nextDouble( ); //get price from keyboard

double tax = 0;
if ( (state = = "Texas") || (state = = "Tx") )
{
        //Execute code here if test above is true
        tax = purchasePrice *.08; //8% tax
}
double totalPrice = purchasePrice + tax;
System.out.println("The total price is " + totalPrice + ".");
```

It won't work!

There is just one difficulty with the above code in Example 2. It won't work! The problem is with how we are trying to compare two *Strings*. It **cannot** be as follows:

```
state = = "Texas"
```

Rather, we must do it this way:

```
state.equals("Texas")
```

A good way to cover all the bases in the event someone mixes upper and lower case on the input is as follows:

(state.equalsIgnoreCase("Texas") | | state.equalsIgnoreCase("Tx"))

What? No braces?

Braces are not needed if only **one line of code** is in the *if* or *else* parts. Likewise, the absence of braces implies only one line of code in *if* or *else* parts.

Example 3:

```
int groovyDude = 37;
if (groovyDude = =37)
        groovyDude++;  //this line is executed if test is true
System.out.println(groovyDude);  //38
```

Example 4:

```
int groovyDude = 105;
if (groovyDude = =37)
        groovyDude++;  //this line is not executed if test is false
System.out.println(groovyDude);  //105
```

The *else if*:

Multiple *if*s can be used in the same structure using *else if*.

Example 5:

```
//Get a grade from the keyboard
Scanner kbReader = new Scanner(System.in);
System.out.println("What is your grade? ");
int theGrade = kbReader.nextInt( );

if (theGrade>=90)
{
        System.out.println("You made an A.");
}
else if (theGrade>=80)
{
        System.out.println("You made a B.");
}
else if (theGrade>=70)
{
        System.out.println("You made a C.");
}
else if (theGrade>=60)
{
        System.out.println("You made a D.");
}
else
{
        System.out.println("Sorry, you failed.");
}
```

Exercise on Lesson 9

Use the following code for problems 1 – 10 and give the value of *true_false* for each:

```
int i = 10, j = 3;
boolean true_false;
```

1. true_false = (j > i);

2. true_false = (i > j);

3. true_false = (i= = j);

4. true_false = ((j <= i) | | (j >= i));

5. true_false = ((i > j) && (j = = 0));

6. true_false = ((j < 50) | | (j != 33));

7. true_false = (!(j >= 0) | | (i <= 50));

8. true_false = (!(! (!true)));

9. true_false = (5 < = 5);

10. true_false = (j != i);

11. Write a statement that will store a true in *boolean b* if the value in the variable *m* is 44 or less.

12. Write a statement that will store a false in *boolean b* if the value in *r* is greater than 17.

13. What is returned by the following expression? (Recall that the precedence order of logical operators is !, &&, and finally | |.)

    !((2>3) | | (5= =5) && (7>1) && (4<15) | | (35<=36) && (89!=34))

In problem 14 – 16 what is the output?

14. String s1 = "school BUS";
```
if ( s1.equals("school bus") )
        System.out.println("Equal");
else
        System.out.println("Not equal");
```

15. String s1 = "school BUS";
```
if ( s1.equalsIgnoreCase("school bus") )
System.out.println("Equal");
else
System.out.println("Not equal");
```

16. int j = 19, m = 200;

```
if (j= =18)
        m++;
        j++;
System.out.println(m);
System.out.println(j);
```

17. Write a statement that will store a *false* in *boolean b* if the value in *g* is not equal to 34.

18. Write a statement that will store a *true* in *boolean b* if integer *k* is even, *false* if it is odd.

19. Write a program that inputs a *String* from the keyboard after the prompt, "Enter your password". If it's entered exactly as "XRay", printout "Password entered successfully."; otherwise, have it printout "Incorrect password."

20. What is output by the following "nested *ifs*" code?

```
int k = 79;
if (k>50)
{
        if (k<60)
        {System.out.println("One");}
        else
        { System.out.println("Two");}
}
else
{
        if (k>30)
                System.out.println("Three");
        else
                System.out.println("Four");
}
```

Project… Even or Odd?

Create a new project called *EvenOrOdd* containing a class called *Tester*. In the *main* method of *Tester* print a prompt that says, "Enter an integer:" Input the user's response from the keyboard, test the integer to see if it is even or odd (use the modulus operator % to do this), and then print the result as shown below (several runs are shown).

```
Enter an integer: 28
The integer 28 is even.

Enter an integer: 2049
The integer 2049 is odd.

Enter an integer: -236
The integer -236 is even.
```

Lesson 10…..The *switch* Statement and *char*

The *if* statement is the most powerful and often used decision-type command. The *switch* statement is useful when we have an integer variable that can be one of several quantities. For example, consider the following menu scenario (enter and run this program):

```
//This code should be placed inside the main method of a class
System.out.println("Make your arithmetic selection from the choices below:\n");

System.out.println("    1. Addition");
System.out.println("    2. Subtraction");
System.out.println("    3. Multiplication");
System.out.println("    4. Division\n");

System.out.print("         Your choice? ");

Scanner kbReader = new Scanner(System.in);
int choice  = kbReader.nextInt( );

System.out.print("\nEnter first operand. " );
double op1 = kbReader.nextDouble( );
System.out.print("\nEnter second operand." );
double op2 = kbReader.nextDouble( );

System.out.println("");

switch (choice)
{
    case 1:  //addition
        System.out.println(op1 + "  plus  " + op2 + "  =  " + (op1 + op2) );
        break;
    case 2:  //subtraction
        System.out.println(op1 + "  minus  " + op2 + "  =  " + (op1 - op2) );
        break;
    case 3:  //multiplication
        System.out.println(op1 + "  times  " + op2 + "  =  " + (op1 * op2) );
        break;
    case 4:  //division
        System.out.println(op1 + "  divided by  " + op2 + "  =  " + (op1 / op2) );
        break;
    default:
        System.out.println("Hey dummy, enter only a 1, 2, 3, or 4!");
}
```

The optional *default*:

The *default* command is optional. You can use it if there might be a possibility of the value of *choice* not being one of the cases.

Give me a *break*:

The *break* statements are normally used. Try leaving them out and see what happens here. In the next section we will look at an application in which they are omitted.

Basically, *break* jumps us out of the *switch* structure and then code execution continues with the first line immediately after the closing *switch* brace. Specifically, you might want to omit the *break* within the *case 1:* section. If *choice* is 1 then the result will be that it prints the answer for **both** addition and subtraction.

The next experiment you might want to do is to leave the parenthesis off of *(op1 + op2)* in the *case 1:* section. Since *op1 + op2* is no longer in parenthesis, the plus between them no longer means addition. It now means concatenation since all the activity to the left of this point in the code was also *String* concatenation.

Leaving off the *break*:

Now, let's look at an example where we intentionally omit *break*:

```
//Suppose at this point in the program we have an integer variable, j. If j equals 1,
//2, or 3 we want to set String variable s to "low" and if j equals 4, 5, or 6 we want
//to set s to "high". If j equals 7, set s to "lucky".
switch ( j )
{
        case 1:
        case 2:
        case 3:
                s = "low";
                break;
        case 4:
        case 5:
        case 6:
                s = "high";
                break;
        case 7:
                s = "lucky";
}
```

A new data type… *char*:

Before we look further at the *switch* statement, we must look at a new data type, *char*. This stands for character. Following is a typical way to declare and initialize a character:

```
char ch = 'h';
```

Notice that a character is always enclosed in single quotes. Characters can be anything, even numbers or symbols:

```
char x = '6';          char pp = '@';
```

Only *int* and *char* are legal:

switch() statements can **only** use **integers** or **characters**. Modify the example on the previous page to use a *char* instead of *int*. See the next page for the necessary modifications:

```
System.out.println("Make your arithmetic selection from the choices below:\n");

System.out.println("    A.  Addition");
System.out.println("    S.  Subtraction");
System.out.println("    M.  Multiplication");
System.out.println("    D.  Division\n");

System.out.print("        Your choice? ");

Scanner kbReader = new Scanner(System.in);
String choice  = kbReader.nextLine( );
//char ch = choice;  //You would think this would work…but it doesn't.
char ch = choice.charAt(0);  //you just learned another String method.

System.out.print("\nEnter first operand. " );
double op1 = kbReader.nextDouble( );
System.out.print("\nEnter second operand ." );
double op2 = kbReader.nextDouble( );

System.out.println(" ");

switch (ch)
{
    case 'A':  //addition
    case 'a':  //Notice we are providing for both capital A and little a.
        System.out.println(op1 + "  plus  " + op2 + "  =  " + (op1 + op2) );
        break;
    case 'S':  //subtraction
    case 's':
        System.out.println(op1 + "  minus  " + op2 + "  =  " + (op1 - op2) );
        break;
    case 'M':  //multiplication
    case 'm':
        System.out.println(op1 + "  times  " + op2 + "  =  " + (op1 * op2) );
        break;
    case 'D':  //division
    case 'd':
        System.out.println(op1 + "  divided by  " + op2 + "  =  " + (op1 / op2) );
        break;
    default:
        System.out.println("Hey dummy, enter only a A, S, M, or D!");
}
```

Exercise on Lesson 10

1. What are the two permissible data types to use for *x* in the following?

```
switch (x){ . . . }
```

2. What is the output of the following code?

```
int x = 3, p = 5, y = -8;
switch(x)
{
        case 2:
                p++;
        case 3:
        case 4:
                y+=(--p);
                break;
        case 5:
                y+=(p++);
}
System.out.println(y);
```

3. Write a *switch* structure that uses the character *myChar*. It should increment the integer variable *y* if *myChar* is either a capital or small letter G. It should decrement *y* if *myChar* is either a capital or a small letter M. If *myChar* is anything else, add 100 to *y*.

4. What is output by the following code?

```
int z = 2, q = 0;
switch(z)
{
        case 1:
                q++;
        case 2:
                q++;
        case 3:
                q++;
        case 4:
                q++;
        default:
                q++;
}
System.out.println(--q);
```

5. Write a line of code that declares the variable *chr* as a character type and assigns the letter *z* to it.

6. What is output by the following?

```
int x = 10, y = 12;
System.out.println( "The sum is  " + x + y );
System.out.println( "The sum is  " + (x + y) );
```

7. Convert the following code into a *switch* statement.

```
if(speed = = 75)
{
        System.out.println("Exceeding speed limit");
}
else if( (speed = = 69) || (speed = = 70) )
{
        System.out.println("Getting close");

}
else if(speed = = 65)
{
        System.out.println("Cruising");
}
else
{
        System.out.println("Very slow");

}
```

8. Is *default* a mandatory part of a *switch* structure?

9. Write a line of code that converts *String s = "X"* into a character called *chr*.

Project...Weight on Other Planets

Write a program that will determine the user's weight on another planet. The program should ask the user to enter his weight (on earth) via the keyboard and then present a menu of the other mythical planets. The user should choose one of the planets from the menu, and use a *switch* (with an integer) statement to calculate the weight on the chosen planet. Use the following conversion factors to determine the user's weight on the chosen planet.

Planet	Multiply weight by
Voltar	0.091
Krypton	0.720
Fertos	0.865
Servontos	4.612

A typical output screen will be similar to the following:

```
What is your weight on the earth? 135

1. Voltar
2. Krypton
3. Fertos
4. Servontos

   Selection? 1

Your weight on Voltor would be 12.28499984741211
```

Lesson 11.....The *for*-Loop

One of the most important structures in Java is the "*for*-loop". A loop is basically a block of code that is **repeated** with certain rules about how to start and how to end the process.

Simple example:

Suppose we want to sum up all the integers from 3 to 79. One of the statements that will help us do this is:

```
sum = sum + j;
```

However, this only works if we repeatedly execute this line of code, ...first with *j = 3*, then with *j = 4, j = 5*, ...and finally with *j = 79*. The full structure of the *for*-loop that will do this is:

```
int j = 0, sum = 0;
for (j = 3; j <= 79; j++)
{
        sum = sum + j;
        System.out.println(sum);  //Show the progress as we iterate thru the loop.
}

System.out.println("The final sum is " + sum);
```

Three major parts:

Now let's examine the three parts in the parenthesis of the *for*-loop.

Initializing expression...*j = 3* If we had wanted to start summing at 19, this part would have read,   *j = 19*.

Control expression...*j <= 79* We continue looping as long as this *boolean* expression **is *true***. In general this expression can be **any** *boolean* expression. For example, it could be:

count = = 3   s + 1 < alphB   s > m +19   etc.

Warning: There is something really bad that can happen here. You must write your code so as to insure that this control statement will eventually become *false*, thus causing the loop to terminate. Otherwise you will have an endless loop which is about the worst thing there is in programming.

Step expression... *j++* This tells us how our variable changes as we proceed through the loop. In this case we are incrementing *j* each time; however, other possibilities are:

j--   j = j + 4   j = j * 3   etc.

For our example above, exactly when does the increment ...*j++* occur? Think of the step expression being at the bottom of the loop as follows:

```
for (j = 3; j <= 79; . . . )
{
        … some code …

        j++;  //Just think of the j++ as being the last line of code inside the
}             //braces.
```

Special features of the for-loop:

The *break* command:

If the keyword ***break*** is executed inside a *for*-loop, the loop is immediately exited (regardless of the control statement). Execution continues with the statement immediately following the closing brace of the *for*-loop.

Declaring the loop variable:

It is possible to declare the loop variable in the initializing portion of the parenthesis of a *for*-loop as follows:

```
for (int j = 3; j <= 79; j++)
{
        . . .
}
```

In this case the **scope** of *j* is confined to the interior of the loop. If we write *j* in statement outside the loop (without redeclaring it to be an *int*), it won't compile. The same is true of any other variable declared inside the loop. Its scope is limited to the interior of the loop and is not recognized outside the loop as is illustrated in the following code:

```
for (j = 3; j <= 79; j++)
{
        double d = 102.34;

        . . .
}
System.out.println(d);  //won't compile because of this line
```

No braces:

If there is only **one line of code** or just one basic structure (an *if*-structure or another loop) inside a loop, then the braces are unnecessary. In this case it is still correct (and highly recommended) to still have the braces…but you **can** leave them off.

```
for (j = 3; j <= 79; j++)        is equivalent to        for (j = 3; j <= 79; j++)
      sum = sum + j;                                      {  sum = sum + j; }
```

When the loop finishes:

It is often useful to know what the loop variable is after the loop finishes:

```
for (j = 3; j <= 79; j++)
{
        . . . some code . . .
}
System.out.println(j);  //80
```

On the last iteration of the loop, *j* increments up to 80 and this is when the control statement *j <= 79* finally is *false*. Thus, the loop is exited.

Nested loops:

"Nested loops" is the term used when one loop is placed inside another as in the following example:

```
for(int j = 0; j < 5; j++)
{
        System.out.println("Outer loop");  // executes 5 times
        for(int k = 0; k < 8; k++)
        {
                System.out.println("Inner loop");  //  executes 40 times
        }
}
```

The inner loop iterates eight times for **each** of the five iterations of the outer loop. Therefore, the code inside the inner loop will execute 40 times.

****

Warning:

A very common mistake is to put a semicolon immediately after the parenthesis of a *for*-loop as is illustrated by the following code:

```
for (j =3; j <= 79; j++);
{
        //This block of code is only executed once because of the inappropriately
        //placed semicolon above.
        . . . some code . . .
}
```

Exercise for Lesson 11

In each problem below state what is printed unless directed otherwise.

1. ```
   int j = 0;
   for (int g = 0; g <5; g++)
           j++;
   System.out.println(j);
   ```

2. ```
   int s = 1;
   for (int j = 3; j >= 0; j--)
   {
           s = s + j;
   }
   System.out.println(s);
   ```

3. ```
   int p = 6;
   int m = 20, j;
   for (j = 1; j < p; j++);  //Notice the semicolon on this line
   {
           m = m + j * j;
   }
   System.out.println(m);
   ```

4. ```
   double a = 1.0;
   for (int j = 0; j < 9; j++)
   {
           a*=3;
   }
   System.out.println(j);
   ```

5. ```
   for (int iMus = 0; iMus < 10; iMus++)
   {
           int b = 19 + iMus;
   }
   System.out.println(b);
   ```

6. ```
   double d = 100.01;
   int b = 0;
   for (int iMus = 0; iMus < 10; iMus++)
           b = 19 + iMus;
           d++;
   System.out.println(d);
   ```

7. Write a for-loop that will print the numbers 3, 6, 12, and 24

8. Write a for-loop that will print the numbers 24, 12, 6, 3

9.
```
int k = 0;
for(int j = 0; j <= 10; j++)
{
        if (j = = 5)
        {
                break;
        }
        else
        {
                k++;
        }
}
System.out.println(k);
```

10. What is the name of the part of the parenthesis of a for-loop that terminates the loop?

11. What is the value of *j* for each iteration of the following loop?
```
        int i, j;
        for( i = 10; i <= 100; i = i+ 10)
                j = i / 2;
```

12. What is the value of *r* after the following statements have executed?
```
        int r, j;
        for (j = 1; j < 10; j = j * 2)
        r = 2 * j;
```

13. What is the worst sin you can commit with a for-loop (or any loop for that matter)?

14. How many times does the following loop iterate?
```
        for (p = 9; p <= 145; p++)
        {
                . . .
        }
```

Project… Name Reversal

Write a program that will allow a user to input his name. The prompt and input data would look something like this:

```
Please enter your name. Peter Ustinov
```

Using a for-loop and the *String* method, *substring(…),* produce a printout of the reversal of the name.

For example, the name *Peter Ustinov* would be:

```
vonitsu retep
```

Notice that the printout is in all lower-case. Use the *String* method, *toLowerCase( )* to accomplish this.

for-Loop… Contest Type Problems

1. What is output?
 	
A. 0
B. 10
C. 15
D. 5
E. None of these
	int sum=0;
	for (int k=0; k<5; k++) {
	    sum+=k;
	}
	System.out.println(sum);

2. What is output?
 	
A. 66
B. 100
C. 101
D. 99
E. None of these
	double kk = 3;
	int j = 0;
	for(j = 0; j <= 100; j++) {
	    kk = kk + Math.pow(j, 2);
	    ++kk;
	}
	System.out.println(j);

3. What is the final value of p?
 	
A. 10
B. 4
C. 5
D. 12
E. None of these
	double p = 0;
	for(m=10; m>6; --m)
	{
	    if(m= =7) {
	        p = p+m;
	    }
	    else {
	        ++p;
	    }
	}

4. Which of the following will print the set of odd integers starting at 1 and ending at 9? A. for(int j=0; j<=9; j++) { System.out.println(j); } B. for(int j=1; j<10; j= j+2) { System.out.println(j); } C. for(int j=1; j<=9; j+=1) { System.out.println(j); } D. for(int j=1; j<=9; j+=2) { System.out.println(j); } E. Both B and D	

5. What is output?
 	
A. 4950
B. 101
C. 100
D. Nothing, it's an endless loop
E. None of these
	double x = 0;
	for(int b=0; b<101; b++)
	{
	    x = x + 1;
	    b--;
	}
	System.out.println(x);

6. What is output?
 	
A. 5 6
B. 6 6
C. 5 10
D. 5 5
E. None of these
	int p, q=5;
	for(p=0; p<5; p++); //notice the semicolon
	    q = q+1;
	System.out.println(p + " " + q);

7. What is output?	

A. 98
B. 3939
C. 109
D. 4039
E. None of these
	<pre>int j, k;
	int count = 0;
	for(j=0; j<4; j++)
	{
	    for(k = 0; k < 10; k++)
	    {
	        count++;
	    }
	}
	System.out.print(count--);
	System.out.println(count);</pre>

Lesson 12…..The *while* & *do-while* Loops

The *while* loop is basically the same as the *for*-loop except the **initializing** and **step** expressions are **not** part of the *while*-loop basic structure. In the following code we show the basic structure (skeleton) of the *while*-loop:

```
while( j <= 79 )
{
        … some code that we want repeated…
}
```

We notice in the above code that the only part similar to the *for*-loop is the **control expression** *j <= 79*. The **initializing** and **step** expressions are **absent**. As with the *for*-loop, the *while*-loop keeps repeating **as long as the control statement is *true***.

Summing numbers:

Now, let's actually do something with a *while*-loop. We will begin with a *for*-loop that sums the numbers from 3 to 79 and then perform this same task with a *while*-loop:

```
int sum = 0, j;
for (j = 3; j <= 79; j++)
{
        sum = sum + j;
}
System.out.println(sum);  //3157
```

An equivalent *while*-loop:

Here's a *while*-loop that does the same thing:

```
int sum = 0;
int j = 3;  //initializing expression…not part of loop.
while (j <= 79)  //control expression…fundamental part of loop
{
        sum = sum + j;
        j++;  //step expression…we have to remember to put this in.
              //It's not part of the basic "skeleton" of a while-loop.
}
System.out.println(sum);
```

The *do-while* loop:

A *do-while* loop is exactly the same as a *while*-loop except the control expression is at the **bottom** of the loop rather that at the **top** as it is with the *while*-loop. Following is the skeleton of a *do-while* loop:

```
do
{
                …some code that gets repeated…
}
while( j<= 79);
```

Note that *while* is not inside the braces. Also, notice the **semicolon**. It is a common mistake to leave it off.

We will now re-implement the *for*-loop above that sums from 3 to 79 as a *do-while* loop:

```
int sum = 0;
int j = 3;  //initializing expression
do
{
        sum = sum + j;
        j++;  //step expression
}while (j <= 79);   //control expression
System.out.println(sum);  //3157
```

What's the difference?

The main difference between the *while* loop and the *do-while* loop is **where** the test for staying in the loop is made (the control expression).

while-loop → test is at the **top** of the loop
do-while-loop → test is at the **bottom** of the loop

The *break* statement:

If *break* is encountered inside a loop, the loop terminates regardless of the status of the control statement. Code execution continues with the first line of code following the loop structure.

The *continue* statement:

If *continue* is encountered inside **any** loop (*for*, *while*, or *do-while*), all remaining code in the loop is skipped for this particular iteration; however, looping continues in accordance with the control expression.

This is illustrated with the following code:

```
int j = 0, boxer =11;
while(j <10)
{
        j++;
        if (j != 5)
        {
                continue;
        }
        boxer = boxer + j;
}
System.out.println(boxer);  //16
```

No braces:

If a *while* loop has no braces then it is understood that **only** the very next line of code (or structure such as another loop, *switch*, or *if* structure) is to be iterated (repeated). Consider the following code examples:

```
while(control expression)  …is equivalent to…  while( control expression)
pk = pk +2;                                     {
x = 97;                                             pk = pk +2;
                                                }
                                                x = 97;
```

Exercise for Lesson 12

1. Show the basic skeleton of a *while* loop.

2. Show the basic skeleton of a *do-while* loop.

3. Implement the following for-loop as a *while* loop.

```
int m;
for (m = 97; m <= 195; m++)
{
        k = k * k + 3 * m;
        p = p + m +1;
}
```

4. Implement the following *for* loop as a *do-while* loop.

```
for (int v = 2; v <= 195; v*=3)
{
        k = k * k + 3 * v;
        q = Math.sqrt(q + v +1);
}
```

5. What is the loop control expression in the code segment below?

```
while (!done)
{
        if (i < 1)
        {done = true;}
        i--;
}
```

6. What is the error in the code segment below?

```
do;
{
        if (i < 1)
        {done = true;}
        i--;
}while (!done);
```

7. How many times will the loop below iterate?

```
int j = 0;
while(j < 50)
{
        System.out.println("Hello World!");
}
```

8. How many times will the loop below iterate?

```
int j = 25;
while (j <= 100 || j >= 25)
{
        System.out.println("Temp variable =" + j);
        j++;
}
```

9. Identify the error(s) in the code below:

```
j = 155
while (!done)
{
        if (j <= 25)
                done = true;
        j = j – 5;
};
```

10. What will be the output of the following code:

```
int i = 0, j = 0;
while(i <= 3)
{
        for(j = 0; j <=2; j++)
        {
                System.out.print(i + "," + j + "   ");
        }
        i++;
}
```

11. What command would you use if something unusual happens in one of your loops and you wish to exit prematurely (even before the control expression says you can)?

12. What loop structure would you use if you want to guarantee that a test condition of the control expression be tested **before** the block of code inside the loop could execute?

13. What is printed when the following code runs?

```
double m = 92.801;
int j = 0;
do
{
        j = j + 2;
        if (j > -100)
                continue;
        m+=3;
}while(j < 6);
System.out.println(m);
```

14. Write a program that will prompt the user to enter an integer. The program should square the number and then print the squared number. Repeat this process until 0 is entered as input. Use a do-while-loop to do this.

while & *do-while* loops… Contest Type Problems

1. Which of the following imitates the action of the *for*-loop to the right?

```
for(int j=0; j<100; j++)
{
        … some code …
}
```

   A. int j =0;
      while(j<100){ j++; …some code…}
   B. int j=0;
      while(j<100){…some code… j++;}
   C. int j=0;
      do{…some code… j++;}while(j<100);
   D. Both B and C
   E. Both A and B

2. How many times does this loop iterate?

```
int z = 19;
while(z < 20)
{
        if(z<100)
            continue;
        z++;
}
```

   A. 0
   B. 1
   C. 2
   D. Infinite number of times
   E. Both A and B

3. What is the output if the initial value of *k* and *p* are both 0?

```
do  {
        if(k= =1)
        {
                p+=3;
        }
        k++;
        p--;
}while(k<3);
System.out.println(p);
```

   A. 0
   B. 3
   C. 2
   D. 1
   E. None of these

4. How many times does this loop iterate if the value of the *boolean b* is **not** known?

```
boolean p = true;
int sum=0;
while(p)
{
        sum+=5;
        if(b || !b)
                break;
}
```

   A. None
   B. 2
   C. Can't be determined
   D. Infinite number of times
   E. None of these

5. What type of loop would you use if the condition for staying in the loop needs to be tested **before** the loop iterates?

   A. *for*-loop
   B. *while*-loop
   C. *do-while* loop
   D. All of these
   E. Both A and B

Lesson 13....ASCII and More on *char*

Things you can't do:

Character type *char* and *String* types can't be stored into each other. The following lines of code are **illegal**:

```
char a = aString;  //where aString is a String…..illegal
char a = "A";  //illegal

String x = xChar;  //where xChar is a char……..illegal
String x = 'X';  //illegal
```

Surprisingly legal:

Strangely enough the following **is** legal:

```
int x =1;
char a = 'A';  //ASCII code for 'A' is 65… (more on ASCII below)
int y = x + a;  //This is legal!
System.out.println(y);  //66

int z = a;  //This is legal!
```

Illegal!

Storing an *int* type into a *char* is illegal.

```
char ch = j;  //Illegal…assuming j is an int
```

Why is this illegal? It's because *char* can take on Unicode values from 0 – 65536 (two bytes)while *int* types can go over 2 billion. The compiler justly complains about "possible loss of precision" and refuses to do it. Use casting as a way around this.

```
char ch = (char)j;   //Legal…assuming j is an int and less than 65,536
```

ASCII (pronounced "ask-key") codes:

Why does the code in middle section above work? It's because characters are just numbers. For example, capital A is stored as a 65. That's why we got 66 above. All characters (letters, numbers, symbols, etc) are stored as numbers. Some ASCII codes that you **should know** are:

Character	ASCII	Character	ASCII	Character	ASCII
0	48	A	65	a	97
1	49	B	66	b	98
2	50	C	67	c	99
. . .	. . .	. . .	. . .	. . .	. . .
8	56	Y	89	y	121
9	57	Z	90	z	122

For more on ASCII codes, see Appendix D.

Conversion between *Strings* and characters:

Let's look back at the top section of this page. What do you do if you absolutely have to convert a *String* into a character or vice versa?

a. **Conversion of a *String* into a character**

```
String s = "W";
char a = s.charAt(0);  //a now equals 'W'
```

b. **Conversion of a character into a *String***

```
char a = 'X';
String s = "" + a;  //concatenation of a string and a character is permit-
                    //ed. The result is a String. The trick is to make the
                    //String we are concatenating an empty String ("").
```

Conversion from capital to small:

A way to convert capital-letter characters into small-letter characters is to add 32. Look in the chart above…capital A is 65……small a is 97…….a difference of 32

.

```
char bigLetter = 'H';
char smallLetter = (char)(bigLetter + 32); //(bigLetter + 32) is an int that must be
                                           //cast…see # 3 on previous page.
System.out.println(smallLetter);  //h
```

What are you? (just ask)

We can ask the following questions of a character (answers are always *true* or *false*),

c. "are you a digit?"

```
char ch = 'a';
System.out.println( Character.isDigit(ch) );  //false

char ch = '3';
System.out.println( Character.isDigit(ch) );  //true
```

d. "are you a letter?"

```
char ch = 'a';
System.out.println( Character.isLetter(ch) );  //true

char ch = '3';
System.out.println(Character.isLetter(ch) );  //false
```

e. "are you a letter or a digit?"

```
char ch = 'a';
System.out.println( Character.isLetterOrDigit(ch) );  //true

char ch = '3';
System.out.println( Character.isLetterOrDigit(ch) );  //true
```

f. "are you whitespace?"….(new line character, space and tabs are whitespace)

```
char ch = ' ';
System.out.println( Character.isWhitespace(ch) ); //true

char ch = 'p';
System.out.println( Character.isWhitespace(ch) ); //false
```

g. "are you lowercase?"

```
char ch = 'a';
System.out.println( Character.isLowerCase(ch) ); //true

char ch = 'A';

System.out.println(Character.isLowerCase(ch) ); //false
```

h. "are you uppercase?"

```
char ch = 'a';
System.out.println( Character.isUpperCase(ch) ); //false

char ch = 'A';
System.out.println( Character.isUpperCase(ch) ); //true
```

Conversion to upper case:

We can convert a character to upper case as follows:

```
char ch = 'd';
char nn = Character.toUpperCase(ch);
System.out.println(nn); //D
```

Conversion to lower case:

We can convert a character to lower case as follows:

```
char ch = 'F';
char nn = Character.toLowerCase(ch);
System.out.println(nn); //f
```

Exercise on Lesson 13

1. What is the ASCII code for 'A'?

2. What is the ASCII code for 'Z'?

3. What is the ASCII code for 'a'?

4. What is the ASCII code for 'z'?

5. How many letters are in the English alphabet?

6. What is the ASCII code for the character '0' (this is the number 0 and not the letter O)?

7. What is the ASCII code for the character '9'?

8. What does the following code do?

```
char c;
for (int j = 97; j <= 122; j++) {
        c = (char)(j –32);
        System.out.print(c);
}
```

9. What does the following code do?

```
String s = "Alfred E. Neuman";
char ch;
for (int x = 0; x < s.length( ); x++) {
        ch = s.charAt(x);
        if ( (ch <= 90) && (ch>=65) )
                ch = (char)(ch + 32);
        System.out.print(ch);
}
```

10. Write code that will convert *char a* into a *String*.

11. Write code that will convert *String p* into a character. (*p* consists of just one letter.)

12. Is this legal?

```
char ch = 'V';
String sd = ch;
```

13. Is this legal?
```
char ch = 'V';
char x = (char)(ch + 56);
```

14. Is this legal?
```
char aa = "X";
```

15. char k = 'B';
```
System.out.println(k + 3);  //What's printed?
```

16. char k = 'B';
```
System.out.println( (char)(k + 3) );  //What's printed?
```

17. Write code that will insure that an uppercase version of *char boy* is stored in *char cv*.

18. Write code that will insure that a lowercase version of *char boy* is stored in *char cv*.

19. If you have a character called *bv*, what could you do to determine if it's a digit?

20. If you have a character called *bv*, what could you do to determine if it's a letter?

21. If you have a character called *bv*, what could you do to determine if it's an uppercase character?

22. If you have a character called *bv*, what could you do to determine if it's either a letter or a digit?

23. If you have a character called *bv*, what could you do to determine if it's a lowercase character?

24. Describe what the following code does.
```
for(int j = 0; j <= 127; j++)
{
        char ch = (char)j;
        if (Character.isWhitespace(ch) )
                System.out.println(j);
}
```

Lesson 14…..Binary, Hex, and Octal

We will examine four different number systems here,…decimal, binary, hexadecimal (hex), and octal. In your study of these number systems it is very important to note the **similarities** of each. Study these similarities carefully. This is ultimately how you will understand the new number systems.

Decimal, base 10

There are only **10** digits in this system:
0, 1, 2, 3, 4, 5, 6, 7, 8, 9

Note that even though this is base **10**, there is no single digit for **10**. Instead we use two of the permissible digits, 1 and 0 to make **10**.

Positional value: Consider the decimal number 5,402.

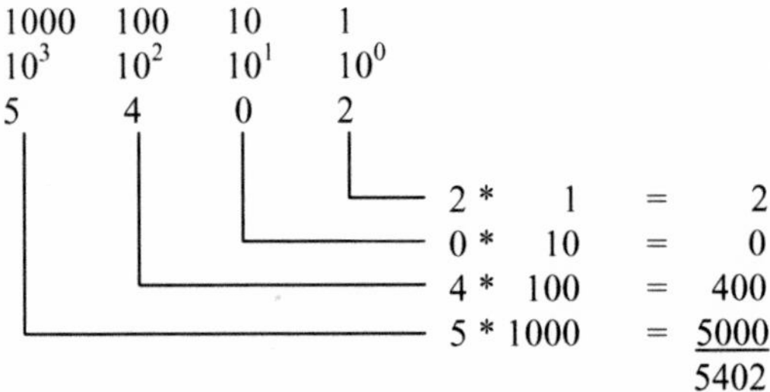

Binary, base 2

There are only **2** digits in this system:
0, 1

Note that even though this is base **2**, there is no single digit for **2**. Instead we use two of the permissible digits, 1 and 0 to make $\mathbf{10_{bin}}$ $\mathbf{(2_{dec})}$.

Positional value: Consider the conversion of binary number 1101_{bin} to decimal form.

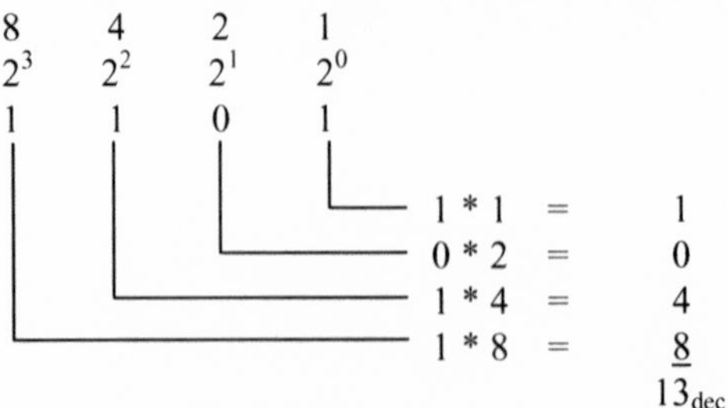

Bits and Bytes: Each of the positions of 1101_{bin} is called a bit… it's a four-bit number. When we have **eight bits** (example, 10110101_{bin}) we call it a **byte**. If we say that a computer has 256mb of memory, where *mb* stands for megabytes, this means it has 256 million bytes. See Appendix Y for more on kilobytes, megabytes, and gigabytes, etc.

Hexadecimal (hex), base 16

There are only **16** digits in this system:
0, 1, 2, 3, 4, 5, 6, 7, 8, 9, A, B, C, D, E, F

A	B	C	D	E	F
10	11	12	13	14	15

Note that even though this is base **16**, there is no single digit for **16**. Instead we use two of the permissible digits, 1 and 0 to make $\mathbf{10_{hex}}$ $\mathbf{(16_{dec})}$.

Positional value: Consider the conversion of hex number $5C02_{hex}$ to decimal form.

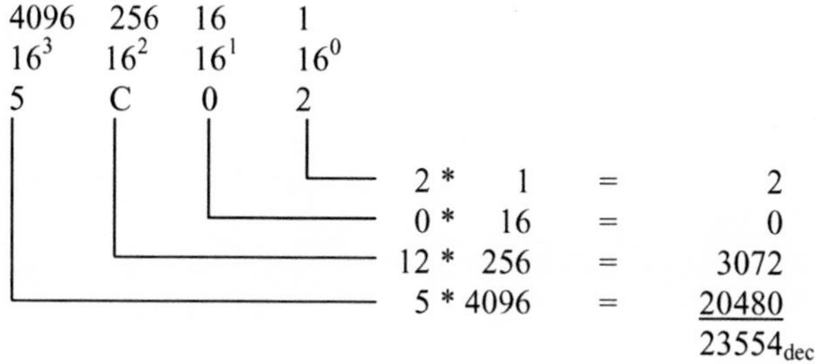

4096 256 16 1
16^3 16^2 16^1 16^0
5 C 0 2
2 * 1 = 2
0 * 16 = 0
12 * 256 = 3072
5 * 4096 = 20480
23554dec

Octal, base 8

There are only **8** digits in this system:
0, 1, 2, 3, 4, 5, 6, 7

Note that even though this is base **8**, there is no single digit for **8**. Instead we use two of the permissible digits, 1 and 0 to make $\mathbf{10_{oct}}$ $\mathbf{(8_{dec})}$.

Positional value: Consider the conversion of octal number 5402_{oct} to decimal form.

512	64	8	1
8^3	8^2	8^1	8^0
5	4	0	2

2 *	1	=	2
0 *	8	=	0
4 *	64	=	256
5 *	512	=	2560
			2818_{dec}

Following are examples that show how we can use these different number systems with Java.

Store a hex number:

```
int x = 0x4CB3; //the leading 0x indicates hex format
System.out.println(x); //19635 …Notice it automatically prints in decimal form
```

Store an octal number:

```
int x = 0734; //the leading 0 indicates octal format
System.out.println(x); //476 ...Notice it automatically prints in decimal form
```

Convert an integer variable to a hex *String*:

```
int x = 3901;
System.out.println( Integer.toHexString(x) ); //F3Dhex
                //...or Integer.toString(x, 16);
```

Convert an integer variable to a binary *String*:

```
int x = 3901;
System.out.println( Integer.toBinaryString(x) ); // 111100111101bin
        //...or Integer.toString(x, 2);
```

Convert an integer variable to an octal *String*:

```
int x = 3901;
System.out.println( Integer.toOctalString(x) ); //7475oct
                //...or Integer.toString(x, 8);
```

Notice in the last three examples above the following method was an alternate way to convert bases:

```
String s = Integer.toString(i, b);
```

The first parameter *i* is of type *int* and *b* is the base to which we wish to convert. *b* (also an *int* type) can be any base ranging from 2 to 36. Just as for hexadecimal numbers where we use the letters A – F, the bases higher than 16 (hex) use the remaining letters of the alphabet. For example, Integer.toString(8162289, 32) returns “7p2vh”.

Base conversion using *parseInt*:

It is also possible to go from some strange base (in *String* form) back to a decimal *int* type. For example, *Integer.parseInt(“3w4br”, 35)* converts $3w4br_{35}$ into 5879187_{dec}.

A technique for converting 147 from decimal to binary:

```
2 147            ; 2 divides into 147   73 times with a remainder of
2   73  1        ;1.  2 divides into 73, 36 times with a remainder of
2   36  1        ;1.  2 divides into 36, 18 times with a remainder of
2   18  0        ;0.  2 divides into 18, 9 times with a remainder of
2    9  0        ;0.  etc.
2    4  1
2    2  0
2    1  0
     0  1
```

Now list the 1’s and 0’s from <u>bottom to top</u>. $\mathbf{10010011_{bin} = 147_{dec}}$

A technique for converting 3741 from decimal to hex:

```
16      3741            ;divide 3741 by 16. It goes 233 times with a
16      233     13      ;remainder of 13.
16      14      9
        0       14
```

Now list the numbers from bottom to top. Notice, when listing the 14 we give its hex equivalent, E, and for 13 we will give D.

$E9D_{hex} = 3741_{dec}$

An octal multiplication example (47_{oct} * 23_{oct}):

```
 2
 47
 23
  5
```

$3 * 7 = 21_{dec}$ — 8 divides into 21 2 times with a remainder of 5. Notice the 5 and the carry of 2

```
12
 47
 23
165
```

$(3*4) + 2 = 14_{dec}$ — 8 divides into 14 1 time with a remainder of 6

```
 1
 47
 23
165
 6
```

$2 * 7 = 14_{dec}$ — 8 divides into 14 1 time with a remainder of 6

```
 11
  47
  23
 165
116
```

$2*4 + 1 = 9_{dec}$ — 8 divides into 9 1 time with a remainder of 1

Now we are ready to add:

```
  1
  165
 116
1345oct
```

Notice in adding 6 + 6 we get 12. 8 divides 12 1 time, remainder 4.

Binary addition:

The rules to remember are:

0 + 0 = 0   0 + 1 = 1   1 + 1 = 0 with a carry of 1

Add the two binary numbers 110011 and 100111.

1			1	1	1	
	1	1	0	0	1	1
	1	0	0	1	1	1
1	0	1	1	0	1	0

The problem we have done here:

$110011_{bin} + 100111_{bin} = 1011010_{bin}$

is equivalent to:

$51_{dec} + 39_{dec} = 90_{dec}$

A trick for converting binary into hex:

Begin with the binary number 10110111010. Starting on the right side, partition this into groups of four bits and get 101 1011 1010 To each four bit group, assign a hex digit.

5 B A

Thus we have $10110111010_{bin} = 5BA_{hex}$. Similarly, partition a binary number into groups of 3 to convert to Octal.

See Appendix D for the decimal, hex, octal, and binary equivalents of 0 – 127.

For an enrichment activity concerning a **Binary** File Editor, see Appendix U. There, you will have an opportunity to specify software, search on the Internet, and publish the information you discover…. Appendix G explains how negative numbers are handled in the binary system.

Project… Basically Speaking

Create a project called *TableOfBases* with class *Tester*. The *main* method should have a *for* loop that cycles through the integer values 65 <= j <= 90 (These are the ASCII codes for characters A – Z). Use the methods learned in this lesson to produce a line of this table on each pass through the loop. Display the equivalent of the decimal number in the various bases just learned (binary, octal, and hex) as well as the character itself:

Decimal	Binary	Octal	Hex	Character
65	1000001	101	41	A
66	1000010	102	42	B
67	1000011	103	43	C
68	1000100	104	44	D
69	1000101	105	45	E
70	1000110	106	46	F
71	1000111	107	47	G
72	1001000	110	48	H
73	1001001	111	49	I
74	1001010	112	4a	J
75	1001011	113	4b	K
76	1001100	114	4c	L
77	1001101	115	4d	M
78	1001110	116	4e	N
79	1001111	117	4f	O
80	1010000	120	50	P
81	1010001	121	51	Q
82	1010010	122	52	R
83	1010011	123	53	S
84	1010100	124	54	T
85	1010101	125	55	U
86	1010110	126	56	V
87	1010111	127	57	W
88	1011000	130	58	X
89	1011001	131	59	Y
90	1011010	132	5a	Z

Exercise on Lesson 14

1. Convert $3C4F_{hex}$ to decimal.

2. Convert 100011_{bin} to decimal.

3. Convert 637_{oct} to decimal.

4. Is the following code legal? If not, why?
```
int v = 04923;
```

5. Is the following code legal? If not, why?
```
int w = 0xAAFF;
```

6. Convert $9A4E_{hex}$ to decimal.

7. Convert 1011011_{bin} to decimal.

8. Convert 6437_{oct} to decimal.

9. Write code that will store $5C3B_{hex}$ in the integer variable *a*.

10. Write code that will store 3365_{oct} in the integer variable *k*.

11. Convert 478_{dec} to binary.

12. Convert 5678_{dec} to hex.

13. Convert 5678_{dec} to octal.

14. Multiply $2C6_{hex}$ times $3F_{hex}$ and give the answer in hex.

15. Add 3456_{oct} and 745_{oct} and give the answer in octal.

16. What is the decimal equivalent of A_{hex}?

17. What is the decimal equivalent of 8_{hex}?

18. What is the base of the hex system?

19. How do you write 16_{dec} in hex?

20. What is the base of the binary system?

21. Add these two binary numbers 1111000 and 1001110.

22. Add these two binary numbers:

1000001 and 1100001

23. Explain the following "joke".

"There are only 10 types of people in the world…those who understand binary and those who don't."

24. Suppose you have *String s* that represents a number that you know is expressed in a base given by *int b*. Write code that will convert this into an equivalent decimal based integer and store the result in *int i*.

25. Show code that will convert $9322gf_{33}$ into *String s* that is the equivalent number in base 28.

26. Add $3FA6_{hex}$ to $E83A_{hex}$ and give the answer in hex.

27. Multiply 7267_{oct} times 4645_{oct} and give the answer in octal.

28. Add 2376_{oct} to 567_{oct} and give the answer in octal.

29. Multiply $3E_{hex}$ times $5B_{hex}$ and give the answer in hex.

Lesson 15.....Classes and Objects

A **class** is like a cookie cutter and the "cookies" it produces are the **objects**:

One cookie cutter.......................many possible cookies.
One **class**..............................many possible **objects**.

Building a *Circle* class:

Let's build a class and begin to understand its parts. Our class will be called *Circle*. When we create one of our *Circle* objects (just like creating a cookie), we will want to specify the radius of each circle. We will want to have the ability to interrogate the various *Circle* objects we might have created and ask for the area, circumference, or diameter.

```
public class Circle
{
        //This part is called the constructor and lets us specify the radius of a
        //particular circle.
        public Circle(double r)
        {
                radius = r;
        }

        //This is a method. It performs some action (in this case it calculates the
        //area of the circle and returns it.
        public double area( ) //area method
        {
                double a = Math.PI * radius * radius;
                return a;
        }

        public double circumference( ) //circumference method
        {
                double c = 2 * Math.PI * radius;
                return c;
        }

        public double radius;  //This is a State Variable...also called Instance
                               //Field and Data Member. It is available to code
                               // in ALL the methods in this class.
}
```

Instantiating an object:

Now, let's use our cookie cutter (the *Circle* class) to create two cookies (*Circle* objects).

```
Circle cir1 = new Circle(5.1);
Circle cir2 = new Circle(20.6);
```

With a cookie-cutter we say we create a cookie. With a class we **instantiate** an object. So, we just instantiated an object called *cir1* having a radius of 5.1 and another object called *cir2* having a radius of 20.6.... From this point on we don't refer to *Circle*. Instead we refer to *cir1* and *cir2*.

Let's suppose we wish to store the radius of *cir1* in a variable called *xx*. Here's the code to do this:

```
double xx = cir1.radius;
```

Now let's ask for and printout the area of *cir2*:

```
System.out.println ( cir2.area( ) );
```

A closer look at methods:

We will now look at the **signature** of this *area* method and then examine each part.

```
public double area( )  //this is the signature
```

Access control (*public*, *private*, etc.):

The word ***public*** gives us access from outside the *Circle* class. Notice above that we used *cir2.area( )* and this code was in some other class…so "public" lets us have access to the *area( )* method from the outside world. It is also possible to use the word ***private*** here. (more on this later)… Strictly speaking, *public* and *private* are not officially part of the signature; however, since they generally always preface the actual signature, we will consider them part of the signature for the remainder of this book.

Returned data type (*double*, *int*, *String*, etc):

The word ***double*** above tells us what type variable is returned. When we issue the statement *System.out.println(cir2.area( ));*, what do we expect to be "returned" from the call to the *area* method? The answer is that we expect a double precision number since the area calculation may very well yield a decimal fraction result.

Method name:

The word ***area*** as part of the signature above is the name of the method and could be any name you like…even your dog's name. However, it is wise not to use cute names. Rather, use names that are suggestive of the action this method performs.

Naming convention:

Notice all our methods begin with a small letter. This is not a hard-and-fast rule; however, it is conventional for variables and objects to begin with lower case letters.

Parameters:

The parenthesis that follows the name of the method normally will contain parameters. So far, in our circle class none of the methods have parameters so the parenthesis are all empty; however, the parenthesis must still be there.

Let's create a new method in which the parenthesis is **not** empty. Our new method will be called *setRadius*. The purpose of this is so that after the object has been created (at which time a radius is initially set), we can change our mind and establish a **new** radius for this particular circle. The new signature (and code) will be as follows:

```
public void setRadius(double nr)
{
        radius = nr;  //set the state variable radius to the new radius
}                     //value, nr
```

We see two new things here:

a. ***void*** means we are **not** returning a value from this method. Notice there is no *return* in the code as with the other methods.

b. *double nr* means the method expects us to send it a *double* and that it will be called *nr* within the code of this method. *nr* is called a **parameter**.

   Here is how we would call this method from within some other class:

   ```
   cir2.setRadius(40.1);  //set the radius of cir2 to 40.1
   ```

   40.1 is called an **argument**. The terms arguments and parameters are often carelessly interchanged; however, the correct usage of both has been presented here.

   Notice that there is no equal sign in the above call to *setRadius*. This is because it's void (returns nothing)… therefore, we need not assign it to anything.

Have you noticed another way we could change the radius?

```
cir2.radius = 40.1;  //We store directly into the public instance field.
```

Understanding *main*:

At this point we are capable of understanding three things that have remained mysterious up to now. Consider the line of code that's a part of all our programs:

```
public static void main(String args[ ])
```

1. ***main*** is the name of this special **method**
2. ***public*** gives us access to this method from outside its class
3. ***void*** indicates that this method doesn't return anything

The other parts will have to remain a mystery for now.

The constructor:

Next, we will look at the constructor for the *Circle* class.

```
public Circle(double r)
{
        radius = r;
}
```

The entire purpose of the constructor is to set values for some of the state variables of an object at the time of its creation (construction). In our *Circle* class we set the value of the state variable, *radius*, according to a double precision number that is passed to the constructor as a parameter. The parameter is called *r* within the constructor method; however, it could be given any legal variable name.

The constructor is itself a method; albeit a very special one with slightly different rules from ordinary methods.

1. **public** is always specified.

2. The name of the constructor method is always the **same** as the name of the class.

3. This is actually a void method (since it doesn't return anything); however, the *void* specifier is omitted.

4. The required parenthesis may or may not have parameters. Our example above does. Following is another example of a *Circle* constructor with **no** parameters. A constructor with no parameters is called the **default constructor**.

   ```
   public Circle( )
   {
           radius =100;
   }
   ```

   What this constructor does is to just blindly set the radii to 100 of all *Circle* objects that it creates.

Project... What's That Diameter?

Create a new method for the *Circle* class called *diameter*. Add this method to the *Circle* class described on page 15-1. It should return a *double* that is the diameter of the circle. No parameters are passed to this method.

In a *Tester* class, test the performance of your new *diameter* method as follows: (Your project should have two classes, *Tester* and *Circle.*)

```
public class Tester
{
        public static void main( String args[] )
        {
                Circle cir1 = new Circle(35.5);
                System.out.println( cir1.diameter( ) );
        }
}
```

The printout should give 71.0 as the answer.

Exercise on Lesson 15

1. double length = 44.0;
   int width =13;
   Rectangle myRect = new Rectangle(length, width);
   a. Identify the class
   b. Identify the object
   c. What type of parameter(s) are passed to the constructor?

2. Write out the signature for the constructor of the *Rectangle* class from #1 above.

3. Suppose a constructor for the *Lunch* class is as follows:
```
public Lunch(boolean diet, int cal)
{
        diet_yes_no = diet;
        calories = cal;
}
```
   Write appropriate code that will create a *Lunch* object called *yummy5*. You should tell the constructor that, yes, you are on a diet, and the number of calories should be 900.

4. BankAccount account39 = new BankAccount(500.43);
   a. Identify the class
   b. Identify the object
   c. What type of parameter(s) are passed to the constructor?

5. A class is like a ____________. An object is like a ______________.
   Fill in the blanks above using the word "cookie" and "cookie cutter".

6. What's wrong (if anything) with the following constructor for the *School* class?
```
public void school(int d, String m)
{ … some code … }
```

7. Which of the following is a correct association?
   a. One class, many objects
   b. One object, many classes

8. Which must exist first?
   a. The class
   b. The object

9. Is the following legal? If not, why?

```
//Constructor
public House(int j, boolean k)
{  …some code…  }
```

```
//This code is in main of Tester class
int p = 3, q = 9;
House myHouse = new House(p, q);
```

10. //Constructor

```
public Band(int numMembers, int numInstruments, String director, double amount)
{  …code…}

Band ourBnd = new Band(mem, instrmnts, "Mr. Perkins", budget);
```

What should be the data types of:

   a. mem
   b. instrmnts
   c. budget

****

```
public class BibleStory
{
    public int var1;
    public double var2;
    public String sss;

    public void Samson(double zorro)
    {  …some code…}

    public String getDelilah( )
    {  …some code…}

    public BibleStory(String x, int y, double z)
    {  …some code…  }
}
```

11. From the *BibleStory* class above, write the signature of the constructor.

12. From the *BibleStory* class above, what is/are the instance field(s).

13. From the *BibleStory* class above, write the signature(s) of the all the method(s).

14. Write code that instantiates an object called *philistine* from the *BibleStory* class. Pass the following parameters to the constructor:

    The integer should be 19, the *String* should be "Ralph", and the *double* should be 24.18.

15. Assume an object called *gravy* has been created from the *BibleStory* class. Write code that will set the state variable *var2* to 106.9 for the *gravy* object.

16. Write code that will print the value of the *BibleStory* data member, *sss*. Assume you have already created an object called *bart*.

17. Again, assume we have an object called *bart* instantiated from the *BibleStory* class. What should you fill in for **<#1>** below in order that *sss* be stored in the variable *jj*?
    <#1> jj = bart.sss;

18. Create a class called *Trail*. It should have instance fields *x* and *y* that are integers. Instance field *s* should be a *String*. The constructor should receive a *String* which is used to initialize *s*. The constructor should automatically set *x* and *y* both equal to 10. There should be a method called *met* that returns a *String* that is the hex equivalent of *x* y*. This method receives no parameters.

19. Suppose you wish to call a method whose signature is:
    public double peachyDandy(int z)

    Write code that would call this method (assume we have an object name *zippo*). Also assume that this code will be placed in the *main* method of a *Tester* class and that the *peachyDandy* method is in some other class.

20. Refer to the information in 19 above. What's wrong with trying to call this method in the following fashion?
    double hamburger = zippo.peachyDandy(127.31);

Project ... Overdrawn at the Bank

Create a class called *BankAccount*. It should have the following properties:

1. Two state variables:
   balance...double... This is how much money is currently in the account.
   *name...String...*The name of the person owning the account.

2. Constructor should accept two parameters.
   a. One should be a *double* variable that is used to initialize the state variable, *balance*.

   b. The other should be a *String* that is used to initialize the state variable, *name*.

3. Two methods:
   a. *deposit...*returns nothing...accepts a *double* that is the amount of money being deposited. It is added to the *balance* to produce a new balance.

   b. *withdraw...*returns nothing...accepts a *double* that is the amount of money being taken out of the account. It is subtracted from the *balance* to produce a new *balance*.

Create a *Tester* class that has a *main()* method. In that method you should input from the keyboard the amount (1000) of money initially to be put into the account (via the constructor) along with the name of the person to whom the account belongs.

1. Use these two pieces of data to create a new *BankAccount* object called *myAccount*.

2. Call the *deposit* method to deposit $505.22.

3. Print the *balance* state variable.

4. Call the *withdraw* method to withdraw $100.

5. Print the remaining *balance* in this form:

```
The Sally Jones account balance is, $1405.22
```

Lesson 16….. More on Classes and Objects

In this lesson we will explore some additional features of classes and objects.

***private* methods and state variables:**

Consider the following class:

```
public class Recipe
{
        public Recipe(String theName )
        {  …some code… }

        public void setServings(int x)
        { …some code… }

        public double getRetailCost( )
        {
                …
                int x = 13;
                double tempCost = pricePerCalorie(x) * calories + cost;
                …
        }

        private double pricePerCalorie(int z)
        { …some code… }

        public int calories;
        public int carbs;
        public int fat;
        private double cost;
        public String name;
}
```

We notice that there is a ***private*** method called *pricePerCalorie* and a **private** instance field called *cost.*

Now let's suppose that we instantiate an object from this *Recipe* class.

```
Recipe yummyStuff = new Recipe("Watermelon Salad");
```

The following code would be illegal from within some other class:

```
double ff = yummyStuff.cost; //illegal! Cost is private
double dj = yummyStuff. pricePerCalorie(3); //illegal! Method is private
```

Notice that from within the *getRetailCost* method that we can **legally** access the **private** data member and the ***private*** method. Thus we learn that

***private* things can only be accessed from <u>within</u> the class itself.**

Declaring and instantiating an object:

Normally when we instantiate an object, we do it in one line of code:

```
Circle cir1 = new Circle(3.0);
```

However, it can be done in <u>two</u> lines:

```
Circle cir1; //Here, cir1 is merely declared to be of type Circle
cir1 = new Circle(3.0); //Here, it is finally instantiated.
```

Anonymous objects:

It is possible to **instantiate an object without a name**. Suppose that in the *Ozzy* class (having an object named *osborne*) there is a method that we wish to call that has the following signature:

```
public void melloJello(Circle cirA)
```

Notice that the parameter is of type *Circle* so in our calling code below, we dutifully pass a *Circle* object to the *melloJello* method:

```
osborne.melloJello(new Circle(5) );
```

The code, *new Circle(5)*, instantiates the object; however, in the region of the calling code it doesn't have a name. In the code of the *melloJello* method it **does** have a name, *cirA*. In that code we can do such things as *cirA.area( )* to find the area of the circle, etc.

Setting two objects equal:

Recall the *Circle* class from the previous lesson. Suppose we have instantiated a *Circle* object called *cir1*.....

```
Circle cir1 = new Circle(5.3); //cir1 has a radius of 5.3
```

We will now demonstrate how to declare a *cir2* object, but not to instantiate it. Then in another line of code, set it equal to *cir1*:

```
Circle cir2; //cir2 has only been declared to be of type Circle
cir2 = cir1; //cir2 and cir1 now refer to the same object. There is only one object.
             //It simply has two references to it.
```

Thus, *cir2.area( )* returns exactly the same as *cir1.area( )*....and *cir1.radius* is exactly the same as *cir2.radius*,...etc.

Determining if two objects are equal:

Look above in #4 at *cir1* and *cir2*. We have said these are equal objects. Since they are equal the following should print a *true*:

```
System.out.println(cir1 = = cir2); //true
```

However, if we recreate *cir1* and *cir2* in the following way and then compare them, they will **not** be equal.

```
Circle cir1 = new Circle(11);
Circle cir2 = new Circle(11);
System.out.println(cir1 = = cir2); //false, in spite of the fact they both have a
                                   //radius of 11
```

We see that various objects of the same class must refer to the **same** object in order to be judged equal using = =. (Of course, we could also test with !=.)

Now suppose we change the code as follows:

```
Circle cir1 = new Circle(11);
Circle cir2 = new Circle(11);
```

```
System.out.println( cir1.equals(cir2) );
```

What would be printed? This would behave **exactly** as the previous code, printing a *false*. In other words, *(cir1.equals(cir2))* is equivalent to *(cir1 = = cir2)*. In a later lesson on inheritance we would say that the *Circle* class inherits the *equals* method from the cosmic superclass *Object* and simply compares to see if we are referring to the **same** object. There is, however, an exception. If the programmer who created the *Circle* class created an *equals* method for it, then that overrides the inherited method and compares the **contents** of the two objects (likely the radii). In this case, the *println* above would print a *true* since the contents of the two objects are the same (they both have a radius of 11).

With regard to the = = operator, *String* objects behave in **exactly** the same way as other objects; however, they can sometimes **appear** to not follow the rule. Consider the following:

```
String s1 = "Hello";
String s2 = "Hello";  //s1 and s2 are String constants
System.out.println(s1 = = s2);  // prints true
```

The *String* constant pool:

Why did this print a *true* when *s1* and *s2* appear to be two separate objects? The reason is that all *String* literals are stored as *String* constants in a separate memory area called the *String constant pool* (as are all *String* literals at compile time). When object *s1* is created, "Hello" is placed in the *String constant pool* with the reference *s1* pointing to it. Then, for efficiency, when the reference (variable) *s2* is created, Java checks the pool to see if the *String* constant being specified for *s2* is already there. Since it is in this case, *s2* also points to "Hello" stored in the *String constant pool*. Physically, *s1* and *s2* are two separate *String* object references, but logically they are pointing to the **same** object in the *String constant pool*. So, in *(s1 = = s2)* from the code above we see that both *s1* and *s2* are referencing the same object, and a *true* is returned.

Now consider *String*s built in the following way and their reaction to the = = operator:

```
String s1 = new String("Felix");
String s2 = new String("Felix");  // s1 and s2 are not String constants
System.out.println(s1 = = s2);  // prints false
```

This code behaves exactly as expected since the two *String* objects, s1 and s2, really are two separate objects referenced in an area of memory apart from the *String constant pool* (as dictated by *new*).

While we are on the subject of *String* storage let's see what happens with the following:

```
String s = new String("my string");
```

This actually results in the creation of *two String* objects. The reference *s* points to the newly created *String* object in "regular" memory. The *String* literal "my string" is encountered at compile time and is placed as a *String* constant in the *String constant pool*.

The moral of all this confusion is that if you want to compare the contents of *String*s, use either the *equals* or the *compareTo* method, not the = = operator.

Reassignment of an object:

The name of an object is simply a reference to the actual object and can be easily made to point to a different object.

```
Plant species = new Plant("ragweed");
System.out.println( species.status( ) );
species = new Plant("redwood");  //species is set equal to the new Plant object
species.endangered = false;
```

The reassignment above is exactly analogous to the following in which the integer *x* is assigned a new value.

```
int x = 3;
. . .
x = 5;
```

Default rule of *public/private*:

Suppose in a class we have the following method and data member:

```
public double method1( )
{     … some code …     }

public int var1;
```

What would these mean if the word *public* was left off of each? By **default** they would be *Package* (see Nug12-1) which for most student applications will behave like *public*.

Initializing state variables at the time of declaration:

Look back at the *Recipe* class on the first page of this lesson. There, you will find the following declaration for the state variable *cost*.

private double cost; //numeric **state variables** are automatically **initialized to 0**.

Notice that *cost* is only declared, not initialized. Typically, initialization is done in the constructor; however, it can be done at the time of declaration as follows:

```
private double cost = 3;
```

Notice that a numeric state variable can be declared, but not initialized as follows:

```
public int idNum;
```

In this case *idNum* is **automatically** initialized to 0.

The rules are different for initialization of a numeric variable in the **body of a method**. Assume that *amount* in the code below is in the body of a method. It is **not** automatically initialized to 0. In fact, trying to use it without initializing will result in a compile error.

```
double amount;
```

Exercise for Lesson 16

Problems 1 – 5 refer to the following code (assume that *equals* is not an explicit, method of this class):

```
MoonRock myRock = new MoonRock(3, "Xeon");
MoonRock yourRock = new MoonRock(2, "Kryptonite");
MoonRock ourRock = new MoonRock(3, "Xeon");
MoonRock theRock;
theRock = ourRock;
```

1. Does *theRock.equals(ourRock)* return a *true* or *false*?

2. Does *theRock.equals(yourRock)* return a *true* or *false*?

3. Does *theRock.equals(myRock)* return a *true* or *false*?

4. Does *myRock = = ourRock* return a *true* or *false*?

5. Does *myRock.equals(yourRock)* return a *true* or *false*?

Problems 6 – 11 refer to the following code:

```
public class Weenie
{
        public Weenie( )
        {       . . .           }

        public String method1(int jj)
        {       . . .           }

        private void method2(String b)
        {       . . .           }

        public int method3( )
        {       . . .           }

        public double x;
        public int y;
        private String z;
}
```

Now suppose from within a different class we instantiate a *Weenie* object, *oscarMeyer*. All of the code in questions 6 – 11 is assumed to be in this other class.

6. Is *int zz = oscarMeyer.method1(4);* legal? If not, why?

7. Is *oscarMeyer.method2("Hello");* legal? If not, why?

8. Is *int cv = oscarMeyer.method3( );* legal? If not, why?

9. Is *int cv = oscarMeyer.method3(14);* legal? If not, why?

10. Is *oscarMeyer.z = "hotdog";* legal? If not, why?

11. Assume the following code is inside *method1*:

```
method2("BarBQ");
```

Is this legal? If not, why?

12. Instantiate an object called *surferDude* from the *Surfer* class using two separate lines of code. One line should declare the object and the other line should instantiate it. (Assume no parameters are sent to the constructor.)

13. Which of the following sets of code (both purport to do the same thing) is correct? (Assume *beco* is an object having a method (*method33*) that receives a *Circle* parameter.)
    a. Circle cir5 = new Circle(10);
       beco.method33(cir5);
    b. beco.method33(new Circle(10)) ;
    c. Both a and b

14. What is the value of *balance* after the following transactions?

```
//Refer to the BankAccount class you created on p 15-8
BankAccount acc = new BankAccount(10, "Sally");
acc.deposit(5000);
acc.withdraw(acc.balance / 2);
```

15. What's wrong with the following code?

```
BankAccount b;
b.deposit(1000);
```

16. What's wrong with the following code?

```
BankAccount b new BankAccount(32.75, "Melvin");
b = new BankAccount(1000, "Bob");
b.deposit("A thousand dollars");
```

17. What is printed in the following?

```
String myString = "Yellow";
String yourString = "Yellow";
String hisString = new String("Yellow");
String ourString = myString;
System.out.println(myString = = yourString);
System.out.println(myString = = ourString);
System.out.println( myString.equals(yourString) );
System.out.println( myString.equals(ourString) );
System.out.println( myString = = hisString );
```

Project… Gas Mileage

Create a class called *Automobile* in which you pass a gas mileage (miles per gallon) parameter to the constructor which in turn passes it to the state variable, *mpg*. The constructor should also set the state variable *gallons* (gas in the tank) to 0. A method called *fillUp* adds gas to the tank. Another method, *takeTrip*, removes gas from the tank as the result of driving a specified number of miles. Finally, the method *reportFuel* returns how much gas is left in the car.

Test your *Automobile* class by creating a *Tester* class as follows:

```
public class Tester
{
        public static void main( String args[] )
        {
                //Create a new object called myBmw. Pass the constructor an
                //argument of 24 miles per gallon
                Automobile myBmw = new Automobile(24);

                //Use the myBmw object to call the fillup method. Pass it an argument
                //of 20 gallons.
                myBmw.fillUp(20);

                //Use the myBmw object to call the takeTrip method. Pass it an
                //argument of 100 miles. Driving 100 miles of course uses fuel and we
                //would now find less fuel in the tank.
                myBmw.takeTrip(100);

                //Use the myBmw object to call the reportFuel method. It returns a
                //double value of the amount of gas left in the tank and this is assigned
                // to the variable fuel_left
                double fuel_left = myBmw.reportFuel( );

                //Print the fuel_left variable
                System.out.println(fuel_left); //prints gallons left, 15.833333333333332
        }
}
```

Classes and Objects… Contest Type Problems

1. What should replace **<#1>** in order that the instance field, *name*, be initialized when a new object is created?

   A. String name = nm;
   B. name = nm;
   C. nm name;
   D. Can't be done because name is private
   E. None of these

2. Assuming **<#1>** is filled in correctly, how would you create a *Student* object called *stu1* and set *name* to "Sally"?

   A. Student stu1 = new Student( );
      name = "Sally";
   B. stu1.name = "Sally";
   C. stu1 = new Student("Sally");
   D. Student stu1 = new Student("Sally");
   E. None of these

3. Assume a *Student* object called *myStd* has been created and grades have been assigned. How would you retrieve this student's average and store the result in the integer variable *sa*?

   A. sa = myStd.getAverage( );
   B. sa = (int)(myStd.sum/myStd.numGrades);
   C. sa = (int)myStd.getAverage( );
   D. Both B and C
   E. None of these

4. Which of the following would print the *name* of the student represented by the object called *sObj*?

   A. System.out.println(sObj.getName( ));
   B. System.out.println(sObj.name( ));
   C. Both A and B
   D. System.out.println(sObj(name));
   E. None of these

5. Which state variable is accessible from outside the *Student* class?

   A. numGrades
   B. name
   C. sum
   D. Both *name* and *sum*
   E. All are accessible

```
public class Student
{
        public Student(String nm)  {
                <#1>
        }

        public String getName( )
        {
                return name;
        }

        public void setGrade(int grd)
        {
                numGrades++;
                sum = sum + grd;
        }

        public double getAverage( )
        {
                return sum/numGrades;
        }

        private String name;
        private double sum=0;
        public int numGrades=0;
}
```

Lesson 17.....Advanced *String* Methods

Following is a list of some of the *String* methods and techniques we encountered in Lesson 3:
Concatenation, *length()*, *substring()*, *toLowerCase()*, *toUpperCase()*, and escape sequences.

In Lesson 9 we studied:
equals( ) and equalsIgnoreCase( )

We will now look at some of the **signatures** (and examples) of some of the more advanced *String* methods. Recall from Lesson 15 that the layout of a signature is as follows:
public return_type method_name(type parameter1, type parameter2, …)

The variable *return_type* and *type* could be *double*, *int*, *boolean*, *String*, *char*, etc.

For the examples below assume that *s* is a *String* as follows:
s = "The Dukes of Hazzard"

For convenience, the indices of the individual characters of this *String* are given below:

```
T h e   D u k e s   o  f     H  a  z  z  a  r  d
| | | | | | | | | | |  |  |  |  |  |  |  |  |  |
0 1 2 3 4 5 6 7 8 9 10 11 12 13 14 15 16 17 18 19
```

public int compareTo(Object myObj)

Notice this method accepts any Object. Here, we will specifically use a ***String*** object. The general syntax for usage of *compareTo* is: *int j = s.compareTo("coat room");*

This method has three rules:

a. If *s* alphabetically precedes "coat room" then it returns a negative *int*.
b. If *s* alphabetically comes after "coat room" it returns a positive *int*.
c. If *s* is alphabetically equal to "coat room" then it returns a zero.

System.out.println(s.compareTo("coat room")); //**prints a negative number**

The reason we get a negative number in the example above is because 'T' alphabetically precedes 'c'. Refer back to Lesson 13 and you will see that the ASCII code for capital 'T' is 84 and the ASCII code for little 'c' is 99. The number 84 comes before 99 so we say that "The Dukes of Hazzard" comes before (or alphabetically precedes) "coat room".

indexOf( )

This method comes in 6 flavors: (All return –1 if the search is unsuccessful.)

a. **public int indexOf(String str)**

Search from left to right for the first occurrence of the *String str*.

int j = s.indexOf("Hazzard");
System.out.println(j); //**13**

b. public int indexOf(String s, int from)

Starting at index *from*, search from left to right for the first occurrence of the *String s.*

```
int j = s.indexOf("Hazzard", 15);
System.out.println(j);  //-1...it couldn't find it when starting at 15

int j = s.indexOf("e", 4);
System.out.println(j);  //7. First "e" is at 2, but we started searching at 4
```

c. public int indexOf(char ch)

Search from left to right for the first occurrence of the *char ch.*

```
int j = s.indexOf('D');
System.out.println(j);  //4
```

d. public int indexOf(int ascii)

This method is very similar to c. above, except, instead of a character we give the ASCII code of the character desired.

```
int j = s.indexOf(68);  // ASCII code for 'D' is 68
System.out.println(j);  //4
```

e. public int indexOf(char ch, int from)

Starting at index *from*, search from left to right for the first occurrence of the *char ch.*

```
int j = s.indexOf('e', 4);
System.out.println(j);  //7
```

f. public int indexOf(int ascii, int from)

This method is very similar to e. above, except, instead of a character we give the ASCII code of the character desired.

```
int j = s.indexOf(101, 4);  // ASCII code for 'e' is 101
System.out.println(j);  //7
```

lastIndexOf( )

This method also comes in 6 flavors: (All return –1 if the search is unsuccessful.)

These are exactly the same as the *indexOf( )* method, except here, we begin searching from the right side of the *String* instead of the left as with *indexOf( ).* Only two examples of the six different types will be given since they are so similar to the previous examples.

a. public int lastIndexOf(String str)

```
int j = s.lastIndexOf("Haz");
System.out.println(j);  //13
```

b. public int lastIndexOf(String s, int from)

```
int j = s.lastIndexOf("Haz", 11);
System.out.println(j);  // -1…can't find since we start at 11.
```

c. public int lastIndexOf(char ch)
d. public int lastIndexOf(int ascii)
e. public int lastIndexOf(char ch, int from)
f. public int lastIndexOf(int ascii, int from)

public char charAt(int indx)

This method returns the character at the specified index.

```
char myChar = s.charAt(6);
System.out.println(myChar);  //k
```

public String replace(char old, char new)

This method replaces **all** occurrences of the character *old* with the character *new*.

```
String myString = s.replace('z', 'L');
System.out.println(myString);  // The Dukes of HaLLard
```

Notice that we replaced **all** occurrences of 'z'.

public String trim( )

This method removes whitespace from both ends of the *String* while leaving interior whitespace intact. (Whitespace consists of the new line character (\n), tab (\t), and spaces.)

```
String s = "\t    Ding Dong  \t   \n   " ;
System.out.println("X" + s.trim( ) + "X");  // XDing DongX
```

Parsing *Strings* with *Scanner*

In Lesson 7 we learned how to use the *Scanner* class to input text from the keyboard. Here, we illustrate further uses of *Scanner* in parsing a *String*. Instead of passing *System.in* to the *Scanner* constructor as we did for keyboard input, we pass a *String* to the constructor as follows:

```
Scanner sc = new Scanner("Please, no more homework!");
```

Delimiters:

A delimiter is a series of characters that separates the text presented to a *Scanner* object into separate tokens. The default delimiter is whitespace, so the separate tokens produced by repeated application of the *next* method in the above example would be "Please,", "no", "more", and "homework!". The *useDelimiter* method allows a custom delimiter to be set using regular expressions (see Appendix AC).

Position:

One of the key concepts here is that of the "position" of the *Scanner* object as it scans its way through the *String*. We will always think of this position as being **between** two characters in the same way that a cursor in a word processor is never **on** a character; rather it is always **between** two characters (or perhaps preceding the first character, or just after the last character). As tokens are returned by *next*, etc., the position advances to just after the last token returned.

Let us consider the following sequence of code where a *String* is passed to the constructor of the *Scanner* class as we illustrate the concept of position. We are also going to introduce the *findInLine*, *useDelimiter*, *hasNext(String regex)*, and *skip* methods (all use regular expression arguments… see Appendix AC). These methods will **not be formally defined**; rather, their functions will be **inferred from these examples**:

Code	Position after code execution
Scanner sc = new Scanner("A string for testing scanner"); //The default delimiter of whitespace will be used.	A string for testing scanner | (before "A")
System.out.println(sc.next( )); //**Prints A**	A string for testing scanner | (after "A")
System.out.println(sc.findInLine("ri")); //**Prints ri and advances the position**	A string for testing scanner | (after "stri")

String ns = sc.next( ); //next( ) returns a String
System.out.println(ns);
//**Prints ng**
	A string for testing scanner
	| (after "string")

sc.useDelimiter("r\\s+"); //**New delim is r followed by 1 or more whitespace chr**	A string for testing scanner | (after "string")
System.out.println(sc.next( )); //**Prints fo (there is a leading blank before f)**	A string for testing scanner | (after "fo")
sc.skip("r\\s*test"); //**Advances the position by skipping over "r test"** //**\\s* stands for zero or more white space characters**	A string for testing scanner | (after "test")
System.out.println(sc.next( )); //**Prints ing scanner**	A string for testing scanner | (after "scanner")

We should take note of several salient features from this example:

1. The position of a *Scanner* object always moves **forward**. It can never be "backed-up". Likewise, searches (as with *findInLine* and *skip*) always move **forward** from the current position.

2. Starting from the current position and moving forward, the *findInLine* method searches ahead **as far as necessary** to find the specified substring. Notice above that the "ri" sought after does **not** have to **immediately** follow the current position.

   If the substring is not found, a *null* is returned.

3. In the *skip* method the specified substring **does** indeed need to **immediately** follow the current position. The "r test" sought after needs to immediately follow the current position.

If the substring is not found, a *NoSuchElementException* is thrown (an error).

In addition to the searching methods *findInLine* and *skip*, there is another that can sometimes be useful, *findWithinHorizon(String regex, int horizon)*. This is identical to *findInLine* except for the additional parameter, *horizon*, which limits the search for *regex* to the next *horizon* characters. If the search is to be successful, *regex* must be found in its **entirety** within *horizon* characters. If *horizon* is zero the search is allowed to continue to the end of the text if necessary.

A quirk:

Let's consider what happens when there are two delimiters **immediately adjacent to each other** as illustrated by the following code:

```
String ss = "abcxyxydef";
Scanner sc = new Scanner(ss);
sc.useDelimiter("xy");
while(sc.hasNext( ))
{
        System.out.println(sc.next( ));
}
```

The resulting printout is:

```
abc

def
```

The blank line is an **empty** *String* that was "between" the two successive delimiters.

Detecting Spam Email:

In order to refine our understanding of the *useDelimiter*, *skip* and *hasNext(String regex) methods*, consider how an email-spammer might try to disguise a word for the purpose of getting past a spam filter. Instead of transmitting something like "Low cost loans", the trick is to send a similar phrase with intervening characters like, "L*o*w* *c*o*s*t* l*o*a*n*s". Notice this is still readable; however, a standard spam filter would be defeated.

In the first line of code below we see an attempt at disguising the word "dirty". The remainder of the code strips away the superfluous characters leaving only the original word so that the spam filter can properly detect it.

```
String s = "d^^*_^^ir....-t***y";  //"dirty"

Scanner sc = new Scanner(s);
sc.useDelimiter(""); //set delimiter to nothing which makes every character a token

String answer = "";
while(sc.hasNext( ))
{
        //skip the stuff we want to get rid of
        while(sc.hasNext("\\W|_"))
```

```
        {
            sc.skip("_*"); //skip underscores
            if(sc.hasNext( ))
                sc.skip("\\W*"); //skip non-word characters.Word characters are[a
                                    //zA-Z_0-9]
        }

        if(sc.hasNext( ))
            answer = answer + sc.next( );
}
System.out.println(answer); //prints dirty
```

In Lesson 7 we learned to input text from the keyboard by creating a *Scanner* object by passing *System.in* to the constructor. There, we directly used this **same** *Scanner* object to parse the input with *next*, *nextInt*, etc. To avoid some strange effects, it is suggested that all the input be immediately stored into a *String* using *nextLine* and then passed to a **new** *Scanner* object. Then parse this second *Scanner* object using *next*, *nextInt*, *findInLine*, etc.

Project… Add 'em Up

Consider the following program that allows something like **8 + 33 + 1,345 +137** to be entered as *String* input from the keyboard. A *Scanner* object then uses the plus signs (and any adjoining whitespace) as delimiters and produces the sum of these numbers(1523).

```
import java.io.*;
import java.util.*;
public class Tester
{
  public static void main(String args[])
  {

    Scanner sc = new Scanner(System.in);

    System.out.print("Enter something like 8 + 33 + 1,345 +137  :  ");
    String s = sc.nextLine( );    //Best to store in a String and then create a new Scanner
                                  //object; otherwise, it can get stuck waiting for input.
    Scanner sc1 = new Scanner(s);
    //Set delimiters to a plus sign surrounded by any amount of white space...or...
    // a minus sign  surrounded by any amount of white space.
    sc1.useDelimiter("\\s*\\+\\s*");

    int sum = 0;
    while(sc1.hasNextInt( ))
    {
      sum = sum + sc1.nextInt( );
    }
    System.out.println("Sum is: " + sum);

  }
}
```

The output will typically look like this:

```
Enter something like 8 + 33 + 1,345 +137  :  8 + 33 + 1,345 + 137
Sum is: 1523
```

Now modify this program so as to allow either plus or minus signs. Don't forget to allow for a leading plus or minus sign on the first number in the sequence. If the leading number has no sign, assume the number is positive. Your output should typically appear as follows:

```
Enter something like 8 + 33 + 1,345 -137  :  8 + 33+ 1,345 -137
Sum is: 1249
```

Exercise on Lesson 17

Use the following code for problems 1 – 15. In each problem state what's printed.

String s = "Lucky hockey puck";
String m = "uck";
int j = 6, z = 99;

1. int k = s.indexOf(m);
   System.out.println(k);

2. int k = s.indexOf("uck", j);
   System.out.println(k);

3. int k = s.indexOf('c');
   System.out.println(k);

4. String str = s.replace('o', 'p');
   System.out.println(str);

5. int k = s.lastIndexOf(m, j + 3);
   System.out.println(k);

6. char p = s.charAt(7);
   System.out.println(p);

7. int k = s.indexOf(z);
   System.out.println(k);

8. int k = s.lastIndexOf(m);
   System.out.println(k);

9. int k = s.indexOf('y', j);
   System.out.println(k);

10. char p = s.charAt(z - 90);
    System.out.println(p);

11. int k = s.indexOf(m,15);
    System.out.println(k);

12. int k = s.indexOf(z + 2, 4);
    System.out.println(k);

13. int k = s.lastIndexOf('h');
    System.out.println(k);

14. int k = s.lastIndexOf(121);
    System.out.println(k);

15. String str = s.replace('y', 'A');
    System.out.println(str);

The following code applies to problems 16 – 22. In each problem, state what's printed.

```
String xyz = "bathtub";
String ddd = "BathTUB";
String ccc = xyz;
String wc = "Whooping crane";
String s = "      \t\tGu daay, mates   \n";
```

16.
```
int j = xyz.compareTo(wc);
boolean bb;
if (j > 0)
{
        bb = true;
}
else
{
        bb = false;
}
System.out.println(bb);
```

17. String v = ddd.toLowerCase( );
    int fg = ccc.compareTo(v);
    System.out.println(fg + 1);

18. System.out.println(ddd.compareTo(ccc));

19. System.out.println(xyz.compareTo(ccc));

20. System.out.println("Stupid".compareTo(ddd));

21. System.out.println(">>>" + s.trim( ) + "<<<");

For the remaining problems assume the following code has already executed:

String m = "Good morning, how may I help you? I289 56";
Scanner sc = new Scanner(m);

In each of the following problems, assume that the code in all of the preceding problems (starting with problem 22) has run and state what is printed. If an exception (error) is generated, state what causes it.

22. System.out.println(sc.next( ));

23. sc.skip("\\s*mo");
    String s = sc.next( );
    System.out.println(s);

24. sc.useDelimiter("\\s+I");
    System.out.println(sc.next( ));

25. sc.findInLine("el");
    System.out.println(sc.hasNext( ));
    System.out.println(sc.next( ));

26. sc.useDelimiter("\\s+");
    System.out.println(sc.nextInt( ));

Project… Encryption/Decryption

You have just been hired by the CIA as a programmer in the encryption department. Your job is to write a class called Crypto. One method, *encrypt*, will accept a *String* that represents the sentence to be encrypted. It will return a *String* that is the sentence with all v's (big or small) replaced with "ag',r", all m's (big or small) with "ssad", all g's (big or small) with "jeb..w", and all b's (big or small) with "dug>?/".

The class contains another method, *decrypt*, that accepts a *String* that represents the sentence to be decrypted. In this method the reverse process described above is performed. It returns a *String* that is the original sentence before encryption.

Use the following *Tester* class to insure that your methods work.

```
import java.io.*;
import java.util.*;
public class Tester
{
        public static void main(String args[])
        {
                Scanner kbReader = new Scanner(System.in);
                System.out.print("Enter a sentence that is to be encrypted: ");
                String sntnc = kbReader.nextLine( );
                System.out.println("Original sentence = " + sntnc);

                Crypto myCryptObj = new Crypto( );
                String encryptdSntnc = myCryptObj.encrypt(sntnc);
                System.out.println("Encrypted sentence = " + encryptdSntnc);

                String decryptdSntnc = myCryptObj.decrypt(encryptdSntnc);
                System.out.println("Decrypted sentence = " + decryptdSntnc);
        }
}
```

Test with this sentence: "This is a very big morning."

After running your program, your screen should appear as follows:

```
Enter a sentence that is to be encrypted: This is a very big morning.
Original sentence = This is a very big morning.
Encrypted sentence = This is a ag',rery dug>?/ijeb..w ssadorninjeb..w.
Decrypted sentence = This is a very big morning.
```

Advanced *String* Methods… Contest Type Problems

1. What is returned by *doStuff("I would if I could")*?

   A. 1
   B. 2
   C. 3
   D. 4
   E. None of these

2. What is returned by *doStuff("fee fi fo fum")*?

   A. 1
   B. 2
   C. 3
   D. 4
   E. None of these

```
public class MyTester
{
   public static int doStuff(String myString)
   {
      int cc = 0;
      int p = myString.length( )/2;
      for (int k=0; k<myString.length( )/2; k++, p++)
      if(myString.charAt(k) == myString.charAt(p))
      cc++;
      return cc;
   }
}
```

3. What is output with the method call, *convert("Abe Lincoln")*?

   A. ABELINCOLN
   B. ABE LINCOLN
   C. aBE lINCOLN
   D. abe lincoln
   E. None of these

4. What is output with the method call, *convert("BR549")*?

   A. Throws an exception
   B. Nothing
   C. BR549
   D. Br549
   E. None of these

```
public class MyTester
{
   public static void convert(String myString)
   {
      String tot = "";
      for(int j=0; j<myString.length( ); j++)
      {
         char ch =
             Character.toUpperCase(myString.charAt(j));
         tot = tot + ch;
      }
      System.out.println(tot);
   }
}
```

5. What is output with the method call, *bailOnM("mumify")*?

   A. 0
   B. 1
   C. 2
   D. 6
   E. None of these

```
public class MyTester
{
   public static int bailOnM(String myString)
   {
      int indx = 0;
      do {
         indx++;
      }while(myString.charAt(indx)!='m');
      return indx;
   }
}
```

6. What is output?

   A. A blank
   B. t
   C. e
   D. Won't compile
   E. None of these

```
public class MyTester
{
   public static void main(String args[]) {
     System.out.println("Nertz to you".charAt(4));
   }
}
```

7. What is output with the method call, *printStuff("A1 USDA prime.")*?

A. AUSDAprime
B. A USDA prime.
C. 1
D. A USDA PRIME.
E. None of these

```
public class MyTester
{
    public static void printStuff(String theString)
    {
        for(int j=0; j<theString.length( ); j++) {
            char chr = theString.charAt(j);
            if(Character.isLetter(chr))
            System.out.print(chr);
        }
    }
}
```

8. What is output with the method call, *elim("ABC1234DEF")*?

A. Throws exception
B. 0
C. 18.0
D. 306.0
E. None of these

```
public class MyTester
{
    public static double elim(String theString)
    {
        int sum = 0;
        for(int j=0; j<theString.length( ); j++) {
            if(theString.charAt(j) > '1' &&
                                theString.charAt(j) < '8')
                sum = sum + theString.charAt(j) * 2;
        }
        return sum;
    }
}
```

9. What is output by *System.out.println("Alf Abrams".indexOf('A'));* ?

A. 0
B. 1
C. 4
D. 65
E. None of these

10. What is output by *System.out.println("Alf Abrams".lastIndexOf('A'));* ?

A. 0
B. 1
C. 4
D. 65
E. None of these

11. What is output with the method call, *doStuff("3872345619")*?

A. 42345>>>0
B. 43456>>>1
C. 42345>>>1
D. 4345619>>>1
E. None of these

```
public static void doStuff(String aString)
{
  int p=1;
  int j = aString.indexOf("23") + p;
  String s;
  System.out.print(j);
  if(j>=0)
      s = aString.substring(j, j+4);
  else
      s = "No can do";
  System.out.println(s + ">>>" + j%3);
}
```

Lesson 18.....Arrays

Let's suppose we need to keep grades for 400 students. Here is one way to do it:

```
int grade1 = 97,   grade2 = 62,   grade3 = 85, ...  grade400 = 76;
```

Clearly this is a tedious process for a large number of variables. Is there a better way? Yes, we should use **array variables** in this application.

Implementing our 400 variables as an array, we will use **an identical name** for all 400 variables. So how will we be able to tell them apart? We will use indices as follows (indices are sometimes called subscripts; in fact, array variables are sometimes called **subscripted variables**).

```
grade[1] = 97;     grade[2] = 62;     grade[3] = 85;   ... grade[400];
```

Actually, this is not quite the way we do it. In reality, the indices always start at 0, so the variables would really look like this:

```
grade[0] = 97;     grade[1] = 62;     grade[2] = 85;   ... grade[399];
```

Notice that even though we have 400 different variables in our array, the last index is 399. It is **very important** to be aware of this little quirk.

Three ways to declare and initialize an array:

Above we looked at how to initialize the various elements of an array. Let's look now at how to declare the array ...and in fact, the entire process. We will present 3 different approaches:

Before we begin to show the various approaches, let's look first at the syntax of declaring an int array called *a*:

```
int []a = ....;   //The square brackets indicate that a is to be an array. This is the
                  //syntax used in most books and in contests.
int a[] =. . . ;  //This is a more natural way to accomplish the same thing. This is
                  // the method we will use.
```

The first way:

```
int a[] = new int[400];
a[0] = 97;
a[1] = 62;
a[2] = 85;
...
```

The second way:

```
int a[] = {97, 62, 85, . . .}; //This is the most popular way
```

The third way:

```
int a[] = new int[] {97, 62, 85, . . .};
```

While the above examples are for an *int* array, arrays for *double*, *String*, *char*, and *boolean* types are also possible. They are done in **exactly** the same way. We can even make **arrays of objects** although their initialization is slightly different. (That will be discussed later.)

We will now look at some examples of array usage, each of which will illustrate a particular feature.

Finding the *length* of an array:

a.length will tell us how many elements the array *a* has.

```
double a[] = new double[7];
int lngt = a.length;  //notice no parenthesis after length (it's a state variable)
System.out.println(lngt);  //7
```

Declaring and initializing on different lines:

In this example we illustrate that it's possible to declare an array on one line and then to initialize its elements on a **different** line. Also, in a *for* loop we will take special note of the technique for cycling through all the elements of the array.

```
int sq[] = new int[1000];  //array is only declared here…indices 0 - 999
for (int j = 0; j < sq.length; j++)
{
        sq[j] = j * j;  //stores the square of each index in the element
}
```

Notice that in the code fragment *int j = 0; j < a.length* that *j* will assume values of 0 through 999. This makes a total of **1000** (0 – 999) different indices…and 1000 times through the loop.

Now let's try to write this same code in the old fashioned way (**without using arrays**):

```
sq0 = 0 * 0;
sq1 = 1 * 1;
sq2 = 2 * 2;
  . . .
sq999 = 999 * 999;
```

This is clearly impractical and we begin to see the value of arrays.

Parallel arrays:

Consider the *String* array, *name*, and the related "parallel" *int* array, *grade*. We will cycle through a loop, inputting students' names and corresponding grades.

```
int numStudents = 25;  //this illustrates that we can use a variable to
                       //determine the length of our array
String name[] = new String[numStudents];
int grade[] = new int[numStudents];

for(int j = 0; j < numStudents; j++) {
        Scanner kbReader1 = new Scanner(System.in);
                System.out.print("Enter the student name: ");
                name[j] = kbReader1.nextLine( );  //input from keyboard
        Scanner kbReader2 = new Scanner(System.in);
                System.out.print("Enter the grade: ");
                grade[j] = kbReader2.nextInt( );
}
```

Because they are "associated", the *name* and *grade* arrays are called **parallel** arrays.

Arrays in calculations:

We can use numeric array variables in calculations as follows:

```
average = (slg[0] + slg[1] + slg[2]) / 3;
```

This code computes the average of the first 3 elements of the *slg* array.

Warning:

Don't produce an ***ArrayIndexOutOfBoundsException*** (an error) with improper subscripts:

```
double zorro[] = new double[15];
zorro[14] = 37;
zorro[15] = 105;  //Illegal! Index 14 is the largest possible.
zorro[0] = 209;
zorro[-1] = 277;  //Illegal! Index 0 is the smallest possible.
```

Passing an array to a method:

Suppose we have the following code:

```
char ch[] = new char[50];  //Yes, we can have character arrays
. . .
ch[4] = 'g';
. . .
double e = 2.718;
method1(e, ch);  //call method1 (see code below) in some other class and
                 //pass our double variable and the array, ch
System.out.println( ch[4] );  //V...notice it's not 'g' anymore
System.out.println( e );  //2.718...unchanged

****************************
public void method1(double xxx, char myArray[])
{
        xxx = 0;
        myArray[4] = 'V';
}
```

Notice that within *method1* that *e* was passed, but locally renamed to *xxx*. Similarly, the *ch* array was renamed there to *myArray*.

a. Notice that changing *xxx* in *method1* does **not** affect the *e* value back in the calling code.

b. Notice that changing *myArray[4]* in *method1* **does** change *ch[4]* back in the calling code.

Automatic initialization of arrays:

With numeric arrays (both *double* and *int*), all elements are automatically initialized to 0.

```
int xyz[] = new int[2000];
System.out.println( xyz[389] );  //0
```

The elements of a *String* array (and other object arrays) are **not** automatically initialized and will result in a *NullPointerException* when trying to reference an element that has not been specifically initialized.

Using the *split* method to produce an array:

The *split* method parses the original *String* into the separate elements of a returned *String* **array** using the rules of "regular expressions" (see Appendix AC) to determine the parsing delimiters.

The signature for the split method is:
public String[] split(String regex)

The following examples assume that test *String s* has been created and that the *String sp* array have already been declared:

String s = "Hello again", sp[];

Example:
sp = s.split("a"); //**sp[0] = "Hello ", sp[1] = "g" , sp[2] = "in"**

Example:
sp = s.split("\\s"); // **"\\s" means white space, sp[0] = "Hello", sp[1] = "again"**
// \\s+ means one or more white space characters, so the same
//split would result from "Hello   again"

Example:
sp = s.split("ga"); // **sp[0] = "Hello a", sp[1] = "in"**

Example:
sp = s.split("m"); // **sp[0] = "Hello again"**

Example:
sp = s.split("e|g"); // **"e|g" means either 'e' or 'g', sp[0] = "H", sp[1] = "llo a",**
// sp[2] = "ain"

Example:
sp = s.split("a|g"); // **"a|g" means a or g (same as [ag]), sp[0] = "Hello ", sp[1] =**
//"" sp[2] = "", sp[3] = "in", (notice the elements of zero
// length)

Example:
sp = s.split("el|ai"); // **"|" means OR, sp[0] = "H", sp[1] = "lo ag", sp[2] = "n"**

The *split* method can be used to **count the number of occurrences** of a specified regular expression within a *String*. For example, consider the following *String*:

String s = "IF THE BOX IS RED IT'S THE RIGHT ONE."

In order to count the occurrences of "THE", use it as the regular expression with the *split* method (*String sp[] = s.split("THE")*). The underlined portions below show the three different elements of the array into which our array is "split."

"IF **THE** BOX IS RED IT'S **THE** RIGHT ONE."

The number of elements in the array is three (*sp.length*); therefore, the number of occurrences of "THE" is *sp.length – 1*. A complication occurs if the delimiter trails the *String* as in the following example:

"ENOUGH USE OF **THE** WORD **THE**"

sp.length –1 yields the wrong answer (1). See the "Count 'em Right" project for how to properly handle this anomaly of the *split* method.

Project… Count 'em Right

At the bottom of page 18-4 we were left with the dilemma of how to use the *split* method to count multiple occurrences of a regular expression when that expression is at the **end** of the *String* to be searched. It is also interesting to see what happens when there is a delimiter at the **beginning** of the *String*. Following is an example of the anomalies caused by having a delimiter at either the beginning or end of the *String*:

```
String s = "cHello good cbuddyc";
int sp[] = s.split("c");
```

One would normally think that this would produce two elements for the *sp* array (sp[0] = "Hello good " and sp[1] = "buddy"). This is **not** the case. In fact, it produces three elements (sp[0] = "", sp[1] = "Hello good ", and sp[2] = "buddy"). This anomaly of an empty *String* occurs when a delimiter is at the beginning of the *String*, but strangely enough, not when a delimiter is at the end.

Fortunately, for the sake of counting delimiters, one at the beginning of a **String** is automatically handled since sp[0] = "". A delimiter at the end of the *String* is easily handled with the concatenation of extra characters to the end of the *String*.

Our project will be to count all occurrences of the letter *s* followed by the letter *a*. Case will be ignored, and it will be permissible to have **any** amount (including none) of white space between the *s* and the *a*.

Call your project *CountEmRight* and create just one class, *Tester*. In the *main* method, do the following:

- Create a loop that asks for *String* input (a sentence).
- Release from the loop if the input *String* is "EXIT".
- So as to ignore case, convert the input *String* into an uppercase version of itself.
- Concatenate some "harmless" *String* to the end of the input *String*. By "harmless" it is meant that it should not contain any occurrences of the delimiter expression. This is the **real secret** to this project… to get any occurrence of the sought after expression off the end and into the "interior" of the *String*.
- Use the *split* method to produce a *String* array (call it *sp*). Then use *sp.length –1* to count the number of occurrences.

A typical run will appear as follows:

```
Type in a sentence and press ENTER. His initials are SA
There are 2 occurrences.

Type in a sentence and press ENTER. Sad but true, their teams are
better.
There are 2 occurrences.

Type in a sentence and press ENTER. S    a sa ssa  s    a
There are 4 occurrences.

Type in a sentence and press ENTER. exit
```

Exercise on Lesson 18

1. Write code that will declare an integer array called *sgt* having 800 elements.

2. double []dfw = new double[21];
   System.out.println(dfw.length);

3. For the code in #1 above, write a for-loop that will cycle through all the elements of *double sgt[]* and store the square root of the index of each element in that element.

4. Assuming *rtl* is the name of an array, what's wrong with this code?
   double rtl_len = rtl.length( );

5. On **one** line of code, both declare a character array called *cr* and initialize its elements to be 'a', 'b', 'c', 'd', and 'e'.

6. Refer to #5 above. What is the value of *cr.length* ?

7. Write code that will print the sum of the squares of the all elements of the *ref* integer array.

8. What's wrong with the following code?
```
for (int k = 2; k < homer.length; k++)
{
        homer[k +1] = k;
}
```

9. Fill in the blanks below to enable us to pass a *double* array called *dbx* to a method called *heroWorship*. Within the method, the array should be called *vb*.
   boolean bbc = heroWorship(____________);
   ****
   public boolean heroWorship(________________) //signature of method

10. Assume the five values an integer array *adc* contains are: 34, 56, -102, 18, and 5. What is the value of *adc[1]* ?

11. Using the *adc* array from #10 above, what would be the value of *adc[3] + adc[4]*?

12. Using the *adc* array from #10 above, what would be the value of *adc[5]* ?

13. Describe what the following code segment does:

```
for (int j = 0; j < b.length; j++)
        b[j] = Math.abs( b[j] );
```

14. For the *int* array *c = {1, 2, 3, 4}*, what would be the output of the following code?

```
String ss = “>>>”;
int len = ss.length( );
for (int j = 0; j < len; j++)
        ss+= c[j];
System.out.println(ss);
```

15. Write a loop that locates the first occurrence of a negative integer in an array, *pg*. When the loop is finished, the variable *indx* should contain the index of the negative number or the length of the array if there were no negative numbers in the array.

16.
```
String wc = “Whooping crane”;
String sp[] = wc.split(“oo”);
for(int j = 0; j < sp.length; j++)
{
    System.out.println(sp[j]);
}
```

17. List the elements of *String [ ]sArray = “fee   fi fo ”.split(“\\s+”);*.

18. List the elements of *String [ ]sp = “One two”.split(“Q”);*.

19. Using the *split* method, write code that will count all of the occurrences of “th” (without regard to upper or lower case) in “The best THERE is is Barth”.

Project… Array of Hope

This project called *ArrayOfHope* will consist of just one class, *Tester*, that in turn, has just one method, *main*. The *main* method will use two *for*-loops:

- The first loop will produce an integer count from 65 to 90 (notice these are the ASCII codes for characters A…Z) and initialize the elements of the character array *ch[ ]* with the characters corresponding to the ASCII codes being generated by the loop. This will fill the *ch[ ]* array as follows: ch[0] = ‘A’, ch[1] = ‘B’, …, ch[25] = ‘Z’.

- The second loop will print the 26 elements of the *ch[ ]* array with one comma followed by one space between adjacent characters as follows:

```
A, B, C, D, E, F, G, H, I, J, K, L, M, N, O, P, Q, R, S, T, U, V, W, X, Y, Z
```

Lesson 19…..Advanced Array Concepts

Arrays of objects:

```
Circle cir[] = new Circle[500];  //declares 500 circles, all null for the moment

//We can initialize each of these 500 Circle objects individually as shown here
cir[117] = new Circle(57.2);  //set radius to 57.2

for (j = 0; j < 500; j++)  //…or we can initialize them in a loop
{
        cir[j] = new Circle(10);  //all radii set to 10
}
```

Comparison of array values:

We will give examples of *boolean* values within fragments of ***if*** statements; however, any other such usage of *boolean* values using arrays would be acceptable:

a. **Numeric** arrays:
```
if ( n[23] = = n[k+1] )
if ( n[23] >= n[k+1] )
```

b. **String** arrays:
```
if ( s[3 +d] .equals("hermit") )
if ( s[3 +d] .compareTo("hermit") > 0 )
```

c. **Object** arrays:
```
if ( BankAccount[1].equals(BankAccount[2]) )
```

The dreaded *NullPointerException*:

```
double mxz[];   //the array mxz has only been declared
mxz[3] = 19.1;  //error! NullPointerException, mxz has not been initialized yet.
```

Different references to the <u>same</u> array:

Because arrays are objects, two or more variables can refer to the same array as in the following example:

```
int []frst = {1, 2, 3, 4, 5}, sec[];  // frst[] declared and initialized.  sec[] just declared

sec = frst;
sec[2] = 99;
System.out.println(frst[2]);  //99 Notice that even though we changed only
                              //sec[2] to 99, frst[2] also changes to 99.
```

Removing an array from memory:

It is possible to erase an array from memory so that it no longer takes up any memory space. To do this, simply set the array name equal to **null** as follows:

```
int myArray[] = new int[500];   //occupies 500 * 4 bytes of memory
. . .
myArray = null;  //occupies almost no memory now
myArray[45] = 2003;  //generates a "null pointer exception"
```

A major lesson here is that you can set <u>any object</u> equal to *null.*

Copying from array to array:

System.arraycopy*(theFromArray, fromIndex, theToArray, toIndex, howMany)* to **copy part of an array to part of another array**. The five parameters are explained as follows:

- **a.** *theFromArray*…the array <u>from</u> which we are copying, i.e., the source.
- **b.** *fromIndex*…the index in *theFromArray* from which copying starts.
- **c.** *theToArray*…the array <u>to</u> which we will copy, i.e., the destination.
- **d.** *toIndex*… the index in *theToArray* at which copying starts.
- **e.** *howMany*…the number of array elements to copy.

If you have trouble remembering the order of <u>from</u> and <u>to</u>, just remember this little ditty, "<u>From</u> me <u>to</u> you."

Example:

```
char ch[] = {'a', 'b', 'c', 'd', 'e', 'f', 'g', 'h'};
char nn[] = {'1', '2', '3', '4', '5', '6', '7', '8'};
System.arraycopy(ch, 1, nn, 2, 3);
```

The destination array, *nn* will now look like this:
{'1', '2', 'b', 'c', 'd', '6', '7', '8'}   *ch* array is unchanged.

Converting a *String* into a character array:

A *String* method we have not previously discussed is the ***toCharArray*** (signature: *public char[] toCharArray()*) method. Here is how it's used:

```
char ch[]; //declared, but not initialized
String s = "ABCDE";
ch = s.toCharArray( ); //this initializes the ch array
```

Here's what the character array *ch* looks like now:
{'A', 'B', 'C', 'D', 'E'}

It is also possible to reverse the process and convert a character array directly into a *String* with:

```
String s = String.copyValueOf(ch); //ch is a character array
```

There is another version of *copyValueOf* whose signature is:

```
static copyValueOf(char[]ch, int offset, int count)
```

Logical versus physical size of an array:

The **logical size** of the array in the following example is 5 since we only store numbers in the first 5 elements of this array. Notice the variable *max* in this particular example determines the logical size. The **physical size** (30 in this example) is always easy to determine. It's always *jk.length*;

```
int jk[] = new int[30]; //physical size… 30
int max = 5;
for (int j = 0; j < max; j++)
{
    jk[j] = j * 36;
}
```

The *Arrays* class:

This special class has some very useful methods that assist in the manipulation of arrays…especially **sorting**. For each of these methods we offer a description, the signature, and an example. To get these methods to work, you must **import** the *Arrays* class by putting ***import java.util.*;*** at the very top of your program. See Appendix I for more on the process of importing.

Sort:

Sort the array in ascending order (uses a merge sort…see Lesson 41).

public static void sort(int a[]) //**Signature**

Example:

```
int b[] = {14, 2, 109, . . . 23, 5, 199};
Arrays.sort(b); //The b array is now in ascending order.
```

See the project at the end of this lesson where you will actually sort an array.

Binary search:

Perform a binary search (see Lesson 51) of an array for a particular value (this assumes the array has already been sorted in ascending order). This method returns the index of the last array element containing the value of *key*. If *key* is not found, a negative number is returned… *–k –1* where *k* is the index before which the *key* would be inserted.

public int binarySearch(int a[], int key) //**Signature**

Example:

```
//Assume array b[] already exists and has been sorted in ascending order.
//The b array now reads {2,17, 36, 203, 289, 567, 1000}.
int indx = Arrays.binarySearch(b, 203); //search for 203 in the array
System.out.println(indx); //3
```

Equality:

Test for the equality of two arrays.

public boolean equals(int a[], b[]) //**Signature**…compare arrays a and b //element by element and returns true if //all are the same…otherwise false.

Example:

```
int x[] = {1, 2, 3, 4, 5};
int y[] = {1, 2, 3, 4, 5};
int z[] = {1, 2, 9, 4, 5};
System.out.println(Arrays.equals(x, y); //true
System.out.println(Arrays.equals(x, z); //false
```

Fill:

Fill an array with some specified value.

public void fill(int [], v) //**Signature**…fill array a with value v.

Example:

```
int pk[] = {1, 2, 3, 4, 5};
Arrays.fill(pk, 77); //Array now looks like this {77, 77, 77, 77, 77}
```

The above discussion is for the *int* type arrays; however, all methods work for arrays of any of the primitive types and *Strings*. The *sort* method works for objects from any class implementing the *Comparable* interface... All methods are <u>*static*</u>.

Command Line arguments:

Let's take a final look at the signature for the *main* method:

```
public static void main(String args[])
```

Now that we know about arrays, we can see that "*String args[ ]*" is declaring *args* as a *String* array. But where and how is this *args[ ]* array to be used? (Incidentally, this *args[ ]* array could be called by **any** legal variable name.)

The *args[ ]* array allows us to pass **command line arguments** to the *main* method. Entering a command line (see <u>Appendix X</u>) at the DOS prompt is one way to run a Java program. To do this you would need to be in a DOS console via the sequence Start | Run | *cmd* (don't use the older *command*) | OK):

```
java MyClass -46 Fleetwood.bat
```

What exactly does all this mean? The leading word *java* means to run the Java executable file (*java.exe*), *MyClass* (shown below) is the class containing the *main* method you wish to run, -46 is a *String* representing the first parameter we are passing (stored in *args[0]*), and *Fleetwood.bat* is a *String* representing the second parameter we are passing (stored in *args[1]*).

```
public class MyClass
{
        public static void main( String args[] )
        {
                System.out.println( args[0] ); //-46
                System.out.println( args[1] ); //Fleetwood.bat
        }
}
```

Using a command line argument from the DOS prompt is a little awkward. Generally, you will need to first issue the command *cd C:\Program Files\Java\jdk1.5.0_04\bin* to change to the folder in which *java.exe* resides. (Your Java folder's name may be different.) You will also need to have compiled your class file (resulting in a file with extension *.class*) and have it stored in this same *bin* folder.

For users of the Blue Jay Environment there is a much easier way to pass command line arguments. When you are ready to launch your *main* method, click on <u>void *main(args)*</u> and then in the resulting dialog, enter your arguments between the two braces as follows:

{"-46", "Fleetwood.bat"}

Be sure to include the quotes. You can have as many arguments as you like. Many times, only two are used. It is customary to interpret those *Stings* starting with a "-" as options and others as file names; however, as a programmer you may assign any desired meaning.

Using an array variable as an index:

Consider the following code that uses an array variable as an index for an array variable:

```
int ary[] = {5, 6, 7, 8, 9, 10};
System.out.println(ary[  ary[0]  ]);  //10 … ary[0] = 5,   ary[5] = 10
```

The enhanced *for* loop ("for-each" style):

With the advent of Java 5.0 comes the much awaited "for-each" style of *for* loop. It is officially referred to as an **enhanced** *for* loop. Fundamentally, it lets us automatically loop through all the elements of a collection of objects, such as an array, from start to finish. This is done without specifying the length of the array and without an artificial, dummy integer index.

Traditional *for*-loop example:

This is illustrated below; first, by showing the traditional way of summing the squares of a sequence of numbers stored in array *x*:

```
int x[] = {4,3,2,1};
int sum = 0;
for(int j = 0; j < x.length; j++)
    sum = sum + x[j] * x[j];
System.out.println(sum);  //30… this is the problem  4^2 + 3^2 + 2^2 + 1^2
```

Enhanced *for*-loop example:

With the "enhanced *for*" style, the equivalent code would be:

```
//Equivalent code using the enhanced for method
int x[] = {4,3,2,1};
int sum = 0;
for(int varName: x)
     sum = sum + varName * varName;
System.out.println(sum);  //30
```

Notice here in the parenthesis of the *for*-loop, *x* is the name of the object collection through which we wish to iterate, while *varName* is the local name given to it for use on each iteration of the loop. Thus, we can state the following syntax rule for the "enhanced *for*" style:

```
for(Type DummyName: ObjectCollectionName)
```

Read-only:

Unfortunately, the enhanced *for* loop is "**read-only**" thus making its usefulness somewhat limited. This is illustrated by the following code in which we loop through all the elements of the *str* array in which we "try" to change their values:

```
String str[] = {"one", "two", "three"};
for(String ss: str)
{  ss = "zero";  }
```

Beware: The expectation would normally be for all three elements of the *str* array to now equal "zero"; however, they remain the same. This is because *ss* is read-only. This code will compile and run; however, it accomplishes nothing.

Exercise for Lesson 19

1. Write code that will create an array of 300 *BankAccount* objects. You are only to instantiate two of them. The object with index 47 should have a beginning balance of $92, and index 102 should have $1007. The name of your array will be *ba*.

2. Write an *if* statement that will decide if *k[3]* is equal to *jm[5]* where it is assumed that *k* and *jm* are numeric arrays.

3. Write an *if* statement that will decide if *s[2]* is equal to *ss[19]* where it is assumed that *s* and *ss* are *String* arrays.

4. Write an *if* statement that will decide if *cir[2]* is equal to *cirr[10]* (with regard to content) where it is assumed that *cir* and *cirr* are object arrays of type *Circle*.

5. What's wrong with the following code?
```
char months[];
months[0] = 'j';
```

6.
```
String suv[] = new String[20];
j = 0;
while(j < 17 )
{
        suv[j] = "Hello";
        j++;
}
```
What is the logical size of the *suv* array?
What is the physical size of the *suv* array?

7. Write code using *toCharArray* to convert *String d = "The quick brown fox jumped over the lazy dog."* into the character array *qbf*.

8.
```
double rub[] = {23.0, -102.1, 88.23, 111, 12.02, 189.119, 299.88};
double dub[] = {1, 2, 3, 4, 5, 6, 7, 8, 9};
```
Write a single line of code (using arraycopy) that will result in *dub* looking like this:
{1, 2, 3, 4, 111, 12.02, 189.119, 8, 9}

9. double[] zz, top;
   top = {12.1, 13.1, 14.1, 15.1, 18};
   zz = top;
   zz[2] = 99;
   top[3] = 100.2;
   Show what both arrays would look like at the completion of the above code.

10. char[] a, b;
    a = "Groovy dude".toCharArray( );
    b = "I like this".toCharArray( );
    System.arraycopy(a, 1, b, 0, 4);
    What do the two arrays look like at the completion of this code?

11. What must be true of any array before we can use *Arrays.binarySearch( )?*

12. Write code that will establish an array called *myArray* having the following elements, {189.01, 2000, -32, 56, 182, 2}. Then sort the array.

13. Assume the array *myArray* in #12 has been correctly sorted. What would be printed with the following?
    ```
    System.out.println( Arrays.binarySearch(myArray, 56) );
    System.out.println( Arrays.binarySearch(myArray, 102) );
    ```

14. What does the following print?
    ```
    int xc[] = {123, 97, -102, 17};
    int pk[] = {123, 79, -102, 17};
    int gs[] = {123, 97, -102, 17};
    System.out.println( Arrays.equals(xc, pk) + "\n" + Arrays.equals(xc, gs));
    ```

15. What does the following print?
    ```
    int pickle[] = {1, 2, 3, 4, 5, 6, 7, 8};
    Arrays.fill(pickle, -1);
    System.out.println( pickle[4] );
    ```

16. If a command line reads, *java BigClass Munster Herman dude*, what will the following line inside the *main* method print?
    ```
    System.out.println("Name=" + args[2] +args[1] );
    ```

17. What's printed by the following?
    ```
    int px[] = {3, 4, 5, 6, 7, 8, 9};
    System.out.println( px[   px[1] + 1   ]);
    ```

18. Write code using the "for-each" style of a *for* loop that will accumulate and print the product of the state variables *int jj* within each object of object array *objArray*. Assume the objects are created from the class *DummyClass*.

Arrays... Contest Type Problems

```
int [] gem = {-102, 14, 5, 100, -100};
```

1. What is the value of *gem[1]* in the code to the right?

   A. –102
   B. 14
   C. 5
   D. 100
   E. –100

2. Which code will sort the *gem* array in the code to the right?

   A. mergeSort(gem);
   B. Arrays.sort(gem[]);
   C. Arrays.sort(gem);
   D. Collections.sort(gem);
   E. Both C and D

3. What is the value of *g* when accessing the code to the right?

```
int [] stk = {1, 5, 19, 2, 20, 180};
int g = nerdStuff(stk) + 1;
```

   A. 3
   B. 2
   C. 0
   D. 7
   E. None of these

```
public static int nerdStuff(int [] cb)
{
        int counter = 0;
        for(int k=0; k<cb.length; ++k)
            if( cb[k] < 3 )
                ++counter;
        return counter;
}
```

4. Which of the following lines of code is a proper way to declare and initialize the *c* array?

   A. int [] c = new int[] {1, 2, 3, 4};
   B. int [10] c = {1, 2, 3, 4};
   C. int c = {1, 2, 3, 4};
   D. int[] c = new int {1, 2, 3, 4};
   E. Both A and B

5. What should replace **<*1>** in the code to the right in order that the *for*-loop variable, *j*, would cycle through all indices of the *a* array?

   A. j < a.length - 1
   B. j < a.length( )
   C. j <= a.length
   D. j < a.length + 1
   E. None of these

```
public static void testLoop(int [] a)
{
        for(int j=0; <*1>; ++j)
            ++a[j];
}
```

6. If **<*1>** has been filled in correctly in the code to the right, and *a[3] = 19* before calling *testLoop*, what is *a[3]* afterwards?

   A. 3
   B. 19
   C. 18
   D. 20
   E. None of these

7. What is output in the code to the right?
 	
A. ancp
B. mbod
C. aocq
D. abcd
E. None of these
	<pre>public class ArrayTest
	{
	  public static void main(String [] args)
	  {
	    String s1 = "abcdefghijk";
	    char [] x = s1.toCharArray( );
	    String s2 = "mnopqrstuvw";
	    char [] y = s2.toCharArray( );
	    int vv[] = {0,1,0,1};
	    for(int j=0; j<vv.length; j++) {
	      switch (vv[j])
	      {
	          case 0:
	            System.out.print(x[j]);
	            break;
	          case 1:
	            System.out.print(y[j+1]);
	      }
	    }
	  }
	}</pre>

8. What is output in the code to the right?
 	
A. 14
B. 15
C. 16
D. Throws an exception
E. None of these
	<pre>public class ArrayTest
	{
	  public static void main(String [] args)
	  {
	    int a[] = {0,1,2,3};
	    int b[] = a;
	    int sum = 0;
	    for(int j=0; j<3; j++) {
	        sum+=(a[j+1] * b[j]) + (a[j] * b[j+1]);
	    }
	    System.out.println(sum);
	  }
	}</pre>

9. What is output in the code to the right?
 	
A. 102
B. 44
C. 56
D. Throws an exception
E. None of these
	<pre>public class ArrayTest
	{
	  public static void main(String [] args)
	  {
	    int [] z1 = {2,3,4,5,6};
	    int [] z2 = {1,2,1,2,1};
	    double d = 0;
	    for(int j=0; j<3; j++)
	    {
	      d = d + Math.pow(z1[j+1], 2) + Math.pow(z2[j], 2);
	    }
	    System.out.println(d);
	  }
	}</pre>

10. What is output in the code to the right?
 	
A. 1002003007080
B. 1002007080500
C. 405030040080
D. 405060300400
E. None of these
	``public class MyTester
	{
	  public static void main(String args[])
	  {
	    int j, src =2, des=3, hm=2;
	    int [] sa = {100,200,300,400,500};
	    int [] da = {40,50,60,70,80};
	    System.arraycopy(sa,src,da,des,hm);
	    for(j=0; j<da.length; j++)
	    System.out.print(da[j]);
	  }
	}```

11. What is output in the code to the right?
 	
A. 6
B. 1
C. 0
D. 2
E. Throws an exception
	``public class MyTester
	{
	  public static void main(String args[])
	  {
	    int [] aleve = new int[] {0,1,2,3,4,5,6,7,8};
	    int n = 6;
	    n = aleve[aleve[n]/2];
	    System.out.print(aleve[n]%2);
	  }
	}```

12. What replaces **<#1>** so that the product of all the elements in array *d* is returned?
 	
A. for(double j: d) product *= d[j];
B. for(int j = 0; j < d.length; j++)
product = product * j;
C. for(int j = 0; j < d.length; j++)
product*= d[j];
D. for(double j: d) product *= j;
E. More than one of these
	``public static double getProduct( )
	{
	    double d[] = {100, -25, 16, 27, -102};
	    double product = 1;
	    <#1>
	    return product;
	}```

Project… Sorting a *String* Array

Create a *String* array call *ss*. It will contain the following *String*s in the order shown.

{"Bill", "Mary", "Lee", "Agnes", "Alfred", "Thomas", "Alvin", "Bernard", "Ezra", "Herman"}

Using the technique described on page 19-3, sort this array and then print the contents of the sorted array (using a loop) from index 0 to the last. Call both your project and class, *SortStringArray*. Confine all of your code to the *main* method.

The printout should look like the following:

```
Agnes
Alfred
Alvin
Bernard
Bill
Ezra
Herman
Lee
Mary
Thomas
```

Project… Two Orders for the Price of One

Modify the project above so as to print two side-by-side columns. Call both your project and class *AscendDescend*. The first column should be in ascending order and the second in descending order. The output should appear as below (Be sure to include the headers):

```
Ascend     Descend

Agnes      Thomas
Alfred     Mary
Alvin      Lee
Bernard    Herman
Bill       Ezra
Ezra       Bill
Herman     Bernard
Lee        Alvin
Mary       Alfred
Thomas     Agnes
```

Lesson 20…..*static* Methods and State Variables

You should be aware that *static* methods are sometimes called **class methods**. Similarly, *static* instance fields (*static* state variables) are called **class variables**. The reason for the class designation is that when we access either *static* methods or variables, **we are accessing them at the class level rather than at the object level.** (In this course, we will primarily use the word <u>*static*</u> rather than <u>*class*</u> as the designation of such methods and variables.). This is a profound statement that you will likely only come to appreciate as we move through the material below. …There are two primary reasons for using the key word *static*.

The first reason for using *static*:

We are accustomed to calling a method or accessing a data member (state variable) by first <u>creating an object</u> and then using that object to reach the method or variable. To recall how we do this, consider this class:

```
public class Nerd
{
        public Nerd( )
        {    . . .    }

        public double methodA(int x)
        {    . . .    }

        public void methodB(String s)
        {    . . .    }
        public double abc;
        public int xyz;
}
```

If we want to call *methodB* or access *abc* from outside the *Nerd* class, here is how we have had to do it in the past:

```
Nerd geek = new Nerd( );  //we create a Nerd object called geek
geek.methodB("Some words");  //Here we call methodB, but notice we must use
                                   //the object (geek) we created to do it
geek.abc = 32.38;  //Similarly we use the object (geek) to access the state variable
```

Now, we are going to show how to do this **without** having to create an object. First we will do a slight rewrite of the *Nerd* class.

```
public class Nerd
{
        public Nerd( )
        {    . . .    }

        public double methodA(int x)
        {    . . .    }

        public static void methodB(String s)
        {    . . .    }
        public static double abc;
        public int xyz;
}
```

Accessing without an object:

Notice the key word *static* has been inserted into two places. Both the data member *abc* and *methodB* are *static* which makes the following legal from the "outside world":

```
Nerd.methodB("Some words");
Nerd.abc = 32.38;
```

Notice that we did **not** need to create an object this time. Rather we used the name of the <u>*class*</u>. (That's why they're sometimes called <u>*class*</u> variables and methods.)

Well, this is all rather strange, isn't it? We just aren't accustomed to doing this....But wait! Oh, yes we **have** done this before. Remember our usage of *Math.PI* ? *Math* is a class within Java and *PI* is a data member there. Guess what? It's *static*. That's why we can access it <u>without</u> creating an object.

***static* method from the past:**

Is there an example of where we have used a *static* method in the past? Yes, again. Recall using *Math.sqrt(56.23)*? In fact, all of the methods we have studied in the *Math* class are *static*. We just need to precede the name of the variable or method with the name of the class.

So, there you have it, the first reason for having *static* variables and methods ...**the ability to access them <u>without</u> having to create an object**. It should be pointed out that we <u>can still</u> access *static* methods and variables by creating objects...

...*obj.methodB("Some words")*, *obj.abc*, etc. if desired.

Finally, while we are on this topic, we are now able to see why *static* is present in the familiar, *public static void main(String args[ ])* signature. It's because we are accessing the *main* method from the "outside world" (the development environment; BlueJ, JCreator, etc.) **without creating an object** and we now know that the key-word *static* is necessary for us to be able to do that.

The second reason for using *static*:

We will now examine a class with *static* state variables and see what happens when we create various instances of this class. (Notice that's the same as saying we create various objects from the class.)

```
public class Dweeb
{
        ... some methods and state variables ...
        public static int x;
}
```

We will now instantiate some objects from this class and manipulate the *static* data member *x*. (The following code is assumed to be in the *main* method of some other class.)

```
Dweeb.x = 79;
System.out.println(Dweeb.x); //79...object not necessary to access x

Dweeb twerp1 = new Dweeb( );      //Create objects and still we access the
System.out.println(Dweeb.x); //79   same, shared value of x
System.out.println(twerp1.x); //79
twerp1.x = 102;
```

```
Dweeb twerp2 = new Dweeb( );
System.out.println(Dweeb.x); //102
System.out.println(twerp2.x); //102
System.out.println(twerp1.x); //102
```

So, we see a second great principle of *static* data members. They are **shared by all instances** (all objects) of the class. In fact, the static variables are still present and available even if no objects are ever instantiated.

Accessing methods and data members from within a *static* method:

If from within a *static* method we try to access another method and/or data member of the same class, then that other method and/or state variable **must also be *static***. This is illustrated in the following code:

```
public class Tester
{
        //Since this method is static, all other methods and state variables
        //in its own class that it accesses must also be static.
        public static void main(String[] args)
        {
                . . . some code . . .
                double yz = methodF( );
                double ab = yz + sv;
        }

        . . .more methods . . .
        public static double methodF( )
        {    . . . some code. . .   }

        public static double sv = 99;
}
```

a. *Static* methods can reference only *static* variables and never the “regular”, non-*static* instance variables.

b. Non-*static* methods can reference either.

Sequence doesn’t matter:

Within some class, we might set up a class variable as follows:

```
public static String s;
```

The key word sequence *public static* **can be reversed**:

```
static public String s; //Can also be written this way, but usually the other way.
```

Even *static* methods can be written with the key-word *static* coming before *public*; however, it’s rare to see this in actual practice.

Static constants:

Constants can also be *static* as demonstrated in the following example:

```
public static final double PI = 3.14159;
```

Static imports:

With the advent of Java 5.0 the cumbersome use of *static* methods and variables can now be simpler and more readable. For example, *Math.sqrt(x)* and *System.out.println(x);* can now be written as just *sqrt(x)* and *out.println(x)*; however, the appropriate *static* imports must be made:

```
import static java.lang.Math.*;
import static java.lang.System.out;
```

Exercise on Lesson 20

The following code will apply to problems 1 – 7:

```
public class TvShow
{
        public TvShow(String nm)
        {
                numShows++;
                showName = nm;
        }

        public static int numberOfShows( )
        {
                return numShows;
        }

        public void setActor1(String act1)
        {
                actor1 = act1;
        }

        public String actor1 = "Don Knots";
        public static String actor2 = "Homer Simpson";
        public static int numShows = 0;
        public static int x = 59;
        public int y = 1059;
        public String showName;
}
```

1. At any time after several *TvShow* objects have been instantiated, how would you find out how many shows were instantiated? (Don't use an object to do this.)

2. Would the code inside the *numberOfShows* method still be correct if *numberOfShows* were non-*static*? If not, why?

3. Suppose the code inside the *numberOfShows* method is replaced with the following line:
   ```
   return y;
   ```
   Is this legal? If not, why?

4. Write code that will print the data member *actor2*. Do this without instantiating any objects.

5. Is the following code legal? If not, why?
   ```
   TvShow.setActor1("Jimmy Stewart");
   ```

6. Create an instance of *TvShow* called *chrs* (pass in the String "Cheers") and use it to access and print the class variable *numShows*.

7. Give the output of the following:
   ```
   System.out.println(TvShow.x);

   TvShow chrs = new TvShow("Cheers");
   System.out.println(TvShow.x);
   System.out.println(chrs.x);

   TvShow hc = new TvShow("History Channel");
   hc.x = 160;
   System.out.println(TvShow.x);
   System.out.println(hc.x);
   ```

****

8. Is the following a legal declaration of a class variable? If not, why?
   ```
   static public char ch = 'K';
   ```

9. Write code that will cause the variable *zxb* to be a *static* state variable. The variable *zxb* is a *double*.

10. Write code that will cause *sn* to be a constant *static* class member. The constant *sn* should be initialized as an empty *String*.

11. What is the significance of the word *Math* when we use *Math.pow(3.2, 4.001)*?

12. Class variables are also called _________ variables.

13. Assuming that the appropriate *static* import has been done, rewrite the following code without using the class name of the *static* methods.
    ```
    double xop = Math.pow(Math.sqrt(x - zv), 3.1);
    ```

14. What are the two primary reasons for using the key-word, *static*?

Project… How Far To The Line?

Create a new project called *DistToLine* having a class by the same name. The purpose of this class will be to calculate the distance from a point (a, b) to a line given by equation Ax + By + C = 0. The formula giving this distance is a standard one from analytic geometry, and is given below.

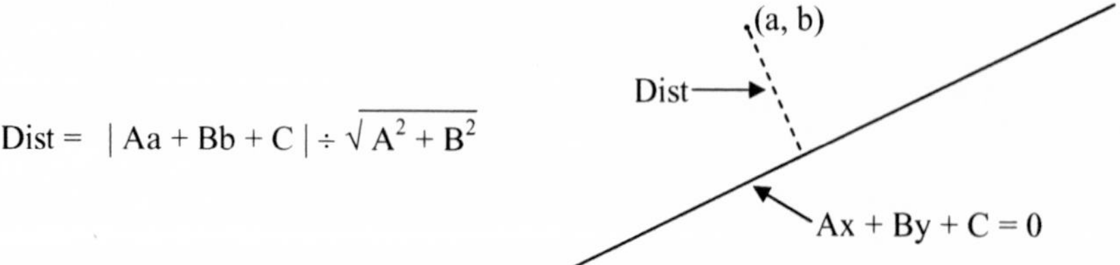

Fig. 20-1 Distance from a point to a line

The class will have no constructor and since we want to be able to compute the above distance **without creating an object**, the three state variables (*A*, *B*, & *C)* and the only method (*getDist*) will all need to be *static*. The method will receive two *double* parameters *a* and *b* that represent the point.

Here is how things will be organized in the class:

- Call the class *DistToLine*.
- Create *static double* state variables *A*, *B*, and *C*.
- Create the signature of the *static* method *getDist*. It will receive doubles *a* and *b*. It will return a *double* representing the calculated distance.
- In the body of this method, implement the distance formula above and return that value.

Create a *Tester* class as part of this project that will:

- Set the *static* state variables *A*, *B*, and *C* with the corresponding values of the desired line.
- Call the method *getDist* and pass as arguments the coordinates of the desired point.
- Print the returned *double* as the distance from the point to the line.

Typical output of the *Tester* class is shown below:

```
Enter the A value for the line: 2.45
Enter the B value for the line: 4
Enter the C value for the line: -8
Enter the x coordinate of the point: 2.17
Enter the y coordinate of the point: -4

Distance from the point to the line is: 3.9831092774319026
```

static Methods and State Variables… Contest Type Problems

```
public class GpsTrack
{
        public GpsTrack(int id)
        {
                vehicleCount++;
                vehicleID = id;
        }

        public static double getLonPos( )
        {
                //Code not shown
        }

        public static double getLatPos( )
        {
                //Code not shown
        }

        public double diffCor( )
        {
                …
                <#1>
                …
        }

        //Other methods not shown

        public static double longitude;
        public static double latitude;
        public int vehicleID;
        public String quad = "";
        public static int vehicleCount = 0;
}
```

1. Which of the following is **not** a legal way to access *vehicleCount* from within some other class? (assume that *gpsZ* is a *GpsTrack* object)

   A. double d = gpsZ.vehicleCount;
   B. vehicleCount = 27;
   C. gpsZ.vehicleCount = 27;
   D. int i = GpsTrack.vehicleCount;
   E. All are legal

2. Which of the following is **not** a class variable?

   A. longitude B. latitude C.vehicleId
   D. vehicleCount E. They are all class variables

3. If no objects have yet been instantiated, what is the value of *GpsTrack.vehicleCount* after the following code executes?

```
GpsTrack gpsA = new GpsTrack(1);
GpsTrack gpsB = new GpsTrack(3);
```

   A. 0 B. 1 C. 2 D. 3 E. None of these

4. Which of the following replacements for **<#1>** are legal?

   A. String s = quad;
   B. int vc = vehicleCount;
   C. int id = vehicleID;
   D. More than one of these
   E. They are all illegal

5. Is it possible for a constant to also be *static*?

   A. Yes B. No C.Yes, but only if the entire class is *static*
   D. Yes, but only if it's a numeric E. No, unless it's leap year

6. The statement *double d = Math.sqrt(pow(3.1, 4.67))* is which of the following?

   A. Evidence that *Math* is a *static* class
   B. Evidence that *sqrt* is a *static* method
   C. Evidence that a *static* import was done so that *pow (3.1, 4.67)* is legal
   D. Only A and C
   E. Only B and C

Lesson 21…..Wrapper Classes

Primitive data types are *int*, *double*, *boolean*, *char,* and some others of less importance that we haven't studied yet. Some of those others are (See Appendix C for a summary of all the numeric data types.):

1. *long*…an integer…gives more digits than *int.*
2. *short* …an integer…gives fewer digits than *int.*
3. *float* …a floating point number (a *double* is also a floating point number)… gives fewer significant digits than *double*.

Objects required instead of primitives:

Shortly, we will begin studying classes that require primitive data types to be stored in them in a special way. The requirement will be for essentially everything to be **stored as objects**. There are special classes that permit us to **convert primitives into objects** and thus satisfy the demands of those other classes that insist on being fed only objects. The classes that convert primitives to objects are called the **Wrapper Classes**…because they "wrap" the number, *boolean, or char* inside an object. Another term for this is "**boxing**" with the number being stored in a "box" (an object).

Four important wrapper classes:

The wrapper classes of greatest importance are *Integer*, *Double*, *Boolean*, and *Character* (notice the capital letters). In the examples below, notice that a **simpler way is given in the comments**. This simpler way is only true for Java 5.0 and higher.

1. *Integer* class examples:
```
Integer ic = new Integer(7); // Integer ic = 7;

int i = 10;
Integer ii = new Integer(i); //Integer ii = i;
```

2. *Double* class examples:
```
Double dc = new Double(1003.45); //Double dc = 1003.45;

double d = -82.19;
Double dd = new Double(d); //Double dd = d;
```

3. *Boolean* class examples:
```
Boolean bc = new Boolean(false); //Boolean bc = false;

boolean b = true;
Boolean bb = new Boolean(b); //Boolean bb = b;
```

4. *Character* class examples:
```
Character wc = new Character('X'); //Character wc = 'X';

char ch = 's';
Character cc = new Character(ch); //Character cc = ch;
```

The Wrappers classes for the other primitives (*float*, *long*, etc.) are done in exactly the same way.

We can take these wrapper objects and store them in those special classes that demand them. While we are not directly storing primitives there, we are at least storing a "version" of them.

Arithmetic operations on wrapper class objects:

What if we want to multiply (or perhaps add) two wrapper class *Integers*? How do we do it? From example 1 above we have *Integer* objects *ic* and *ii*. Do we just say *ic * ii*? "Yes," if Java 5.0 is being used because it uses "auto-unboxing" to convert the object versions back into primitive types before doing the actual multiplication. Here's how it must be done with the older versions of Java:

```
//First, convert back to int form
int j = ic.intValue( ); //Get the int value of object ic and store in j.
int k = ii.intValue( ); //Similarly, get the int value of object ii and store in k.

//Now perform the multiplication with the int versions j and k
int product = j * k;
```

Converting back to primitives:

We just looked at some "backwards" conversions above in which we converted from wrapper class *Integer* objects **back** to primitive *int* versions (also called "unwrapping" or "unboxing"). Let's look at **all** such conversions from Wrapper Class object back to primitives, but before presenting these examples it should be stated again that if Java 5.0 or higher is being used, "auto-unboxing" takes place as illustrated by:

- int i = iObj; //iObj is an Integer object
- double d = dObj; //dObj is a Double object
- ...etc...

1. Assume *iObj* is an *Integer* object.
    a. int i = iObj.**intValue( )**; //**most often used**...convert to int
    b. short s = iObj.shortValue( ); //convert to short
    c. long el = iObj.longValue( ); //convert to long
    d. float f = iObj.floatValue( ); //convert to float
    e. double d = iObj.doubleValue( ); //convert to double

2. Assume *dObj* is a *Double* object
    a. int i = dObj.intValue( ); //convert to int...loses fractional part
    b. short s = dObj.shortValue( ); //convert to short...loses fractional part
    c. long el = dObj.longValue( ); //convert to long...loses fractional part
    d. float f = dObj.floatValue( ); //convert to float...might lose some precision
    e. double d = dObj.**doubleValue**( ); //**most often used**...convert to double

3. Assume *bObj* is a *Boolean* object
    boolean b = bObj.booleanValue( ); //convert to boolean

4. Assume *cObj* is a *Character* object
    char ch = cObj.charValue( ); //convert to char

Likewise, the Wrapper classes for the other numeric types (*float*, *short*, etc.) have conversion methods.

Exercise on Lesson 21

1. The classes that convert primitives to objects are called ___________ classes.

2. Name the four primitive data types with which wrapper classes primarily deal.

3. Write code that will convert *double dx* into a wrapper class object. Call the object *dd*.

4. Write code that will produce a *Boolean* type wrapper object called *bj* ("wrap" a *true* inside it).

5. Write code that will convert the integer *ip* into an *Integer* wrapper class object. Call the object *ozzie*.

6. Assume you have the object *Character cw*. Write code to convert this to a primitive character.

7. Assume you have *Double* objects *d1* and *d2*. Show how you would multiply the values stored in these objects and then store the answer in primitive *double dd*.

8. Assume you have *Integer* objects *i1* and *i2*. Show how you would add the values stored in these objects and then store the answer in a third *Integer* object called *i3*.

9. Write code that will extract the *boolean* wrapped in the *Boolean wnOh* and test it with an *if* statement.

   if(______________)

10. Convert the object *jj* (of type *Double*) into a primitive *float* called *ff*.

11. Convert the object *pk* (of type *Double*) into a primitive *int* called *gurg*. What is the danger of doing this?

12. What is the primary purpose of wrapper classes?

Lesson 22…..Additional Methods of Wrapper Classes

Main purpose:

As was stated in the last lesson, the **main purpose** of the Wrapper classes is to **convert the primitive data types into their object equivalents**. Here, in this lesson we explore some of the other methods of the Wrapper classes.

Looking for a home:

These particular methods have **nothing** to do with the objects the Wrapper Classes produce. They could have been included in any class; however, as a matter of convenience they were placed in the Wrapper Classes…and especially the *Integer* class.

Notice that all methods given in this lesson are ***static***, i.e. **they do not require an object.**

Most frequently used:

The description and signatures of the two very most useful methods are given here:

Conversion from a *String* to an *int* type:

public static int parseInt(String s) //signature…from Integer class

Example:
String s = "139";
int i = Integer.parseInt(s);

The method *parseInt* is overloaded. Its other form is *parseInt(s, base)* where the second parameter, *base*, is the base of the number represented by *String s*.

Example:
String s = "3w4br";
int base = 35;
int i = Integer.parseInt(s, base); //i = 5879187

Conversion from a *String* to a *double* type:

public static double parseDouble(String s) //signature…from Double class

Example:
String s = "282.8026";
double d = Double.parseDouble(s);

The equivalents of these for the *Boolean* and *Character* classes do not exist.

When using either the *parseInt* or *parseDouble* methods there is a danger of throwing an exception (causing an error). Suppose we have *String s = "123"* and we wish to convert to an *int* type. This makes perfect sense, and the following line of code using this *s* will yield an integer value of *123*.

int i = Integer.parseInt(s); //yields i = 123

But what if *s* equals something like *"abc"*? How will the *parseInt* method react? It will throw an exception. Specifically, it will throw a *NumberFormatException*.

Base conversion methods:

In Lesson 14 we became familiar with some base conversion methods of the *Integer* class. They all converted *int* types to the *String* equivalent of various number systems. Below are examples of usage where *s* is assumed to be a *String* and *i* is assumed to be an *int* type:

1. s = Integer.toHexString(i);
   //…or use Integer.toString(i, 16); …see page 14-3

2. s = Integer.toOctalString(i);
   //…or use Integer.toString(i, 8);

3. s = Integer.toBinaryString(i);
   //…or use Integer.toString(i, 2);

Additional methods:

A description of each is given followed by the method signature and then an example of usage:

Conversion of an *int* type to a *String*:

public String toString(int i); //Signature…from Integer class
//See 1, 2, & 3 above for a two-parameter version.

Example:
int i = 104;
String ss = Integer.toString(i);

You should be aware that there is an easier way to convert an integer into a *String*. Just append an *int* type to an empty *String* and the compiler will think you want to make a *String* out of the combination.

Example:
int j = 3;
String s = "" + j; // s will be equal to "3"
s = "" + 56; // s will be equal to "56"

Conversion of a *String* to an *Integer* object.

public static Integer valueOf(String s); //Signature…from Integer class

Example:
String s = "452";
Integer iObj = Integer.valueOf(s);

Data member constants of the *Integer* class

- *Integer.MIN_VALUE* has a value of -2,147,483,648
- *Integer.MAX_VALUE* has a value of 2,147,483,647

These two constants (see Appendix C) give the two extreme possible values of *int* variables.

Exercise on Lesson 22

1. Write code that will convert a *String* called *rr* into an *int* type called *i*.

2. The *String s* contains "123.456". How would you convert this into a *double* type variable?

3. What evidence is there in the following statement that the method is *static*?

```
int v = Integer.parseInt(s);
```

4. How would you convert *String s* to hex form?

5. Suppose you have an *int* type stored in *jj*. How would you convert this into a *String*?

6. Suppose you must pass the *Integer* object equivalent of 1000 as a parameter to a *methodA*; however, all you have is a *String* representation *ss* of that integer. Show how you would manipulate *ss* and change it into an object called *obj* so that it could be used as a parameter for *methodA*.

7. What is output by the following code?

```
String pdq = "-772.29";
System.out.println( 3 + Double.parseDouble(pdq) );
```

8. Assume *iObj* is an *Integer* object "wrapping" the value -186. What is output by the following code?

```
int ip = iObj.intValue( );  //java 5.0, int ip = iObj;
String mz = "3" + Integer.toString(ip) + "3";
System.out.println(mz);
```

9. Write code that will convert "3pfh" (a *String* representation of a base 33 number) to *int i*.

10. Write code that will convert *int i* into its *String* equivalent in base 6.

Wrapper Class Objects… Contest Type Problems

<table>
<tr><td>1. What is the output?

A. 0
B. 6
C. 1
D. 2
E. None of these</td><td>

```
public class MyTester
{
   public static void main(String args[])
   {
      int j=2, k=3;
      Integer bj, bk;
      while(k>0) {
         j = j*k;
         k = k/2;
      }
      bj = j;
      bk = k;
      System.out.println(bj.intValue( ) + bk);
   }
}
```

</td></tr>
<tr><td>2. What is printed when we make the call getAsum("22222")?

A. 9
B. 7
C. 5
D. 2
E. None of these</td><td>

```
public static void getAsum(String a)
{
      int total=0;
      Integer p1, p2;
      for(int j = a.length( ) - 1; j > 1;j--)
      {
         p1 = j-1;
         p2 = new Integer(j);
         total+=j;
      }
      System.out.println(total);
}
```

</td></tr>
<tr><td>3. What is returned when we make the call theTest(2)?

A. 3.14
B. 3
C. 2
D. 1
E. 0</td><td>

```
public static int theTest(int div)
{
      Integer trial;
      double d = Math.PI/div;
      trial = new Integer( (int)d );
      return trial.intValue( );
}
```

</td></tr>
<tr><td>4. What gets printed?

A. 235
B. 234
C. 235.6
D. Throws an exception
E. None of these</td><td>

```
 …
Calc myObj = new Calc( );
System.out.println( myObj.adjust(117.8) );
 …

public class Calc
{
   public static int adjust(double d)
   {
      d *= 2;
      Double dw = d;
      return dw;
   }
}
```

</td></tr>
</table>

Lesson 23…..*StringTokenizer* Class

Consider the *String*, "The quick brown fox jumped over the lazy dogs." Suppose we wanted to take this sentence apart, word-by-word, and then test or process each word? Right now it's a little hard to see what might be the application of doing something like that or why it might be practical. Rest assured there **are** plenty of applications (for example, virus detection, email filtering, etc); however, those apps are a bit advanced for us right now.

Instead, let's look at another, more practical *String* for us:
"128 65 1 586 108 79222"

What we have above are several numbers, all separated by spaces. We might also have the same list in which commas separate the numbers as follows:
"128,65,1,586,108,79222"

Tokens:

In either case, what can we do to separate the individual words of a sentence …or as in the last example, the individual numbers? We call the individual words or numbers, **tokens**. The characters that separate them (spaces, commas, etc), are called **delimiters**.

A class that lets us choose delimiters and then automatically separates out the tokens is called the ***StringTokenizer*** class.

***StringTokenizer* methods:**

Let's take a look at the various methods available to us from the *StringTokenizer* class (we must import *java.util.*)*. For each method, we will give a description and then the signature of the method. These are **not** *static* methods, so we must first show how to create an object:

```
String theString = "128,65,1,586,108,79222";
StringTokenizer t = new StringTokenizer(theString, ",  \n"); //comma, space, & \n
                                                              //are delimiters
```

countTokens( )

Returns the number of tokens in the specified *String* that **remain** to be processed.

public int countTokens( ) //**Signature**

Example:

```
System.out.println ( t.countTokens( ) ); //6
//See next example for more on countTokens
```

nextToken( )

Returns the next token in the specified string. Gives an exception (error) if no more tokens.

public String nextToken( ) //**Signature**

Example:

```
String x = t.nextToken( ); //x is now equal to "128"
String y = t.nextToken( ); //y is now equal to "65"
System.out.println ( t.countTokens( ) ); //4 remain to be processed
```

Also, see the example for *hasMoreTokens( )* below for how to prevent *nextToken* from throwing an exception.

nextToken(delim)

Establishes a **new** set of delimiters via *String delim* and then returns the next resulting token. Gives an exception (error) if no more tokens.

```
public String nextToken(String delim)  //Signature
```

Example: (Assume the code in the previous examples has already executed)

```
String m = t.nextToken(" ,8\n");  //space, comma, 8, and \n specified as new
                                  //delimiters. Returns a 1.
System.out.println( t.nextToken( ) );  //5... as a result of 8 also acting as a
                                       //delimiter.
```

hasMoreTokens( )

Returns either a *true* or *false* depending on the presence of more unprocessed tokens.

```
public boolean hasMoreTokens( )  //Signature
```

Example: (Assume the code in the previous examples has already executed)

```
if ( t.hasMoreTokens( ) )
    System.out.println( t.nextToken( ) );  //6
```

Note that the above *if* statement is equivalent to:

```
if ( t.countTokens( ) > 0 )
    System.out.println( t.nextToken( ) );  //6
```

Constructors:

There are **two constructors** that you should be aware of when creating *StringTokenizer* objects. Each type is illustrated below:

One parameter:

```
StringTokenizer stok = new StringTokenizer(myString);
```

There is only one parameter, *myString* (the *String* we desire to tokenize). The delimiters are by default:

" \t\n\r\f" i.e., the space, tab, new line, carriage-return, and form-feed characters.

Two parameters:

```
StringTokenizer stok = new StringTokenizer(myString, delimString);
```

Again, *myString* is the *String* we desire to tokenize. *String delimString* is a list of desired delimiter characters. For example, if we desire a space, a plus sign, and the letter "p" as delimiters, then set *delimString* = *" +p"*.

You should be aware that another way to tokenize *Strings* is by using the *split* method of the *String* class. See Lesson 18, Appendix J, and Appendix AC for more on the *split* method.

Exercise on Lesson 23

1. Create a *StringTokenizer* object called *st*. We wish to tokenize *String zulu* and specify only a plus sign as a delimiter.

2. What are the "things" called that separate the "words" within a *String* that is to be tokenized?

3. What are the individual parts or "words" called in a *String* that is to be tokenized?

4. What is the import we need in order to get the *StringTokenizer* to work?

5. What is the output of the following code?
```
StringTokenizer t = new StringTokenizer("Hello there good buddy");
String m = t.nextToken( );
System.out.println(m + ">>>" + t.countTokens( ) + "  tokens left.");
```

6. Rewrite the following *if* statement using *countTokens()* rather than *hasMoreTokens()*.
```
if ( jj.hasMoreTokens( ) )
{ …. }
```

7. What is the output of the following code?
```
StringTokenizer g = new StringTokenizer("Rumplestillskin", "me");
System.out.println( g.nextToken( ) );
System.out.println( g.nextToken("s") );
```

8. Write a class called *SpecialToken* that has a *static* method called *thirdToken*. This method should return as a *String*, the third token of a *String* that you pass as a parameter. You may assume that spaces will serve as delimiters.

9. Which constructor for the *StringTokenizer* class would be simplest to use if you wanted spaces and tabs as delimiters?

In problems 10 – 13 state what's printed. Use the following code and assume for each question that the code in the previous questions has been executed.

```
StringTokenizer gt = new StringTokenizer("Humpty Dumpty", "  pu\n\t");
```

10. System.out.println(gt.countTokens( ));

11. String radString = gt.nextToken( );
    System.out.println(gt.nextToken( ) + radString);

12. System.out.println(gt.countTokens);

13. What should replace ??? below in order to insure that we don't get an exception?

```
while ( ??? )
{
        System.out.println( gt.nextToken( ) );
}
```

14. What is output by the following code?

```
StringTokenizer tux = new StringTokenizer("Ignoramus");
System.out.println( tux.countTokens( ) );
System.out.println( tux.nextToken( ) );
System.out.println( tux.nextToken( ) );
```

Project… Military Censor

You are in the Army and have been assigned the task of censoring soldiers' outgoing mail for security reasons. Let's assume that the troops all know about an upcoming offensive that will involve an assault on the Hermes bridge that crosses the Muddy River. Develop an algorithm that uses the *StringTokenizer* to examine each word of outgoing email. If any of the following words are found, print the word REJECTED. If none are found, then print OK.

Taboo words are: Hermes, bridge, Muddy, River, assault, and offensive

Call your class *Censor* and use the following sentences for testing.

"I hope I survive the assault tomorrow."

"I want to talk to you about Bobby, but we'll cross that bridge later."

"Tell sis and Larry that I'll be Ok and I will see them in 6 months"

"Your last letter was a little muddy on exactly what you meant."

"I see no point in us trying to take the hermes crossing."

Notice the last sentence uses "hermes" instead of "Hermes". Your code should not be sensitive to case and should reject this sentence.

You should input these sentences via the keyboard using the *Scanner* class. Your output screen should look like the following after testing all the sentences:

```
Enter next sentence: I hope I survive the assault tomorrow.
I hope I survive the assault tomorrow.>>>REJECTED

Enter next sentence: I want to ask about Bobby, but we'll cross that
bridge later.
I want to ask about Bobby, but we'll cross that bridge
later.>>>REJECTED

Enter next sentence: Tell sis and Larry that I'll be ok and I will see
them in 6 months.
Tell sis and Larry that I'll be ok and I will see them in 6
months.>>>OK

Enter next sentence: Your last letter was a little muddy on exactly
what you meant.
Your last letter was a little muddy on exactly what you
meant.>>>REJECTED

Enter next sentence: I see no point in us trying to take the hermes
crossing.
I see no point in us trying to take the hermes crossing.>>>REJECTED
```

StringTokenizer... Contest Type Problems

<table>
<tr><td>1. What is output?

A. 54593
B. 54+593
C. 54+5=93
D. 59=93
E. None of these</td><td>

```
import java.util.*;
public class MyTester
{
   public static void main(String args[]){
      int m=3, n=4, p=5;
      String s="5;4+5=9;3";
      StringTokenizer st=new StringTokenizer(s,";");
      while(st.hasMoreTokens( ))
      {
         System.out.print(st.nextToken( ));
      }
   }
}
```

</td></tr>
<tr><td>2. What should be passed as a parameter to the total method in order for it to return a 17?

A. “11”
B. “3 8 0”
C. “7\n2 1\n1”
D. “15 –1 –2 –1”
E. All of the above</td><td>

```
public static int total(String str) {
      StringTokenizer t = new StringTokenizer(str);
      int sum = 5;
      while(t.hasMoreTokens( ))
      {
         sum = sum+Integer.parseInt(t.nextToken( ));
      }
      return sum+1;
}
```

</td></tr>
<tr><td>3. What is output?

A. 100.4
B. 101.4
C. 101.5
D. 102.5
E. None of these</td><td>

```
import java.util.*;
public class MyTester
{
   public static void main(String args[]){
      double [] md = {100.3, 100.4, 100.5, 100.6};
      int k=0;
      String b = "0 1 2";
      StringTokenizer st=new StringTokenizer(b);
      while(st.hasMoreTokens( ))
      {
         String str = new String(st.nextToken( ));
         //System.out.println(str);
         double val = Double.parseDouble(str);
         ++k;
         md[k]+=val;
      }
      System.out.print(md[1]);
   }
}
```

</td></tr>
</table>

4. What is output?

A. 6
B. 8
C. 2
D. Throws exception
E. None of these

```
import java.util.*;
public class MyTester {
   public static void main(String args[]){
      double [] md = {1, 2, 3, 4};
      int j;
      String b = "0 1 2";
      StringTokenizer st=new StringTokenizer(b);
      int k=st.countTokens( );
      for(j=1; j<=k; j++) {
         double f=Double.parseDouble(st.nextToken( ));
         //System.out.println(j + "   " + f + "   " + md[j]);
         if(j%2==1){
            md[j]*=f;
         }
         else {
          md[j]/=f;
         }
      }
      System.out.println(md[j-1]);
   }
}
```

5. What is output?

A. Fourscoreandsevenyearsago
B. Four-scoreandsevenyears
C. Fourscoreandsevenyears
D. Fourscore and seven years ago
E. None of these

```
String s = "Four-score and seven years ago";
StringTokenizer st = new StringTokenizer(s, "  -");
for(int j=0; j<5; j++)
        System.out.print(st.nextToken( ));
```

6. How would the output change if the *for*-loop was changed to *for(int j=1;j<=5;j++)*?

A. Throws an exception
B. No change
C. "ago" would be appended to the end of the output.
D. Four-score would be omitted
E. None of these

Lesson 24.....Input from a Disk File

Before we look at the code necessary to input data from a disk file, let's first create a text file. We will use a text editor for this purpose. Microsoft Notepad (preferred) or Microsoft WordPad is recommended. Students sometimes have problems getting the proper extension for the file name, etc., so it is recommended that we take a brief detour to Appendix E so as to avoid problems in this area.

Create a file:

Create a text file called *MyData.in*. Store it in a folder specified by the following path (unless directed otherwise by your instructor):

C:\temp_Larry

It is assumed that your name is Larry and you have already created the folder, *temp_Larry*.

The contents of *MyData.in* should be as follows:

```
One for all and all for one.
Little House on the Prairie
11 22 33 44 55 66 77 88    << notice the spaces between the numbers
Sticks and stones
```

After the *s* in *stones* press the *Enter* key **just once**. If the programs that follow give a *NullPointerException*, then first suspect the problem of "multiple *Enter*s".

Read the file:

We finally get down to business and begin writing a class called *FileTester* that will read and display the contents of the file, *MyData.in*.

```
import java.util.*;
import java.io.*;
public class FileTester
{
        public static void main(String args[])
        {
                Scanner sf = new Scanner(new File("C:\\temp_Larry\\MyData.in"));
                ... more code to come ...
                sf.close( ); //We opened a file above so close it when finished.
        }
}
```

To read the file, we need to create a *Scanner* object, and this necessitates the import of *java.util.** (package name is *java.util*...see Appendix I for more on packages). *File* requires the import of java.io.*. In the above code it is the object *sf* that will be used to input data from the file.

Notice in *C:\\temp_Larry\\MyData.in* the use of the double back-slashes. Recall that \\ is the escape sequence for the back-slash character. Otherwise, if we had specified *C:\temp_Larry\MyData.in* the *\t* would have been interpreted as the escape sequence for a tab .... and *\M* would have been interpreted as yet another escape sequence.

Won't compile:

Unfortunately, this code won't even compile. The *File* object is capable of producing errors beyond our control. For example, suppose the file doesn't exist or is corrupted. What if we try to do successive inputs beyond the end of the file? These would all produce errors (exceptions). To correctly allow for these errors, we need to change the signature of the *main* method as follows:

public static void main(String args[]) **throws IOException**

This *throws IOException* is very mysterious right now. In a later lesson we will learn all about exceptions. For now, we simply accept by faith that *throws IOException* needs to be there in case of a file error.... If you are incurably curious and need to know, we **can** tell you briefly that for a method that is capable of throwing a **checked** exception (of which, *IOException* is a classic example) you can either handle the error in your code with *try*, *catch*, and *finally*...or you can **defer** the response to the error up the calling chain with *throws IOException*. Incidentally, the *IOException* class also requires the importing of the *java.io.** package.

At this point your *FileTester* class should compile successfully.

We will now add some more code that will actually bring in the data from the *MyData.in* file one line at a time. We will use a *while* loop to do this, and inside the loop on each iteration we will assign the lines in the text file to the *String* array, *text[ ]*. When finished with the loop, we should find that we have four array values as follows:

text[0] = "One for all and all for one."
text[1] = "Little House on the Prairie"
text[2] = "11 22 33 44 55 66 77 88"
text[3] = "Sticks and stones"

The amended class:

```
import java.io.*;  // necessary File and IOException
import java.util.*;  // necessary for Scanner
public class FileTester
{
    public static void main(String args[]) throws IOException
    {
        Scanner sf = new Scanner(new File("C:\\temp_Larry\\MyData.in"));

        int maxIndx = -1;  //-1 so when we increment below, first indx is 0
        String text[] = new String[100];  //to be safe, declare more than we need

        while(sf.hasNext( ))
        {
            maxIndx++;
            text[maxIndx] = sf.nextLine( ) ;
        }
        //maxIndx is now the highest index of text[], -1 if no text lines
        sf.close( );  //We opened a file above so close it when finished.
    }
}
```

One line at a time:

A little explanation is in order. The most critical line above is *text[maxIndx] = sf.nextLine( )*. This is where we pull an entire line in from the disk file. The control part of the *while*-loop, *sf.hasNext( )*, lets us gracefully end the loop after all lines have been input.

The final version:

This is all well and good, but how do we know if it really worked? After the *sf.close( )* statement above, let's add a loop to cycle through all the appropriate *text[ ]* values and print them out. The final class is:

```
import java.io.*;  // necessary for File and IOException
import java.util.*;  // necessary for Scanner
public class FileTester
{
        public static void main(String args[]) throws IOException
        {
            Scanner sf = new Scanner(new File("C:\\temp_Larry\\MyData.in"));

            int maxIndx = -1;  //-1 so when we increment below, first indx is 0
            String text[] = new String[100];  //to be safe, declare plenty

              while(sf.hasNext( ))
              {
                      maxIndx++;
                      text[maxIndx] = sf.nextLine( ) ;
              }
              //maxIndx is now the highest index of text[], -1 if no text lines
              sf.close( );  //We opened a file above so close it when finished.

              for(int j = 0; j <= maxIndx; j++)
              {
                      System.out.println( text[j] );
              }
        }
}
```

The final output:

After running this program, your printout should look like this:

```
One for all and all for one.
Little House on the Prairie
11 22 33 44 55 66 77 88
Sticks and stones
```

Exercise on Lesson 24

Unless otherwise indicated, the following questions refer to the final *FileTester* class on the previous page.

1. Create a *Scanner* object called *scr* suitable for reading in the file *DaffyDuck.txt*. This file resides in the *C:\Disney\Cartoons* folder.

2. Consider the code fragments:

```
maxIndx++;
text[maxIndx] = sf.nextLine( );
```

   Which of the following could replace this code?
   a. text[++maxIndx] = sf.nextLine( );
   b. text[maxIndx++] = sf.nextLine( );
   c. text[maxIndx] = sf.nextLine( );
   d. None of these

3. Write an expression that tells the number of elements in the *text[ ]* array (after exiting the loop) that contain meaningful data.

4. Why do we initialize *maxIndx* with a value of –1?

5. What are the conditions for exiting the *while* loop?

6. The *Scanner* class requires what import?

7. Rewrite the *while* loop so that it prints each line of input from the file just after it's stored in the *text[ ]* array.

8. What would be the value of *maxIndx* (at the completion of the *while* loop) if the *MyData.in* file was completely empty?

9. What does *sf.close( )* accomplish?

10. With the statement *String text[ ] = new String[100];* why do we dimension *text[ ]* so large?

11. What might account for the following?

You used Notepad to create a file and thought you named it *Dat.xx*. Later when you look in the folder (in which it resides) with Windows Explorer, you notice that the file name is actually *Dat.xx.txt*.

12. Write the signature of the *nextLine* method.

Project… Reading Files

Write a class called *FileNerd* that will input the lines of text from a file named *NerdData.txt* that is stored in the *C:\temp_Larry* folder (assuming your name is Larry). After the file input loop, create a loop in which you printout only those lines that begin with the word "The".

The contents of NerdData.txt are:

Every man tries as hard as he can.
The best way is this way.
The schedule is very good.
Cosmo Kramer is a doofus.
The best movie was cancelled.

Output will look like this:

```
The best way is this way.
The schedule is very good.
The best movie was cancelled.
```

Warning:
Now that we know how to input files there is a danger of bringing a virus into our computers. See Appendix T for a discussion on viruses and how to protect against them.

Lesson 25…..Processing File Input with *Scanner*

We are going to illustrate the use of the *Scanner* class with lines of text that we input from a file. First, we will look at how to process **numbers** that are embedded in the text that makes up the various lines of an ASCII text file.

Suppose we consider text files with the following properties:

1. They will have an unknown number of lines of text.
2. Each line of text consists of an unknown number of integers separated by spaces.

Following is an example of the contents of such a file (*NumData.in* stored in your standard *temp_Name* folder):

```
12 10 3 5
18 1 5 92 6 8
2 9 3 22 4 11 7
```

Adapting to unpredictability:

When we write our program, we want to remember that this file has elements of unpredictability. There are an **unpredictable number of lines of text**. Furthermore, each line of text contains an **unpredictable number of integers**.

Here is our task. We are to input the lines of text and then print the sum of the numbers in each line. For example, the sum of the numbers in the first line is:

12 + 10 + 3 + 5 = 30

Similarly, the other lines of text yield:

18 + 1 + 5 + 92 + 6 + 8 = 130
2 + 9 + 3 + 22 + 4 + 11 + 7 = 58

We are required to process the data in such a way that the final printout appears as follows:

```
12 + 10 + 3 + 5 = 30
18 + 1 + 5 + 92 + 6 + 8 = 130
2 + 9 + 3 + 22 + 4 + 11 + 7 = 58
```

Begin the new class:

Let's begin our new *InputNumData* class as follows:

```
import java.io.*; //necessary for File and IOException
import java.util.*; //necessary for Scanner
public class InputNumData
{
  public static void main( String args[] ) throws IOException
  {
      Scanner sf = new Scanner(new File("C:\\temp_Name\\NumData.in"));
      int maxIndx = -1; //-1 so when we increment below, the first index is 0
```

```
                String text[] = new String[100]; //To be safe, declare more than we need
                while(sf.hasNext( ))
                {
                        maxIndx++;
                        text[maxIndx] = sf.nextLine( );
                        //System.out.println(text[maxIndx]); //Remove rem for testing
                }
                //maxIndx is now the highest index of text[], -1 if no text lines
                sf.close( ); //We opened a file above, so close it when finished.

                ...process the text[] array...
        }
}
```

Notice that the *while*-loop automatically adjusts to an unpredictable number of lines of text. We exit the loop with the lines of text stored in *text[ ]* and with *maxIndx* being the highest index.

Processing the text:

Our real job here is to fill in code in the area of **...process the *text[ ]* array...**. To do this, we will set up a loop to process the *text[ ]* elements. As the first line inside the loop, we will create another *Scanner* object where *text[j]* is the *String* to be tokenized (parsed).

```
for(int j =0; j <= maxIndx; j++)
{
        Scanner sc = new Scanner(text[j]);
        //Notice we create a new object each time through the loop
        . . .
}
```

Now, we will adjust to the unpredictable number of integers in each line of text by using a *while* loop and the *Scanner* method *hasNext( )* as follows:

```
String answer = “”; //We will accumulate the answer string here.
int sum; //accumulates sum of integers
for(int j =0; j <= maxIndx; j++)
{
        Scanner sc = new Scanner(text[j]);
        sum = 0; //important to set to 0; otherwise it will remember the last sum
        answer = “”; //otherwise it will remember last answer String

        while( sc.hasNext( ) ) //We could also have used hasNextInt( ) here
        {
                int i = sc.nextInt( );
                answer = answer +  “ + ”  + i;
                sum = sum + i;
        }
        answer = answer +  “ = ”  + sum;
        System.out.println(answer);
}
```

As we learned in Lesson 7, use of the *Scanner* class necessitates the import of *java.util.**.

The resulting printout:

```
+ 12 + 10 + 3 + 5 = 30
+ 18 + 1 + 5 + 92 + 6 + 8 = 130
+ 2 + 9 + 3 + 22 + 4 + 11 + 7 = 58
```

Project… Get Rid of That Leading Plus Sign!

The above is fairly close to what we want except that we have a leading " + " to eliminate from each line. This is left as an exercise for the student.

A more complex task:

For our next application of file input using *Scanner*, we will consider lines of pure alphabetical characters. The text file we will use will be called *Names.in* and will be stored on a floppy. The path to the floppy will be "*A:\Names.in*". (Your instructor may have you put the file on your hard drive if you do not have a functioning floppy drive.)

The contents of this file will be:
Sally Jones
Laura Bush
Charlene Tilton
Marilyn Monroe
Judy Ellison
Felecia Garza
Minerva Perez

Output will be:

```
Bush, Laura
Ellison, Judy
Garza, Felecia
Jones, Sally
Monroe, Marilyn
Perez, Minerva
Tilton, Charlene
```

There are two things required of the output that we observe above.

1. The names have been reversed with the last name occurring first followed by a comma and then the first name.
2. The reversed names are listed in alphabetical order.

Reversing the names:

We will call our class *AlphNames*; however, for now we will skip immediately to the code that follows the *while*-loop that inputs the lines of text from the file into the array, *text[ ]*. Our code begins with the assumption that we have the following:

text[0] = "Sally Jones"
text[1] = "Laura Bush"
. . .

The first thing we will do is produce a new unsorted array *reversedName[ ]* that will appear as follows:

reversedName[0] = "Jones, Sally"
reversedName[1] = "Bush, Laura"
. . .

Here is the code that will accomplish all this:

```
String reversedName[] = new String[maxIndx + 1];
for (int j = 0; j <= maxIndx; j++)
{
        Scanner sc = new Scanner( text[j] );

        String firstName = sc.next( );
        String lastName = sc.next( );
        reversedName[j] = lastName +   ", "   + firstName;
}
```

Sorting the new array:

Finally, we need a way to sort the array, *reversedName[ ]*. Recall from Lesson 19 that it's done like this: (The *for*-loop prints the sorted array.)

```
Arrays.sort(reversedName);  //requires import java.util.*
for (int j =0; j <= maxIndx; j++)
{
        System.out.println( reversedName[j] );
}
```

Finally, the entire class is as follows:

```
import java.io.*;  //for File and IOException
import java.util.*;  //necessary for Arrays.sort( ) and Scanner
public class AlphNames
{
        public static void main(String args[]) throws IOException
        {
                Scanner sf = new Scanner(new File("A:\\Names.in"));

                int maxIndx = -1;  //-1 so when we increment below, the first index is 0
                String text[] = new String[100];  //to be safe, declare more than we need

                while(sf.hasNext( ))
                {
                        maxIndx++;
                        text[maxIndx] = sf.nextLine( );
                }
                //maxIndx is now the highest index of text[], = -1 if no text lines
                sf.close( );  //We opened a file above, so close it when finished.

                String reversedName[] = new String[maxIndx + 1];
                for (int j = 0; j <= maxIndx; j++)
                {
                        Scanner sc = new Scanner( text[j] );

                        String firstName = sc.next( );
                        String lastName = sc.next( );
                        reversedName[j] = lastName +   ", "   + firstName;
                }
```

```
            Arrays.sort(reversedName);
            for (int j =0; j <= maxIndx; j++)
            {
                System.out.println( reversedName[j] );
            }
        }
    }
```

Project... Student Averages

Create the following text file called *StudentScores.in* and store in your standard folder (*temp_Name*).

File contents:

```
Agnes 56 82 95 100 68 52
Bufford 87 92 97 100 96 85 93 77 98 86
Julie 99 100 100 89 96 100 92 99 68
Alice 40 36 85 16 0 22 72
Bobby 100 98 92 86 88
```

Program output:

```
Agnes, average = 76
Bufford, average = 91
Julie, average = 94
Alice, average = 39
Bobby, average = 93
```

Each line of the file consists of a student's name followed by an unpredictable number of test scores. The number of students is also unpredictable. The desired output is as shown where the numbers there represent the average test score rounded to the nearest whole number.

Create a class called *StudentAverages* that will input the *StudentScores.in* text file and produce the indicated output.

Lesson 26.....Writing to a Text File

Writing/overwriting a file:

Writing to a text file is very simple. We will again need to do two things we are already accustomed to doing when **reading** text files:

1. *java.io.** must be imported.

2. Use *throws IOException* as part of the signature of the method containing our file output code.

Create *FileWriter* and *PrintWriter* objects:

FileWriter fw = new FileWriter("C:\\temp_Name\\Output1.out");

Notice here that we specify the name of the file we wish to create. This object sends **one character at a time** to the file. This could be a bit inconvenient. For example, if we need to output "Hello good buddy", we would need to output all 16 characters **separately**.

PrintWriter output = new PrintWriter(fw);

This final object, *output*, permits us to use a **single command** to write entire sentences (or numbers) to the file. This *PrintWriter* class has two methods of which we need to be aware.

a. *print()*
b. *println()*

print() and *println()* are used in exactly the same way in which they are used with *System.out*.

Complete class in which we write to a file:

```
import java.io.*;
public class WriteToFile
{
	public static void main(String args[]) throws IOException
	{
		FileWriter fw = new FileWriter("C:\\temp_Name\\Output1.out");
		PrintWriter output = new PrintWriter(fw);

		output.print("Four-score and ");
		double d = 7.023;
		output.println(d);
		output.println("years ago.");

		output.close( );  //These two lines are very important. Some of the data
		fw.close( );      //may not actually be put on disk until you close.
	}
}
```

Load Notepad and look at the file *Output1.out*. The following is what you should see.

```
Four-score and 7.023
years ago.
```

Project…. Write Student Averages

Modify the project (Determining Student Averages) from Lesson 25 so that it will print the output to a file rather than a console screen. Your output file should be stored in your standard folder, *temp_Name* and the file name should be *StudentScores.out*. At the completion of the program, the contents of *StudentScores.out* should be:

```
Agnes, average = 76
Bufford, average = 91
Julie, average = 94
Alice, average = 39
Bobby, average = 93
```

Call this new class *StudentAverages_Out*.

****

Appending to a file:

Occasionally it may be desirable to append new content to the end of an existing file rather that overwriting it as is the case with all of the previous code in this lesson. To accomplish this, just make the following modification to the creation of the *FileWriter* object:

```
FileWriter fw = new FileWriter("C:\\temp_Name\\Output1.out", true);
```

The new parameter, *true*, simply says, "Yes, we want to append."

Flushing the buffer:

The *PrintWriter* constructor will also accept a second parameter that indicates if we wish to **flush** the buffer after each *println*. This forces storage to the disk **at that moment** rather than waiting for the *close* method. This second parameter is not necessary if the *close* method is issued at the end of output to the disk. The syntax for this is:

```
PrintWriter output = new PrintWriter(fw, true);
```

As an enrichment activity, take a look at Appendix F. There, you will learn the difference between text and binary files.

Lesson 27…. Formatting (rounding-off)

One method of rounding off is to use the *NumberFormat* (requires *import java.text.*;*) class to create a *String*, and then convert that *String* back into the desired primitive number type.

A "rounding-off" example:

For example, to round 34.982665 to the nearest thousandths:

```
double d = 34.982665;

NumberFormat formatter = NumberFormat.getNumberInstance( );
formatter.setMaximumFractionDigits(3);
formatter.setMinimumFractionDigits(3);

String s = formatter.format(d);
System.out.println(s);  //34.983
double d3 = Double.parseDouble(s);
System.out.println(d3);  //34.983 ...Perfect, just the answer we expected!
```

Analyzing the details:

Let's examine four important details about the above code:

1. *setMaximumFractionDigits(3)* gives us **no more** than 3 decimal places… i.e. it rounds off to **3** decimal places.

2. *setMinimumFractionDigits(3)* **guarantees** at least 3 decimal places. For example, if we round off 34.9997 to 3 decimal places we would ordinarily get 35.0; however, with *setMinimumFractionDigits(3)* we would get 35.000.

3. *formatter.format(d)* returns a ***String***, not a numeric.

4. You may ultimately want a numeric instead of a *String*, hence the *Double.parseDouble(s)* part of the code.

More *NumberFormat* objects:

Notice above that the way we create a *NumberFormat* object is by calling the *getNumberInstance static* method. It returns a *NumberFormat* object. There are two other similar methods that return *NumberFormat* objects. These are detailed below along with sample usage.

1. The object returned by *getCurrencyInstance* is used for formatting money.

```
NumberFormat nf = NumberFormat.getCurrencyInstance( );
String str = nf.format(81.09745);
System.out.println(str);  //$81.10

str = nf.format(.358);
System.out.println(str);  //$.36
```

2. The object returned by *getPercentInstance* is used for formatting percents. The number to be formatted is multiplied by 100 and then a percent sign is appended. The settings determined by *setMinimumFractionDigits( )* and *setMaximumFractionDigits( )* are applied **after** multiplication by 100. If these methods are not specifically called, then their settings are automatically 0.

```
NumberFormat nf = NumberFormat.getPercentInstance( );
nf.setMinimumFractionDigits(2);
nf.setMaximumFractionDigits(2);
String str = nf.format(.35838);
System.out.println(str); //35.84%
```

For even more formatting flexibility use the *DecimalFormat* class. Its usage is detailed in Appendix Z. There, you will learn, for example, to specify a pattern like "#,###.000", and then format a number like 3847.2 as 3,847.200.

The Formatter Class:

The *Formatter* class (new to Java 5.0) is used to format numbers (and other data too) and to produce *String*s containing the formatted data. Begin the process by creating a *Formatter* object:

```
Formatter fmt = new Formatter( );
```

Actual formatting is done with the *format* method. It has several parameters, the first of which is a *String* with embedded **format specifiers**. This is followed by a corresponding sequence of data to be formatted. The **sequence** of embedded specifiers matches the **sequence** of data parameters as illustrated by the following example:

%f means floating point

```
fmt.format("My number>>>%f, and my string>>>%s", 237.647, "hello");
```

%s means *String*

Finally, produce the formatted *String* with *fmt.toString( )* and get:

```
My number>>>237.647000, and my string>>>hello
```

In this example we formatted a floating-point number using **%f** and a *String* using **%s**. See Appendix AD for other format specifiers.

Minimum Field Width:

The output above is especially useful when we are able to specify a field width as in the next example where we allocate a width of 15 characters to the number and a width of 8 characters to the *String*. Each field is padded with spaces to insure it occupies the specified number of characters. If the *String* or number is longer than the setting, it will still be printed in its entirety.

```
fmt.format("My number>>>%15f, and my string>>>%8s", 237.647, "hello");
```

A subsequent application of *fmt.toString( )* will yield (notice the padding with spaces):

```
My number>>>      237.647000, and my string>>>   hello
```

15 characters   8 characters

The ability to set field widths is especially useful in the printing of tables since it helps keep columns aligned.

Precision:

Next, we examine the notion of precision (typically, the number of decimal places). The precision specifier follows the minimum field width specifier (if there is one) and consists of a period followed by an integer. It can be applied to **%f**, **%e**, **%g**, or **%s**. The default precision for numerics is 6 decimal places.

The following examples show how to use the precision specifier:

1. **Example 1**... **%9.3f**... a decimal floating point number in a field 9 characters wide and having 3 decimal places... 187.9207 formats as "`  187.921`"

2. **Example 2**... **%9.2e**... a scientific notation number in a field 9 characters wide and having 2 decimal places... 46238.123 formats as "` 4.62e+04`"

3. **Example 3**... **%.4g**... either a decimal floating number or scientific notation (whichever is shorter) having no minimum field width and having 4 **significant digits**.... 187.0853211 formats as "`187.1`"

4. **Example 4**... **%6.8s**... displays a *String* of at least 6 but not exceeding 8 characters long. If the *String* is longer than the maximum, characters toward the end of the *String* will be truncated... "abc" formats as "`   abc`"; "123456789A" formats as "`12345678`"

Format Flags:

It is possible to use special format flags to control various aspects of formatting. These flags **immediately** follow the **%**. Some of the more often used flags are detailed here (see Appendix AD for a more complete list):

- \- Left justification... **%-9.2f**... 72.45822 formats as "`72.46    `"

- 0 Pad with zeros instead of the default spaces... **%09.2f**... 72.45822 formats as "`000072.46`"

- , Numeric values include grouping separators... **%-,10.2f**...1726.46 formats as "`1,726.46  `"

It is possible to pass a *Formatter* object as an argument to the *println* method where its *toString* method is **automatically** called with *System.out.println(fmt);*

An even handier shortcut is to dispense with the *Formatter* object entirely and use the *printf* method (new to Java 5.0). The parameters in the example below are **exactly** the same as for *Formatter*.

```
System.out.printf("One number, %0,10.2f, followed by another, %-9e, %s",
1267.657, 56.71, "number.");
```

The output is:

```
One number, 001,267.66, followed by another, 5.671000e+01, number.
```

Exercise on Lesson 27

1. Using the *NumberFormat* class, write code that will create a *double* called *cv*, assign it a value of 18.7713, and then convert it to a *String* rounded off to the nearest hundredth. Assure that at least 1 decimal place is printed. Print the *String*.

2. What type variable is returned by the *format( )* method of the *NumberFormat* class?

3. Using the *NumberFormat* class, write code that will create a *double* called *dv*, assign it a value of 184.767123, and then convert it to a *String* rounded off to the nearest thousandth. Assure that at least 2 decimal places are printed.

4. Using the *NumberFormat* class, write code that will input a *double* called *db* from the keyboard and then convert it to a *String* in which there are at least 3 decimal places… and at most 4.

5. Assume you already have a floating type variable *mn* that you want to display as dollars and cents (example, $127.15). Using the *NumberFormat* class, write code that will produce such a printout (including the dollar sign).

6. What import does the *NumberFormat* class require?

7. What is the output of the following code?
   ```
   NumberFormat nf = NumberFormat.getCurrencyInstance( );
   System.out.println(nf.format(487.0871));
   ```

8. What is the output of the following code?
   ```
   NumberFormat nf = NumberFormat.getPercentInstance( );
   nf.setMinimumFractionDigits(3);
   nf.setMaximumFractionDigits(3);
   String str = nf.format(4.708832);
   System.out.println(str);
   ```

9. What class lets you specify patterns like "0,000,000.##" in determining the formatting of a number?

10. In calling the *getNumberInstance( )* method of the *NumberFormat* class, why do we have to preface it with *NumberFormat.* as in *NumberFormat.getNumberInstance( )*?

11. What is printed by the following code? Indicate each space (if any) with a tilde(~).

```
Formatter fmt = new Formatter( );
fmt.format("%s--->%-,10.3f--->%08.1e", "Formatting example", 189.11081, .07642);
System.out.println(fmt);
```

12. Suppose you have a *Formatter* object called *f*. Write code that will use *f* to produce *String s* having *double d* left justified in a field 12 characters wide and rounded to 4 decimal places.

13. Suppose you have a *Formatter* object called *f*. Write code that will use *f* to produce *String s* having *int i* left justified in a field 11 characters wide. Use comma separators.

14. What is output by the following code? Indicate each space (if any) with a tilde(~).

```
System.out.printf("--->|%3.6s|<---", "x");
```

15. Suppose you need to produce a table that looks like the following:

```
57012        $1,200,586.22
00026        $       187.91
00729        $  571,267.03
```

Here is a code fragment that produces this table:

```
for(int j = 0; j < 3; j++)
        System.out.printf("???????", num[j], money[j]);
```

Supply the correct syntax for "???????" so that there are 13 spaces between the end of the first column and the start of the visible part of the second column. The *num* array is an *int* array and *money* is a *double* array.

16. What does the following print?

```
Formatter fmt = new Formatter( );
int i = 4893;
fmt.format("start%012dend",i);
String s = fmt.toString( );
System.out.println(s);
```

Project... BaseClass (Shell)

We will create a generic class (sometimes called a shell) for reading/processing files that also includes a *NumberFormat* object as well as *StringTokenizer* and *Scanner* objects. We will call this class *BaseClass* and every time we have a programming project that requires file input, we will begin by simply pasting in this code. We would then change the name of the class from *BaseClass* to whatever the new class name is to be and finally, lay in the additional code to accomplish the task at hand.

```
import java.io.*; //necessary for File and IOException
import java.util.*; //necessary for StringTokenizer and Scanner
import java.text.*; //necessary for NumberFormat
public class BaseClass
{
   public static void main( String args[] ) throws IOException
   {
      NumberFormat formatter = NumberFormat.getNumberInstance( );
      formatter.setMinimumFractionDigits(3); //may need to change value
      formatter.setMaximumFractionDigits(3); //may need to change value

      Scanner sf = new Scanner(new File("c:\\temp_Name\\FileName.in"));
      int maxIndx = -1; //-1 so when we increment below, the first index is 0
      String text[] = new String[100]; //To be safe, declare more than we need
      while(sf.hasNext( ))
      {
               maxIndx++;
               text[maxIndx] = sf.nextLine( );
               //System.out.println(text[maxIndx]); //Remove rem for testing
      }
      //maxIndx is now the highest index of text[]. Equals -1 if no text lines
      sf.close( ); //We opened a file above, so close it when finished.
      //System.exit(0);  //Use this for testing… to temporarily end the program here

      for (int j = 0; j <= maxIndx; j++)
      {
            //Typically, only one of the following two will be used.
               //StringTokenizer st = new StringTokenizer( text[j] );
               //Scanner sc = new Scanner(text[j]);

            //…code specific to the task…

            //System.out.println(text[j]);  //Remove rem for testing
      }
   }
}
```

Project… Gymnastics

Use your new *BaseClass* class to implement the following project. Call the new class *Gym*:

Ten people are judging an international gymnastics competition. Each judge gives a contestant a performance score between 0.0 and 10.0, inclusive, with the score given to one decimal place. Since some judges favor their own country's competitors and/or give lower scores than deserved to their country's rivals, the highest and lowest scores are discarded before averaging the eight other scores. Write a program that will read in the judges' ten scores, discard the highest and lowest score, and compute the average of the eight other scores to **four** decimal places.

Input

Read in one or more data sets (assume you don't know ahead of time how many) of 10 scores from the file *DataGym.in*. Each data set will use exactly one line of the input text file. There will be ten floating point numbers (each separated from the others by spaces) between 0.0 and 10.0, inclusive (to one decimal place) on each line of the file.

Input file

```
8.7  6.5  0.1  3.2  5.7  9.9  8.3  6.5  6.5  1.5
0.0  0.0  0.0  0.0  0.0  0.0  0.0  0.0  0.0  0.0
1.0  1.0  1.0  1.0  1.0  1.0  1.0  1.0  1.0  1.0
```

Output

Print, for each data set that is input, the average to **four** decimal places. This average should be preceded each time by "For Competitor #X, the average score is ", where X denotes the competitor's position (starting with 1) in the input file.

Output to screen for above input file

```
For Competitor #1, the average is 5.8625
For Competitor #2, the average is 0.0000
For Competitor #3, the average is 1.0000
```

On the next page is a flowchart that shows the flow of the logic involved in solving this problem. Notice two nested loops whose starting points are depicted with diamonds. Typically, diamonds are used for decisions (*if* statements); however, they are used here to depict the decisions of whether to stay in the loops or not.

On highly complex problems it is common practice to begin program design with a flow chart. The gymnastics program is not a very complicated program; however, most students find the flowchart a significant aid on this problem.

The teacher's answer key shows two solutions to this problem, the first of which follows the flow chart exactly. The second solution uses a completely different approach.

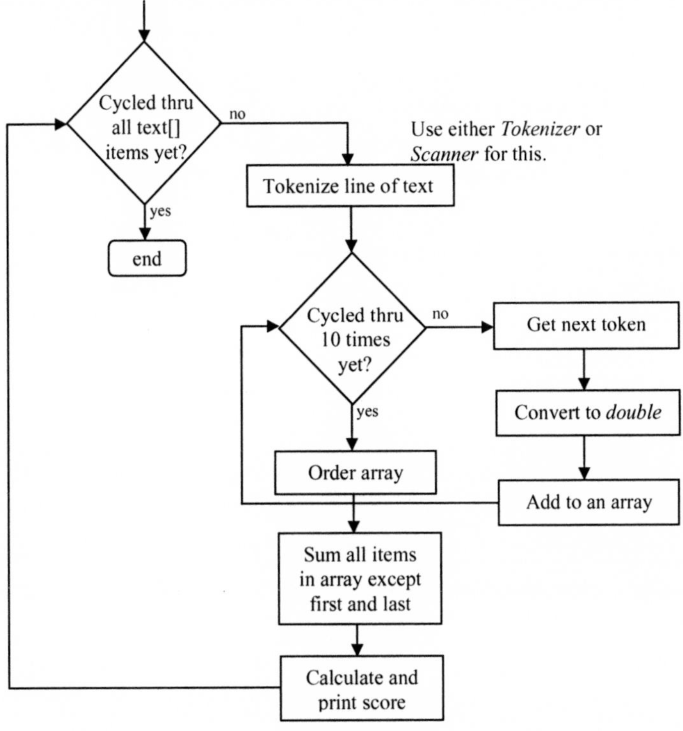

Fig. 27-1 Flow chart for gymnastics project. This assumes the lines of text from the input file have already been stored in the *text[ ]* array.

Lesson 28…..Bitwise Operators

Just as we can **AND** and **OR** *boolean* quantities we can also **AND** and **OR** numbers. This is called bitwise **AND-ing** and **OR-ing**, whereas the *boolean* symbols are && and ||, their bitwise counterparts are denoted by & and |. (It turns out that there are some other bitwise operations too.) Here are the bitwise binary operators and their rules (using only 1's and 0's):

Bitwise-AND, & (Notice we must have all 1's to yield a 1.)

```
         0          1          1
         0          0          1
  answer 0   answer 0   answer 1
```

Bitwise-OR, | (Notice if we have at least one 1, it yields a 1.)

```
         0          1          1
         0          0          1
  answer 0   answer 1   answer 1
```

Bitwise-exclusive-OR (also called XOR) ^ (Same as bitwise-OR except all 1's yields a 0)

```
         0          1          1
         0          0          1
  answer 0   answer 1   answer 0
```

Bitwise-NOT (also called inverting) ~

```
      ~0         ~1
  answer 1   answer 0
```

Bitwise-AND example, & :

```
System.out.println( (90) & (107) ); //74
```

$90_{dec} = 0101\ 1010_{bin}$
$107_{dec} = \underline{0110\ 1011}_{bin}$
$0100\ 1010_{bin} = 74_{dec}$

Bitwise-OR example, | :

```
System.out.println( (90) | (107) ); //123
```

$90_{dec} = 0101\ 1010_{bin}$
$107_{dec} = \underline{0110\ 1011}_{bin}$
$0111\ 1011_{bin} = 123_{dec}$

Bitwise-exclusive-OR examples, ^ :

System.out.println((90) ^ (107)); //**49**

$90_{dec} = 0101\ 1010_{bin}$
$107_{dec} = \underline{0110\ 1011}_{bin}$
$0011\ 0001_{bin} = 49_{dec}$

****

Now let's think of the **exclusive-OR** problem 0x4BA ^ 0x132

Let's break up each into its binary form.

0x4BA = 0100 1011 1010 (4 B A)   0x132 = 0001 0011 0010 (1 3 2)

Stack them and do an **exclusive-OR** remembering that two 1's yields a 0.

```
0x4BA= 0100 1011 1010
0x132 = 0001 0011 0010
        0101 1000 1000 = 1416dec = 0x588, the answer
         5    8    8
```

Bitwise-NOT example, ~ :

int zx = 46; // 010 1110 $_{bin}$
System.out.println(~ 46); // -47

Why does this print a negative number? The positive integer (four bytes), 46, is represented in binary as follows:

00000000 00000000 00000000 00101110
|
This most significant bit (msb) is the "sign-bit". An msb value of 0 means the number is positive while 1 would mean it's negative.

The NOT (~) operation changes all 1's to 0's and vice versa, so we get:

11111111 11111111 11111111 11010001
|
Clearly, the sign bit, 1, is now representing a negative number.

It is beyond us at the present to understand what the value of this negative number might be. This negative number is represented in "two's complement notation". This is a topic for the advanced student and is presented in Appendix G.

For now it is enough for us just to know that ~(positive integer) yields a negative integer and that ~(negative integer) yields a positive integer.

Exercise on Lesson 28

1. What is the bitwise operator for **AND**?

2. What is the *boolean* operator for **AND**?

3. What is the bitwise operator for **OR**?

4. What is the *boolean* operator for **OR**?

5. What is the bitwise operator for exclusive-**OR**?

6. What is the bitwise operator for **NOT**?

7. What is the *boolean* operator for **NOT**?

Use the following code to tell what's printed in problems 8 – 18. (The code in some problems may not compile. If that's the case then state, "Won't compile.")

```
int j = 79, k = 82, p = 112, q = 99;
```

8. System.out.println((137) | q);

9. System.out.println((137) & (121));

10. System.out.println((137) && (0x3A));

11. System.out.println((137) ^ (121));

12. System.out.println((p) | (j));

13. System.out.println(~ 465);

14. System.out.println(j ^ (0x4B));

15. System.out.println((j) & (k));

16. System.out.println(p || j);

17. System.out.println(p ^ q);

18. System.out.println(~ (-k));

19. What does msb stand for?

20. What do you get if you bitwise-exclusive-**OR** two 1's?

21. What can be said about an integer if its most significant bit is 1?

22. An integer's msb is 1. If this integer is multiplied by –27 what will be the resulting sign?

Project… Masking Telemetry Data

In a telemetry system in a spacecraft each bit position within the first eight bits of an integer sent to ground control have meaning with regard to the status of certain switches onboard the spacecraft. Assuming a 1 indicates the switch is **on** and a 0 indicates that it's **off**, these meanings are illustrated below:

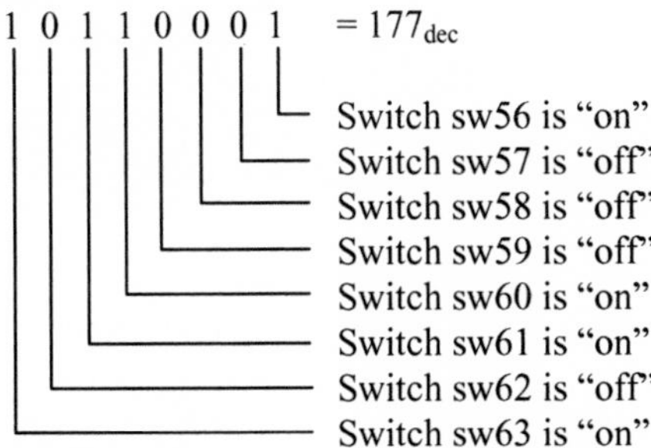
1 0 1 1 0 0 0 1 = 177dec
Switch sw56 is "on"
Switch sw57 is "off"
Switch sw58 is "off"
Switch sw59 is "off"
Switch sw60 is "on"
Switch sw61 is "on"
Switch sw62 is "off"
Switch sw63 is "on"

The numbers sent to ground control never exceeds 255 (first eight bits all set to 1). Suppose we wish to look at the third bit from the left. Use a mask as illustrated below to bitwise **AND** with the original number in order to look **only** at the third bit.

$1\,0\,1\,1\,0\,0\,0\,1_{bin} = 177_{dec}$
$\underline{0\,0\,1\,0\,0\,0\,0\,0}_{bin} = 32_{dec}$ (this is the mask)
$0\,0\,1\,0\,0\,0\,0\,0_{bin} = 32_{dec} = (177 \,\&\, 32)$

Notice this scheme of bitwise **AND-ing** a mask value of 32 (2^5, since the third bit position from the left has a positional value of 2^5) yields a value in the third bit position exactly equal to the third bit position of the original number. All other bit positions are guaranteed to be 0's. Thus, this result of bitwise **AND-ing** can be tested to see if its entire value is 0. If it's greater than 0, this means that the bit in the tested position was a 1.

Write a program that will input the following data file, *Switches.in*, containing decimal numbers that represents successive switch information telemetry. Print the status of all eight switches.

Switches.in

```
 22
194
203
 97
```

Your output should be as shown on the next page:

```
Switch status for data value 22:
  Switch sw56 is "off"
  Switch sw57 is "on"
  Switch sw58 is "on"
  Switch sw59 is "off"
  Switch sw60 is "on"
  Switch sw61 is "off"
  Switch sw62 is "off"
  Switch sw63 is "off"

Switch status for data value 194:
  Switch sw56 is "off"
  Switch sw57 is "on"
  Switch sw58 is "off"
  Switch sw59 is "off"
  Switch sw60 is "off"
  Switch sw61 is "off"
  Switch sw62 is "on"
  Switch sw63 is "on"

Switch status for data value 203:
  Switch sw56 is "on"
  Switch sw57 is "on"
  Switch sw58 is "off"
  Switch sw59 is "on"
  Switch sw60 is "off"
  Switch sw61 is "off"
  Switch sw62 is "on"
  Switch sw63 is "on"

Switch status for data value 97:
  Switch sw56 is "on"
  Switch sw57 is "off"
  Switch sw58 is "off"
  Switch sw59 is "off"
  Switch sw60 is "off"
  Switch sw61 is "on"
  Switch sw62 is "on"
  Switch sw63 is "off"
```

Lesson 29…..Advanced Bitwise Operations

Decimal shifting:

We will briefly discuss shifting by considering the decimal number 283.0. If we hold the decimal place fixed and shift all numbers to the right we get:

28.3

Thus, we see shifting a decimal number to the right is equivalent to **dividing by 10** (the base of the decimal system). If we take the same number and shift to the left we get:

2830.0

Thus, we see shifting a decimal number to the left is equivalent to **multiplying by 10**.

Binary shifting:

We can apply this same principle to the binary system with the following two rules:

1. Shifting a binary number to the right is equivalent to **dividing by 2**.
2. Shifting a binary number to the left is equivalent to **multiplying by 2**.

Bitwise shift left (sign is preserved), << :

System.out.println(7 << 3); // **56**

7 is the number we will be shifting to the left. We are to shift 3 times. Since each shift to the left is equivalent to a multiplication by 2, then 3 shifts is 2 * 2 * 2 = 2^3 = 8. So, the problem 7 << 3 is really 7 * 8 = 56.

System.out.println(-7 << 3); // **-7 * 8 = -56** Notice the sign is preserved

Bitwise shift right (sign is preserved), >> :

System.out.println(32 >> 3); // **4**

32 is the number we will be shifting to the right. We are to shift 3 times. Since each shift to the right is equivalent to a division by 2, then 3 shifts is really dividing by 2 * 2 * 2 = 2^3 = 8. So, the problem 32 >> 3 is really 32 / 8 = 4.

System.out.println(-32 >> 3); // **-4** Notice the sign is preserved
System.out.println(35 >> 3); // **4** Notice fractional part disappears since we are dealing
// with integers.

Bitwise shift right (sign is not preserved), >>> :

System.out.println(-16 >>> 3); // **536870910**

Think of this number (-16) as a long series of 1's and 0's. We know that the msb (most significant bit) will be a 1 since it's negative. When shifted right the msb is vacated and a 0 always takes its place. That's why it turns into a positive number.

Don't worry about the actual number we get as an answer for this last example. **It's enough just to know it's positive.**

```
System.out.println( 16 >>> 3 );  // 2
```

What does it mean?

Now we are going to show something **really weird**. If bitwise **AND-ing** and **OR-ing** is done on numbers, and *boolean* **AND-ing** and **OR-ing** is done on *boolean* quantities (*true* or *false*), then we would guess that the following would be illegal:

```
System.out.println( (y = = z) & (z > p) );  //try to bitwise-AND two booleans
```

That guess would be wrong! It **is** legal, so what could it mean to bitwise-**AND** two *boolean* quantities? After all, *booleans* are not numbers that have "bits", so how can we do bitwise operations on them? To answer that we must go back to *boolean* operations and discuss a subject called "short circuiting".

Short-Circuiting

Consider the following program fragment:

```
int j = 34;
int p = 0;
if( (p > 2) && (++j = =19) )
{
        …some code…
}
System.out.println(j);
```

What do you think would be printed? 35? Actually, 34 is printed. Here's what happens. The *boolean* quantity (*p> 2*) is evaluated to be *false*. Java is wise enough to know that since the first parenthesis is *false*, there is no point in continuing with the **AND** (&&) evaluation. Regardless of what the second parenthesis, (*++j = =19*), evaluates to be, the entire **AND** must come out *false*.

Therefore, for the sake of time efficiency, **"short-circuiting"** takes place and the second parenthesis is never executed. Hence, the *++j* never gets a chance to increment *j*. This is why *j* stays at its original value of *34*.

"Bitwise" operation on *booleans*

If we rewrite the above code as follows it performs a traditional ***boolean* AND,** but with **no** short-circuiting:

```
int j = 34;
int p = 0;
if( (p > 2) & (++j = =19) )  //notice a single & now
{
        …some code…
}
System.out.println(j);  //35
```

Even though we use the & symbol it is **really doing *boolean* AND-ing (with no short-circuiting)**.

Bitwise AND-ing, or OR-ing more than two numbers:

What would be the value of *j* in the following?

int j = 23 & 19 & 106; //2

Let's "stack" these three numbers as follows:

23_{dec} = 001 0111 $_{bin}$
19_{dec} = 001 0011 $_{bin}$
106_{dec} = <u>110 1010</u> $_{bin}$
000 0010 $_{bin}$ = 2_{dec}

(Notice the rules for **AND-ing** are essentially the same as before.... We must have **all** 1's to get a 1.)

****

What would be the value of j in the following?

int j = 27 | 19 | 106; //123

Again, let's "stack" the three numbers as follows:

27_{dec} = 001 1011 $_{bin}$
19_{dec} = 001 0011 $_{bin}$
106_{dec} = <u>110 1010</u> $_{bin}$
111 1011 $_{bin}$ = 123_{dec}

(Notice the rules for **OR-ing** are essentially the same as before...the presence of **any** 1 will yield a 1.)

Precedence of operators:

Just as PEMDAS (see <u>Lesson 4</u> and <u>Appendix H</u>) gives the precedence (order) for math operators, there is also a precedence for bitwise operators. That order is:

Example 1

System.out.println(117 & 46 | 98); //**102**
Do the 117 & 46 first and get 36.
Then do 36 | 98 and get 102.

Example 2

System.out.println(117 | 46 & 98); //**119**
Do the 46 & 98 first and get 34.
Then do 117 | 34 and get 119.

Recall that <u>Lesson 8</u> gives a precedence order for *boolean* operators (!, = =, !=, ^, &&, ||)

Exercise on Lesson 29

This code applies to problems 1 - 7:

```
int m = 45;
int k = 102;
int p = 4;
```

In each problem state what's printed.

1. `System.out.println(m << 2);`

2. `System.out.println( (m/2) >> 2 );`

3. `System.out.println(k << p);`

4. `System.out.println(-m >>> 2);`

5. `System.out.println (k << 1);`

6. `System.out.println( 222 >>> 2);`

7. `System.out.println( p >> p );`

8. What gets printed?

```
int jz= 3;
int ii = 5;
if( (ii > 2) & (jz = =ii--) ) //notice a single &
{
        …some code…
}
System.out.println(ii);
```

9. What gets printed?

```
int mk= 3;
int sd = -4;
if( (sd > 2) & (   sd = = ++mk )   ) //notice a single &
{
        …some code…
}
System.out.println(mk);
```

10. What gets printed?

```
int mk= 3;
int sd = -4;
if( (Math.abs(sd ) > 2) | (   sd = = ++mk )   ) //notice a single |
{     …some code…     }
System.out.print(mk++); //notice print, not println
System.out.println(mk++);
```

In the following problems, what gets printed?

11. System.out.println(122 & 18 & 79);

12. System.out.println(122 | 18 | 79);

13. System.out.println(122 | 18 & 79);

14. System.out.println(122 & 18 | 79);

Bitwise Operators… Contest Type Problems

1. Suppose we wish to subtract the bitwise-**OR** of *m* and *n* from the bitwise-**AND** of *m* and *n*. To which of the following should we set *z*?

   A. (m && n) – (m ^ n)
   B. (m & n) – (m | n)
   C. m – n
   D. (m && n) – (m || n)
   E. None of these

```
public static int Herman(int m, int n)
{
        int z = ???;
        return z;
}
```

2. What is output by the code to the right?

   A. 9 true
   B. 10 true
   C. 9 false
   D. 10 false
   E. None of these

```
int p = 9;
int q = -1;
boolean sim = (q-- > 5) & (p++ > 22)
System.out.println(p + "   " + sim);
```

3. What is the value of *w*?

```
int xz[] ={6, 0, 3, 3, 5, -1, 12, 7, 3, 3};
int w = theMethod(xz);
```

   A. Exception is thrown
   B. 5
   C. 6
   D. 0
   E. None of these

4. What is the value of *w*?

```
int xz[] ={2, 0, 3, 3, 5, 4, 2, 7, 3, 3};
int w = theMethod(xz);
```

   A. Exception is thrown
   B. 5
   C. 6
   D. 0
   E. None of these

```
public static int theMethod (int k[] )
{
    int p=0;
    for(int j =0; j < k.length; j++)
      if (k[j] >= 0  &  k[j]<=k.length  &  k[k[j]]
                                                = =3)
          p++;
    return p;
}
```

5. What is the value of *w*?

```
int xz[] ={6, 0, 3, 3, 5, -1, 12, 7, 3, 3};
int w = theMethod(xz);
```

   A. Exception is thrown
   B. 3
   C. 4
   D. 5
   E. None of these

```
public static int theMethod (int k[] )
{
    int p=0;
    for(int j =0; j < k.length; j++)
      if (k[j] >= 0  &&  k[j]< k.length  &&  k[k[j]]
                                                = =3)
          p++;
    return p;
}
```

Project… Tweaking for Speed

Since most computers are very fast, we are not normally concerned with how fast our code runs. However, consider the following code that may be inside a loop that iterates many times.

```
int p = 386; q = 581, n = 0;
n = ((p * 2) + q)/2;
```

Just a slight reduction in execution time of this code may result in the loop being completed in a significantly shorter time. There are two things we can do to this code to make it run faster.

- Algebraically simplify the right side to *p + q/2*. Notice that where we originally had **both** a multiplication **and** a division, we now have only a **single** division in this simplified version. This, of course, will execute faster.
- Replace */2* with *>>1*. (It turns out that a shift to the right is faster than a division by 2; however, it produces the same results.)

Use the following code to time the two different loops for the sake of comparison. You supply the missing code using the two "speed enhancements" mentioned above.

```
public class Tester
{
    public static void main(String gg[])
    {
        int p = 386, q = 581, n = 0;

        System.out.println("Hello"); //Start timing first loop when "Hello" is printed
        for(int j=0; j<2000000000; j++)
        {
            n = ((p * 2) + q) / 2;
        }
        System.out.println(n); //When this line prints, stop timing the first loop and
                               //begin timing the second loop.

        for(int j=0; j<2000000000; j++)
        {
            n = ..appropriate code for speed.. ;
        }
        System.out.println(n);
    }
}
```

The second loop should run about 30% - 40% faster than the first loop.

There is a way to have the computer automatically time these two loops. See page 48-2 for more on this technique.

Lesson 30…..Random Numbers

Why random?

Why would we want random numbers? What possible use could there be for the generation of **unpredictable** numbers? It turns out there are plenty of applications, and the following list suggests just a few:

1. Predictions for life expectancy …used in insurance
2. Business simulations
3. Games …gives users a different experience each time
4. Simulations for scientific research, etc.

Important methods:

The *Random* class (requires the import of *java.util.Random*) generates random numbers and has three methods, besides the constructor, that are of interest to us. These are not *static* methods, so we must first create an object:

Constructor

public Random( ) // **Signature**

Example:
Random rndm = new Random( );

nextInt( )

public int nextInt( ) // **Signature**

This yields a randomly selected integer in the range Integer.MIN_VALUE to Integer.MAX_VALUE. (-2,147,843,648 to 2,147,843,647 as specified in Appendix C).

Example:
int x = rndm.nextInt( ); //x could be any integer from -2,147,843,648 to
//2,147,843,647

nextInt(n)

public int nextInt(int n) // **Signature**

This yields a randomly selected integer (0, 1, 2, …, n-1).

Example:
int x = rndm.nextInt(21); //x could be any integer from 0 to 20, inclusive for both

nextDouble( )

public double nextDouble( ) // **Signature**

This yields a randomly selected *double* from 0 (inclusive) to 1 (exclusive) and behaves exactly as does Math.random( ) (discussed in Lesson 6).

Example:
double d = rndm.nextDouble( ); //generates doubles in the range $0 \leq d < 1$

Because of the two versions of *nextInt*, we notice that our *Random* class has two methods of the same name (but different parameters). We say the methods named *nextInt* are

overloaded. In some contexts overloading is bad (example, overloading a truck). However, in the software sense of overloading, it is perfectly normal and acceptable.

Typical Problems:

1. Suppose we want a range of integers from 90 to 110, inclusive for both.

   First we subtract (110 – 90 = 20). Then add 1 to get 21. Now set up your code as follows to generate the desired range of integers:

   ```
   int r = 90 + rndm.nextInt(21);
   ```

   Put this last line of code in a *for*-loop, and you will see a range of integers from 90 to 110. Loop through 1000 times, and likely you will see every value…most will be repeated several times.

   ```
   int r = 0, count = 0;
   Random rndm = new Random( );
   for(int j = 0; j < 1000; j++) {
           r = 90 + rndm.nextInt(21);
           System.out.print(r + "  ");

           //For convenience in viewing on a console screen, the following loop
           //produces a new line after 15 numbers are printed side-by-side.
           count++;
           if(count >15) {
                   System.out.println(" ");
                   count = 0;
           }
   }
   ```

2. Suppose we wish to generate a continuous range of floating point numbers from 34.7838 (inclusive) to 187.056 (exclusive). How would we do this?

   First, subtract (187.056 – 34.7838 = 152.2722). Now set up your code as follows to generate the desired range.

   ```
   Random rndm = new Random( );
   double r;
   r = 34.7838 + 152.2722 * rndm.nextDouble( );
   // Generates continuous floating point numbers in the range
   // 34.7838  ≤  r  <  187.056
   ```

Project… Generate Random Integers

As described in problem 1 above, generate 33 random integers in the inclusive range from 71 to 99.

Project… Generate Random Doubles

As described in problem 2 above, generate 27 random *doubles* in the inclusive range from 99.78 to 147.22.

Exercise on Lesson 30

In the following problems assume that *rndm* is an object created with the *Random* class. Assume *d* is of type *double* and that *j* is of type *int*.

1. What range of random numbers will this generate?
   j = 201 + rndm.nextInt(46);

2. What range of random numbers will this generate?
   d = 11 + 82.9 * rndm.nextDouble( );

3. What range of random numbers does *nextDouble( )* generate?

4. List all numbers that rnd*m.nextInt(10)* might generate.

5. Write code that will create an object called *rd* from the *Random* class.

6. Write code that will create a *Random* object and then use it to generate and print 20 floating point numbers in the continuous range 22.5 $\leq$ r $<$ 32.5

7. What import is necessary for the *Random* class?

8. Write code that will randomly generate numbers from the following set. Printout 10 such numbers.
   18, 19, 20, 21, 22, 23, 24, 25

9. Write code that will randomly generate and print 12 numbers from the following set.
   100, 125, 150, 175

10. Write a line of code to create a *Random* class object even though *Random* wasn't imported.

Random Numbers… Contest Type Problems

1. Which of the following is a possible output?

   A. 0
   B. 36
   C. 37
   D. Throws an exception
   E. None of these

```
Random rd = new Random( );
System.out.println( rd.nextInt(36) );
```

2. To simulate the result of rolling a normal 6-sided die, what should replace **<*1>**

   A. rdm.nextDouble(6);
   B. rdm.nextInt(7);
   C. 1+ rdm.nextDouble(7);
   D. 1 + rdm.nextInt(6);
   E. 1 + rdm.nextDouble(6)

```
public static int dieOutcome( )
{
        Random rdm = new Random( );
        int die = <*1>
        return die;
}
```

3. Which of the following is a possible output of the code to the right?

   A. 0
   B. .9999
   C. 5.0
   D. 6.0
   E. None of these

```
java.util.Random rd = new java.util.Random( );
System.out.println( 1+ 5 * rd.nextDouble( ) );
```

4. What would be the range of possible values of *db* for the following line of code?

   double db = genRndDbl(4, 1);

   A. $1 \le db < 5$
   B. $0 \le db < 5$
   C. $1 \le db < 4$
   D. $1 \le db \le 5$
   E. $0 \le db \le 5$

```
public static double genRndDbl(int m, int a)
{
    Random r = new Random( );
    double d = a + m * r.nextDouble( );
    return d;
}
```

5. What would be the replacement code for **<*1>** to generate random numbers from the following set?

   {20, 35, 50, 65}

   A. 20 * 15 + ri.nextInt(4);
   B. 20 + 15 * ri.nextInt(5);
   C. 15 * 20 + ri.nextInt(4);
   D. 15 + 20 * ri.nextInt(5);
   E. None of these

```
Random ri = new Random( );
int ri = <*1>
```

6. When a class has more than one method of the same name, this is called which of the following?

   A. overloading B. inheritance C. overriding D. polymorphism

   E. None of these

7. Which of the following "tosses" a *Coin* object named *theCoin*, and produces a *true* when the *toss()* method yields a *HEADS*?

A. theCoin.toss = = HEADS
B. toss = = 0
C. theCoin.toss( ) = = Coin.HEADS
D. theCoin.HEADS = = HEADS
E. Both C and D

8. Assuming that the *Random* class is "perfect" and generates all of the integers with equal probability, what is the probability that *toss()* returns a head?

A. slightly over .5
B. slightly under .5
C. 1
D. exactly .5
E. None of these

```
public class Coin
{
    public Coin( )
    {
        r = new Random( );
    }

    public int toss( )
    {
        int i = r.nextInt( );
        if(i < 0)
        {
            return TAILS;
        }
        else
        {
            return HEADS;
        }
    }

    public static final int HEADS =  0;
    public static final int TAILS = 1;

    private Random r;
}
```

Project… Monte Carlo Technique

Imagine a giant square painted outdoors, on the ground, with a painted circle inscribed in it. Next, image that it's raining and that we have the ability to monitor every raindrop that hits inside the square. Some of those raindrops will also fall inside the circle, and a few will fall in the corners and be inside the square, but not inside the circle. Keep a tally of the raindrops that hit inside the square (*sqrCount*) and those that also hit inside the circle (*cirCount*).

The ratio of these two counts should equal the ratio of the areas as follows: (Understanding this statement is essential. It is the very premise of this problem.)

sqrCount / cirCount = (Area of square) / (Area of circle)

sqrCount / cirCount = $side^2 / (\pi * r^2)$

Solving for π from this equation we get

$$\pi = cirCount * (side^2) / (sqrCount * r^2)$$

So why did we solve for π? We already know that it's $\cong$ 3.14159. We simply want to illustrate that by a simulation (raindrop positions) we can solve for various things, in this case something we already know. The fact that we already know π just makes it that much easier to check our answer and verify the technique.

We are going to build a class called *MonteCarlo* in which the constructor will establish the size and position of our square and circle. Public state variables inside this class will be *h*, *k*, and *r*. These are enough to specify the position and size of our circle and square as shown in the figure to the right.

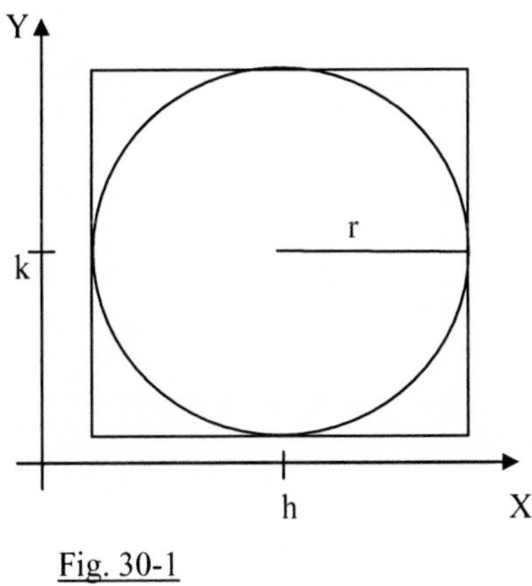

Fig. 30-1

The requirements of your *MonteCarlo* class are:

1. The constructor should receive *h*, *k*, and *r* as described above and use them to set the instance fields (state variables).

2. State variables *h*, *k*, and *r* are public *doubles*. Create a *private* instance field as an object of the *Random* class. Call it *rndm*.

3. The *nextRainDrop_x()* method should return a *double* that corresponds to a random raindrop's *x* position. The range of *x* values should be confined to the square shown above. No parameters are passed to this method.

4. The *nextRainDrop_y()* method should return a *double* that corresponds to a random raindrop's *y* position. The range of *y* values should be confined to the square shown above. No parameters are passed to this method.

5. The method *insideCircle(double x, double y)* returns a *boolean*. A *true* is returned if the parameters *x* and *y* that are passed are either <u>inside</u> or <u>on</u> the circle.

   In writing this method, you must remember that the equation of a circle is
   $(x - h)^2 + (y - k)^2 = r^2$ ...where *(h,k)* is the center and *r* is the radius.

   Also, the test for a point *(x, y)* being either <u>inside</u> or <u>on</u> a circle is
   $(x - h)^2 + (y - k)^2 <= r^2$

You will need to build a *Tester* class with the following features:

1. Class name, *Tester*

2. There is only one method, the *main()* method.

3. Create a *MonteCarlo* object called *mcObj* in which the center of the circle is at (5, 3) and the radius is 2.

4. Set up a *for*-loop for 100 iterations:

5. Inside the loop obtain the random coordinates of a rain drop using the *nextRainDrop_x()* and *nextRainDrop_y()* methods.

6. Using the *x* and *y* just obtained, pass them as arguments to the *insideCircle()* method to decide if our "raindrop" is inside the circle. If *insideCircle()* returns a *true* then increment *cirCount*.

7. Increment *sqrCount* on each pass through the loop.

8. After the loop, calculate and print your estimate for π according to the solution for π on the previous page.

9. Change the number of iterations of the loop to 1000 and run the program again. Repeat for 10,000, 100,000, and 1,000,000 iterations. The estimate for π should improve as the number of iterations increases.

Lesson 31….. *StringBuffer* Class

The problem:

Manipulating *Strings* can be very inefficient for the computer with regard to both memory usage and time of processing. This is especially true if there is a need to concatenate many small *Strings*. Each of these small *Strings* is an object that is only used once and unfortunately persists in memory…not to even mention the time it takes to create them.

The solution:

This can lead to significant degradation of performance if multiple concatenations are done inside loops that iterate a large number of times. In such cases, there is a more efficient way to handle this problem. Create a *StringBuffer* and do the desired concatenations using the *append( )* method of the *StringBuffer* object. When finished, simply convert the contents of the *StringBuffer* object to a *String* via the *toString( )* method.

Traditional solution with *Strings*:

Consider the following **traditional way** of printing a pattern of X's:

```
String myXs = "";
for(int j = 1; j <= 8; j++)  //generates 8 rows
{
        for(int k = 1; k <= j; k++)
        {
                myXs = myXs + "X";
        }
        myXs = myXs + '\n';
}
System.out.println(myXs);
```

Resulting output

```
X
XX
XXX
XXXX
XXXXX
XXXXXX
XXXXXXX
XXXXXXXX
```

And now with *StringBuffer*:

Here is the same program **using the *StringBuffer* class**:

```
StringBuffer sb = new StringBuffer( );
for(int j = 1; j <= 8; j++)  //generates 8 rows
{
        for(int k = 1; k <= j; k++)
        {
                sb.append("X");
        }
        sb.append('\n');
}
String s = sb.toString( );
System.out.println(s);
```

Resulting output

```
X
XX
XXX
XXXX
XXXXX
XXXXXX
XXXXXXX
XXXXXXXX
```

Using the Appendix:

Rather than go into a detailed explanation of the additional methods of the *StringBuffer* class, the reader is referred to page J-3 in the Appendix. For the exercises that follow in this lesson, the reader is expected to sharpen his or her skills at reading and interpreting a reference such as Appendix J.

Important facts:

Besides what you will learn from Appendix J, you should additionally know the following important two facts:

1. The *println* or *print* methods will print the contents of a *StringBuffer* **directly** without having to convert to a *String* first (the *toString* method is automatically called).

```
StringBuffer sb = new StringBuffer( );
sb.append("xyz");
System.out.println(sb);  //xyz
```

2. One of the *StringBuffer* constructors allows an **initial *String*** to be put into the *StringBuffer*.

```
StringBuffer sb = new StringBuffer("Help, I'm trapped in a StringBuffer!");
```

Project… Concatenations Gone Wild

Supply code for the *cat* method in the class below. Use ordinary *String* concatenation to implement this method, then rewrite *cat* using a *StringBuffer* object.

```
public class Tester
{
   public static void main(String args[]) {
            String t1 = cat(68, 108);
            System.out.println(t1);

            String t2 = cat(35, 59);
            System.out.println(t2);
   }

   //Enter this method with a starting ASCII code(start) and an ending ASCII code(end).
   //Return a String that is the concatenation of all the characters represented
   //by the continuous range of ASCII codes, start through end.
   private static String cat(int start, int end)
   {        ...        }
}
```

The output should appear as follows:

```
DEFGHIJKLMNOPQRSTUVWXYZ[\]^_`abcdefghijkl
#$%&'()*+,-./0123456789:;
```

Exercise on Lesson 31

1. Write code to create a *StringBuffer* and store "Hello" in it. Then convert it to a *String* and print.

Use this code in the following problems: (Assume that any changes you make to *sb* in a problem do not affect any future problems.)

```
StringBuffer sb = new StringBuffer( );
sb.append("Humpty Dumpty sat on a wall.");
```

2. What is the value of *str*?

```
String str = sb.substring(3, 8);
```

3. What is the value of *str*?

```
String str = sb.substring(3);
```

4. Write code to printout the contents of the buffer after the following code executes. What will be printed?

```
sb.append('K');
```

5. What is the output?

```
StringBuffer sss = new StringBuffer( );
 sss.append("Hello");
sb.append(sss);
String s = sb.toString( );
System.out.println(s);
```

6. What is the value of *len*?

```
int len = sb.length( );
```

7. What is the output?

```
System.out.println( sb.charAt(4) );
```

8. What is output?

```
sb.setCharAt(7,'C');
String s = sb.toString( );
System.out.println(s);
```

9. What is output?

```
sb.delete(7,9);
String s = sb.toString( );
System.out.println(s);
```

10. What is output?

```
sb.deleteCharAt(9);
String s = sb.toString( );
System.out.println(s);
```

11. What is output?

```
sb.insert(0, 'B');
String s = sb.toString( );
System.out.println(s);
```

12. What is output?

```
sb.insert(1, "xxx");
String s = sb.toString( );
System.out.println(s);
```

StringBuffer … Contest Type Problems

1.What is the output?
 	
A. Du
B. t (leading space)
C. on
D. nothing
E. None of these
	public class StrBuf
	{
	  public static void main(String args[])
	  {
	    StringBuffer sb = new StringBuffer( );
	    int t[] = {1,2,8,9,2};
	    String s = "Do unto others as you would have...";
	    char [] sc = s.toCharArray( );
	    for(int j=0; j<t.length; j++) {
	      if(t[j] == 2)
	        sb.append(sc[j]);
	    }
	    System.out.print(sb.toString( ));
	  }
	}

2.What is the output?
 	
A. 10
B. 9
C. 8
D. Throws exception
E. None of these
	public class StrBuf
	{
	  public static void main(String args[])
	  {
	    StringBuffer sb = new StringBuffer("groovy");
	    String st = "dude";
	    sb.append(st);
	    System.out.print(sb.length( ));
	  }
	}

3.What is the output?
StringBuffer asb = new StringBuffer("abcdef_mnopqrst");
StringBuffer nsb = StrBuf.sbStuff(asb);
System.out.println(nsb);
 	
A. nothing
B. abcdef_mxxxxxxx
C. abcdef_mnxxxxxx
D. abcdef_mnoxxxxx
E. None of these
	public class StrBuf
	{
	  public static StringBuffer sbStuff(StringBuffer sb)
	  {
	    for(int j=0; j<sb.length( ); j++)
	      if(sb.charAt(j) >= 'q' -1)
	        sb.setCharAt(j, 'x');
	    return sb;
	  }
	}

4.What is returned by the method call *lefty("Rubber ducky")?*
 	
A. ducky
B. bber ducky
C. Rubbeb d ckc
D. Throws exception
E. None of these
	public static String lefty(String s)
	{
	    StringBuffer sb = new StringBuffer(s);
	    for(int j=0; j<sb.length( ); j++)
	      if(sb.charAt(j) >= 'q' -1)
	        sb.setCharAt(j, sb.charAt(j-2));
	    return sb.toString( );
	}

5.What is the output? A. PeCokepsi Cola B. PepCokesi Cola C. Pepsi ColaCokeCoke D. Throws exception E. None of these	StringBuffer sb = new StringBuffer("Pepsi Cola"); sb.insert(2, "Coke"); System.out.println(sb);

Lesson 32…..Boolean Algebra and DeMorgans's Theorem

Yes, it's Algebra. The nightmare continues:

When manipulating complex arrangements of *boolean* variables, they are found to follow many of the rules of ordinary algebra. This is easily seen if we think of **AND-ing as multiplication** and **OR-ing as addition**. Consider, for example, the following *boolean* expression where *a*, *b*, and *c* are *boolean* variables:

a &&(b || c)

Let us agree to rewrite this with "&&" replaced with "*" and "||" replaced with "+". So, our expression becomes,

a * (b + c) = a*b + a*c,

where we have taken the liberty of "multiplying" *a* into the parenthesis just as we would in regular algebra. Converting this back in terms of the familiar && and || symbols we have,

a && b || a && c which can be rewritten as (a && b) || (a && c) for clarity. The reason we can use the parenthesis like this is because && has higher precedence than does ||.

In summary we can state the following rule: **In *boolean* expressions in which each AND is expressed as a * (multiplication) and each OR is expressed as a + (addition), most simplification is done exactly as would be done with ordinary algebra.**

*From this point on in this lesson, we will use * for **AND** and + for **OR** when writing and simplifying* Boolean *expressions. Also, we will take the liberty of writing things like ab. Just as in ordinary algebra where this means "a times b," here it will mean "a*b" which of course ultimately means a **AND** b.*

DeMorgan's Theorem:

Before we offer more examples of Boolean simplification, we need the services of the most important theorem in Boolean algebra, **DeMorgan's Theorem**. Following are its two forms:

!(a + b) = (!a) * (!b) and !(a * b) = (!a) + (!b)

Thus, we see a way to turn **OR**s into **AND**s and vice versa. This is a **very powerful** tool. We can even use it where there isn't a "not" (!) in the original expression:

(a + b) = !!(a + b) = !(!(a + b)) = !(!a * !b))

Obvious Theorems:

Some other more obvious but still very useful theorems are(*a* and *b* are *booleans*):

a + false = a	a * true = a	a * false = false
a + true = true	! !a = a	a + !a = true
a + a = a	a * !a = false	
a * a = a		

The three examples in the top row just above are easy to obtain if we substitute 0 for *false* and 1 for *true*. The rules of ordinary algebra are then followed to produce the answers.

This illustrates one of the reasons why we express && as a multiplication sign and || as a plus sign…because it lets us work in terms of something with which we are already familiar (hopefully), regular algebra.

A Subtle Theorem:

This is subtle and not very obvious; however, it can be easily confirmed with a truth table.

a + b = a + (!a)(b) …same as a || b = a || (!a) && (b)

Law of Absorption:

In these theorems, the value of *boolean b* **does not matter** (it could just take a hike).

a = a * (a + b) …same as a = a && (a || b)
a = a + (a * b) …same as a = a || (a && b)

Now we are ready to present some examples of *boolean* simplification:

1. **Example:**
   a(!b) + ab
   = a(!b + b) = a(true) = **a**

2. **Example:**
   ab + !ab + !ba + !b(!a)
   = b(a + !a) + !b(a + !a)
   = b(true) + !b(true) = b + !b = **true** (Amazing! Always true, doesn't depend on a and b)

3. **Example:**
   !(!a + b + c)
   = (! !a)(!b)(!c) = **a(!b)(!c)** (notice ! ! a = a)

4. **Example:**
   Express a || b || c using **AND**s instead of **OR**s.
   a || b || c
   = (a || b || c)
   = ! !(a || b || c)
   = ! (!(a || b || c))
   = **! (!a && !b && !c)**

5. **Example:**
   Illustrate the equivalence of !(a + b) and !a * ! b using truth tables.

a	**b**	**a + b**	**!(a + b)**
false	false	false	true
false	true	true	false
true	false	true	false
true	true	true	false

a	b	!a	!b	!a * !b
false	false	true	true	true
false	true	true	false	false
true	false	false	true	false
true	true	false	false	false

Notice the two gray sections are identical. Also, notice that the two black sections are the same.

6. **Example:**
Derive the Boolean expression that produces the following truth table. This table uses 1's and 0's. Just thinks of a 1 as a *true* and a 0 as a *false*:

A	B	C	D
(input)			(output)
0	0	0	0
0	0	1	0
0	1	0	1
0	1	1	0
1	0	0	1
1	0	1	0
1	1	0	1
1	1	1	0

Choose only the rows that produce a 1 in the output.

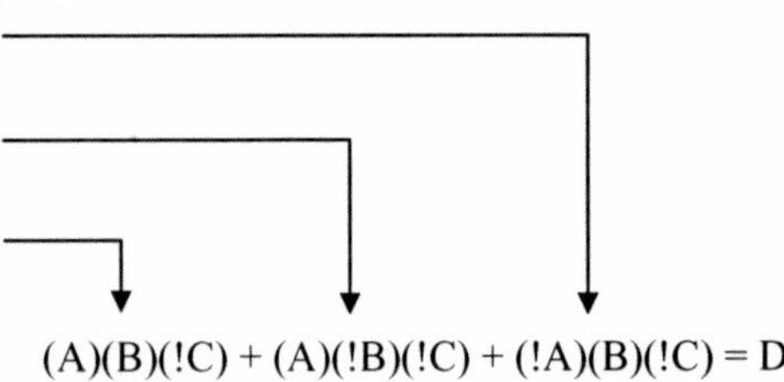

Notice that we always **AND** the inputs together that produce an output of 1. Then **OR** all of these groups. When **AND**-ing, any input that is a 0 should be inverted. Thus, for example, the A, B, and C values of 1, 1, 0 produce (A)(B)(!C).

Now let's simplify the above expression by factoring out (!C)(A) from the left two terms as follows:

!CA(B + !B) + !AB !C

The parenthesis evaluates to 1, so we have:

!CA + !AB !C

Now factor out !C and get:

!C (A + !AB)

Apply the "subtle theorem" on page 2 of this lesson and get:

!C (A + B) = D

Exercise on lesson 32

Assume in the following *boolean* expressions that *a*, *b*, *c*, and *d* are *boolean* quantities.

1. Show the algebraic simplification of ab(!c) + !ab(!c) to b(!c).

2. Show the algebraic simplification of a(!b)c + abc + !abc + !ab(!c) + a(!b) to !ba + !ab + ac

3. Show the algebraic simplification of !(!a * !c) + !b + !(ad) to *true*.

4. Show the algebraic modification of !((a + bc) (a + c)) to !a(!b + !c) + !a(!c).

5. Express ab(!c) + !ab(!c) using proper Java syntax (&&, ||, and !).

6. Express a(!b)c + abc + !abc + !ab(!c) + a(!b) using proper Java syntax (&&, ||, and !).

7. Express !(!a * !c) + !b + !(ad) using proper Java syntax (&&, ||, and !).

8. Simplify x + (x * y) where *x* and *y* are *boolean* variables.

9. Express !((a + bc) (a + c)) using proper Java syntax (&&, ||, and !).

10. Express !(a && b && c) using **OR**s instead of **AND**s.

11. Express (a && b && c) using **OR**s instead of **AND**s.

12. Illustrate the equivalence of !(a * b) and !a + !b using truth tables.

13. Which of the following is the equivalent of ((p > 3) || (q < b)) ?
    a. !(!(p>3) && !(q<=b))
    b. !((p <= 3) && (q >= b))
    c. !((p > 3) || (q < b))
    d. !(!(p <= 3) || (q >= b))
    e. More than one of these

14. Write a Boolean expression that produces the following truth table:

A	B	C	D
(input)			(output)
0	0	0	1
0	0	1	0
0	1	0	1
0	1	1	0
1	0	0	1
1	0	1	0
1	1	0	0
1	1	1	0

Boolean Algebra and DeMorgan's Theorem… Contest Type Problems

1. If we call *bolTest(x, y)* in the code to the right, which of the following is equivalent to what it returns? (assume that *x* and *y* are *boolean* types)

   A. !(x && y)
   B. !(x && !y)
   C. !x && y
   D. x || !!y
   E. None of these

```
public static boolean bolTest(boolean a, boolean b) {
        boolean temp = !a || b;
        return temp;
}
```

2. What is output in the code to the right?

   A. Throws an exception
   B. *false*
   C. *true*
   D. !bv
   E. None of these

```
boolean bv = true;
for(int j=0; j<79; j++) {
        bv = !bv;
}
System.out.println(bv || false);
```

3. The ???? column of this table is represented by which of the following?

   A. p && q
   B. p && !q
   C. !p && q
   D. p || q
   E. p || !q

p	q	!p	!q	?????
false	false	true	true	false
false	true	true	false	false
true	false	false	true	true
true	true	false	false	false

4. Which of the following is the equivalent of !x && (a || b || !c)?

   A. !x&&a || !x&&b || !x&&(!c)
   B. x && !c
   C. !x || a && !x || b && !x || !c
   D. Both A and C
   E. None of these

5. In the code to the right, which of the following would equivalently replace the line of code marked with a rem?

   A. return !sv || b
   B. return !(!sv || b)
   C. return !(sv && !b)
   D. return !sv && b
   E. None of these

```
public class smallClass {
        public smallClass(boolean sv1) {
                sv = sv1;
        }

        public boolean decide(boolean b, int j) {
                if (j >30) {
                    return !!!(sv || !b); //
                }
                else {
                    return false;
                }
        }
        private boolean sv;
}
```

Lesson 33…..Selection Operator (?:)

A strange syntax:

Consider the code fragment:

```
double d = m > 0? x + 1.1 : x * x;
```

It is easy to understand this syntax if we see the equivalent code implemented with an ordinary *if* statement.

```
double d;
if (m > 0)
{
        d = x + 1.1;
}
else
{
        d = x * x;
}
```

General form of the selection operator:

(a boolean test) ? value1 : value2 …where value1 is returned if *boolean* is true; otherwise, value2 is returned

Below, are three examples of usage of the selection operator.

1. **Example:**
```
int m = 15;
double pos1 = b ? m + 1:m * 2;
System.out.println(pos1); //If b is true, prints 16. If b is false, prints 30.
```

2. **Example:**
```
int jack = 19;
double jill = 19.2;
double merv = 22.02;
 int jDark = (jack = = jill) ? (int)(merv + 20) : (int)merv++;
System.out.println(jDark); //22
```

3. **Example:**
```
 int j = 4, k =5;
 int p = (j <= k * 2) ? j= =k?-j:-k : k;
System.out.println(p); //-5
```

This is more easily understood if we rewrite

```
int p = (j <= k * 2) ? j= =k?-j:-k : k;
```

as `int p = (j <= k * 2) ? (j= =k?-j:-k) : k;`

Nested selection operators:

It is possible to "nest" selection operators as was seen above in example 3. Unfortunately, this can become quite confusing as the following example illustrates.

```
int i = s.equals("Busy Bee") ? 3 * j : p > q ? 3 : 5;
```

In the author's opinion, writing such confusing code is inexcusable. This line of code would be clearer if written as follows:

```
int i = s.equals("Busy Bee")  ?  (3 * j)  :  (   (p > q) ? 3 : 5  );
```

Of course, an even clearer way would be to write it like this:

```
int i;
if(s.equals("Busy Bee"))
{
        i = 3 * j;
}
else
{
        if(p > q)
        {
                i = 3;
        }
        else
        {
                i = 5;
        }
}
```

It is recommended to **not** use the selection operator in code that you create. Use an *if* statement instead; however, it is sometimes valuable to know selection operator syntax when reviewing the code of others.

Exercise for Lesson 33

1. Write the equivalent of the following code using an *if* statement.

   ```
   j = kimTrq < jDorch ? Math.pow(3,p) : p * p;
   ```

2. What is output if *a = true*, *b = false*, *m = 200*?

   ```
   System.out.println(a && b? m*m:--m);
   ```

3. What is the value of *v* if *m = true* and *n = true*?

   ```
   boolean v = m||n ? (m && !n) : (m || !n);
   ```

4. ```
   double g = 5.0, h = -2.0, s = 9.0;
   int ii = (g>=h) ? (int)(h+2) : (int)(s++);
   ```
   What is the value of ii?

5. What is output by the following code?

   ```
   int soy = 12, tabasco = 10, noodles = 4, sauce = 0;
   int ugh = (Math.pow(soy, noodles)<tabasco) ? 12 : sauce= =tabasco?11:122;
   System.out.println(ugh);
   ```

6. Rewrite the following code fragment using the selection operator instead of the *if* statement.
   ```
   if (bq < j +1)
   {
           z = 1;
   }
   else
   {
           z = 2;
   }
   ```

7. What is output by the following code?
   ```
   String toy = "Tickle Me Elmo";
   double price = 20.13;
   String s = (toy.equals("Barbie")) ? (price>20.13)? "maybe": "yes": "no way";
   System.out.println(s);
   ```

8. What would have been the answer to problem 7 if *toy* had been equal to "Barbie"?
   ```

Selection Operator… Contest Type Problems

1. What would be an appropriate way to call *vogue* from some other class besides *Tire*? (assume *a* and *b* are booleans)
 	
A. String s;
s = vogue(false, a&&b?a:!b);
B. int i;
i = vogue(false, a&&b?a:!b);
C. vogue(false, a&&b?a:!b);
D. boolean bb;
Tire obj = new Tire( );
bb = obj.vogue(false, a&&b?a:!b);
E. boolean bol;
Tire obj = new Tire( );
bol = obj.vogue(3, a&&b?a:!b);
	public class Tire
	{
	…
	public boolean vogue(boolean p, boolean q)
	{
	boolean perk;
	perk = !p || q ? p&&q : p||q;
	return perk;
	}
	…
	}

2. What is returned by the method call, *vogue(true, false)*? A. 0 B. *false* C. *true* D. Nothing E. None of these	

3. Which of the following selection operator statements does the equivalent of the code to the right?
 	
A. m = (j= =g)?++j:37;
B. m = if(j = =g)?j++:37;
C. m = (j= =g)?37:j++;
D. m = (j= =g)?j:37;
++j;
E. None of these
	if(j = = g)
	{
	m = j++;
	}
	else
	{
	m = 37;
	}

4. What will be the value of *ht* after the method call, *ht = nerdMethod(false, false);*?
 	
A. 15.70796327
B. 18.3
C. 3.141592654
D. *nerdMethod* is *static* and can't be called without creating an object
E. *false*
	public static double nerdMethod(boolean x, boolean y)
	{
	double coneHeight;
	coneHeight = !(x&&y) ? 18.3 : 5 * Math.PI;
	return coneHeight;
	}

Lesson 34.....Passing by Value and by Reference

Consider the following class:

```
public class Tester
{
        public static void main(String[] args)
        {
                double b[]= new double[10];
                b[3] = 19;
                BankAccount myAccount = new BankAccount(79); //sets balance to
                int y =39;                                   //79
                method1(y, b, myAccount);
                System.out.println(y + "     " + b[3] + "     " + myAccount.balance);
                   //prints .... 39   -54    702
        }

        public static void method1(int x, double a[ ], BankAccount theAccount)
        {
                x =332;
                a[3] = -54;
                theAccount.balance = 702;
        }
}
```

Passing by value:

This demonstrates that primitive data types like *int*, *double*, etc. are **passed by value**; i.e. a new copy of the variable is temporarily created in the method and any changes to that variable in the method are **not** made to the original. Notice above that we pass an *int* type *y* to the method where the temporary copy is called *x*. The *x* is changed to 332; however, back in the calling code, *y* stays at its original value of 39.

Passing by reference:

Arrays (the *b[ ]* array) and **objects** (*myAccount*) are **passed by reference**. Notice both of these are modified in *method1,* and sure enough, back in the calling code these changes are reflected there.

> *Actually, arrays are objects, so our rule is simply stated,* ***"Objects are passed by reference."***

There is an exception to the above rule. A *String* is an object; however, it acts like a primitive data type and is passed by value.

Passing an array to a method:

Now we are going to look a little deeper into passing arrays to methods. We must remember that the array may be named something different in the method; however, that new name is just a **reference** back to the original array. Passing an array **does not create a new array** in the method.

Consider the following code:

```
public class Tester
{
        public static void main(String args[])
        {
                int s[] = {1,2,3,4,5,6};

                for(int g = 0; g < s.length; g++)  //prints first
                        System.out.print(s[g] + "  ");
                 System.out.println("\n");

                testMethod(s);

                for(int g = 0; g < s.length; g++)  //prints last
                        System.out.print(s[g] + "  ");
        }

        public static void testMethod(int pp[])
        {
                //pp references the s array in main
                int len = pp.length;
                int t2[] = new int[len];
                for(int j=0; j<len; j++)
                   t2[j] = pp[len -j -1];

                for(int k=0; k<t2.length; k++)  //prints t2 array
                        System.out.print(t2[k] + "  ");
                System.out.println("\n");

                pp = t2;  //pp now references the local t2 array
        }
}
```

The output looks like this:

```
1  2  3  4  5  6
6  5  4  3  2  1
1  2  3  4  5  6
```

Everything about this printout looks normal except this last line. How do we explain that the *s* array is completely unchanged in the *main* method even though *t2* is clearly reversed in *testMethod* and is then assigned to *pp* (which seems to be a reference back to *s*)?

The explanation is in realizing that *testMethod* initially **does** assign a reference for *pp* back to the *s* array. However, *pp* is later assigned as a reference to the local array *t2* and no longer references the *s* array in *main*. From this point, *pp* cannot affect the *s* array back in *main*. The assignment *pp = t2* **does not assign numbers** in one array to another; rather, it **reassigns a reference** to an array.

Exercise for Lesson 34

State what's printed for each *println* in the code below:

```
public static void main(String args[ ])
{
        MyClass theObj = new MyClass( );
        theObj.gravy = 107.43;

        String s = "hello";

        int xray[] = {1, 2, 3, 4, 5};
        double floozy = 97.4;
        myMethod(floozy, theObj, xray, s );

        System.out.println(floozy); // Problem 1:
        System.out.println(theObj.gravy); //Problem 2:
        System.out.println(xray[2]); //Problem 3:
        System.out.println(s); //Problem 4:
}

public static void myMethod(double floozy, MyClass anObj, int a[ ], String s)
{
        floozy = 13.1;
        anObj.gravy = 10.001;
        a[2] = 100;
        s = "good bye";
}
```

Project… Pass the Gravy, Please

Create a new project called *PassingValues* and put the two above methods in a *Tester* class. Then create a class called *MyClass* having no constructor, no methods and only one *public static double* data member called *gravy*. The *gravy* instance field (data member) should only be declared, not initialized in the *MyClass* class.

Run the *main* method and confirm your answers in the exercise above.

Passing by Value and by Reference… Contest Type Problems

1. What is the output of *System.out.println(d);* in *main*?

   A. 30.89
   B. 31.89
   C. 29.89
   D. 0
   E. None of these

2. What is the output of *System.out.println(prf[2]);* in *main*?

   A. 89
   B. 16
   C. 122
   D. 22
   E. None of these

3. What is the output of *System.out.println(myCir.rad);* in *main*?

   A. 13
   B. 14
   C. 122
   D. 16
   E. None of these

4. What is the output of *println* in the *fg* method?

   A. 0
   B. 32.89
   C. 30.89
   D. 31.89
   E. None of these

5. Remove the block rem symbols from within the *fg* method. What will be the resulting change in the array *prf* in *main*?

   A. 0 and 3rd index elements exchanged
   B. 1st and 3rd index elements exchanged
   C. No change
   D. All elements in reverse order
   E. None of these

```
public class Tester
{
    public static void main(String args[])
    {
        int [] prf = {13,22,89,15};
        double d = 30.89;
        Circle myCir = new Circle(18);
        myCir.rad = 14;

        fg(prf, d, myCir);

        System.out.println(d);
        System.out.println(prf[2]);
        System.out.println(myCir.rad);
    }

    public static void fg(int [] x, double d, Circle c)
    {
        d++;
        x[2] = 16;
        c.rad = 122;
        System.out.println(d++);

        /*int nn[] = new int[x.length];
        nn[3] = x[0];
        x = nn; */
    }
}
```

6. What is output by the following code if the *harvest* method is given in the code to the right?

```
int []gem = {2,3,4,5,6};
harvest(gem);
for(int k=0; k<gem.length; k++)
    System.out.print(gem[k] + "  ");
```

A. 2 3 7 5 6
   0 2 4 6 8
   2 3 7 5 6

B. 2 3 4 5 6
   0 2 4 6 8
   2 3 4 5 6

C. 2 3 7 5 6
   0 2 4 6 8
   0 2 4 6 8

D. 2 3 4 5 6
   8 6 4 2 0
   2 3 4 5 6

E. None of these

```
public static void harvest(int h[])
{
        int z[] = new int[h.length];
        for(int j=0; j<z.length; j++)
                z[j] = j * 2;

        h[2] = 7;

        for(int k=0; k<h.length; k++)
                System.out.print(h[k] + "  ");
        System.out.println("\n");

        h = z;

        for(int k=0; k<h.length; k++)
                System.out.print(h[k] + "  ");
        System.out.println("\n");
}
```

Lesson 35.....Two-Dimensional Arrays

Consider the following array (3 rows, 2 columns) of numbers:

```
22  23
24  25
26  27
```

Let's declare our array as follows:

```
int a[ ] [ ] = new int [3] [2];
```

Subscript convention:

Notice that in both mathematics **and** computer science, designations for a two dimensional array (subscripted variable) conventionally have **rows first** and **columns second**. Just think of RC Cola, …RC (rows, columns).

Initializing a two-dimensional array:

Now let's initialize the *a* array, i.e. store values in the various positions. There are **three** ways to do this:

The first way:

```
int a[ ] [ ] = new int [3] [2];  //declaration
a[0] [0] = 22;  //initialization from here on down
a[0] [1] = 23;
a[1] [0] = 24;
a[1] [1] = 25;
a[2] [0] = 26;
a[2] [1] = 27;
```

The second way:

```
int a[ ] [ ]  = {  {22, 23},
                   {24, 25},
                   {26, 27}  };  //Notice that declaration and initialization
                                 // must both take place on the same line.
```

The third way:

```
int a[ ] [ ]  = new int[][] {  {22, 23},
                               {24, 25},
                               {26, 27}  };
```

How many rows and columns?

Determine the number of rows and columns in a two-dimensional array (sometimes called a **matrix** or **subscripted variables**) as follows:

For the matrix above, *a.length* returns a value of 3…the numbers of rows.

For the matrix above,

a[0].length returns a value of 2…the number of columns in row 0
a[1].length returns a value of 2…the number of columns in row 1
a[2].length returns a value of 2…the number of columns in row 2

"Ragged" arrays:

The previous discussion seems redundant, since **all** rows have 2 columns. So we begin to wonder if it's possible for various rows to have **different** number of columns? Is it really possible to produce a "ragged" looking array with uneven rows? The answer is, "Yes," even though it's highly unusual and seldom used.

Suppose we want the following matrix structure:

```
X  X  X  X
X  X
X  X  X
```

Here's the code that would declare such an array:

```
int a[ ] [ ] = new int[3] [ ];  //array has 3 rows, unspecified number of columns
a[0] = new int[4];  //row 0 has 4 columns
a[1] = new int[2];  // row 1 has 2 columns
a[2] = new int[3];  // row 2 has 3 columns
```

Incidentally, the first line of code above (int a[ ] [ ] = new int[3] [ ];) could be equivalently replaced with the following; however, the former is preferred:

```
int a[ ] [ ] = new int[3] [0];  //3 rows, unspecified number of columns
```

While on the subject of working with a single row of a two-dimensional array, consider an array *a* of three rows declared as was done above. How would we pass a single row of this array to a method called *myMethod* in which each element would be initialized?

```
a[2] = new int[3];  //Row 2 has 3 columns. Before passing a[2] below, we must
                    //have specified the number of columns.
myMethod(a[2]);  // Call the method and pass the row with index 2.
. . .
public void myMethod(int [] x)  //Notice how we receive the row
{
        x[0] = 36;  // Initialize the three columns.
        x[1] = 101;
        x[2] = -45;
}
```

Automatic initialization of arrays:

As with all one-dimensional numeric arrays, all elements of two-dimensional arrays are also automatically initialized to 0 until specific values are given.

```
int abc[][] = new int[20][30];
System.out.println(abc[5][22]);  //0
```

Using the *Arrays* class:

In Lesson 19 (page 3), several methods of the *Arrays* class were discussed. Below we present their equivalents as used with two-dimensional arrays.

```
int a[][] = {  {3, 9, 2, 1},
               {5, 7, 6, 0}  };
int b[][] = {  {0, 2, 8, 4},
               {3, 9, 2, 1}  };
```

```
System.out.println(Arrays.equals(a, b)); //always false...won't compare entire two-
                                         //dimensional arrays.
System.out.println(Arrays.equals(a[0],b[1])); //true, compares row 0 of a to row 1 of b.

Arrays.sort(a); //illegal (run-time exception), can't sort entire two-dimensional array.
Arrays.sort(a[0]); // sorts the 0 row of the a matrix. Row 0 is now {1, 2, 3, 9}

System.out.println(Arrays.binarySearch(a[0], 9)); //1, returns index of the 9 in row 0.
                                                  //This row must have been sorted first.
Arrays.fill(a, 22); //illegal, can't fill entire two-dimensional array
Arrays.fill(a[1], 22); //fills this row with 22 in each position
```

Exercise on Lesson 35

Consider the following *a* matrix for problems 1 - 11:

5	-16	9	21
22	19	-101	36
18	17	64	-2

1. Write a single line of code that will create the above integer array. Call the array *a*.

2. Write a line of code that will printout the array element occupied by –101.

3. The above table can be described as:
(a) an Array (b) a Matrix (c) numbers that could be represented as subscripted variables (d) a, b, and c (e) none of these

4. Write a line of code that will print the number of rows in matrix *a*.

5. Write a line of code that will print the number of columns (in matrix a) in the row given by index 2.

6. What is printed by *System.out.println(a[1][3]);* ?

7. Show what the printout will look like:

```
for (int row = 0; row < a.length; row++)
{
        for(int col = 0; col < a[row].length; col++)
```

```
            {
                System.out.print(a[row][col] + "\t");
            }
            System.out.println(" ");
    }
```

8. What is printed by the following?

```
Arrays.sort(a[0]);
System.out.println(Arrays.binarySearch(a[0],5));
```

9. What is printed by the following?

```
Arrays.sort(a[0]);
System.out.println( Arrays.binarySearch(a[0],0) );
```

10. Show what the matrix *a* would look like after the following code executes:

```
for (int row  = 0; row < a.length; row++)
{
        for(int col = 0; col < a[row].length; col++)
                a[row][col] = row * col;
}
```

11. Show what the matrix *a* would look like after the following code executes:

```
Arrays.fill(a[2], -156);
```

12. Must all two-dimensional arrays have the same number of columns in each row?

In the remaining problems, some of the code might not compile or will give a run-time exception. If that's the case then state, "Won't compile" or "Run-time exception."

13. What is printed by the following?

```
double d[][] = new double[8][25];
System.out.println(d[4][2]);
```

14. If *x* and *y* both represent two-dimensional *int* arrays and have identically the same elements, what does the following print?

```
System.out.println( Arrays.equals(x,y) );
```

15. Is it possible to sort *z* (a two-dimensional array) with *Arrays.sort(z);* ?

16. Is it possible to use one of the *sort* methods of the *Arrays* class to sort a single row (index 3) of the two-dimensional matrix *g*? If so, show the code that will accomplish this.

Project… Matrix Multiplication

The primary objective in this project will be to write code that will multiply the following two matrices and produce the indicated answer.

$$\begin{pmatrix} 1 & 2 & -2 & 0 \\ -3 & 4 & 7 & 2 \\ 6 & 0 & 3 & 1 \end{pmatrix} \text{X} \begin{pmatrix} -1 & 3 \\ 0 & 9 \\ 1 & -11 \\ 4 & -5 \end{pmatrix} = \begin{pmatrix} -3 & 43 \\ 18 & -60 \\ 1 & -20 \end{pmatrix}$$

If you are not familiar with the intricacies of matrix multiplication, Appendix AA is supplied to provide a brief overview of the subject. In fact, the above example is used in that appendix.

Create a project called *MatrixStuff* that consists of two classes. These two classes will be called *Tester* and *MatrixMult* and will meet the specifications listed below.

The *Tester* class (*main* method):

1. Hard code the *int a[][]* array so as to be comprised of the 3 X 4 matrix on the left in the example above.

2. Hard code the *int b[][]* array so as to be comprised of the 4 X 2 middle matrix in the example above.

3. Call a *static* method of the *MatrixMult* class called *mult* in which we pass the *a* and *b* arrays (matrices) as arguments and receive back an integer array as the product matrix.

4. Print the product matrix.

5. The output of *main* should appear as follows:

```
-3    43

18    -60

1     -20
```

The *MatrixMult* class:

1. No constructor.

2. Create a single *static* method called *mult* that receives two *int* arrays (matrices) as parameters that are to be multiplied in the order in which they are received.

3. The *mult* method is to return an array that is the product matrix of the two parameter arrays it receives.

4. The code in the *mult* method is to determine the dimensions of the matrices that it receives and set up a "product" array (matrix) to be returned with the appropriate dimensions.

5. The code in *mult* should be general so as to adapt to any two matrices to be multiplied; however, for the sake of simplicity, you may assume that the matrices received as parameters **are** always compatible with each other for multiplication.

6. The code in the *mult* method will multiply the two incoming matrices so as to correctly produce each element of the product matrix.

Project… Matrix Multiplication with File Input

Modify the previous project so that the matrices to be input are input from a text file. The "rules" of the text file are:

> The start of a new matrix will be indicated with "matrix". The start of a new row will be indicated with "row" followed by the numbers assigned to each column of that row.

Call your data file *MatrixData.txt*. It should have the following content:

```
matrix
row
1
2
-2
0
row
-3
4
7
2
row
6
0
3
1
matrix
row
-1
3
row
0
9
row
1
-11
row
4
-5
```

Output should be identical to that in the previous project (since the two matrices to be multiplied are the same as before).

Two-Dimensional Arrays… Contest Type Problems

1. Which of the following is the resulting array after running the code to the right?

```
int [][] zorro = new int[3] [4];
for(int row=0; row<zorro.length; row++)
{
    for(int col=0; col<zorro[row].length; col++)
    {
        zorro[row][col] = col + 1;
    }
}
```

A.

0	0	0	0
1	1	1	1
2	2	2	2

B.

0	1	2	3
0	1	2	3
0	1	2	3

C.

1	2	3	4
1	2	3	4
1	2	3	4

D.

1	1	1	1
2	2	2	2
3	3	3	3

E. None of these

2. Which of the following is the resulting array after running *main* in the *Tester* class to the right?

```
public class Tester
{
    public static void main(String args[])
    {
        int z[][] = {   {5,6,7,8},
                        {1,2,3,4},
                        {0,1,2,3}   };
        MatrixManip f = new MatrixManip( );
        f.adjust(z);
    }
}


public class MatrixManip
{
    . . .
    public void adjust(int[][] mat)
    {
        for(int p=0; p<mat.length; p++)
            for(int q=0; q<mat[p].length; q++)
                --mat[p][q];
    }
    . . .
}
```

A.

4	5	6	7
0	1	2	3
-1	0	1	2

B.

5	6	7	8
1	2	3	4
0	1	2	3

C.

6	7	8	9
2	3	4	5
1	2	3	4

D.

1	1	1	1
2	2	2	2
3	3	3	3

E. None of these

```java
int [][] intArray = {  {11,2}, {20,30}, {7,9}, {0,1}  };
```

3. What is printed by *System.out.println(intArray.length);*?

   A. 2
   B. 4
   C. 8
   D. 0
   E. None of these

4. What is printed by *System.out.println(intArray[2].length);*?

   A. 2
   B. 4
   C. 8
   D. 0
   E. None of these

5. Initialize the array *d* and call *doStuff* as follows:

```java
int d[][] = {  {-1,0,1},
               {5,6,7},
               {2,3,4}  };
doStuff(d);
```

What does the array *d* look like now?

```java
public static void  doStuff (int [][] frst)
{
    int len = frst.length;
    int sec[][] = new int[len] [];
    for(int j=0; j<len; j++)
        sec[j] = frst[len –j -1];
    frst = sec;
}
```

A.

-1	5	2
0	6	3
1	7	4

B.

1	0	-1
7	6	5
4	3	2

C.

2	3	4
5	6	7
-1	0	1

D.

-1	0	1
5	6	7
2	3	4

E. None of these

Lesson 36…..Inheritance

Within a new project we will create three classes……*BankAccount*, *SavingsAccount*, and *Tester*. First, the *BankAccount* class:

```
public class BankAccount
{
        public BankAccount(double amt) //Constructor
        { balance = amt; }

        public double getBalance( )
        { // You supply code here that returns the state variable, balance.}

        public void deposit(double d)
        { //You supply code here that adds d to balance. }

        public void withdraw(double d)
        { //You supply code here that subtracts d from balance. }

        private double balance;
}
```

Subclass and Superclass:

This *BankAccount* class will be known as our **Superclass**. We will now create a *SavingsAccount* class that will be known as a **Subclass**. This *SavingsAccount* class is a perfect candidate to use as a subclass of *BankAccount* since it needs all the methods and state variable of the superclass, *BankAccount*. To make the *SavingsAccount* class **inherit** those methods and the state variable, use the key word **extends** as follows:

```
public class SavingsAccount extends BankAccount
{
        public SavingsAccount(double amount, double rate) //Constructor
        {
                super(amount);              //Calls the constructor in
                interestRate = rate;        //BankAccount and sets balance
        }

        public void addInterest( )
        {
                double interest = getBalance( ) * interestRate / 100;
                deposit(interest);
        }
        private double interestRate;
}
```

There are some significant features of the constructor in *SavingsAccount*. In the absence of *super(amount),* it would have tried to **automatically** call the *BankAccount* constructor and would have failed, since that constructor requires a parameter and we would not have supplied one. By making *super(amount)* **the first line** of code, we are able to supply the needed parameter. When used, it **must** be the first line of code in the constructor.

There is also something interesting in the *addInterest* method above. Notice that we are calling the *getBalance* and *deposit* methods. This is completely legal even though they are not *static* methods and we are not accessing them with a *BankAccount* object. Why is it legal? It is because we have **inherited** these methods from *BankAccount* by virtue of the *extends BankAccount* portion of our class signature.

Testing the subclass and superclass:

And finally, we will create a class called *Tester* that we will use to test the interaction of our superclass and subclass:

```
public class Tester
{
    public static void main(String[] args)
    {
        //This begins a new account in which the initial balance is 200
        // and the interest rate is 5%.
        SavingsAccount myAccount = new SavingsAccount(200, 5);

        //Make a deposit...notice we use an inherited method, deposit
        myAccount.deposit(132.14);

        myAccount.addInterest( );

        //Here, we use another inherited method, getBalance
        System.out.println( "Final balance is: " + myAccount.getBalance( ) );
    }
}
```

Important terms and ideas:

Superclass…the “original” class (sometimes called the base class)

Subclass…the one that says “extends” (sometimes called the derived class)

abstract

a. As applied to a **class**…Example, *public abstract class MyClass…* prevents objects from being instantiated from the class. Why would we want to do this? Perhaps the only way we would want our class used is for it to be inherited.

b. As applied to a **method**…Example, *public abstract void chamfer( );* …means that no code is being implemented for this method in this class. This forces the subclass that inherits this class to implement the code there.

   Note that the signature of an abstract method is immediately followed by a semicolon and that there can be no body (curly braces) for the method.

   If any method in a class is abstract, then that **forces** its class to be abstract too.

final

a. As applied to a **class**…*public final class MyClass*…means no other class can inherit this one.

b. As applied to a **method**...*public final void bisect( )*...means it can't be overridden in a subclass. See the discussion below for the meaning of "overriding".

Overriding...if a method is defined in a superclass and is also defined in a subclass... then when objects are made from the subclass, the redundant method in the subclass will take precedence over the one in the superclass. This is overriding.

There is a way to access a method in a superclass that has been overridden in the subclass. Let's suppose the method's signature in both classes is:

```
public void trans(double x)
```

From within some method of the subclass you can access the method *trans* in the superclass via a command like this:

```
super.trans(15.07);
```

***private* methods not inherited:**

Methods and state variables in the superclass that are designated as *private* are **not** inherited by the subclass.

Shadowing...is when a state variable in a subclass has a name identical to that of a state variable in the superclass. We do not say that the subclass variable overrides the other, rather that it **shadows** it. In such cases, uses within the subclass of the redundant variable give precedence to the subclass variable. It is, however, possible to access the shadowed variable in the superclass by creating a method in the superclass to access it. Suppose that the shadowed public variable in question is *double y*. Then, in the superclass create this method.

```
public double getY( )
{    return y;    }
```

Since this method is inherited by your subclass, use it to obtain the *y* value in the superclass. Assuming that an object created with your subclass is called *myObj*, consider the following code within the subclass:

```
double d = myObj.getY( );  //  returns y from the superclass
double p = myObj.y;  //  returns y from the subclass
```

There is also another type of shadowing. Let's look at a method that brings in the variable *z* as a parameter. Complicating things is a state variable also named *z*.

```
public class MyClass
{
        . . .
        public void aMethod(int z)
        {
                z++; //This increments the local z which has precedence here within
                     //this method.

                this.z = 19;  //only way to access the state variable z from within
                              //this method.

        } . . .
        public int z;
}
```

Cosmic Superclass... Every class that does not extend another class automatically extends the class *Object* (the cosmic superclass). Following are the signatures and descriptions of four of the most important methods of the *Object* class.

Signature	Description
String toString( )	Returns a string representation of the object. For example, for a BankAccount object we get something like *BankAccount@1a28362*
boolean equals(Object obj)	Tests for the equality of objects. This tests to see if two variables are references to the same object. It does not test the contents of the two objects.
Object clone( )	Produces a copy of an object. This method is not simple to use and there are several pitfalls and is therefore, rarely used.
int hashCode( )	Returns an integer from the entire integer range.
In many classes it is commonplace to override the inherited methods above with corresponding methods that better suit the particular class. For example, the *String* class overrides *equals* so as to actually test the contents.	

Table 36-1

Creation of objects:

Suppose we have a superclass called *SprC* and a subclass called *SbC*. Let's look at various ways to create objects:

a. SbC theObj = new SbC( );
   SprC anotherObj = theObj;

   Since *anotherObj* is of type *SprC* it can **only** access methods and state variables that belong to *SprC*.

b. SprC hallMark = new SbC( );

   Since *hallMark* is of type *SprC* it can only access methods and state variables that belong to *SprC*.

c. SbC obj = new SprC( ); //illegal

Expecting a particular object type:

Any time when a parameter is **expecting** to receive an object of a particular type, it is acceptable to send it an object of a subclass, but never of a superclass. This is because the passed subclass object **inherits** all the methods of the object. Otherwise, the expected object may have methods **not** in a superclass object. Consider the following hierarchy of classes where each class is a subclass of the class immediately above it.

Person
Male
Boy

Suppose there is a method with the following signature:

```
public void theMethod(Male ml)
```

The method *theMethod* is clearly **expecting a *Male* object**; therefore, the following calls to this method would be legal since we are either sending a ***Male*** object or an object of a **subclass**:

```
Male m = new Male( );
theMethod(m);  //ok to send m since its expecting a Male object
Boy b = new Boy( );
theMethod(b); //ok to send b since b is created from a subclass of Male
```

Since *theMethod* is expecting a *Male* object, we **can't** send an object of a **superclass**.

```
Person p = new Person( );
theMethod(p);  //Illegal
theMethod( (Male)p );  //Legal if we cast p as a Male object
```

Using the same classes from above, the following examples illustrate legal and illegal object creation. Notice when we use a class on the left, the class on the right must be either the **same** class or a **subclass**.

```
Person p = new Male( );  //legal
Person p = new Boy( );  //legal
Male m = new Boy( );  //legal
Boy b = new Male( );  //illegal
Boy b = new Person( );  //illegal
Male m = new Person( );  //illegal
```

instanceof

This method tells us if an object was created from a particular class. Suppose *Parent* is a superclass, *Child* is one of its subclasses, *objP* is a *Parent* object, and *objC* is a *Child* object. Also, assume that *Circle* is some unrelated class.

d. (objC instanceof Child) returns a *true*

e. (objC instanceof Parent) returns a *true*

f. (objC instanceof Circle) returns a *false*

g. (objP instanceof Child) returns *false*

h. (objP instanceof Parent) returns *true*

i. (objP instanceof Circle) returns *false*

Notice the syntax of *instanceof* is that an **object precedes** *instanceof* and a **class, subclass or interface follows**.

The big picture:

The following shows the function of each part in the declaration and creation of an object in which a superclass, subclass, or interface may be involved.

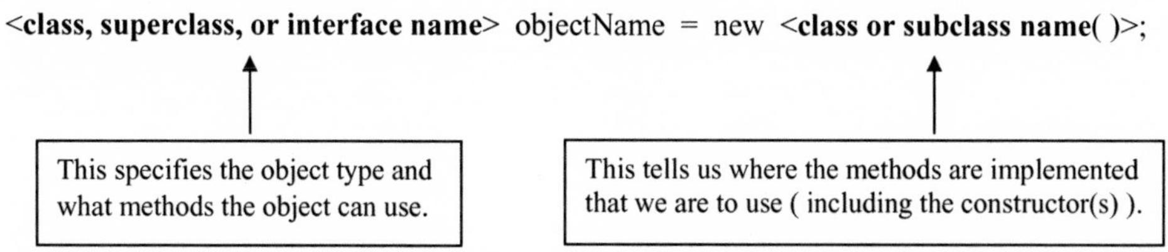

<class, superclass, or interface name> objectName = new **<class or subclass name( )>**;

This specifies the object type and what methods the object can use.

This tells us where the methods are implemented that we are to use (including the constructor(s)).

Fig. 38-1 Determining object type, legal methods, and where the methods are implemented.

Inheritance is considered one of the most important, but, unfortunately, one of the most difficult aspects of Java. See Appendix U for an enrichment activity in which you would be able to participate in electronic communities in the form of message boards (forums). Investigate the questions and answers that other programmers post concerning this topic.

Exercise (A) on Lesson 36

```
public class Red extends Green
{
        public int blue(double x)
        {   . . .   }

        public String s;
        private int i;
}

public class Green
{
        public double peabody(double y)
        {
                return mm;
        }

        private boolean crunch( )
        {   . . .   }

        private double mm;
        public long xx;
}
```

1. Which of the above two classes is the base class?

2. Which of the above two classes is the subclass?

3. Which of the above two classes is the superclass?

4. Which of the above two classes is the derived class?

5. Is this legal? If not, why not? (Assume this code is in some class other than the two above)

```
Red myObj = new Red( );
boolean bb = myObj.crunch( );
```

6. Is this legal? If not, why not? (Assume this code is in some class other than the two above)

```
Red myObj = new Red( );
int bb = myObj.blue( 105.2);
```

7. Write code for the *blue* method that will printout the *mm* state variable.

8. Write code for the *blue* method that will printout the *xx* state variable.

Use the following two classes for problems 9 - 12:

```
public class Red extends Green
{
        public int blue(double x)
        {    . . .    }

        public double peabody(double vv)
        {

        }

        public String s;
        private int i;
}

public class Green
{
        public Green(long j)
        {
                xx = j;
        }

        public double peabody(double y)
        {
                return mm;
        }

        private Boolean crunch( )
        {   . . .   }
        private double mm;
        public long xx;
}
```

9. Consider the following constructor in the *Red* class:

```
public Red( )
{
        //What code would you put here to invoke the constructor in the
        //superclass and send it a parameter value of 32000?
}
```

10. Is there any method in *Red* that is overriding a method in *Green*? If so, what is it?

11. Look at the *peabody* method inside *Red*. Write the code inside that method that will allow you to access the same method inside its superclass, *Green*. Let the parameter have a value of 11.

12. Consider the following constructor in the *Red* class:

```
public Red( )
{
        String s = "Hello";
        super(49);
}
```

Is this code legal? If not, why not?

13. Assume that the following fragments of code are all in a subclass. Match each to an item from the "sentence bank" to the right.

_____ this.(x,y)	a. refers to a constructor in the superclass
_____ this.z	b. refers to a constructor in the subclass
_____ super(j)	c. refers to an overridden method in the super class
_____ super.calc( )	d. refers to a data member in the subclass

Exercise (B) on Lesson 36

The following code applies to problems 1 - 3:

```
public abstract class Hammer
{
        public abstract void duty( );
        public abstract int rule(int d);
}

public class Lurch extends Hammer
{
        public void duty( )
        {
                int x = Y;
        }

        public int rule( int d)
        {
                Y = d + 1;
                return Y;
        }

        private int Y = 30;
        private int x;
}
```

1. What is the purpose of making the two methods above abstract?

2. Write out the full signature of the *rule* method.

3. Which class actually implements the *duty* method?

4. A class for which you cannot create objects is called a (an)___________ class.

5.
```
public abstract class Felix
{
        . . .
}
```

   Is the following attempt at instantiating an object from the *Felix* class legal? If not, why?

```
        Felix myFelix = new Felix( );
```

6. Is the following legal? If not, why?

```
public abstract class Lupe
{
        public abstract void fierce( )
        {   . . .   }

        public final double PI = 3.14;
}
```

7. What is the main reason for using abstract classes?

8. Modify the following class so it is impossible to make subclasses from it.

```
public class MyClass
{
        . . .
}
```

9. Why would the following code be pointless?

```
public final abstract class MyClass
{
        . . .
        //there are no static methods
}
```

10.
```
public class ChevyChase
{
        public void Chicago(int x)
        {
                . . .
        }
}
```

    Modify the above code so as to make it impossible for a subclass that extends *ChevyChase* to override the *Chicago* method.

11. Is it possible to override instance fields (also called state variables)?

12. What is shadowing (as the term applies to superclasses and subclasses)?

The following code applies to problems 13 – 14, 18 - 20:

```
public class Parent
{
        public void rubyDoo( )
        { . . . }
        • • •

        public int  x = 0;
}

public class Child extends Parent
{
        public void busterStein( )
        { . . . }
        • • •

        public int x = 39;
}
```

13. Consider the following code in a *Tester* class:

```
Child myChild = new Child( );
System.out.println(myChild.x);  //What gets printed?
```

14. Consider the following code in a *Tester* class:

```
Child myChild = new Child( );
```

Is there any way using the *myChild* object to retrieve the *x* state field within the *Parent* class? Write the code that will do this. You may write a new method for either class if you need to.

15. What is the name of the Cosmic Superclass?

16. What is the name of the class that every class (that does not extend another class) automatically extends?

17. What are the three main methods of the *Object* class?

18. Is the following legal? If not, why not?

```
Child theObj =  new Child( );
Parent newObj = theObj;
newObj.busterStein( );
```

19. Is the following legal? If not, why not?

```
Child theObj =  new Child( );
Parent newObj = theObj;
newObj.rubyDoo( );
```

20. Is the following legal? If not, why not?

```
Parent meatloaf = new Child( );
```

For problems 21-25, consider the following. In each problem either state what is printed or indicate that it won't compile:

```
public class A
{
        public A (int x)
        {
                this.x = x;
        }

        public int f( )
        {
                return x;
        }

        public int g( )
        {
                return x;
        }

        public int x;
}
```

```
public class B extends A
{
        public B (int x, int y)
        {
                super(x);
                this.x = y;
        }

        public int f( ) { return x + g( ); }

        public int zorro( ) { return x + g( ); }

        public int x;
}
```

21. A a = new B(5, 10);
    System.out.println(a.g( ));

22. A a = new B(5, 10);
    System.out.println(a.f( ));

23. A a = new B(5, 10);
    System.out.println(a.x);

24. B a = new B(5, 10);
    System.out.println(a.x);

25. A a = new B(5, 10);
    System.out.println(a.zorro( ));

****

26. Consider the classes *Food*, *Cheese*, and *Velveta* where *Cheese* is a subclass of *Food* and *Velveta* is a subclass of *Cheese*. State which of the following lines of code are legal.

```
Cheese c = new Food( );
Velveta v = new Food( );
Cheese c = new Velveta( );
Food f = new Velveta( );
Food f = new Cheese( );
```

Inheritance… Contest Type Problems

1. What replaces **<*1>** and **<*2>** in the code to the right to indicate that objects cannot be instantiated and that the methods are not being defined?

   A. **<*1>**: abstract **<*2>**: abstract
   B. **<*1>**: abstract **<*2>**: final
   C. **<*1>**: final **<*2>**: abstract
   D. **<*1>**: final **<*2>**: final
   E. None of these

```
public <*1> AccountDetails {
    public <*2> double getPrinciple( );
    public <*2>  String getName( );
}

public <*1> class Financial {
    public <*2>  double interestEarned( );
    public <*2>  double paymentDue( );
}
```

2. The interest earned on a loan is the product of 1/12, the *principle*, the *rate*, and the *months*. What replaces **<*3>** in the code to the right to correctly compute the *interestEarned( )* method?

   A. months / 12 * rate * ad.getPrinciple( )
   B. months * rate * ad.getPrinciple( ) / 12
   C. Loan.months /12 * Loan.rate * ad.getPrinciple
   D. months * rate * ad.getPrinciple( ) * (1/12)
   E. More than one of these

3. Assume that the class *Info* is a subclass of *AccountDetails* and has a constructor which receives a *double* and a *String*. Which of the following builds a *Loan p* object with *rate* .07, *months* 4, and *principle* $450?

   A. Loan p (.07, 4, new Info(450, "Bob"));
   B. Loan p = Loan(.07, 4, new Info(450, "Bob"));
   C. Loan p = new Loan(.07, 4, Info(450, "Bob"));
   D. Loan p = new Loan(.07, 4, new Info(450, "Bob"));
   E. None of these

```
public class Loan extends Financial {
    public Loan(double rate, int months,
                                AccountDetails ad)
    {
        this.rate = rate;
        this.months = months;
        this.ad = ad;
    }

    public double interestEarned( )
    {
        return <*3>;
    }

    public double paymentDue( )
    {
        //code not shown
    }

    private double rate;
    private int months;
    AccountDetails ad;
}
```

4. What is output by the code below?

```
Parent pr = new Parent(7);
System.out.print(pr.work( ));
```

   A. 1 B. 0 C. 3 D. 7
   E. None of these

5. What is output by the code below?

```
Parent pr = new Child(4, 11);
System.out.print(pr.work( ));
```

   A. 11 B. 4 C. 1 D. 0
   E. None of these

```
public class Parent {
    public Parent(int q)  {this.q = q;}
    public int work( ) {return q;}
    private int q;
}

public class Child extends Parent
{
    public Child(int q, int y) {
        super(q);
        this.y = y;
    }

    public int work( ) {
        return y + super.work( );
    }
    private int y;
}
```

6. What replaces **<*1>** in the code to the right that causes *Z* to inherit class *A*?

A. implements A
B. subclass of A
C. subclass of class A
D. extends A
E. inherits A

```
public class Z <*1>
{
    //methods and data not shown
}
```

7. Which of the following replaces **<*1>** in the code to the right so that the default constructor builds a *Triangle* object with *base* 2 and *altitude* 5?

A. this(2, 5);
B. Triangle (2, 5);
C. super(2, 5);
D. this(base) = 2;   this(altitude) = 5;
E. More than one of these

8. Assume that **<*1>** has been filled in correctly. Which of the following returns the area of *EquilateralTri et*?

A. (EquilateralTri)et.area( )
B. et.super.area( )
C. et.(EquilateralTri)area( )
D. et.area( )
E. None of these

9. Given a *Triangle tri* that is initialized to hold a *Triangle* and an *EquilateralTri et* that is initialized to hold a *Triangle*, which of the following expressions evaluates to *true*?

A. Triangle instanceof *EquilateralTri*
B. tri instanceof et
C. tri instanceof *EquilateralTri*
D. Triangle instanceof Object
E. None of these

```
public class Triangle {
    public Triangle( )
    {
        <*1>
    }

    public Triangle(int bs, int alt) {
        base = bs;
        altitude = alt;
    }

    public double area( )
    {
        return .5 * base * altitude;
    }

    private int base;
    private int altitude;
}

public class EquilateralTri extends Triangle {
    public EquilateralTri (int s) {
        super(s, s * Math.sqrt(3)/2);
        this.s = s;
    }
    private int s;
}
```

10. Suppose *st* is a *Street object*. Which of these is a valid call to method *House.getInfo( )* using *st* as an argument?

A. st.getInfo(Town t)
B. House.getInfo((Town)st)
C. House.getInfo(Town(st))
D. House.getInfo(Town.st)
E. None of these

11. Suppose *st* is a *Street* object. What is the value of this expression?   *st instanceof Town*

A. 0
B. true
C. 1
D. false
E. None of these

```
public class Town
{
        //code not shown
}

public class Street extends Town
{
        //code not shown
}

public class House
{
      public static void getInfo(Town t)
      {   //code not shown     }
}
```

12. Given the declarations below, which of the following expressions is *true*?

```
Car cr = new Car( );
Chevy chv = new Chevy( );
Lumina lm = new Lumina( );
```

A. cr instanceof Chevy
B. chv instanceof Lumina
C. cr instanceof Lumina
D. lm instanceof Car
E. More than one of these

```
public class Car
{
    //methods and data not shown
}

public class Chevy extends Car
{
    //methods and data not shown
}

public class Lumina extends Chevy
{
    //methods and data not shown
}
```

13. Suppose that the *static* method *doStuff( )* of class *Engine* takes a parameter of type *Lumina*. Given the declarations below, which of these is a valid call to *doStuff( )*?

```
Car cr = new Lumina( );
Chevy chv = new Lumina( );
Lumina lm = new Lumina( );
```

A. Engine.doStuff(chv)   B. Engine.doStuff(cr)
C. Engine.doStuff(lm)   D. doStuff((Car)lm)
E. None of these

14. Suppose that *Insect* is an abstract class, that *Bee* is a class that extends *Insect*, and that *Drone* is a class that extends *Bee*. Given the following declaration, which of these is *true*?

```
Drone d = new Drone( );
```

A. d instanceof Object   B. d instanceof Insect   C. d instanceof Bee
D. d instanceof Drone   E. All of these

15. If *class Man* is a subclass of *class Person*, what is the syntax for calling a *private* method of *Person* named *meth( )* from within a *private* method of *Man*?

A. this.meth( )   B. meth( )   C. super.meth( )
D. super(meth( ))   E. None of these

16. Which of the following replaces **<*1>** in the code to the right to call the constructor for the *Pasta* class with the parameter *g*?

A. this(g);
B. super(g);
C. x.super( );
D. Pasta(g);
E. None of these

```
public class  Spaghetti extends Pasta
{
    public Spaghetti(int g, int h)
    {
        <*1>
    }
    ...remaining code not shown
}
```

Lesson 37…..Exceptions

What is an exception?

An exception is simply an error. Instead of saying an error occurred, we say that an **exception is thrown**.

How Java handles exceptions:

Suppose we have a "chain" of methods. The *main* method is the first in the chain. An expression in it calls some other method, and an expression in it calls yet another. Let's assume some piece of code deep in this chain throws an exception. The code immediately surrounding the offending code is examined for a *try-catch* statement. (More on this later; however, for now, suffice it to say that if a *try-catch* is present, it handles the error gracefully without the entire program coming to a halt). If no *try-catch* is found, control immediately passes up the chain to the code that called the method in which the error just occurred. Again, a *try-catch* statement is sought, and if none is found, control is passed back up the calling chain one level. This continues until the *main* method is reached. If it has no *try-catch*, the program is halted with a trace of the method calls, the type of exception, and its error message.

Actually, the above is oversimplified just a bit. In the absence of a *try-catch* statement, control is passed up the calling chain one level **only when we specify it to happen**. This is done with a **throws** specifier in the method signature. (More on **throws** on the next pg)

Forcing an error:

You can **force Java to <u>appear</u> to give an error** as in the following example from a *BankAccount* object. In this example we look at **preconditions** that we require before this method is called. The method we will discuss is *withdraw()*. Certainly, we can't withdraw more than what we have in the account. Also, it would be meaningless to withdraw a negative or zero amount, so we detail these preconditions in the rems above the method signature.

```
/* precondition: amount <= balance
 * precondition: amount > 0 */
public void withdraw(double amount)
{
        if (amount > balance)
        {
                String s = "Can't withdraw more than the balance.";
                IllegalArgumentException e = new IllegalArgumentException(s);
                throw e;  //Presents the s message and the entire program stops
        }

        if (amount <= 0)
        {
                String s = "Withdrawal amount must be greater than 0.";
                IllegalArgumentException e = new IllegalArgumentException(s);
                throw e;  //Presents the s message and the entire program stops
        }
        . . . remainder of code for this method. . .
}
```

In the above code we used the exception class, *IllegalArgumentException*. See Appendix K for a list of some other exception classes.

Two types of exceptions:

Checked... those that Java requires handling by the programmer. These are typically errors over which the programmer has no control. The IOException is a classic example.

Mnemonic memory aide: For errors that are out of your control, such as an *IOException* due to a corrupt file, etc., Java is **extra vigilant** and **checks** for errors for you.

Unchecked... those that the programmer may or may not handle. These are errors that are the programmer's fault. A typical example would be a division by 0 giving an *ArithmeticException*. Another example would be a *NumberFormatException* that might occur when you try to do *Integer.parseInt(m)* and the *String m* can't convert to an *int*. (The example code on the previous page concerned unchecked exceptions.)

Two choices for handling checked exceptions:

Now let's suppose we have a method that has the **potential** of throwing a **checked** exception. We **must handle** the exception with one of two choices. Notice that with checked exceptions, doing nothing is **not** a choice, it won't even compile unless you do one of the following:

1. Handle the exception with ***try, catch, finally*** as we will see later in this lesson.

2. Put a *throws IOException* (or some other appropriate checked exception) tag on the method signature as in the following example:

```
public void readTheDisk( ) throws IOException
{
    ... code that uses a file reader...might encounter a corrupt file...
}
```

So, what's the purpose of this ***throws*** specifier in a method? The **purpose** is so the calling-method (the method that called the *readTheDisk* method) is signaled that an *IOException* **may** occur in *readTheDisk* and that the calling method is to handle the exception. Of course, in the calling-method you can make the choice of putting another ***throws*** specifier in **its** signature, or to actually handle the exception right there with *try*, *catch*, and *finally*.

Thus, we see that the ***throws*** specifier is a way to **defer** the handling of an exception. We can keep postponing the actual handling of the exception right up the calling chain. Of course we can defer it all the way up to the *main* method and if no *try-catch* is there, then the program terminates.

The ***throws*** specifier can provide for **multiple** exceptions as in the following example:

```
public void aMethod(int x) throws IOException, ClassNotFoundException
{

}
```

We should also mention that unchecked exceptions can also make use of ***throws*** to defer handling of the exception…or you can handle them at any level in the calling chain with ***try***, ***catch***, and ***finally***. Unchecked exceptions need not be handled at all. You can just let the program terminate (crash) immediately upon detection of such an error.

Catching exceptions…(referred to above as "handling" the exception):

```
public class MyClass
{
        public void myMethod(double d)
        {
                …some code in which you are not
                     worried about an exception occurring….

                try  //if error occurs, rest of code doesn't execute...jumps to
                     //appropriate catch
                {
                        …some code where you might expect an exception…
                     String s = in.nextLine( );      //might produce an IOException
                     int x = Integer.parseInt(s);  //bad s might produce a
                                                   // NumberFormatException
                        …more code …
                }

                catch (IOException e)
                {
                        System.out.println("Input/output error " + e);
                        // Continues execution after last catch below.
                }

                catch (NumberFormatException e)
                {
                        System.out.println("Input was not a num " + e);
                        // Continues execution immediately after this catch.
                }

                …code execution continues here after try block is finished…or, if an
                exception occurs, execution continues here after catch block finishes…

        }
}
```

Usage of the *finally* block: (this block is optional)

```
try
{ … }

catch( … )
{ … }

finally
{
        …This block of code is guaranteed to execute, regardless of whether there was
        an exception or not. …This is typically used to release resources, such as
        closing a file or releasing a network connection. If an exception occurs in the try
        block and none of the catch statements are appropriate to handle the exception,
        control passes to this finally block and the code here executes… then the
        exception is actually thrown and passed up the calling chain where we can
        attempt to catch it.

        Even if a catch block throws an exception of its own, control is still passed to the
        finally block.
}
```

Designing your own Exception Types:

```
if (amount > balance)
{
        GoofyException e = new GoofyException( "You made a dumb mistake!");
        throw e;
}


public class GoofyException extends RunTimeException
{
        public GoofyException( )  // It is customary to provide a default constructor,
        {                         // even if empty.
        }

        public GoofyException(String reason)  //Your own constructor
        {
                super(reason);
        }
}
```

Some unusual facts concerning exceptions:

1. If you use the following two *catch* statements, they must go in the order shown…subclass on the top, superclass on the bottom. (Note that *FileNotFound* is a subclass of *IOException*)

```
catch(FileNotFoundException e)
{
   System.out.println("FileNotFound");
}

catch(IOException e)
{
   System.out.println("IOException");
}
```

In this particular case, if the *try* block generated a *FileNotFoundException*, only "FileNotFound" would be printed. The second *catch* would be ignored.

2. If you have a method that throws an *IOException* up to the next level in the calling chain, we should be aware that in addition to *IOException* being thrown to the next level, all its subclasses are also thrown to the next level in the chain.

3. If you put a *try* inside a block of code (such as those belonging to loops and *if* statements), then the corresponding *catch* statements must also reside in that same block.

Exercise for Lesson 37

1. Rewrite the method below so as to consolidate the two error messages (that signal violation of preconditions) into a <u>single</u> error message.

```
/*
 * precondition: amount <= balance
 * precondition: amount > 0
 */
public void withdraw(double amount)
{
        if (amount > balance)
        {
                String s = "Can't withdraw more than the balance.";
                IllegalArgumentException e = new IllegalArgumentException(s);
                throw e;  //Presents the s message and the entire program stops
        }

        if (amount <= 0)
        {
                String s = "Withdrawal amount must be greater than 0.";
                IllegalArgumentException e = new IllegalArgumentException(s);
                throw e;  //Presents the s message and the entire program stops
        }
        . . . remainder of code for this method. . .
}
```

2. Write a method called *setStudentScore( )*. Its signature is:

```
public void setStudentScore(int score)
```

You need not worry about the bulk of the code inside this method. Establish some preconditions on the score parameter and detail those preconditions in rems up above the signature. Then, just inside the code body, throw an *IllegalArgumentException* if the preconditions are not met.

3. In Java we don't say, "The program generated an error"; rather, we say what?

4. What are the two types of exceptions?

5. Which type of exception requires being handled?

6. What are the two ways to handle checked exceptions?

7. Is it permissible for unchecked exceptions to be handled with *throws* or with *try-catch*?

8. Give an example of a checked exception and what conditions might cause it.

9. Give an example of a unchecked exception and what conditions might cause it.

10. Modify the following method, so that if an *ArithmeticException* occurs, the actual handling of that exception with *try-catch* is deferred one layer up the calling chain.

```
public String car(int xs)
{
    ...some code that might produce an ArithmeticException...
}
```

11. Modify the following method, so that if an *ArithmeticException* occurs, the handling of that exception with *try-catch* is handled in this method.

```
public String car(int xs)
{

        ...some code that might produce an ArithmeticException...

}
```

12. Create your own exception type by creating a class called *StuffyException*.

13. Write code that will use the above *StuffyException* class by creating an object with it. Specify the error "announcement" with "Hey, you messed up" and then throw the exception.

Exceptions … Contest Type Problems

<table>
<tr><td>1. What is output by the code to the right on the input below?

big mamma
2

A. mamma B. big mamma C. g
D. i E. big mamma2

2. What is output by the code to the right on the input below?

big mamma
22

A. b B. Error: 22 C. a
D. Nothing E. None of these</td><td><pre>
//Assume nextLine( ) and nextInt( ) are static methods in
//a class named Scanner that reads a String and an integer
//from the keyboard.

Scanner rdr = new Scanner(System.in);
String str = rdr.nextLine( );
int j = rdr.nextInt( );

try
{
        System.out.print(str.charAt(j));
}

catch(StringIndexOutOfBoundsException e)
{
        System.out.print("Error: " + j);
}
</pre></td></tr>
<tr><td>3. Which of the following replaces <*1> in the code to the right to make it do what the remarks suggest?

A. prd = 1;
B. return 1;
C. System.exit( );
D. No code is needed
E. None of these

4. Assume <*1> has been filled in correctly. What is returned by product("two", "5")?

A. 10
B. 5
C. 1
D. 2
E. None of these</td><td><pre>
//Returns the product of two integers represented as
//strings. If either string is not a number, returns the other
//number. If both are not numbers, returns 1.

public static int product(String str1, String str2) {
    int prd = 1;
    try {
        prd*=Integer.parseInt(str1);
    }
    catch(NumberFormatException) {
        <*1>
    }

    try {
        prd*=Integer.parseInt(str2);
    }
    catch(NumberFormatException) {
        <*1>
    }
    return prd;
}
</pre></td></tr>
<tr><td>5. What is output by the code to the right if the static method called test( ) encounters the following line of code? Assume the test signature includes throws NumberFormatException.

int j = Integer.parseInt("Two Thousand");

A. Nothing
B. Error with number format Error
C. Error with number format
D. Error
E. None of these</td><td><pre>
try{
    test( );
}

catch(NumberFormatException e)
{
    System.out.println("Error with number format");
}

catch(RuntimeException e)
{
    System.out.println("Error");
}
</pre></td></tr>
</table>

6. If the code designated by **<*1>** to the right does not throw any exceptions, which of the remaining code sections will execute?

   A. <***2**>
   B. <***2**> and <***3**>(if no errors in <***2**>)
   C. <***3**>
   D. <***2**> and <***3**>
   E. None of these

```
try {
    <*1>
}

catch(RunTimeException e) {
    <*2>
}

finally {
    <*3>
}
```

7. What exceptions thrown by method *mental()* are passed up the calling chain?

   A. All exceptions
   B. IOException
   C. IOException, its subclasses, and unchecked exceptions
   D. IOException and its subclasses
   E. None of these

```
public static void mental( ) throws IOException {
    // code not shown
}
```

8. Suppose the *main* method does not include a *try* or *catch*. Futhermore, the code which inputs disk values may throw an *IOException*. Which of these should replace **<*1>** in the code to the right?

   A. throws IOException
   B. throw IOException
   C. throws new IOException
   D. extends IOException
   E. None of these

```
public static void main(String[] args) <*1>
{
    // input some values from disk
}
```

9. Which of these is not a keyword in Java?

   A. short   B. continue   C. finally   D. final   E. None of these

Project… Keep Trying

Create a new project called *ExceptionsProjects* that will contain two classes, *Tester* and *FileInput*. Create the *FileInput* class by modifying your *BaseClass* (see Lesson 27) project as follows:

```
import java.io.*; //necessary for File and IOException
import java.util.*; //necessary for Scanner
public class FileInput
{
        public static void readTheFile(String fileName) throws IOException
        {
           Scanner sf = new Scanner(new File("C:\\temp_Name\\" + filename));

           int maxIndx = -1; //-1 so when we increment below, the first index is 0
           String text[] = new String[100]; //declare more than we need

           while(sf.hasNext( ))
           {
                maxIndx++;
                text[maxIndx] = sf.nextLine( );
           }
           //maxIndx is now the highest index of text[], = -1 if no lines of text.
           sf.close( ); //we opened file so we must close it

           for (int j = 0; j <= maxIndx; j++)
           {
              System.out.println(text[j]);
           }
        }
}
```

Now create a *Tester* class with a *main* method in which you repeatedly loop while inputting a file name from the keyboard. Also, inside the loop call the *readTheFile* method of the *FileInput* class and pass the file name input from the keyboard as a parameter. Set up a *try-catch* pair in *main* so as to keep looping if *readTheFile* passes an *IOException* up the calling chain. If everything in *readTheFile* completes successfully, then in *main* release from the loop and output "It worked."

Provide for an escape from the loop by informing the user that he can enter the word "exit". This should provide a release from the loop and print "It did not work".

Lesson 38…..Interfaces

There are basically two viewpoints when considering interfaces in Java:

The implementation viewpoint:

Consider the following superclass:

```
public abstract class Parent
{
        public abstract void method1( );
        public abstract void method2( );
        public abstract int method3(double d);
}
```

…and now the subclass:

```
public class Child extends Parent
{
        public void method1( )
        {    //some code…}

        public void method2( )
        {    //some code…}

        public int method3(double c )
        {    //some code…}

        public int statevar1;
}
```

****

Notice that the above superclass does **absolutely nothing**. All methods there are abstract. Also, there are **no** state variables. All it does is force us to implement its methods in the subclass. If this is all a particular superclass does, then it could be equivalently replaced with an **interface**. Alter the *Parent* class by converting it to an interface as follows:

```
public interface Parent
{
        void method1( );  //notice the semicolons at the ends of these signatures
        void method2( );
        int method3(double d);
}
```

Notice that with the methods above it would be legal to start their signatures with ***public abstract***; however, even if we leave them off, they are automatically *public* and *abstract*…all because this is an **interface**. It is conventional in interfaces **not** to use *public* and *abstract* in the signatures.

Now adjust the subclass as follows:

```
public class Child implements Parent
{
        public void method1( )
        {   //some code…}

        public void method2( )
        {   //some code…}

        public int method3(double c )
        {   //some code…}

        … some other methods…

        public int statevar1;
}
```

Notice that all the interface does here is to **force** us to implement those methods in the subclass…..**big deal**. (Actually it's a very big deal. Take a look at a short essay presented in Appendix L for four compelling reasons to use interfaces.) The *Child* class above will **refuse to compile** until **all** methods in the *Parent* interface have been implemented in *Child.*

The object viewpoint:

Expect to eventually make an **object** out of the following interface…you probably thought we could only make objects out of classes! This interface describes some of the methods found in a robot related class. As with the previous viewpoint on interfaces, this one will also force other classes implementing *RobotArm* to provide code for each of these methods (i.e. to implement the methods):

```
public interface RobotArm
{
        void moveUp( double rate, double howFar );
        void moveDown( double rate, double howFar );
        void twistLeft(double deg);
        void twistRight(double deg);
}
```

What we really want to look at here is how the *Robot* interface provides the "glue" that holds together several **cooperating classes**, specifically two different industrial robots supplied by two different robot manufacturers. They are the Lexmar 234 and the General Robotics 56A.

Let's suppose we have two classes (*Lexmar234* and *GR56A*) that each implement *RobotArm*:

```
//The implemented methods give detailed instructions on how to manipulate the
//"arm" of this particular robot.
public class Lexmar234 implements RobotArm
```

```
{
        public Lexmar234( ) { Constructor}
        public void moveUp(double rate, double howFar) {     //some code       }
        public void moveDown(double rate, double howFar) {   //some code       }
        public void twistLeft(double deg) {      //some code        }
        public void twistRight(double deg) {     //some code        }
}

public class GR56A implements RobotArm
{
        public GR56A( ) { Constructor}
        public void moveUp(double rate, double howFar) { //some code, different
                                                                 from above  }
        public void moveDown(double rate, double howFar) {//some code,
                                                              different from above}
        public void twistLeft(double deg) { //some code, different from above }
        public void twistRight(double deg) { //some code, different from above }
}
```

So far, this is no different from the **implementation** viewpoint we previously discussed. In other words, the interface forces us to write code for those methods in classes where we specifically say *implements RobotArm*.

Now let's find out what's different about the **object** viewpoint of interfaces. We will look at a *Tester* class with a *main* method in which we will **create objects** from the *RobotArm* interface.

```
public class Tester
{
        public static void main(String[] args)
        {
                RobotArm lx = new Lexmar234( );
                RobotArm gr = new GR56A( );

                // Do something with the Lexmar robot
                lx.moveDown(3, 27.87);
                lx.twistRight(22.0);

                // Do something with General Robotics machine
                gr.moveUp(16.1, -23.19);
                gr.twistLeft(18);
        }
}
```

It is significant that nowhere in the above class did we say *implements* in the code. Also, notice, for example, that when we declare

```
RobotArm lx = new Lexmar234( );
```

that ***lx* is of type *RobotArm*** even though *RobotArm* is not a class; it's just an interface! This is specified by the **left side** of the above statement, and it means that *lx* can **only** use methods given in the *RobotArm* interface. The object *lx* will use these methods as **implemented in the *Lexmar234* class**. Notice this is specified on the **right side** of the above statement.

Important generalization:

All this brings us to an important generalization about classes and interfaces as illustrated in Fig 38-1.

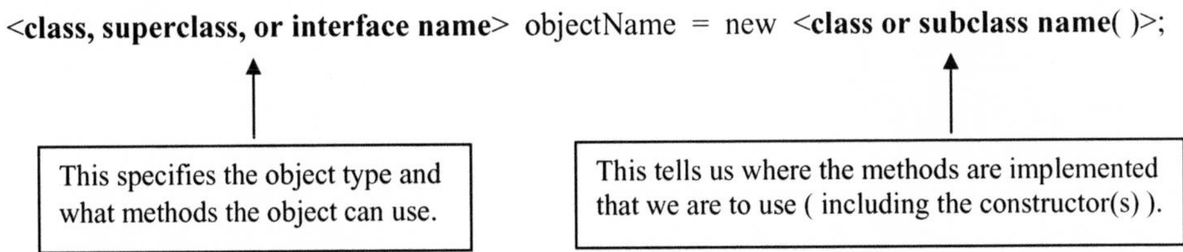
<**class, superclass, or interface name**> objectName = new <**class or subclass name( )**>;
This specifies the object type and what methods the object can use.
This tells us where the methods are implemented that we are to use (including the constructor(s)).

Fig. 38-1 Determining object type, legal methods, and where the methods are implemented.

Miscellaneous facts concerning interfaces and implementations:

1. *instanceof* as applied to the example on the previous page:

    (gr instanceof RobotArm) returns a *true*, and

    (gr instanceof GR56A) also returns a *true*.

    Notice that the syntax is *anObject instanceof ClassOrInterface* and that it returns a *boolean*.

2. **Polymorphism** is the property of being able to have methods **named the same**, while having possibly **different implementations**. For example, *twistLeft* is a method in **both** the *Lexmar234* and *GR56A* classes above, yet the implementations would likely be radically different because the two different manufacturers of these robots probably control their machines differently.

3. Saying that a class **realizes** an interface is the same as saying that it *implements* that interface.

4. It is possible to simultaneously extend another class and implement an interface. It is possible for a particular class to only extend a **single** class, however it can implement as many interfaces as desired. Below, we show the *Redwood* class extending the *Tree* class and implementing both the *Limb* and *Leaf* interfaces.

```
public class Redwood extends Tree implements Limb, Leaf
{
        //code not shown
}
```

    Notice that when simultaneously extending and implementing, ***extends*** **must come first**.

Exercise for Lesson 38

```
public interface Sports
{
        void method1( );
        void method2( );
        int method3(double d);
}

public class Baseball implements Sports
{
        public Baseball( )
        {     . . .   }

        public void method1( )
        {   //some code...}

        public void method2( )
        {   //some code...}

        public int method3(double c )
        {   //some code...}

        public int statevar1;
}


public class Football implements Sports
{
        public Football( )
        {     . . .   }
        public void method1( )
        {   //some code...}

        public void method2( )
        {   //some code...}

        public int method3(double c )
        {   //some code...}

        public int statevar1;
}

public class Tester
{
        public static void main(String[] args)
        {
                Sports x = new Baseball( );
                Sports y = new Football( );
```

```
            x.method2( );
            y.method2( );

            . . . more code . . .
        }
    }
```

Use the above code in the following questions:
****

1. Which methods, if any, in the *Sports* interface are abstract?

2. public class Hockey implements Sports
```
{
    //What methods, if any, must we implement here?
}
```

3. Look at the classes *Baseball* and *Football*. Both implement *method1*. Do both implementations have to have identical code? If so, why?

4. In the "more code" section of *Tester* what would the following return?

   (x instanceof Sports)

5. In the "more code" section of *Tester* what would the following return?

   (y instanceof Football)

6. The property of two classes being able to have methods of the same name (but with possibly different implementations) is known as ______________.

7. Modify the following class so that it will simultaneously inherit the *Red* class and implement both the *Eagle* and *Bobcat* interfaces.

```
public class Austria
{
    . . .
}
```

Interfaces…Contest Type Problems

1. What replaces **<*1>** so that *VectorManip* simultaneously implements the *Vector* interface and inherits the *Tensor* class?

   A. implements Vector extends Tensor
   B. implements Tensor extends Vector
   C. extends Tensor implements Vector
   D. extends Vector implements Tensor
   E. None of these

2. Assuming **<*1>** has been filled in correctly, which of the following is of correct syntax and is *true* if the object *vm* is created by:

   VectorManip vm = new VectorManip(b);

   A. vm instanceof VectorManip
   B. vm instanceof Vector
   C. VectorManip instanceof vm
   D. Vector instanceof vm
   E. More than one of these

3. Assuming **<*1>** has been filled in correctly, which of the following is *true* if *v1* is created by:

   Vector v1 = new VectorManip(b);

   A. *v1* can use all the methods in the *VectorManip* class
   B. The syntax is incorrect
   C. *v1* is a *VectorManip* object
   D. *v1* is a *Vector* object
   E. None of these

4. Assuming **<*1>** has been filled in correctly, which of the following is *true* if the *crossProduct* method is omitted from the *VectorManip* class?

   A. *VectorManip* won't compile
   B. Omitting *crossProduct* is completely legal
   C. Omitting *crossProduct* would be completely legal if *VectorManip* did not implement *Vector*
   D. Both A and C
   E. None of these

```
public interface Vector
{
        double dotProduct(double b[]);
        double[] crossProduct(double b[]);
        double absoluteValue(double b[]);
}

public class VectorManip <*1>
{
        public VectorManip(double v[])
        {
                iComp = v[0];
                jComp = v[1];
                kComp = v[2];
        }

        public double dotProduct(double b[])
        {   …code not shown …   }

        public double[] crossProduct(double b[])
        {   …code not shown …   }

        public double absoluteValue(double b[])
        {   …code not shown …   }

        public double[] sum(double b[])
        {   …code not shown …   }

        private double iComp;
        private double jComp;
        private double kComp;
}
```

5. Saying that *Jackson* realizes the *President* interface is the same as saying which of the following?

   A. *Jackson* inherits *President*
   B. *Jackson* implements *President*
   C. *President* extends *Jackson*
   D. *President* implements *Jackson*
   E. None of these

Project… Linear Function

You are a software engineer with the Blue Pelican Engineering Corporation. Your immediate supervisor has need of a class called *LinearFunction* and she knows exactly the methods that it needs to include. Not having time to write it herself, she assigns the job to you. To insure that you produce exactly the methods she wants, she is providing the interface below and requiring that you implement this interface in the *LinearFunction* class you produce. When your project is complete, she will simply look at your class signature and if she sees *implements LinearFunctionMethods*, she will know for certain that you have implemented all the methods she originally specified in the interface; otherwise, your code would not compile.

```
public interface LinearFunctionMethods
{
    double getSlope( );
    double getYintercept( );
    double getRoot( );

    double getYvalue(double x);  //return the y value corresponding to x
    double getXvalue(double y);  //return the x value corresponding to y
}
```

For simplicity we will assume that the linear function's graph can never be vertical or horizontal. (This eliminates some complications with the math). In writing your methods, simply recall the $y = mx + b$ portion of your algebra studies. The constructor of your class should allow you to pass the slope (m) and y-intercept(b) of the *LinearFunction* object you are instantiating.

****

Test your *LinearFunction* class with the *Tester* class below:

```
import java.io.*;
import java.util.*;
public class Tester
{
    public static void main(String args[])
    {
        Scanner kbReader = new Scanner(System.in);

        System.out.print("What is the slope of your line? ");
        double slope = kbReader.nextDouble(System.in);

        System.out.print("What is the y-intercept of your line? ");
        double yIntc = kbReader.nextDouble( );

        LinearFunction line = new LinearFunction(slope, yIntc);

        System.out.println("\nSlope of this line is: " + line.getSlope( ));

        System.out.println("Y-intercept of this line is: " + line.getYintercept( ));
```

```
        System.out.println("Root of this line is: " + line.getRoot( ));

        System.out.print("\nWhat is an x value for which you wish to solve for y? ");
        double x = kbReader.nextDouble( );
        double yValue = line.getYvalue(x);
        System.out.println("The y value corresponding to x = " + x + " is " + yValue);

        System.out.print("\nWhat is a y value for which you wish to solve for x? ");
        double y = kbReader.nextDouble( );
        double xValue = line.getXvalue(y);
        System.out.println("The x value corresponding to y = " + y + " is " + xValue);
    }
}
```

Below is a typical run:

```
What is the slope of your line? -3
What is the y-intercept of your line? 2.5

Slope of this line is: -3.0
Y-intercept of this line is: 2.5
Root of this line is: 0.8333333134651184

What is an x value for which you wish to solve for y? -4.61
The y value corresponding to x = -4.610000133514404 is 16.329999923706055

What is a y value for which you wish to solve for x? 5.0
The x value corresponding to y = 5.0 is -0.833333313465118
```

This completes our study of interfaces. At this point many students often complain that they "just don't see why we need interfaces." If this is the case with you, please read the essay presented in Appendix L and you should come away convinced of the usefulness of interfaces.

Lesson 39….. Complexity Analysis (Big O)

Two types of complexity analysis:

Complexity analysis takes two forms. One form analyzes **how many steps** an algorithm takes to run… ultimately this means the **time that it takes to run**. The other type of complexity analysis has to do with how much space (in bytes) it takes to run the algorithm. With memory so abundant and inexpensive today, space analysis is not as important as it once was. We will confine our studies here to the time-analysis variety.

Introducing Big O:

Consider the following algorithm:

```
for(int j = 0; j < n; j++)
{…some code, no loops  }
```

How many times do we go through the loop? The answer is *n*, of course, so we say that the time complexity is **of the order of n**. A short-hand equivalent is written as **O(n)**. This is known as **Big O** notation. Another valuable way to look at this is that the time it takes to run this algorithm is approximately proportional to *n*. The larger *n* is, the better the approximation. This is true of all Big O values.

A variety of Big O problems:

Now, let's look at some other specific examples and obtain Big O values for each.

Example 1:

```
for(j = 0; j < n; j++)
{
    for(k = 0; k < n; k++)
    {  …some code… }
}
```

We go through the outer loop n times and for each of these iterations we go through the inner loop n times. The code designated as "…some code…" is executed n^2 times so we assign a Big O value of $\mathbf{O(n^2)}$ to this algorithm.

Example 2:

```
for(j = 0; j < (n +50); j++)
{
    for(k = 0; k < n; k++)
    {  …some code… }
}
```

We go through the outer loop n + 50 times and for each of these iterations we go through the inner loop n times. The code designated as "…some code…" is therefore executed

$(n + 50)n = n^2 + 50n$ times. Recalling that Big O notation is an approximation for only very large n, we realize that 50n pales in comparison to n^2 so we **keep only the part with the highest exponent**. Finally, we assign a Big O value of $\mathbf{O(n^2)}$ to this algorithm.

Example 3:

```
for(j = 0; j < n ; j++)
```

```
{
    for(k = 0; k < (22 * n); k++)
    { ...some code... }
}
```

We go through the outer loop *n* times and for each of these iterations we go through the inner loop 22n times. The code designated as "...some code..." is therefore executed $n(22n) = 22n^2$ times. In Big O notation we ignore all coefficients, no matter their size, and assign a Big O value of $\mathbf{O(n^2)}$ to this algorithm.

Example 4...Suppose by a time complexity analysis, we obtain $(3/5)n^3 + 15n^2 + (1/2)n + 5$, the corresponding Big O value would just simply be $\mathbf{O(n^3)}$, since we **ignore all coefficients and use only the term with the highest exponent**.

Example 5:

```
public static int[] addStuff(int x[][])
{
        int row, col;
        int b[] = new int[x.length];
            for(row =0; row < x.length; row++)
            {
                    for(col= 0; col < x[row].length; col++)
                {
                            b[row]  += x[row][col];
                }
            }
            return b;
}
```

Yes, this one is a bit more complicated than the previous ones. Let's assume we call this method with the following code:

```
int dfg[][] = {  {1,2,...},
                 {0,4,...},
                   ...      }; //Assume this array has r rows and c columns for a
int newArray[] = addStuff(dfg);                        //total of rc = n elements
```

Studying the *addStuff* method, we note that we go through the outer loop *x.length* times which is the number of rows, *r*. For the inner loop we go through *x[row].length* which is the number of columns, *c*. Therefore, the total number of times through the code in the inner loop is *rc*, which in turn is just the number of elements in the entire matrix, *n*. We can write the Big O value as either **O(rc)** or **O(n)**.

Example 6:

```
for(j = 0; j < n; j+=5)
    for(k =1; k < n; k*=3)
    { ...some code... }
```

We go through the outer loop (1 / 5)n times and $\log_3(n)$ times through the inner loop for a total of $(1 / 5)n \log_3(n)$. The final Big O value is **O(n log(n))**. Notice that we have dropped the coefficient of 1 / 5 as is the custom with Big O. Also, we have dropped the base 3 on the log since all logs of the same quantity (but with various bases) differ from each other only by a mulplicative constant.

Example 7:

```
m = -9;
for(j = 0; j < n; j+=5)
{
    ... some code ...
        if (j < m)
        {
                for(k =0; k < n; k*=3)
                {... some code...}
        }
}
```

We go through the outer loop n/5 times and because *j* will never be less than *m*, we never go through the inner loop. Thus the Big O value is **O(n)**.

Example 8:

```
for(j = 0;  j < n; j++)
{
    for(k = j; k < n; k++)
    {  ...some code...  }
}
```

On the first iteration of the outer loop, the inner loop iterates *n* times. On the second iteration of the outer loop, the inner loop iterates n – 1 times. On the third iteration of the outer loop, the inner loop iterates n - 2 times. This continues until the last iteration of the outer loop results in n – (n –1) iterations of the inner loop. Adding these we get

$n + (n - 1) + (n - 2) + \ldots + (n - (n - 1))$

Since the outer loop iterated *n* times we know there are *n* terms here. Simplifying, we get $n(n - 1) + \text{constant} = n^2 - n + \text{constant}$. The Big O value is therefore $\mathbf{O(n^2)}$.

Example 9:... Consider a **sequential search** (sometimes called a **linear search**) through an unordered list looking for a particular item. On the average we will need to search halfway through before we find the item. So, on the average, the Big O value should be O(n /2). Again, we drop the coefficient and get **O(n)**.

Example 10:... Consider a **binary search** on an ordered list. In fact, a binary search can only be done on an **ordered** list since this type of search works as follows. In the beginning we go halfway down the ordered list and ask, "Is this the item? If not, is the item above or below this point?" Then we take that indicated half of the list and cut it in half. The process repeats until we eventually find the item. Since we repeatedly cut the list by a factor of two, the run time is proportional to $\log_2(n)$ when n is the number of elements in the original list. We drop the base and write O (log(n)).

Example 11:... When we have just a simple block of code with no repetition, the Big O value is O(1). Consider the following block of code that yields a Big O value of **O(1)**:

```
x = 3 * Math.pow(p,2.1);
y = 46.1 * q/2.3;
d = Math.sqrt(Math.pow((x –x1),2) + Math.pow((y –x1),2));
```

Calculating run times:

Example 1:

Suppose a certain algorithm has a Big O value of $O(n^2)$ and that when n = 1000 the run time is 19 sec. What will be he run time if n = 10,000?

We set up a proportion as follows:

$$1000^2 / 19 = 10000^2 / T$$

$$(10^3)^2 / 19 = (10^4)^2 / T$$

$$10^6 / 19 = 10^8 / T \text{, cross multiply to get}$$
$$T(10^6) = 19(10^8)$$
$$T = 1900$$

Example 2:

Sometimes questions are worded such that we are looking for a ratio as in this problem. …Suppose a certain algorithm has a Big O value of $O(n^3)$. How many times slower is this algorithm when n = 1500 as compared to n = 500?

We set up a proportion as follows:

$500^3 / T_1 = 1500^3 / T_2$, cross multiply and rearrange things so as to solve for the ratio T_2 / T_1

$$T_2 / T_1 = 1500^3 / 500^3$$
$$T_2 / T_1 = (1500 / 500)^3$$
$$T_2 / T_1 = (3)^3$$
$T_2 / T_1 = 27$, so the answer is that it's 27 times slower.

Example 3:

Consider the following table in which the number of times that a block of code executes is contrasted with the time it takes to run.

Number (n) of times to execute a block of code	Time(sec)
500	3
1000	24
1500	81

Table 39-1

What Big O value is represented by the data in this table?

When *n* doubles (going from 500 to 1000) the time is multiplied by 8. Since 2^3 is eight we conclude that the Big O value should be n^3. This is consistent with a comparison of the first and last rows of the table above. There, we notice that in tripling *n* when moving from an *n* value of 500 to 1500, that the time is multiplied by 27 (3 * 27 = 81). Since 3^3 is 27, we are, once again, led to n^3.

From fastest to slowest:

In summary, we will state what should be obvious by now. We will list in order, Big O values with the most efficient time-wise (fastest) at the top and the slowest at the bottom.

O(log n)
O(n)
O(n log n)
$O(n^2)$
$O(n^3)$
$O(2^n)$

Using graphs to compare Big O values:

Let's compare just two of the Big O values above so we can get a sense of why one is better than the other. In Fig. 39-1 below we will compare O(log n) and O(n).

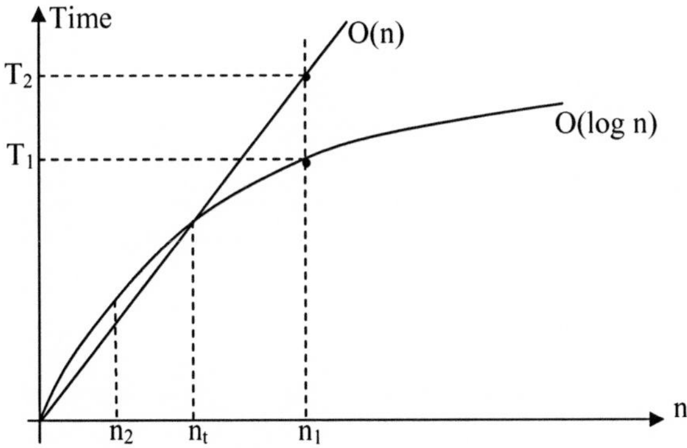

Fig 39-1 Comparison of O(n) and O(log n)

For a particular value of *n* (*n1*, for example) notice that O(log n) gives a corresponding run time of T_1 while n_1 corresponds to T_2 on the O(n) curve. A smaller run time is desired, so the O(log n) curve is superior for n_1 (and all values of *n* higher than n_t).

Beware of false statements:

When comparing Big O values, we must be careful in assuming something like the following:

> An algorithm with a Big O value of O(log n) will **always** be faster than one with a Big O value of O(n).

This is generally a **false** statement. For **some** values of *n* (large ones) O(log n) **will**, indeed, be faster than O(n); however, we do not generally know this "transition" n_t value. For Fig 39-1 above this "transition" n_t value occurs at the intersection point of the curves. You would need to know specific details of each to know which is faster for any particular value of *n*. It is interesting to note that for the *n* value of n_2 in the drawing above, that the O(n) curve actually represents the fastest time.

The moral of all this is that Big O values are generally only valid for **large values of *n***.

Exercise on Lesson 39

1. What is the Big O value for a sequential search on an unordered list?

2. What requirement must we impose on a list before we can apply a binary search to it?

3. What is the time complexity order of a binary search on an ordered list?

4. Suppose an algorithm with a Big O value of $O(n^2)$ has a runtime of 20 sec for n = 5000. What will be the runtime for n = 1000?

5.
```
for(j = 0;j < n + 5; j++)
{
        ...some code...
}
```
What is the Big O value?

6.
```
for(j = 0;j < n + 5; j++)
        for(k = 0; k < n; n+=8)
                for(z = 0; z <= (n*n); z++)
                {   ...some code...   }
```
What is the Big O value?

7.
```
for(j = 0;j < n - 5; j++)
{
        for(k = 0; k < 7; k++)
        {   ...some code...   }
}
```
What is the Big O value?

8.
```
for(j = 2; j < n + 5; j*=7)
{
        ...some code...
}
```
What is the Big O value?

9. There are two types of complexity analysis. What two things can be analyzed?

10. Which of these two types does Big O address?

11. Suppose a time complexity analysis yields $5000n^2 + (1/1000)\ n^3 + n - 2$. What would be the Big O value?

12. Will a O(n) algorithm generally always win in a time-race over a $O(n^3)$ algorithm?

13. Which is generally the fastest, O(log n) or $O(2^n)$?

14. An algorithm has a time complexity of the order 2^n. How many times more slowly would this algorithm run when n= 200, as compared to n = 100?

15.
```
for(j = 0 ;j < n - 5; j++)
{
        for(k = 0; k < n; k++)
        {  ...some code...  }
}
```
What is the Big O value?

16.
```
for(j = 0 ;j < n; j++)
{
        for(k = j; k < n; k++)
        {  ...some code...  }
}
```
What is the Big O value?

17. From the following table, determine the time complexity of the algorithm.

Number of times to execute a block of code	Time(sec)
1000	5
2000	20
4000	80

18. From the following table, determine the time complexity of the algorithm.

Number of times to execute a block of code	Time(sec)
1000	5
2000	10
6000	30

Big O… Contest Type Problems

1. Which of the following would generally indicate the fastest algorithm for large *n*?

A. O(n^2) B. O(n log n) C. O(n) D. O(log n) E. Need more info

2. What is the order of the time complexity of calling the method, *doIt(tam)*. Assume that *tam* is a *double* array with *m* rows.

A. O(m)
B. O(m^2)
C. O(log m)
D. O(sum + m)
E. None of these

```
public double doIt(double vc[])
{
    int k = vc[0];
    int sum = 0;
    for(int p=0; p<vc.length; p++)
        for(q=0; q<vc.length; q++, k--)
        {
            sum+= k + vc[q] + p;
        }
    return sum;
}
```

3. For the algorithm represented in the table to the right, what would be the corresponding Big O value?

A. O(n)
B. O(n^2)
C. O(n^3)
D. O(log n)
E. None of these

Number of times to execute a block of code	Time required to run (sec)
1000	2
2000	16
3000	54

4. Which of the following most closely represents the time order complexity of the following call to method to the right? (Assume all rows have equal length in the *gryLion* array.)

```
...
m = gryLion.length;
n = gryLion[0].length;
int apro[] = pooch(gryLion);
```

A. O(mn)
B. O(m^2)
C. O(n^2)
D. O(m^2n^2)
E. None of these

```
public static int[] pooch(int zzTop[][])
{
    int row, col;
    int barb[] = new int[zzTop.length];
    for(k =0; k < zzTop.length; k++)
    {
        for(j=0; j < zzTop[k].length; j++)
        {
            barb[k]  += k * k + xxTop[k][j];
        }
    }
    return barb;
}
```

5. What is the Big O value for the code to the right?

A. O(n/2 log d)
B. O(log (nd))
C. O(d log n)
D. O(n log d)
E. None of these

```
for(j = 0; j < n; j+=2)
    for(k =0; k < d; k = k * 8)
        { ...some code... }
```

Lesson 40… Recursion

What is recursion?

Software **recursion**, very simply, is the **process of a method calling itself**. This at first seems very baffling…somewhat like a snake swallowing its own tail. Would the snake eventually disappear?

The classical factorial problem:

We will begin with the classical problem of finding the factorial of a number. First, let us define what is meant by "factorial". Three factorial is written as 3!, Four factorial is written as 4!, etc. But what, exactly, do they mean? Actually, the meaning is quite simple as the following demonstrates:

3! = 3 * 2 * 1 = 6
4! = 4 * 3 * 2 * 1 = 24

The only weird thing about factorials is that we define 0! = 1. There is nothing to "understand" about 0! = 1. It's a definition, so just accept it.

Here is an iterative approach to calculating 4!.

```
int answer = 1;
for(int j = 1; j <= 4; j++)
{
        answer = answer * j;
}
System.out.println(answer);  //24
```

Before we present the recursive way of calculating a factorial, we need to understand one more thing about factorials. Consider 6!.

6! = 6 * 5 * 4 * 3 * 2 * 1 = 6 * (5 * 4 * 3 * 2 * 1)

We recognize that the parenthesis could be rewritten as 5!, so 6! could be rewritten as

6! = 6 * (5!)

In general we can write n! = n(n –1)!. It is this formula that we will use in our recursive code as follows:

```
public static int factorial(int n)
{
        if(n = = 1)
        {     return 1;   }
        else
        {     return n * factorial(n – 1);  //notice we call factorial here    }
}
```

Call this code with System.out.println(factorial(4)); //**24**

What really happens when the method calls itself? To understand this, we should pretend there are several copies of the *factorial* method. If it helps, you can think of the next one that is called as being named *factorial1*, and the next *factorial2*, etc. Actually, we need not pretend. This is very close to what really takes place. Analyzing the problem in this way, the last *factorial* method in this "chain" returns 1. The next to the last one returns 2, the next 3, and finally 4. These are all multiplied so the answer is 1 * 2 * 3 * 4 = 24.

Short cuts:

Let's look at some recursion examples using short cuts. For each problem, see if you can understand the pattern of how the answer (in bold print) was obtained.

1. System.out.println(adder(7)); // **46**

```
public static int adder(int n)
{
        if (n<=0)
                return 30;
        else
                return n + adder(n-2);
}
```

On the first call to *adder*, *n* is 7, and on the second call it's 5 (7 - 2), etc. Notice that in the *return* portion of the code that each *n* is **added** to the next one in the sequence of calls to *adder*. Finally, when the *n* parameter coming into *adder* gets to 0 or less, the returned value is 30. Thus, we have:

7 + 5 + 3 + 1 + 30 = 46

2. System.out.println(nertz(5)); // **120**

```
public static int nertz(int n)
{
        if (n = = 1)
                return 1;
        else
                return n * nertz(n-1);
}
```

On the first call to *nertz*, *n* is 5, and on the second call it's 4 (obtained with 5 - 1), etc. Notice that in the *return* portion of the code that each *n* is **multiplied** times the next one in the sequence of calls to *nertz*. Finally, when the *n* parameter coming into *adder* gets to 1, the returned value is 1. Thus, we have:

5 * 4 * 3 * 2 * 1 = 120

3. System.out.println(nrd(0)); // **25**

```
public static int nrd(int n)
{
        if (n > 6)
                return n - 3;
        else
                return n + nrd(n +1);
}
```

On the first call to *nrd*, *n* is 0, and on the second call it's 1 (obtained with 0 + 1), etc. Notice that in the *return* portion of the code that each *n* is **added** to the next one in the sequence of calls to *nrd*. Finally, when the *n* parameter coming into *adder* gets above 6, the returned value is n – 3 (obtained with 7 – 3 = 4). Thus, we have:

0 + 1 + 2 + 3 + 4 + 5 + 6 + 4 = 25

4. System.out.println(festus(0)); // **12**

```
public static int festus(int n)
{
        if (n > 6)
                return n - 3;
        else
        {
                n = n * 2;
                return n + festus(n + 1);
        }
}
```

On the first call to *festus*, *n* is 0 (and is modified to 0*2 = 0), and on the second call it's 1 (0 + 1 = 1, but quickly modified to 1 * 2 = 2), etc. Notice that in the *return* portion of the code that each **modified** *n* is **added** to the next one in the sequence of calls to *festus*. Finally, when the *n* parameter coming into *festus* gets above 6, the returned value is n – 3 (7 – 3 = 4). Thus, we have:

0 + 2 + 6 + 4 = 12

5. What is displayed by *homer(9);* ? **1,2,4,9**

```
public static void homer(int n)
{
        if (n <= 1)
                System.out.print(n);
        else
        {
                homer(n / 2);
                System.out.print(“,” + n);
        }
}
```

Notice on this method that we successively pass in these values of *n*.

9 4 2 1

Nothing is printed until the last time when we are down to a 1. Then we start coming back up the calling chain and printing.

6. What is displayed by *method1(7);* ? **1,3,5,7**

```
public static void method1(int n)
{
        if (n <= 1)
                System.out.print(n);
        else
        {
                method1(n-2);
                System.out.print("," + n);
        }
}
```

7. In this problem we will generate the Fibonacci sequence. This important sequence is found in nature and begins as follows:

   0, 1, 1, 2, 3, 5, 8, 13, 21, …

   We notice that beginning with the third term, each term is the sum of the preceding two. Recursively, we can define the sequence as follows:

   fibonacci(0) = 0
   fibonacci(1) = 1
   fibonacci(n) = fibonacci(n - 1) + fibonacci(n -2)

   Using these three lines, we can write a recursive method to find the kth term of this sequence with the call, *System.out.println(fib(k));* :

```
public static int fib(int n)
{
        if (n = = 0)
        {
                return 0;
        }
        else if(n = = 1)
        {
                return 1;
        }
        else
        {
                return fib(n – 1) + fib(n – 2);
        }
}
```

8. Let's try one similar to #7. What is returned by *pls(4);* ? **85**

```
public static int pls(int n)
{
        if (n = = 0)
        {
                return 5;
        }
        else if (n = = 1)
        {
                return 11;
        }
        else
        {
                return pls(n - 1) + 2 * pls(n - 2);
        }
}
```

The way we approach this is to just build the sequence from the rules we see expressed in the code. Term 0 has a value of 5 and term 1 has a value of 11.

Term number	→0	1	2	3	4
Value	→5	11			

How will we get term 2? Well, the rule in the code says it's the previous term plus twice the term before that. That gives us 11 + 2*5 = 21. Continue this to obtain the other terms.

Term number	→0	1	2	3	4
Value	→5	11	21	43	**85**

9. We are going to use these same ideas to easily work the next problem that in the beginning just looks hopelessly complicated.

```
public void f(int z)
{
        if(z = = 0)
        {
                System.out.print("x");
        }
        else
        {
                System.out.print("{");
                f(z-1);
                System.out.print("}");
        }
}
```

Let's begin analyzing this by observing the output of *f(0)*. It simply prints an "x".

Term number	→0	1	2	3
Value	→x			

Now, what about *f(1)*? It first prints a "{" followed by *f(z-1)*. But *f(z-1)* is simply the previous term, and we already know that it's an "x". A "}" follows. So our 2nd term is "{x}".

Term number	→0	1	2	3
Value	→x	{x}		

Similarly, each subsequent term is the previous term sandwiched in between "{" and "}" and so we have:

Term number	→0	1	2	3
Value	→x	{x}	{{x}}	{{{x}}}

So, if we are asked for *f(3)* the answer is **{{{x}}}.**

10. What is returned by *g(6, 2)*?

```
public static void g(int x, int y)
{
      if (x/y != 0)
      {
         g(x/y, y);
      }
      System.out.print(x / y + 1);
}
```

To analyze this problem the following pairs will represent the parameters on subsequent recursive calls to *g*. Under each pair is what's printed.

6, 2	3, 2	1, 2
4	2	1

Realizing that we don't print until we reach the end of the calling chain, we see that **124** is printed as we "back-out" of the chain.

Exercises on Lesson 40

In each of the following recursion problems, state what's printed.

1. System.out.println(rig(4));

```
public static int rig(int n)
{
        if ( (n = = 0) )
        {
                return 5;
        }
        else if ( n = = 1)
        {
                return 8;
        }
        else
        {
                return rig(n – 1) - rig(n – 2);
        }
}
```

2. System.out.println(mm(6));

```
public static int mm(int n)
{
        if (n<=0)
                return 10;
        else
                return n + mm(n-1);
}
```

3. System.out.println(adrml(5));

```
public static int adrml(int n)
{
        if (n<=1)
                return n;
        else
                return n * adrml(n-2);
}
```

4. System.out.println(bud(1));

```
public static int bud(int n)
{
        if (n>5)
                return n - 2;
        else
                return n + bud(n +1);
}
```

5. System.out.println(zing(0));

```
public static int zing(int n)
{
        if (n > 10)
                return n - 2;
        else
        {
                n = n * 3;
                return n + zing(n + 2);
        }
}
```

6. crch(12);

```
public static void crch(int n)
{
        if (n <= 0)
                System.out.print(n);
        else
        {
                crch(n / 3);
                System.out.print("," + n);
        }
}
```

7. elvis(11);

```
public static void elvis(int n)
{
        if (n <= 3)
                System.out.print(n + 1);
        else
        {
                elvis(n-3);
                System.out.print(">>" + (n – 1));
        }
}
```

8. sal(5);

```
public static int sal(int n)
{
        if (n = = 2)
        {       return 100;     }
        else if (n = = 3)
        {       return 200;     }
        else
        {
                return  (2 * sal(n - 1) +  sal(n - 2) + 1);
        }
}
```

9. puf(4);

```
public static void puf(int n)
{
        if(n = = 1)
        {       System.out.print("x");      }
        else if( n%2 = = 0) //n is even
        {
                System.out.print("{");
                puf(n-1);
                System.out.print("}");
        }
        else  //n is odd
        {
                System.out.print("<");
                puf(n-1);
                System.out.print(">");
        }
}
```

10. bc(6, 2);

```
public static void bc(int p, int q)
{
        if (p/q = = 0)
        {
                System.out.println(p + q + 1);
        }
        else
        {
                System.out.println(p);
                bc(p/q, q);
        }
}
```

Project… Fibonacci

You are to write a recursion routine to generate the kth term of a "modified" Fibonacci sequence. Our modified sequence will be defined as follows:

modFibonacci(0) = 3
modFibonacci(1) = 5
modFibonacci(2) = 8
modFibonacci(n) = modFibonacci(n - 1) + modFibonacci(n -2) + modFibonacci(n-3)

For your convenience several terms of this sequence are:

3 5 8 16 29 53 98 . . .

Call your new class *ModFib* and create a *static* method in it called *modFibonacci.*

Test your new class with the following *Tester* class:

```
import java.io.*;
import java.util.*;
public class Tester
{
   public static void main(String args[])
   {
      Scanner kbReader = new Scanner(System.in);
      System.out.print("Generate which term number? ");
      int k = kbReader.nextInt( );

      System.out.println("Term #" + k + " is " + ModFib.modFibonacci(k));
   }
}
```

Typical runs should look like this:

```
Generate which term number? 5
Term #5 is 53

Generate which term number? 6
Term #6 is 98
```

Lesson 41…..Sorting Routines

What is sorting?

Sorting simply means **arranging items in ascending or descending order**. Two types of approaches to sorting are described here:

1. The **incremental** approach

2. The **divide-and-conquer** approach (typically uses recursion)

Of the two, divide-and-conquer is by far the **<u>fastest</u>** (in most cases)…but also the most complicated.

****

In each of the sorting routines on the following pages we illustrate sorting an *int* array; however, the code could easily be adapted to sorting with other data types.

A class for testing sorting routines:

Test the various methods of sorting with the following code:

```
public class Tester
{
        public static void main(String args[])
        {
          int theArray[] = {4,2,5,1,3,18,0,9,6};
          sort(theArray);

          for(int j = 0; j < theArray.length; j++)
          {
            System.out.print(theArray[j] + "   ");
          }
          System.out.println(" ");
        }

        public static void sort(int a[ ])
        {
          ...specific code for a particular sorting method...
        }
}
```

Bubble Sort $O(n^2)$ for all cases

The Bubble sort uses an **incremental** approach. The following shows the sequence of steps in a Bubble Sort:

4	2	5	1	3	Original data.
4	**2**	5	1	3	Compare the shaded pair. 4 > 2, so we need to swap.
2	**4**	5	1	3	Swap completed.
2	**4**	**5**	1	3	Compare the shaded pair. No swap needed.
2	4	**5**	**1**	3	Compare the shaded pair. 5 > 1, so we need to swap.
2	4	**1**	**5**	3	Swap completed.
2	4	1	**5**	**3**	Compare the shaded pair. 5 > 3, so we need to swap.
2	4	1	**3**	**5**	Swap completed.

After the first pass we notice that the largest value (5) has "bubbled" its way to the end of the list; however, the array is still not in order. Continue to repeat this process **until no swaps are made**. Only then is the list in order. On each subsequent pass the next largest value will "bubble" its way to its correct position near the end of the list.

Making the swap:

Before presenting a method that will perform a Bubble sort we need to first understand how to swap the contents of two variables. This procedure is at the heart of several types of sorting. Suppose we wish to interchange the value of integers *p* and *q* and that their original values are:

p = 5 and q = 79

When finished with the swap, their values will be:

p = 79 and q = 5

This is accomplished with the following code where you will notice the presence of *int temp* which serves as a safe haven for the first variable while the swap is being made.

```
temp = p;
p = q;
q = temp;
```

A Bubble Sort method:

The following method makes use of a similar swap where, instead, array values are used. You will also notice the use of a *boolean loopSomeMore* variable. Just under the sample sequence of steps above, the instruction, "Continue to repeat this process until no swaps are made.", is implemented by usage of this *boolean* variable.

```
public static void sort(int a[])  //Bubble Sort
{
        boolean loopSomeMore;
        do
        {
                loopSomeMore = false;
                for(int j = 0; j < a.length -1; j++)
                {
                        if(a[j] > a[j+1])
                        {
                                //swap a[j] and a[j+1]
                                int temp = a[j];
                                a[j] = a[j+1];
                                a[j+1] = temp;

                                loopSomeMore = true;
                        }
                }
        }
        while(loopSomeMore);
}
```

Very, very slow:

This Bubble Sort is the slowest and most inefficient of all the sorting routines. It should only be used if you have a very few items to sort (say, 50 items or less). If you had, for example, 10,000 items to sort, this routine could literally take hours to run. **It is dreadfully slow**. So, why do we present it if it is so slow? Of all the sorting routines, it is also the **simplest to understand** and is therefore, a starting point for our study of sorting.

Project... Bubble Sort

Run the above code with the Tester class on page 41-1.

Selection Sort $O(n^2)$ for all cases

The Selection Sort uses an **incremental** approach. During the first pass the smallest value is **selected** from the entire array and swapped with the first element. On the second pass the smallest value is **selected** from the array beginning with the 2nd element and swapped with the second element, etc….the above description is for an ascending sort. The following shows the sequence of steps in a Selection Sort:

4	2	5	1	3	Original data.
1	**2**	5	4	3	1st **pass**: Select smallest value in gray area just above…It is 1. 1 and 4 have now been swapped.
1	2	**5**	4	3	2nd **pass**: Select smallest value in gray area just above…It is 3 No swap necessary since the 2 above is less than 3.
1	2	3	**4**	5	3rd **pass:** Select smallest value in gray area just above…It is 3 3 and 5 have now been swapped.
1	2	3	4	5	4th **pass:** Select smallest value in gray area just above…It is 5. No swap necessary since the 4 above is less than 5.

A Selection Sort method:

```
public static void sort(int a[ ])
{
        int min, minIndex;
        for(int i = 0;i < a.length; ++i)
        {
                min = a[i];
                minIndex = i;
                for (int j = i + 1; j < a.length; ++j)  // Find minimum
                {
                        if (a[j] < min)  //salient feature
                        {
                                min = a[j];
                                minIndex = j;
                        }
                }
                a[minIndex] = a[i];  // swap
                a[i] = min;
        }
}
```

Disadvantage:

A disadvantage of the selection sort is that it will not allow an early exit from the entire process if the list becomes ordered in an early pass.

Project… Selection Sort

Run the above code with the *Tester* class on page 41-1.

Selection Sort Exercise

1. What is a disadvantage of the Selection Sort?

2. What is the Big O value for the Selection Sort in best, worst, and average cases?

3. In a sentence or two, describe the basic operation of the Selection Sort.

4. Is the Selection Sort "incremental" or "divide-and-conquer" in its approach?

5. What line or lines of code from the previous page determines the smallest value in the "shaded" region?

6. Which loop from the previous page takes us through the "shaded" region looking for the smallest value?

7. Consider applying an ascending **Selection Sort** to: 3, 7, 6, 4, 5. Make a sequence of charts showing the results of each "pass".

3	7	6	4	5

Original data.

1st pass:

2nd pass:

3rd pass:

4th pass:

Insertion Sort

Best	Average	Worst
O(n)	O(n^2)	O(n^2)

The Insertion Sort uses an **incremental** approach. It works similar to the way you might organize a hand of cards. The unsorted cards begin face down on the table and are picked up one by one. As each new unsorted card is picked up, it is inserted into the correct order in your organized hand of cards.

The following shows the sequence of steps in an Insertion Sort:

2	**5**	1	4	3	Original data. The 2 is our "hand" so insert the 5 into it.
2	5	1	4	3	**End of 1st pass**: The 5 is already in the right place. No need to move.
2	5	**1**	4	3	Our "hand" is now 2, 5. Think of inserting the 1 into it.
1	2	5	4	3	**End of 2nd pass:** Notice the 1 has been **inserted** in the right place.
1	2	5	**4**	3	Our "hand" is now 1, 2, 5. Think of inserting the 4 into it.
1	2	4	5	3	**End of 3rd pass:** Notice the 4 has been **inserted** in the right place.
1	2	4	5	**3**	Our "hand" is now 1, 2, 4, 5. Think of inserting the 3 into it.
1	2	3	4	5	**End of 4th pass:** Notice the 3 has been **inserted** in the right place.

```
public static void sort(int a[ ] ) { //This will do an ascending sort
        int itemToInsert, j;
        boolean keepGoing;
        //On kth pass, insert item k into its correct position among the first k items in the array
        for(int k = 1; k < a.length; k++)
        {
                //Go backwards through the list, looking for the slot to insert a[k]
                itemToInsert = a[k];
                j = k -1;
                keepGoing = true;
                while((j >= 0) && keepGoing)
                {
                        if (itemToInsert < a[j] )
                        {
                                a[j + 1] = a[j]; //Salient feature
                                j--;
                                if(j == -1) //special case for inserting an item at [0]
                                        a[0] = itemToInsert;
                        }
                        else //Upon leaving loop, j + 1 is the index where itemToInsert belongs
                        {
                                keepGoing = false;
                                a[j + 1] = itemToInsert;
                        }
                }
        }
```

An advantage:

The Insertion Sort has an advantage over the Selection Sort since it takes advantage of a partially ordered list. This is evidenced by the fact that in a best case, Big O for an Insertion Sort is O(n), whereas for a Selection Sort, it is always $O(n^2)$.

Project… Insertion Sort

Run the above code with the *Tester* class on page 41-1.

Insertion Sort Exercise

1. What is an advantage of the Insertion sort as compared to the Selection Sort?

2. What is the Big O value for the Insertion Sort in best, worst, and average cases?

3. In a sentence or two, describe the basic operation of the Insertion Sort. You may use an analogy if desired.

4. Is the Insertion Sort "incremental" or "divide-and-conquer" in its approach?

5. What is the purpose of the variable *keepGoing*?

6. Why is the *k* loop started at index 1 instead of index 0?

7. What code would you change to implement a **descending** sort?

8. Consider applying an ascending **Insertion Sort** to: 3, 7, 6, 4, 5. Fill in the sequence of charts showing the results of each "pass".

3	7	6	4	5	Original data.
					End of 1st pass:
					End of 2 rd pass:
					End of 3rd pass:
					End of 4th pass:

Quick Sort

Best	Average	Worst
O(n log(n))	O(n log(n))	O(n^2)

Two partitions:

The Quick Sort uses a **divide-and-conquer** approach. It begins by breaking the original list into two partitions (sections) based on the value of some "pivot value". One partition will eventually contain all the elements with values greater than the pivot value. The other will eventually contain all the elements with values less than or equal to the pivot value. (This description is not always completely true, but close.) Repeat this process on each partition.

Notice the word **partition** above. This is a **salient feature** of the Quick Sort. To identify this type of sort, look for the word "partition" (or equivalent term) in a rem or perhaps as a variable name.

A Quick Sort method:

Initially, enter this method with *left* = the left most index (0) and with *right* = right most index (*a.length* – 1). This is also a **salient feature**.

```
public static void sort(int a[ ], int left, int right)
{
        if (left >= right) return;
        int k = left;
        int j = right;
        int pivotValue = a[ (left + right) / 2 ]; // salient feature
        while ( k < j )
        {
                while (a[k] < pivotValue) //salient feature (pivot point)
                {
                        k++;
                }

                while ( pivotValue < a[j] )
                {
                        j--;
                }
                if ( k <= j)
                {
                        int temp = a[k]; //swap a[k] and a[j]
                           a[k] = a[j];
                        a[j] = temp;
                        k++;
                        j--;
                }
        }
        sort(a, left, j); //salient feature (recursion)
        sort(a, k, right);
}
```

Summary of how Quick Sort works:

A "pivot value" is selected. Usually this is the element at the center position of the array. Elements in the array are moved such that all elements less than the pivot value are in one half (partition) and all elements larger than or equal to the pivot value are in the other half (partition). This process is continually repeated on each partition. The partitions become smaller until they each consist of just a single element. At that point the array is ordered.

Project… Quick Sort

Run the above code with the *Tester* class on page 41-1.

Quick Sort Exercise

1. What is an advantage of the Quick Sort as compared to Selection and Insertion Sort?

2. What is the Big O value for the Quick Sort in best, worst, and average cases?

3. Is the Quick Sort "incremental" or "divide-and-conquer" in its approach?

4. Suppose the signature of a Quick Sort routine is:
   public void quickSort(int a[ ], int start, int end)
   If *a.length* yields a value of 32, what should be the values passed by *f* and *g* when the routine is initially called via:
   quickSort(a, f, g);

5. Into how many partitions is the array divided upon each recursion?

6. Explain how the pivot value is used to separate the list into two halves.

7. How is the pivot value usually calculated?

8. Pick out the line or lines of code that demonstrate that Quick Sort is recursive.

9. Assume that 6 is the pivot value and that we are operating under the rules:
   While a[i] < pivot value, increment i.
   While a[j] >= pivot value, decrement j.
   Interchange a[i] and a[j] as long as i <= j.

4	7	9	1	6	2	3	5	8
i								j

   What two values will get interchanged first?

Merge Sort O(n log(n)) for all cases

The Merge Sort uses the **divide-and-conquer** approach. It begins by placing **each** element into its own individual list. Then each pair of adjacent lists is combined into one **sorted** list. This continues until there is one big, final, sorted list. The process is illustrated below:

Put each element into its own list of one element.	72	83	40	90	51	30	18	75
Merge every two lists above into a single sorted list.	72,83		40,90		30,51		18,75	
Merge every two lists above into a single sorted list.	40,72,83,90				18,30,51,75			
Merge the two lists above into the final sorted list.	18,30,40,51,72,75,83,90							

The above, however, is a very simplistic approach. In reality, the merge sort is often implemented **recursively** as illustrated with the following code:

A Merge Sort method:

```
//Enter this method with left = the beginning index (initially 0) and right = the last index
//(initially a.length-1)
public static void sort (int a[ ], int left, int right)
{
        if (right = = left) return;
        int middle = (left + right) /2;  //salient feature
        sort(a, left, middle); //salient feature #1 (recursion)
        sort(a, middle + 1, right);  //salient feature #2
        merge(a, left, middle, right);  //salient feature #3
}
//...see two pages forward for the merge method, an important component of this sorting
technique.
```

How it works:

The recursive calls to *sort* and the resulting recalculation of *middle = (left + right) / 2* continually subdivide the lists until we get individual "lists" of one element each. Due to the nature of recursion, that subdivision process continues until we reach the final lists of one element each **before** the *merge* method actually begins merging the lists together, two at a time.

Subdividing the list:

On the following page we see this process of recursively subdividing the lists. We will consider the following original order of some numbers to be sorted:

7	8	6	2	3	5

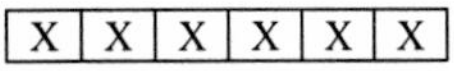

X X X X X X

We begin the process by subdividing the list in half. For the time being we will just ignore the numbers and put in X's.

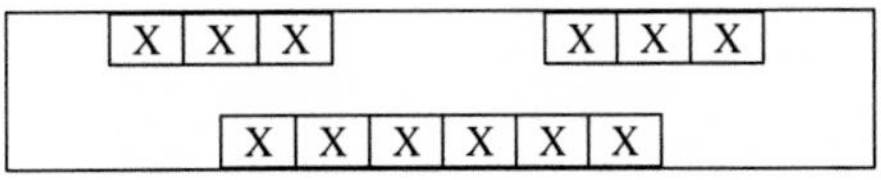

X X X   X X X

X X X X X X

Notice that we have started at the bottom and our picture is growing in the **upward** direction as we subdivide according to *middle = (left + right)/*2 using integer arithmetic.

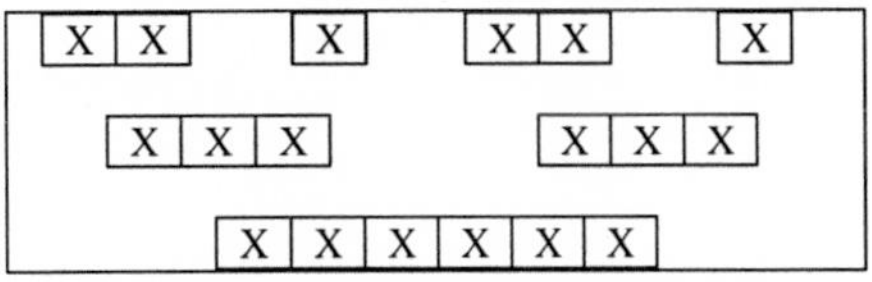

X X   X   X X   X

X X X   X X X

X X X X X X

Now subdivide again. The two lists of three elements above do not divide into two equal parts. When unequal, the left part has one more element.

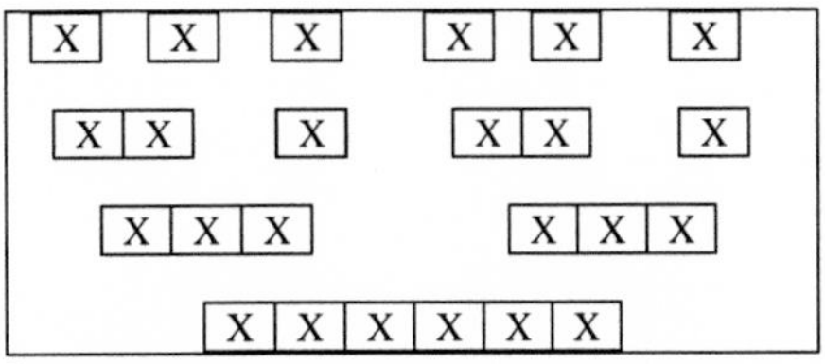

X   X   X   X   X   X

X X   X   X X   X

X X X   X X X

X X X X X X

Left half of the above illustrates **salient feature #1**

Right half of the above illustrates **salient feature #2**

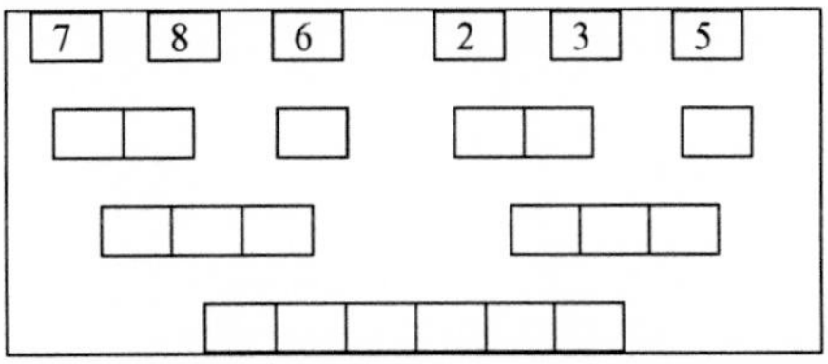

Divide the remaining lists of two elements again and we arrive at our final arrangement of 6 individual lists with each "list" containing only one element.

7   8   6   2   3   5

Now let's consider what our individual elements are in the top row of individual "lists". These are the numbers we wish to order.

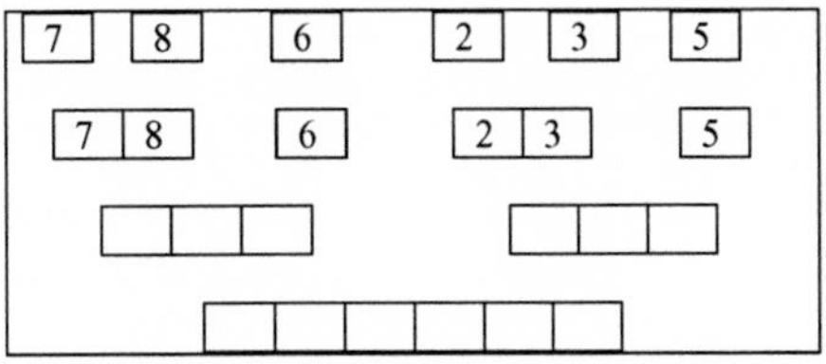

7   8   6   2   3   5

7 8   6   2 3   5

Here we merge some adjacent lists into sorted lists according to the subdivisions predetermined above.

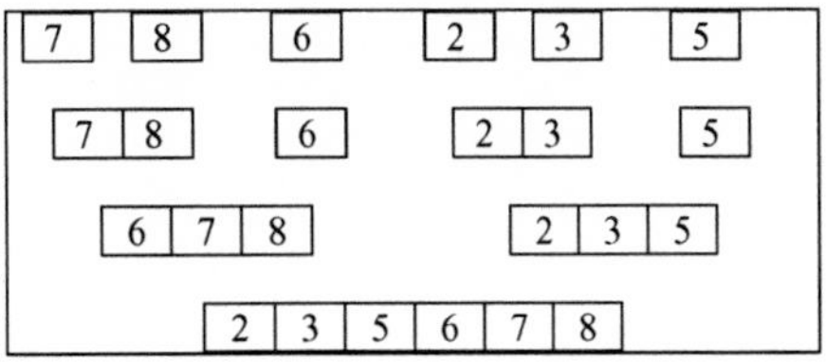

7   8   6   2   3   5

7 8   6   2 3   5

6 7 8   2 3 5

2 3 5 6 7 8

The process continues until we have one, big, sorted list.

//**salient feature #3** (merging)

The *merge* method (used by Merge Sort):

```
private static void merge(int a[ ], int left, int middle, int right)
{
        //This temporary array will be used to build the merged list
        int tmpArray[ ] = new int[right – left +1];
        //This creation of a temporary array is a BIG feature of the merge sort.

        int index1 = left;
        int index2 = middle + 1;
        int indx = 0;

        //Loop until one of the sublists is finished, adding the smaller of the first
        //elements of each sublist to the merged list.
        while (index1 <= middle && index2 <= right)
        {
                if ( a[index1] < a[index2] )
                {
                        tmpArray[indx] = a[index1];
                        index1++;
                }
                else
                {
                        tmpArray[indx] = a[index2];
                        index2++;
                }
                indx++;
        }

        //Add to the merged list the remaining elements of whichever sublist is
        //not yet finished
        while(index1 <= middle)
        {
                tmpArray[indx] = a[index1];
                index1++;
                indx++;
        }
        while(index2 <= right)
        {
                tmpArray[indx] = a[index2];
                index2++;
                indx++;
        }

        //Copy the merged list from the tmpArray array into the a array
        for (indx = 0; indx < tmpArray.length; indx++)
        {
                a[left + indx] = tmpArray[indx];
        }
}
```

Project… Merge Sort

Run the above code (both the *sort* and *merge* methods) with the *Tester* class on page 41-1.

Big O Summary

It will probably be easier to learn the Big O designation for each sorting and search routine when simultaneously viewing all of them in a table:

Algorithm	Best Case	Average Case	Worst Case
Sorts			
Bubble Sort	$O(n^2)$	$O(n^2)$	$O(n^2)$
Selection Sort	$O(n^2)$	$O(n^2)$	$O(n^2)$
Insertion Sort	O(n)	$O(n^2)$	$O(n^2)$
Quick Sort	O(n log n)	O(n log n)	$O(n^2)$
Merge Sort	O(n log n)	O(n log n)	O(n log n)
Searches			
Linear or Sequential	O(1)	O(n)	O(n)
Binary	O(1)	O(log n)	O(log n)
Binary Search Tree	O(1)	O(log n)	O(n)

Occasionally, "best case" is referred to as the **least restrictive** or **fastest executing** case. Similarly, "worst case" is referred to as the **most restrictive** or **slowest executing** case.

****

Prepare for the following "Contest Type Problems":

In the following contest type questions you will encounter *Comparable* type objects. The *Comparable* interface is not introduced until Lesson 45. There, you will learn that this interface has only one method, *compareTo*. This method behaves exactly the same as does the *String compareTo* method described in Lesson 17.

Another question in this section concerns a binary search. The discussion in Lesson 39, example 10, will be of some assistance in this problem. A later lesson, Lesson 51, is devoted to the details of a binary search.

Sorting … Contest Type Problems

1. If *theName* is an array of *Strings* defined in *class Alf*, which of these would be a correct call to the *mSort( )* method from the *Alf* class?

   A. mSort(theName[ ])
   B. MergeSort.mSort(theName)
   C. mSort(theName, 0, theName.length)
   D. MergeSort.mSort(theName, 0, theName.maxLength)
   E. None of these

2. Suppose the array of *Integer* objects below is sorted with the *mSort( )* method. What is the final state of the array after the two recursive calls to *mSort( )* complete, but before the final call to *merge( )?*

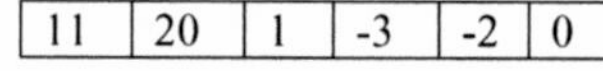

11	20	1	-3	-2	0

A.

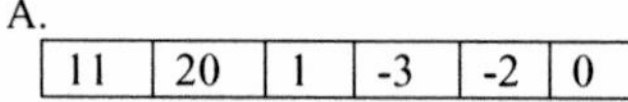

11	20	1	-3	-2	0

B.

1	-3	-2	0	11	20

C.

-3	-2	0	1	11	20

D.

1	11	20	-3	-2	0

E. None of these

3. Which of these has the same worst case Big O as the *mSort* method to the right?

   A. Binary search
   B. Sequential search
   C. Insertion Sort
   D. Quick Sort
   E. None of these

```
public class MergeSort
{
    private static void mSort(Comparable[] S,
                              int first, int last)
    {
        int mid = (first + last) / 2;
        if(mid = = first)  return;
        mSort(S, first, mid);
        mSort(S, mid, last);
        merge(S, first, last);
    }

    public static void mSort(Comparable[] S)
    {
        mSort(S, 0, S.length);
    }

    private static void merge(Comparable[] S, int
                                    first, int last)
    {
        Comparable tmp[] = new
                        Comparable[last - first];
        int i=first, j=(first+last)/2, k=0;
        int mid=j;

        while(i<mid && j<last)
        {
            if(S[j].compareTo(S[j])<0)
                tmp[k++]=S[j++];
            else
                tmp[k++]=S[j++];
        }

        while(i<mid)   tmp[k++] = S[i++];
        while(j<last)  tmp[k++]=S[j++];

        for(i=0; i<last-first; ++i)
            S[first + i] = tmp[i];
    }
}
```

4. Which of the following could be a legal parameter for the *mSort* method above to receive as its first parameter?

   A. an array of *Strings* B. an array of integers C. an array of *HashMaps*
   D. an array of *doubles* E. All of these

5. What is the purpose of the *aSort* method?

A. Perform a Selection Sort
B. Perform a Binary Search
C. Perform an Insertion Sort
D. Perform a Merge Sort
E. Perform a Quick Sort

```
public static void aSort(Comparable array[])
{
    int length =  array.length;
    for( int j = 1; j<length; ++j)
    {
        int pos1 = 0, pos2 = j-1;
        while(pos1 <= pos2)
        {
            int mid = (pos1 + pos2) / 2;
            if( array[mid].compareTo(array[j]) < 0 )
                pos1 = mid + 1;
            else
                pos2 = mid – 1;
        }

        Comparable tmp=array[j];
        for(int j=1; j>pos1; --j)
        {
            array[j]=A[j-1];
        }

        array[pos1] = tmp;
    }
}
```

6. If the array below is passed to the *aSort* method, what will it look like after the outer for-loop completes its first iteration?

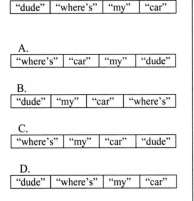

"dude"	"where's"	"my"	"car"

A.

"where's"	"car"	"my"	"dude"

B.

"dude"	"my"	"car"	"where's"

C.

"where's"	"my"	"car"	"dude"

D.

"dude"	"where's"	"my"	"car"

E. None of these

7. What is the worst case Big O value for *aSort()* when it receives an array of length *n*?

A. O(log(n))
B. O(n^2)
C. O(n log n)
D. O(n)
E. None of these

8. To do a binary search of an array of *Object* type objects, which of the following must be true?

A. The objects must be sorted
B. The objects must have been of the same original type
C. The original objects must have all been *String* types
D. Both A and B
E. All of these

9. The Arrays.*sort() static* method of the *java.util* package sorts an array. What is the best case Big O value of this method on an array of randomly ordered double precision numbers?

A. O(n^2) B. O(2^n) C. O(n log n) D. O(log n) E. None of these

10. Which sorting algorithm is implemented by the method to the right?
 	
A. Quick Sort
B. Selection Sort
C. Merge Sort
D. Insertion Sort
E. None of these
 	
11. Time complexity analysis yields what value if *array.length* equals *n*? Choose the smallest correct answer.
 	
A. O(n log n)
B. O(n)
C. $O(n^2)$
D. O(log n)
E. None of these
	`public static void mysterySort(int [] array) {`
	`int minIndx=0, minVal=0;`
	
	`for(int k=0; i<array.length; ++k) {`
	`minVal = array[k];`
	`minIndx = k;`
	`for( int j = k+1; j < array.length; ++j) ) {`
	`if( array[j] < array[minIndx] )`
	`{`
	`minVal = array[j];`
	`minIndx = j;`
	`}`
	`array[minIndx] = array[k];`
	`array[k] = minVal;`
	`}`
	`}`
	`}`

12. How many times is the *equals()* method called when executing *bSrch(B, 0, 5, "ff")* where *B* is the array below?
 	
"aa" | "bb" | "ee" | "ff" | "yy" | "zz"
 	
A. 1
B. 3
C. 2
D. 0
E. None of these
 	
13. If you are limited to examining only *n* elements, what is the largest size array upon which a binary search can be implemented?
 	
A. n^2
B. 2^n
C. 2n
D. 2^n-1
E. None of these
	`// Binary Search method`
	`public static boolean bSrch(Comparable [] Array, int start, int end, Comparable thing)`
	`{`
	`if(start>end)`
	`return false;`
	`int mid = (start + end) / 2;`
	`if(Array[mid].equals(thing))`
	`{`
	`return true;`
	`}`
	`else if(Array[mid].compareTo(thing) < 0)`
	`{`
	`return bSrch(Array, mid+1, end, thing);`
	`}`
	`else`
	`{`
	`return bSrch(Array, start, mid-1, thing);`
	`}`
	`}`

14. What code replaces **<*1>** in the code to the right so that *j* will always be less than the number of elements in the *ary* array?
 	
A. ary.length+1 B. ary.length
C. ary.length-1 D. (length)ary
E. None of these
 	
15. Assume that **<*1>** has been filled in correctly. Which sorting routine is being implemented?
 	
A. Selection B. Quick C. Merge
D. Insertion E. None of these
	`public static void mysterySort(int ary[]) {`
	`for(int j=0; j < <*1>; ++j)`
	`{`
	`int min = ary[j], minIndx = j;`
	`for(int k=j+1; k < <*1>; ++k)`
	`if(ary[k] < ary[minIndx])`
	`{`
	`min=ary[k];`
	`minIndx = k;`
	`}`
	`ary[minIndx]= ary[j];`
	`ary[j] = min;`
	`}`
	`}`

16. How would you call the sorting routine that's a part of the *java.util* package, to sort the array *tinyArray* (shown to the right)?

A. Arrays.sort(tinyArray)
B. mergeSort(tinyArray)
C. tinyArray.sort( )
D. (Arrays)sort(tinyArray)
E. None of these

```
int [] tinyArray;
   tinyArray[0] = 89;
   tinyArray[1] = 511;
   tinyArray[2] = -18;
   tinyArray[3] = 29;
   tinyArray[4] = 67;
```

17. For the *mrgSort* method to the right to implement a merge sort on *Array*, what should the *merge( )* method accomplish?

A. Do a Selection sort on the combination of the two halves.
B. Sort the first half of *Array*
C. Combine the unsorted list stored in the front half of *Array* with the unsorted list in the back half of *Array*.
D. Combine the sorted list stored in the first half of *Array* with the sorted list the in second half of *Array* in such a way that the combination is sorted.
E. None of these

```
public static void mrgSort(Comparable[] Array, double
                                        start, double end)
{
    double mid = (start + end) / 2;
    if(mid = = start)
    {
        return;
    }
    mrgSort(Array, start, mid);
    mrgSort(Array, mid, end);
    merge(Array, start, end);
}
```

18. Assume that *merge( )* has been done correctly. What is the worst case Big O value of *mergeSort(Array, 0, Array.length)*, where *n* equals *Array.length*?

A. $O(n^2)$
B. O(log n)
C. O(n log n)
D. O(log n)
E. None of these

Project... Multiple Key Sorting

Create a text file named *Names_ages.txt* with the following content:

```
Jones 14
Abrams 15
Smith 19
Jones 9
Alexander 22
Smith 20
Smith 17
Tippurt 42
Jones 2
Herkman 12
Jones 11
```

Each line is a person's last name followed by a space and then his age. We want to sort these names alphabetically and in the case of duplicate names, sort by age in an ascending fashion. A properly sorted list will appear as follows:

```
Abrams, 15
Alexander, 22
Herkman, 12
Jones, 2
Jones, 9
Jones, 11
Jones, 14
Smith, 17
Smith, 19
Smith, 20
Tippurt, 42
```

Paste in code from your *BaseClass* to input this file and then use a modified Selection Sort. Call you project *MultiKeySort*. (Notice the commas in the output.)

Lesson 42..... *List interface*

Classes that implement the *List interface*:

Java includes three classes (*LinkedList*, *ArrayList*, and *Vector*) that **implement** the *List* ***interface*** This *interface* and the three classes are made available by importing *java.util.**:

List interface methods:

***List* method signature**	**Action**
void add(int index, Object o)	Inserts the object o at the position specified by *index* after all existing objects at that index and greater are moved forward one position.
void add(Object o)	Appends the specified object to the end of the list.
boolean contains(Object o)	Returns true if this list contains the specified object.
Object get(int index)	Returns the object at the position specified by *index.*
int indexOf(Object o)	Returns the index of the first occurrence of the specified object…searching from left to right….or –1 if not found.
int lastIndexOf(Object o)	Returns the index of the **first** occurrence of o… when searching from **right to left**….or –1 if the object is not found.
Object remove(int index)	Removes the object at the position specified by *index* and returns the object.
Object removeLast( )	Removes the object at the end of the list and returns the object that occupied that position.
boolean remove(Object o)	Remove the first occurrence of o (searching from left to right).
Object set(int index, Object o)	Replaces the object at the position specified by *index* with o…Returns old object.
boolean isEmpty( )	Returns true if this list contains no objects.
int size( )	Returns the number of objects in the list
void clear( )	Removes all elements from the list
boolean equals(Object o)	Returns true if this list is exactly the same as the list specified by o.
Iterator iterator( )	Returns an Iterator object for this list**…Important…to be discussed later.**
ListIterator listIterator( )	Returns a ListIterator object for this list… **Important…to be discussed later.**

Printing a *List* object:

It is possible to print the contents of an entire list named *lst* with *System.out.println(lst)*. A typical printout would look like the following if characters 'a' – 'g' are stored as the individual elements of the list (notice the surrounding square brackets):

```
[a, b, c, d, e, f, g]
```

Creating a *List* object:

There are three ways to **create a *List* object** since there are three classes (mentioned above) that implement the *List* interface.

1. **List lst = new LinkedList( );**

2. **List lst = new ArrayList( );**

3. **List lst = new Vector( );**
   This is basically an array with an initial *capacity* and having the ability to increase its size with a specified *increment* amount when a new storage attempt exceeds the present size.

Important features:

Here are some salient facts about these three *List* types:

1. The lists consist of nothing but objects of **type *Object*. Any** type object can be stored in a list; however, they are immediately and automatically converted into *Object* type objects for storage.

2. A list can have **different** types of objects initially stored in it; however, in actual practice most lists are restricted to just one type.

3. The objects retrieved from a list generally need to be **cast** to a **specific** object type before being used. For example, unless the object *lst* was created using type parameters, *Double d = lst.get(2);* won't work but *Double d = (Double)lst.get(2);* will.

Exercise on Lesson 42

Fill in the blanks below, except the comment column. Only put a note in the comment column if there is an exception (error). The letters *e*, *j*, *p*, *x*, *y*, and *z* all represent objects.

Method	State of list after method is executed	Value Returned	Comment
			Initially, list is empty
add(0,z)			
add(1,y)			
add(1,x)			
add(5,p)			
isEmpty( )			
size( )			
indexOf(x)			
contains(x)			
indexOf(j)			
contains(j)			
get(1)			
get(3)			
set(2,e)			
remove(0)			
remove(2)			
remove(1)			
add(x)			
lastIndexOf(x)			
clear( )			
isEmpty( )			
remove(0)			
set(0,z)			

1. Assume that *lst* is an *ArrayList* object and that the object at index 2 was originally a wrapper class *Integer* before being added to the list. Also assume that *lst* was **not** created with type parameters. The following code will "almost" work. Put in the modification that will make it work.

```
Integer iw = lst.get(2);
```

2. public static void theMethod(List opal)

```
{
        Iterator iter = ??????;
        … more code …
}
```

What code replaces ?????? so that an *Iterator* object is created from *opal*?

Lesson 43….. *ArrayList*

You will recall from Lesson 42 the *ArrayList* is one of several classes that implement the *List* interface. As its name suggests, *ArrayList* also involves arrays. Basically, everything we learned in Lessons 18 and 19 concerning arrays can also be applied to *ArrayList* objects, however, with slightly different methods.

Comparing *ArrayList* to ordinary arrays:

So, a legitimate question to ask at this point is, "Why clutter our brains with a new set of commands for the *ArrayList* if it serves the same purpose as do ordinary arrays?" We are going to discuss the advantages of the *ArrayList* class over ordinary arrays and, to be fair, its disadvantages.

Advantages… Ordinary arrays are fixed in size. When we create an array, we anticipate the largest possible size it will ever need to be, and when instantiating the array, dimension it to that size. We call this the physical size of the array and it always remains that size even though at some point in your program you may wish to only use a portion of the array. The size of that portion is called the logical size. Your own code must keep up with that size. By contrast, the *ArrayList* expands and contracts to meet your needs. If you remove items from or add items to your *ArrayList*, the physical and logical sizes are always identical. This could be very important if you wish to be conservative of memory usage. With memory being so abundant and inexpensive today, this is no longer the advantage it once was.

One of the *add* methods allows very easy insertions of new items in the interior of the list without the nuisance of having to pre-move preexisting items.

A final advantage is that iterator objects are provided, whereby we can easily traverse the list. See Lesson 44 for an explanation of iterators.

Disadvantages… *ArrayList* can only store objects. If we wish to store primitives such as integers, *double*s, or *boolean*s, they must be converted into their wrapper class counterparts (see Lesson 21). This was once a nuisance because the had to be converted manually, but is now circumvented with the advent of Java 5.0 and its autoboxing feature. Similarly, when we retrieve things from an *ArrayList*, they come out as objects. "Big deal", you say….certainly, if we store objects in the list, then we expect to get objects back when we retrieve from the list. Yes, but it's worse than one might think. When retrieving an object from the list, it doesn't come back as the same type object that was originally stored. Rather, it comes back as an *Object* type object (recall the cosmic superclass from Lesson 36). It will be necessary to cast it down to its original object type…yet another nuisance (partially circumvented by Java 5.0 if type parameters are used as discussed below).

So, what are the methods we use with *ArrayList*? Look back at Lesson 42 on the *List* interface. Since ***ArrayList* implements the *List* interface**, those are the methods. We will now offer sample usage and/or discussion of several of the more important methods.

In each of the following examples we are to assume an *ArrayList* object has been created via

ArrayList aryLst = new ArrayList( );   or   List aryLst = new ArrayList( );

Generics (type parameters):

With the addition of generics (type parameters) to Java 5.0, it is also possible to create an *ArrayList* object as follows (this is somewhat reminiscent of templates in c++):

```
ArrayList<String> aryLst = new ArrayList<String>( );
```

The *<String>* part indicates that objects we add to the list can only be *String* types. (Instead of *String* we could use any object type.) This insures "type safety" and would result in a compile time error if we ever tried to add some other type object to *aryLst*. Type parameters also remove the burden of casting *Object* type objects retrieved from a list back to their original type. Unfortunately objects retrieved from a list using an iterator must still be cast.

In the following examples, assume that only *Integer* type objects have been stored in the list and that *aryLst* was created with *List<Integer>aryLst = new ArrayList<Integer>( );*

void add(Object o) //**signature**

Example:

```
aryLst.add(13); //Java 5.0 accomplishes all with just this single line.
        Integer jw = new Integer(j); //pre Java 5.0
        aryLst.add(jw); // add jw to the end of the list
```

void add(int index, Object o) //**signature**

Example:

```
aryLst.add(3, 13); //Java 5.0 accomplishes all with just this single line.
        Integer jw = new Integer(j); //pre Java 5.0
        aryLst.add(3, jw); //inserts jw at index 3 after moving the existing object at index
                           //3 and greater up one notch.
```

Object get(int index) //**signature**

Example:

```
int q = aryLst.get(3); //Java 5.0 accomplishes all with just this single line.
        Object obj = aryLst.get(3); //pre Java 5.0,... retrieve object at position 3
        Integer qw = (Integer)obj; //cast down from Object to Integer
        int q = qw.intValue( ); //convert back to int type.
```

Object remove(int index) //**signature**

Example:

```
int q = aryLst.remove(3); //Java 5.0 accomplishes all with just this single line.
        Object obj = aryLst.remove(3); //pre Java 5.0,... returns and removes object at
                                       //position 3 (then compacts the list)
        Integer qw = (Integer)obj; //cast down from Object to Integer
        int q = qw.intValue( ); //convert back to int type.
```

Object removeLast( ) //**signature**

Example:

```
int q = aryLst.removeLast( ); //Java 5.0 accomplishes all with just this line
        Object obj = aryLst.removeLast( ); // pre Java 5.0,...removes object at end of list
                                           //and returns that object
        Integer qw = (Integer)obj; //cast down from Object to Integer
        int q = qw.intValue( ); //convert back to int type
```

Object set(int index, Object o) //**signature**

Example:

```
//int q = aryLst.set(3, 13); //Java 5.0 accomplishes all with just this single line.
    Integer jw = new Integer(13); //pre Java 5.0
    Object obj = aryLst.set(3, jw); // replaces object at position 3 with jw and returns
                                    //the original object
    Integer qw = (Integer)obj; //cast down from Object to Integer
    int q = qw.intValue( ); //convert back to int type.
```

boolean isEmpty( ) //**signature**

Example:

```
aryLst.isEmpty( ); // returns true if there are no objects in the list
```

int size( ) //**signature**

Example:

```
aryLst.size( ); //returns the number of objects in the list
```

void clear( ) //**signature**

Example:

```
aryLst.clear( ); //removes all objects from the list
```

With Java 5.0, autoboxing makes the following three methods (signatures are shown) easy to use. For example, if we are seeking the integer 13, the argument sent to the method would simply be 13.

```
int indexOf(Object o)
int lastIndexOf(Object o)
boolean contains(Object o)
```

```
ArrayList( )       //Default constructor
ArrayList(int j)   //Constructor that preallocates space for j number of elements to be
                   //stored in the list; however, more than j can be stored. The advantage in
                   //doing this is that the first j elements are stored very quickly.
```

Big O values:

Determine the efficiency of algorithms using *ArrayList* methods with the following table:

List Methods Used With ArrayList	Big O values
add(int index, Object o)	O(n)
add(Object o)	O(1)
contains(Object o)	O(n)
get(int index)	O(1)
indexOf(Object o)	O(n)
remove(int index)	O(n)
clear( )	O(1)
set(int index)	O(1)
size( )	O(1)

Table43-1

Two very important methods, *iterator( )* and *listIterator( )* will be discussed in Lesson 44.

Exercise on Lesson 43

1. Write code that will instantiate an *ArrayList* object called *alst* and have the restriction that only *String* objects can be stored in it.

2. *ArrayLists* are restricted in that only ____________ can be stored in them.

3. What is the main advantage in using an *ArrayList* object as opposed to an ordinary array?

4. What is a disadvantage of using primitive variable types with an *ArrayList* object.

In problems 5 - 9 an operation is performed with the "ordinary" array *ary*. Write equivalent code that performs the same operation on the *ArrayList* object called *a*. Assume that Java 5.0 is being used and give two answers for each problem (parts A and B). For A part assume that *a* was created with *List a = new ArrayList( );* and for B part assume *List<Integer>a = new ArrayList<Integer>( );* was used:

5.
```
int x = 19;
ary[5] = x;
```

6.
```
int gh = ary[22];
```

7.
```
int sz = ary.length;
```

8.
```
int kd = ary[101];
ary[101] = 17;
```
   Use the set method:

9.
```
//Before inserting a new number, 127, at position 59, it will be necessary to move all
//up one notch. Assume that the logical size of our array is logicalSize.
for(int j = logicalSize; j >=59, j--)
{
        ary[j+1] = ary[j];
}
ary[59] = 127; //insert the new number, 127, at index 59.
```

   What code using *List* method(s) does the equivalent of the above code?

10. What does the following code accomplish? (*alist* is an *ArrayList* object)
```
while(!alist.isEmpty( ) )
{
        alist.removeLast( );
}
```

11. What one line of code will accomplish the same thing as does the code in #10 above?

12. Write a <u>single</u> line of code that will retrieve the *String* object stored at index 99 of the *ArrayList* object *buster* and then store it in a *String* called *myString*.

13. What type variable is always returned when retrieving items from an *ArrayList* object?

ArrayList... Contest Type Problems

1. What replaces **<*1>** in the code to the right to throw an appropriate exception when it violates the precondition?

   A. throws RunTimeException;
   B. throw new RunTimeException( );
   C. throw new NumberFormatException( );
   D. throws NumberFormatException( );
   E. throw new NullPointerException( );

2. What replaces **<*2>** in the code to the right to access the individual weight of the player in the *plyrs* list with index *i*?

   A. ((Player) plyrs.get(i).weight( ))
   B. ((Player)plyrs.get(i)).weight( )
   C. (Player) (plyrs).get(i).weight( )
   D. plyrs.get(i).weight( )
   E. More than one of these

3. The *class PlayerInfo* is an implementation of the interface *Player*, and the *PlayerInfo* constructor receives no parameters. Which of the following are valid declarations/instantiations?

   A. Player p = new PlayerInfo( );
   B. PlayerInfo pi = new Player( );
   C. Player p = new Player;
   D. PlayerInfo pi = new PlayerInfo;
   E. More than one of these

```
public interface Player
{
   public double height( );
   public int weight( );
}

public class Team
{
   public Team( )
   {
      plyrs =  new ArrayList( );
   }

   //precondition: p != null
   public Computer addPlayer(Player p)
   {
      if (p = = null) <*1>
      else {
         plyrs.add(p);
         return this;
      }
   }
      ... more methods

   public double weight( ) //weight of entire team
   {
      int sum = 0;
      for (int k=0; k<=plyrs.size( ); ++k)
         sum += <*2>;
      return sum;
   }

   private ArrayList plyrs;
}
```

4. What could be the type of *kbal* to insure that the *add* method is used correctly?

   A. int
   B. String
   C. Both A and B
   D. Both A and B, but first cast as *Object* types
   E. None of these

```
ArrayList al = new ArrayList( );
al.add(kbal);
```

5. What would replace **<*1>** in the code to the right so that the *Integer* stored at index 3 of the list be stored in the primitive integer *j*?

   A. Integer j = (Integer) aList.get(3);
   B. Integer j = aList.get(3);
   C. int j= (Object)aList.get(3).intValue( );
   D. int j= (Integer)aList.get(3);
   E. None of these

```
ArrayList aList = new ArrayList( );
//add some integers to the list
<*1>
```

6. Which of the following is an appropriate way to create an *ArrayList* object to which we could immediately begin adding *Cabinet* type objects?

A. ArrayList obj = new ArrayList(Cabinet);
B. ArrayList obj;
C. ArrayList(Cabinet) = new ArrayList( );
D. ArrayList obj = new ArrayList( );
E. None of these

7. If *ArrayList objAL* contains objects of type *Cabinet*, which of the following will cause *Cabinet cab* to be set equal to the object at index 8 of *objAL*?

A. cab = (Cabinet)(objAL.get(8));
B. cab = (Cabinet)(objAL).get(8);
C. cab = objAL.get(8);
D. More than one of the above
E. None of these

8. Suppose *cab1* is an object of type *Cabinet*. Which of the following returns a *Description* object?

A. Cabinet.cab1.getDescription( );
B. cab1.getDescr( );
C. cab1.descr;
D. (Description)cab1.getDescription( );
E. None of these

```
//Assume that the classes PositionName, Officer,
//Assistant, and Description already exist
public class Cabinet
{
        public Description getDescr( )
        {
                return descr;
        }
        …constructor and other methods not
        shown…

        //State variables
        private PositionName positionName;
        private Officer indivName;
        private Assistant underlings;
        private Description descr;
}
```

9. What replaces **<#1>** in the code to the right so that the value of the *Integer* stored at index 2 of the *lst* object is placed into *int j*?

A. int j = lst.get(2);
B. Object ob = lst.get(2);
   Integer ij = (Integer)ob;
   int j = ij.intValue( );
C. int j = (Integer)lst.get(2);
D. int j = lst.getValue(2);
E. More than one of these

```
List<Integer> lst = new ArrayList<Integer>( );
lst.add(57);
lst.add(-102);
lst.add(57);
<#1>
```

Project… Big Bucks in the Bank

Create a project called *BigBucks*. It will have two classes in it, a *Tester* class and a *BankAccount* class. If you still have your *BankAccount* class from Lesson 15, just paste it into the new project. If not, the code for *BankAccount* follows:

```
public class BankAccount
{
        public BankAccount(String nm, double amt)
        {
           name = nm;
           balance = amt;
        }

        public void deposit(double dp)
        {
           balance = balance + dp;
        }

        public void withdraw(double wd)
        {
           balance = balance - wd;
        }
        public String name;
        public double balance;
}
```

You will need to create a *Tester* class that has a *main* method that provides a loop that lets you enter several *BankAccount* objects. As each is entered, it will be added to an *ArrayList* object. After several accounts have been entered, a loop will step through each *BankAccount* object in the *ArrayList* and decide which account has the largest balance that will then be printed. Following is the output screen after a typical run:

```
Please enter the name to whom the account belongs. ("Exit" to abort) Jim Jones
Please enter the amount of the deposit. 186.22

Please enter the name to whom the account belongs. ("Exit" to abort) Bill Gates
Please enter the amount of the deposit. 102.15

Please enter the name to whom the account belongs. ("Exit" to abort) Helen Hunt
Please enter the amount of the deposit. 1034.02

Please enter the name to whom the account belongs. ("Exit" to abort) Charles Manson
Please enter the amount of the deposit. 870.85

Please enter the name to whom the account belongs. ("Exit" to abort) exit

The account with the largest balance belongs to Helen Hunt.
The amount is $1034.02.
```

A partially complete *Tester* class is presented below. You are to complete the parts indicated in order to achieve the screen output above.

```
import java.io.*;
import java.util.*; //includes ArrayList
import java.text.*; //for NumberFormat
public class Tester
{
   public static void main(String args[])
   {
         NumberFormat formatter = NumberFormat.getNumberInstance( );
         formatter.setMinimumFractionDigits(2);
         formatter.setMaximumFractionDigits(2);
         String name;
         //Instantiate an ArrayList object here called aryList
         do
         {
                  Scanner kbReader = new Scanner(System.in);
                  System.out.print("Please enter the name to whom the account belongs.
                                                                      (\"Exit\" to abort)");
                  name = kbReader.nextLine( );

                  if( !name.equalsIgnoreCase("EXIT") )
                  {
                           System.out.print("Please enter the amount of the deposit. ");
                           double amount = kbReader.nextDouble();
                           System.out.println(" "); //gives an eye-pleasing blank line
                           // Create a BankAccount object
                           // Add it to the ArrayList object
                  }
         }while(!name.equalsIgnoreCase("EXIT"));

         //Search aryList and print out the name and amount of the largest bank account
         BankAccount ba = get first account in the list
         double maxBalance = ba.balance;
         String maxName = ba.name;
         for(int j = 1; j < aryLst.size( ); j++)
         {
                  ?
                  ? Step through the remaining objects and decide which one has
                    largest balance (compare each balance to maxBalance)
                  ?
         }
         Print answer
      }
   }
```

Lesson 44….. *Iterator/ListIterator*

What is iteration?

If someone asks, "Have you studied iteration yet?", you should answer, "Yes." **Loops** are iteration structures. Each pass through a loop is an iteration. Granted, if you say "iteration," it sounds like you are trying to impress someone with your vocabulary; nevertheless, iteration is a continual repeating of something…so looping fits the definition.

Position of an iterator:

Here, we wish to loop through the various objects in a list... or in other words, simply to step through positions of these objects. The concept of **position** for an iterator is central to our understanding of *Iterator* and *ListIterator* objects. Consider the following objects in a list:

```
A B C D E F G H I J
```

These objects have positions as indicated below:

```
0 1 2 3 4 5 6 7 8 9
A B C D E F G H I J
```

However, this familiar indexing scheme for the object in a list is **not** the scheme for indexing the **position of an iterator**.

For an iterator, think of the cursor in a word processor. The cursor is never **on** any particular character; rather, it is always **between** two characters. And so it is with the position of an iterator: it is always **between** two of its list objects.

```
A B C,D E F G H I J
```

Notice that we are symbolically letting a comma indicate the iterator position and that it is **between** the C and D objects above.

But what is the index of this position? In the above example, it is 3 since it comes **before** the object of index 3…D in this case.

Possible positions:

In general the possible positions of an iterator are:

1. Just before the first item (index would have a value of 0)
2. Between two adjacent list objects
3. Just after the last item (index would be the size of the list)

Two iterator interfaces:

We have two iterator interfaces available to us. The first is very simple and the other is considerably more robust.

1. *Iterator* .... interface specified in *java.util.Iterator*
   Recall that in the *List* interface that we previously studied, one of the method's signature was *Iterator iterator( )*. We **create** an *Iterator* object by calling this method.

2. *ListIterator*.....interface specified in *java.util.ListIterator*
   Recall that in the *List* interface that we previously studied, one of the method's signature was *ListIterator listIterator( )*. We **create** a *ListIterator object by calling this method.*

Iterator

The *Iterator* interface has only three methods. It is commonly used with *List* objects but can be used with other classes as well.

Iterator method signature	Action
boolean hasNext( )	Returns *true* if there are any items following the current position.
Object next( )	Returns item following current position and then advances the position… providing there is at least one item after the current position.
void remove( )	Removes the item returned by last successful *next( )* …providing there were no other intervening remove operation.

Code example:

```
List lst = new ArrayList( );  //first, create a List object
Iterator itr = lst.iterator( );  //now we have the object we want, itr.
//The position of the Iterator is at the head of the list (preceding the first object)
```

ListIterator

The *ListIterator* **has the above three methods** (action for *remove* is slightly different) **plus** some additional ones. It is only used with *List* objects, hence the name ***ListIterator***.

ListIterator method signature	Action
void remove( )	Removes the item returned by last successful *next( )* or *previous( )* …providing there were no intervening *add* or *remove* operations.
boolean hasPrevious( )	Returns *true* if there are any items preceding the current position.
Object previous( )	Returns the item preceding the current position and moves the position back.
int nextIndex( )	Returns index of next item (-1 if none). In effect this is the current position of the *ListIterator*.
int previousIndex( )	Returns index of previous item (-1 if none).
void add(o)	Insert object o just left of the current position.
void set(o)	Replaces the last item returned by last successful *next( )* or *previous( )* with object o …providing there were no intervening *add* or *remove* operations.

Creating an iterator:

An iterator object (either *Iterator* or *ListIterator*) is created in the following way:

Code example:

```
List lst = new ArrayList( );  //first, create a List object
ListIterator itr = lst.listIterator( );  //now we have the object we want, itr.
//The position of the ListIterator is at the head of the list (preceding first object)
```

Special usage of the *for*-loop:

It is possible to use either an *Iterator* or a *ListIterator* object directly with a for-loop.

Code example:

```
List lst = new ArrayList( );
...add some items to the list...
ListIterator itr = lst.listIterator( );

for(itr.next( ); itr.hasNext( ); itr.next( ))
{
        ...do something with the list...
}
```

Using generics (type parameters) with an iterator:

Notice in the following code example a cast is required in the last line even when type parameters are used to instantiate the *ArrayList* object:

Code example:

```
ArrayList<String>aryLst = new ArrayList<String>( );
aryLst.add("hello");
aryLst.add("goodbye");
Iterator itr = aryLst.iterator( );
String s = (String)itr.next( );  //Won't compile without this cast
```

If the iterator is built using a type parameter, the cast is not required:

Code example:

```
ArrayList<String>aryLst = new ArrayList<String>( );
aryLst.add("hello");
aryLst.add("goodbye");
Iterator<String>itr = aryLst.iterator( );  //Type parameter used here
String s = itr.next( );  //Cast not required
```

Although the above two examples used *Iterator*, the same is also true for *ListIterator*.

Warning:

- When running an *Iterator* or *ListIterator* on a list, don't modify the list with *List* methods. Errors will result.
- Also, it's not a good idea to simultaneously have two *Iterator*s and/or *ListIterator*s where both of them modify the list in some way. Errors will result.

Exercise A on Lesson 44

Fill in the blanks in the following table. A comma will indicate the position of the *ListIterator* whose methods are shown in the left column. Assume that we begin with a list of objects *x*, *y*, *z*, and *j* as shown in the first line of the table. A few answers are given so that you will know if you are getting them right as you go.

Method	Current Position after method executes	State of List after method executes	Value Returned
	0	,x y z j	
hasNext( )			
remove( )			
next( )			
previous( )			
remove( )			
add(y)			
next( )			
next( )			
next( )			
hasNext( )	4	y y z j,	false
hasPrevious			
previous( )			
remove( )			
previous( )			
set(p)	2	y y, p	
add(y)			
add(z)			
remove( )			
previous( )			
previous( )	2	y y, y z p	y

Exercise B on Lesson 44

In problems 1 – 5, assume the *Iterator iter* has just been created for a list containing the *Strings* "1" "2" "3". For each line of code, supply information in the rem that indicates the state of the list upon completion of code (indicate the cursor position with a comma). Also, state what's returned.

```
Object obj = iter.next( ); //1.
iter.remove; //2.
obj = iter.next( ); //3.
boolean state = iter.hasNext( ); //4.
for (int i = 1; i <= 3; i++)
{
        iter.next( ); //5.
}
```

In problems 6 – 10, write code segments to accomplish the tasks with *ListIterator iter*. Assume the code for these problems is performed in sequence so that the result of each problem is the starting point for the next problem. Also assume that the list initially consists of **"1", "2" "3".** (Notice the initial position of the iterator.)

6. Move to the last item and display it.

7. Move to the first item and display it.

8. Remove the item at the middle position.

9. Replace the last item with the *String* "last".

10. Insert the *String* "middle" at the middle position.

11. Write code that will display the last *String* object in a list of *String* objects in which we do not know how long the list is, but we do know it's not empty. Assume a *ListIterator* object, *iter* has just been created. Use it in your code instead of *List* methods.

In questions 12 – 13 assume a *List* object has been created as follows:

List myList = new ArrayList( );

12. Use *myList* to create an *Iterator* object called *itr*.

13. Use *myList* to create a *ListIterator* object called *lstIter*.

Iterator/ListIterator… Contest Type Problems

1. What replaces **<*1>** in the code to the right to make *itr* an *Iterator* type for the *myList* object?

   A. Iterator itr = iterator(myList);
   B. Iterator itr = myList.iterator( );
   C. Iterator itr = (List) myList.iterator( );
   D. Iterator itr = List.myList.iterator( );
   E. None of these

2. If **<*1>** has been filled in correctly in the code to the right, what is printed when the *main* method executes?

   A. 5.04.03.02.01.00.0
   B. 543210
   C. 0.01.02.03.04.05.0
   D. 012345
   E. None of these

```
import java.util.*;
public class Tester
{
    public static void main(String args[])
    {
        List<Double>dblList = new ArrayList<Double>( );
        for(double d=5; d>=0; d--)
        {
            dblList.add( d );
        }

        traverseAndPrint(dblList);
    }

    public static void traverseAndPrint(List myList)
    {
        <*1>
        while( itr.hasNext( ) )
        {
            System.out.print( itr.next( ) );
        }
    }
}
```

3. What would be the appropriate replacement code for **<*1>** to the right that will cause all of the members of the linked list to be printed?

   A. lnkLst.itr.next( )
   B. lnlLst(itr)
   C. itr.next( )
   D. Iterator.next(itr)
   E. None of these

4. Assuming that **<*1>** has been filled in correctly, what inherited method from the cosmic superclass *Object* is ultimately called inside the *println* method that converts the contents of the returned *Objects* to a printable form?

   A. hashCode( )
   B. equals( )
   C. clone( )
   D. toString( )
   E. None of these

```
public static void doSomething(LinkedList lnkLst)
{
        Iterator itr = lnkLst.iterator( );

        while(itr.hasNext( ))
        {
            System.out.println(<*1>);
        }
}
```

5. What would be the replacement code for **<*1>** to the right in order that items be removed from the list?
 	
A. itr.remove( )
B. Iterator.itr.remove( )
C. lst.remove( )
D. itr.remove(lst.next( ))
E. More than one of these
	```List<String>lst = new ArrayList<String>( );```
	```String s[] = "Hello to you".split("\\s");```
	```for(int j = 0; j < s.length; j++)```
	```{```
	``` lst.add(s[j]);```
	```}```
	
	```Iterator itr = lst.iterator( );```
	```for(itr.next( ); itr.hasNext( ); itr.next( ))```
	```{```
	``` <*1>;```
	```}```
	```System.out.println(lst);```

6. What is the output of the code to the right? A. you B. Hellotoyou C. [ ] D. [you] E. Nothing is printed	
7. What would be the resulting change in the output if *ArrayList* in the code to the right was replaced with *LinkedList*? A. No change B. List would print in reverse order C. Illegal, would not compile D. Nothing would be printed E. None of these	
8. What is the running time of the loop to the right containing **<*1>** if there are *n* items in the list? A. O(1) B. O(n) C. O(n^2) D. O(log n) E. None of these	

9. What replaces **<#1>** in the code to the right so that all floating point numbers in *myLst* are printed?
 	
A. Double d = itr.next( );
B. Double d = (Double)itr.next( );
C. Double d = <Double>itr.next( );
D. Double d = (Double)myLst.next( );
E. More than one of these
	```ArrayList<Double>myLst = new```
	``` ArrayList<Double>( );```
	```myList.add(101.24);```
	``` //...add more doubles...```
	
	```Iterator<Double>itr = myLst.iterator( );```
	```while(itr.hasNext( )```
	```{```
	``` <#1>```
	``` System.out.println(d);```
	```}```

10. What other type objects could be added to *myLst*? A. *Float* B. *String* C. *Integer* D. More than one of these E. None of these	

Project… Big Bucks Revisited

Look back in Lesson 43 at the *BigBucks* Project. Load that project and modify it so that you use a *ListIterator* object to add *BankAccount* objects to the list. Then use the *ListIterator* object to iterate through the list and identify the account with the largest balance. The output will be exactly as it was for the previous project. See the code below for suggested modifications in bold print.

```
import java.io.*;
import java.util.*;
import java.text.*; //for NumberFormat
public class Tester
{
  public static void main(String args[])
  {
    NumberFormat formatter = NumberFormat.getNumberInstance( );
    formatter.setMinimumFractionDigits(2);
    formatter.setMaximumFractionDigits(2);

    String name;
    ArrayList aryLst = new ArrayList( );
    …Create a ListIterator object called iter…
    do
    {
      Scanner kbReader = new Scanner(System.in);
      System.out.print("Please enter the name to whom the account belongs. (\"Exit\" to abort) ");
      name = kbReader.nextLine( );

      if( !name.equalsIgnoreCase("EXIT") )
      {
        System.out.print("Please enter the amount of the deposit. ");
        double amount = kbReader.nextDouble( );
        System.out.println(" "); //gives an eye pleasing blank line between accounts

        BankAccount theAccount = new BankAccount(name, amount);
        …Use iter to add theAccount to the list…
      }
    }while(!name.equalsIgnoreCase("EXIT"));

    //Search aryLst and print out the name and amount of the largest bank account
    BankAccount ba = use iter to get the last bank account in the list
    double maxBalance = ba.balance; //set last account as winner so far
    String maxName = ba.name;
    while( …use iter to see if we should continue looping…)
    {
      …Step through all objects and decide which has the largest balance…
    }

    System.out.println(" ");
    System.out.println("The account with the largest balance belongs to " + maxName + ".");
    System.out.println("The amount is $" + formatter.format(maxBalance) + ".");
  }
}
```

Lesson 45….. *Comparable* and *Comparator* Interfaces

The purpose:

The purpose of both the *Comparable* and *Comparator* interfaces is to enable us to **compare objects.**

***Comparable* Interface:**

The *Comparable* interface contains only **one** method and is specified in *java.util.Arrays*:

```
public interface Comparable
{
        int compareTo(Object otherObject);  // a.compareTo(b)...returns a neg number if
                                            //a < b; returns a pos number if a > b; returns
                                            //0 if a = b.
}
```

Comparing objects:

The most obvious standard Java class that implements the *Comparable* interface is the *String* class. You can implement *Comparable* for your own classes too. Following is an example of a *BankAccount* class in which we will implement *Comparable*. First, we must decide what it means to compare two bank accounts.

1. Do we mean to compare the dates of when the two accounts were opened?
2. Do we mean to compare the amount on deposit (the balance)?
3. Do we mean to compare a "flaky factor" (number of times the account was overdrawn)?

For our example we will compare the amount on deposit (the balance) since this seems the most natural; however, it should be emphasized that **we can define the comparison in any way we might desire**.

First, let's examine how we will call this *compareTo* method. Assume that in some *Tester* class we have the following code.

```
//Create an account called myAccount with a balance of $40.
BankAccount myAccount = new BankAccount("Hilary", 40);

//Create an account called yourAccount with a balance of $135.
BankAccount yourAccount = new BankAccount("Kallie", 135);

//Now, compare these two objects using the compareTo method
int j;
j = myAccount.compareTo(yourAccount);

// If we test j with an if-statement we should see that it's a negative number since
// the balance in myAccount, 40, is less than the balance in yourAccount, 135.
```

And now here is the *BankAccount* class in which we will implement the *Comparable* interface:

```
public class BankAccount implements Comparable
{
	public BankAccount(String nm, double bal)  //Constructor
	{
		name = nm;
		balance = bal;
	}
	. . . other methods . . .

	public int compareTo(Object otherObject)
	{
		//otherObject is passed in as an Object type so let's convert it into
		//a BankAccount type object.
		BankAccount otherAccount = (BankAccount) otherObject;

		int retValue;
		if (balance < otherAccount.balance)
		{
			retValue =  –1;
		}
		else
		{
			if (balance > otherAccount.balance)
			{
				retValue = 1;
			}
			else
			{
				retValue = 0;
			}
		}
		return retValue;
	}
	public String name;
	public double balance;
}
```

You may be concerned that the following line of code in *Tester*,

```
j = myAccount.compareTo(yourAccount);
```

is incompatible with the following line of code (the signature of the *compareTo* method)

```
public int compareTo(Object otherObject),
```

since *yourAccount* is a ***BankAccount*** object and *otherObject* is of type ***Object***. This is not a problem since **any** type object **can be** stored in an *Object* type object. However, if you wish to store an *Object* type object in some other object **it must be cast**.

Using *Comparable* with wrapper class numerics:

Integer and *Double* type variables work directly with the *compareTo* method as shown in the following examples:

***Integer* example:**

```
Integer x = new Integer(5); //Java 5.0, Integer x = 5;
Integer y = new Integer(17); //Java 5.0, Integer y = 17;
System.out.println( x.compareTo(y) ); //negative number
```

***Double* example:**

```
Double x = new Double(52.5); //Java 5.0, Double x = 52.5;
Double y = new Double (11.8); //Java 5.0, Double y = 11.8;
System.out.println( x.compareTo(y) ); //positive number
```

Casting *Object* type objects to *Comparable:*

Suppose you have the following type method that receives an *Object* type parameter. The reason we receive an *Object* type is so as to make this method as **general** as possible, i.e., so it can receive **any** type object:

```
public static void theMethod(Object obj)
{                    }
```

There is, however, a problem if we wish to use *obj* with a *compareTo* method in the code portion of *theMethod. Object* does not implement the *Comparable* class nor does it have a *compareTo* method. There are two ways to solve this problem:

Receive *obj* as a *Comparable* object :

```
public static void theMethod(Comparable obj)
```

Cast *obj* as *Comparable*:

```
public static void theMethod(Object obj1)
{
        …some code…
        //assume obj2 is also of Object type
        int c = ( (Comparable)obj1 ).compareTo( (Comparable)obj2 );
        //Notice the nesting of the parenthesis above
        …some code…
}
```

Using the *compareTo* method for sorting

Recall from Lesson 19 that we used *Arrays.sort(a)* to sort a numeric array. We use exactly this same syntax to sort an array of objects **if** the class for those objects has implemented the *Comparable* interface. To sort the array named *ba_array* of type *BankAccount* in which *Comparable* has been implemented, simply issue the command:

```
Arrays.sort(ba_array);
```

***Comparator* Interface:**

Occasionally, we might need a *compareTo* method in a class that we don't own or is otherwise impossible for us to modify. Or, perhaps there is already a *compareTo* method in the class of interest; however, we might want to sort objects in a way different from the standard specifications for the *compareTo* method. In these cases we need a **different** way. That alternative way is provided with the *Comparator* interface.

The *Comparator* interface also has only **one** method:

```
public interface Comparator
{
        int compare(Object firstObject, Object secondObject);
                // returns a neg number if firstObject < secondObject;
                //returns a pos number if firstObject > secondObject; returns 0 if
                //firstObject = secondObject.
}
```

This *Comparator* interface is generally used to declare a *Comparator* object (let's call it *comp*) that could then be used to sort using either:

1. Arrays.sort(a, comp); //Sorts the a[] array of **objects** in ascending order. This //method is overloaded. There is also a single parameter //version presented in Lesson 19

2. Collections.sort(al, comp); //uses a merge sort and sorts the **ArrayList** al

***Comparator* example:**

As an example let's use a *BankAccount* class again, but this time **without** implementing any interface.

```
public class BankAccount
{
        public BankAccount(double bal)
        {
                balance = bal;
        }
        . . . other methods . . .

        public double balance;
}
```

We will now need to create a *BankAccount* comparator class; let's call it *BA_comparator*. Notice this one **does** implement the *Comparator* interface.

```
import java.util.*; //necessary for Comparator interface
public class BA_comparator implements Comparator
{
        public int compare(Object firstObject, Object secondObject)
        {
                BankAccount ba1 = (BankAccount) firstObject;
                BankAccount ba2 = (BankAccount) secondObject;

                int retValue;
                if (ba1.balance < ba2.balance)
                {
                        retValue = -1;
                }
                else
```

```
                {
                        if (ba1.balance > ba2.balance)
                        {
                                retValue = 1;
                        }
                        else
                        {
                                retValue = 0;
                        }
                }
                return retValue;
        }
}
```

Following is code for a *Tester* class in which we would sort an array of *BankAccount* objects:

```
//Create an array, BankAccount[ ]
BankAccount ba[ ] = new BankAccount[500];
ba[0] = new BankAccount(128);
ba[1] = new BankAccount(1200);
ba[2] = new BankAccount(621);
. . .

// Now create a comparator object using the BA_comparator class above.
Comparator comp = new BA_comparator( );

//Sort the array
Arrays.sort(ba, comp);
```

Sorting contents of a *List* object:

Similarly, to sort an *ArrayList object (also works for LinkedList and Vector objects)*:

```
ArrayList recipeList = new ArrayList( );
...some code to add Recipe objects to the list...

// This assumes we have already written another class called
// RecipeComparator (in which we compare calories) that is similar to the
// BA_comparator class above.
Comparator comp = new RecipeComparator( );

//Now do the sort
Collections.sort(recipeList, comp);  //Makes it possible for iterator to step through
                                     //the list in the prescribed order.
```

This *ArrayList* can also be sorted using *Collections.sort(recipeList);* if the objects comprising the list implement the *Comparable* interface and have an appropriate *compareTo* method.

The most difficult objects to **compare** are images. For an enrichment activity, see Appendix U in which an activity is described that involves scanning a printed document and then applying OCR (optical character recognition) software.

Adapting to either *Comparable* or *Comparator*

There are occasions in which we wish create a class where there is a need to compare two objects and we have no knowledge ahead of time of whether the objects to be compared are *Comparable* or if a comparator is provided. The desire is to make our class as general as possible so as to adapt to **either** possibility. Here is how to do it:

- In the constructor for the class, receive as a parameter a *Comparator* object. A *null* may possibly be passed for this parameter in case the objects used in the class are *Comparable* rather than having a comparator. Initialize a state variable with this *Comparator* object as shown below (even if a null is passed):

```
public YourClass(…other parameters as needed…, Comparator cp)
//Constructor
{
        …
        cmptr = cp;
        …
}

//State variables
Comparator cmptr;
…
```

- Create a method in which the comparison will be done. Assuming that the objects to be compared are of the *Object* type, the method will receive two parameters, *obj1* and *obj2,* both of *Object type*. The method will return an integer that is:

    - less than 0 if *obj1* < *obj2*
    - greater than 0 if *obj1* > *obj2*
    - 0 if *obj1* equals *obj2*

  It is assumed that the *cmptr* object adheres to these same rules if it is not *null*. The method shown below implements all these ideas.

```
private int compareObjects(Object obj1, Object obj2)
{
        if(cmptr = = null)
        {   return ((Comparable)obj1).compareTo(obj2);  }
        else
        {  return cmptr.compare(obj1, obj2);  }
}
```

- Call the *compareObjects* methods when a comparison of two objects is needed.

Exercise for Lesson 45

1. What is the central purpose of both the *Comparable* and *Comparator* interfaces?

2. Name a standard Java class that implements the *Comparable* interface.

For problems 3 – 4, consider the following *PoochyPavy* class:

```
public class PoochyPavy implements Comparable
{
        public PoochyPavy(int k)
        {
                value = k;
        }

        public int compareTo(Object nerd) //This method doesn't follow the normal rules
        {
                PoochyPavy  pp = (PoochyPavy) nerd;

                int r;
                if (value = = 6 * pp.value)
                {
                        r = 136;
                }
                else
                {
                        r = -137;
                }
                return r;
        }

        ...other methods...

        public int value;
}
```

3.
```
PoochyPavy mpp = new PoochyPavy(30);
PoochyPavy vvv = new PoochyPavy(5);
System.out.println(mpp.compareTo(vvv)); //What's printed?
```

4. Of course the above implementation of *compareTo* is ridiculous. If it had been done correctly, what would have been printed in #3 above?

5. Rewrite the code for the *compareTo* method in *PoochyPavy* so that it works according to the specifications in the *Comparable* interface.

6. Suppose you have an array of objects, *obj[ ]*. Also, assume a *Comparator* class implementing *Comparator* has been created and that its name is *CompClass*. Write code that will let you sort the *obj[ ]* array using the sort method of the *Arrays* class. Assume that *CompClass* appropriately compares two *obj* objects.

7. Realizing that if *String x1* comes alphabetically before *String x2*, then it can be said that *x1* < *x2*….what is printed by the following?

```
String s1 = "larry";
String s2 = "curly";
if (s1.compareTo(s2) > 0)
{
        System.out.println("ABC");
}
if (s2.compareTo(s1) = = 0)
{
        System.out.println("XYZ");
}
if (s1.compareTo(s2) < 0)
{
        System.out.println("Yes");
}
```

8. Assume that you have written a date class, called *TheDate*, that implements *Comparable*. Its *compareTo* method correctly compares dates where an earlier date is considered "less than" a later date. Consider the creation of the following two objects:

```
TheDate date1 = new TheDate("11/25/2003");
TheDate date2 = new TheDate("12/03/1945");
```

What will *date2.compareTo(date1)* return?

9. Monster munster= new Monster("Herman");
   Object myObj = munster;
   Monster myMonster = myObj; //Modify this line so it will work.

10. On your own paper, write a class called *Vaulter* that has two state variables…. *name*, a *String*, and *highest_vault*, an integer. The constructor should allow a person's name to be passed in (and then handed-off to *name*) and also a number that represents in inches that person's highest vault (pass it off to *highest_vault*). Furthermore, this class implements the *Comparable* interface.

11. Write code that will compare two *Integers* *p* and *q* and print one of three things… “p>q”, “p<q”, or “p=q”.

12. Repair the following code so that it will work.

```
public static void doSomething(Comparable ob, Object job)
{
        …some code…
        String s = ob.compareTo(job);
        …some code…
}
```

13. Repair the following code so that it will work.

```
public static void doSomething(Object ob, Comparable job)
{
        …some code…
        String s = ob.compareTo(job);
        …some code…
}
```

Comparable/Comparator... Contest Type Problems

1. Which of these signatures represents the method that must be added to the *Car* class so that it implements the *Comparable* interface?

   A. public int equals(Object o)
   B. public boolean equals(Object o)
   C. public boolean compareTo(Object o)
   D. public int Comparable(Object o)
   E. None of these

2. What replaces **<*1>** in the code to the right so that the methods of the *Car* class are forced to include those of the *Comparable* interface?

   A. (Comparable)
   B. implements Comparable
   C. extends Comparable
   D. is Comparable
   E. None of these

```
public class Car <*1>
{
        //code not shown
}
```

3. What replaces **<*1>** in the code to the right to determine if *obj[mid]* is the same as the object being searched for?

   A. comp = = 0
   B. !comp
   C. comp = = -1
   D. comp > 0
   E. None of these

4. What is replacement code for **<*2>** in the code to the right to determine if *obj[mid]* is smaller than *lookFor*?

   A. !comp
   B. comp > 0
   C. comp = = -1
   D. comp = = 0
   E. None of these

```
//Binary Search
//Return true if Object lookFor is found in the obj
//array(ascending order)…otherwise false.
public static boolean bSrch(Comparable[] obj, Object
                                                lookFor)
{
    int start=0, end=obj.length-1;
    int mid;
    do
    {
        mid=(start + end) / 2;
        int comp = obj[mid].compareTo(lookFor);
        if(<*1>)
            return true;
        else if(<*2>)
            start = mid + 1;
        else
            end = mid – 1;
    }while(start <= end);
    return false;
}
```

5. Which of the following is possible as the return value of *s1.compareTo(s2)* if *s1* is a lower case *String*, *s2* is an upper case *String*, and with *s1* coming before *s2* in the dictionary?

A. 2 B. 0 C. -1 D. “<” E. None of these

6. Which of the following is not a subclass of *Object*?

A. String B. Comparable C. Both A and B D.Integer E. None of these

Project… Sorting *BankAccount* Objects

Back in Lesson 43 we created a *BigBucks* project. In Lesson 44 we modified it and called it the *ListIterator* project. We are going to modify it yet again. Of primary interest is the *BankAccount* class. It will now include a *compareTo* method that we will use to sort an array of *BankAccount* objects.

First, add the *compareTo* method to the *BankAccount* class. This method is given on page 45-2 of this lesson. Don't forget to designate *implements Comparable* in the class signature.

Next, modify the *Tester* class as detailed below.

```
import java.io.*;
import java.util.*;
import java.text.*;  //for NumberFormat
public class Tester
{
   public static void main(String args[])
   {
          NumberFormat formatter = NumberFormat.getNumberInstance( );
          formatter.setMinimumFractionDigits(2);
          formatter.setMaximumFractionDigits(2);

          String name;
          int j;
          Create a BankAccount object array ba[ ], length 5
          for(j =0; j < ba.length; j++)
          {
                 Scanner kbReader = new Scanner(System.in);
                 System.out.print("Please enter the name to whom the account belongs. ");
                 name = kbReader.nextLine( );

                 System.out.print("Please enter the amount of the deposit. ");
                 double amount = kbReader.nextDouble( );
                 System.out.println(" ");  //gives a blank line between accounts

                 Instantiate object ba[j] using name and amount
          }

          Sort the ba array using the sort method in the Arrays class

          Print the ordered array in this format
                 Harry Houdini >>> 298.44
   }
}
```

The following is a typical run:

```
Please enter the name to whom the account belongs. Bill Gates
Please enter the amount of the deposit. 473.92

Please enter the name to whom the account belongs. George Bush
Please enter the amount of the deposit. 3873.20

Please enter the name to whom the account belongs. Colin Powell
Please enter the amount of the deposit. 379.23

Please enter the name to whom the account belongs. Jim Carey
Please enter the amount of the deposit. 372.82

Please enter the name to whom the account belongs. Dennis Quaid
Please enter the amount of the deposit. 3721.49

    Jim Carey >>> 372.82
    Colin Powell >>> 379.23
    Bill Gates >>> 473.92
    Dennis Quaid >>> 3,721.49
    George Bush >>> 3,873.20
```

Project… Sorting *BankAccount* Objects Alphabetically

Modify the last project so that it sorts alphabetically on the names instead of on the balances in the accounts. The only thing that needs to be changed is the *compareTo* method in the *BankAccount* class. The output should appear as follows:

```
Bill Gates >>> 473.92
Colin Powell >>> 379.23
Dennis Quaid >>> 3,721.49
George Bush >>> 3,873.20
Jim Carey >>> 372.82
```

Project… Sorting *BankAccount* Objects using a *Comparator*

Modify the last project so that it again sorts on the balances in the accounts; however, this time we will use a Comparator object. Delete the *compareTo* method from the *BankAccount* class, and eliminate *implements Comparable* from the class signature. Create a *Comparator* class and call the *Arrays.sort* method as detailed on pages 45-4 and 45-5. The output will appear as follows:

```
Jim Carey >>> 372.82
Colin Powell >>> 379.23
Bill Gates >>> 473.92
Dennis Quaid >>> 3,721.49
George Bush >>> 3,873.20
```

Document all aspects of your project using *javaDoc* as described in Appendix AE. View the following link to see how your final documentation will appear:

http://www.bluepelicanjava.com/javaDoc/index.html

Lesson 46….. *HashSet/TreeSet*

Pros and cons:

We saw the *List* interface applied to the *ArrayList*, *LinkedList*, and *Vectors* classes. These lists are all **ordered** in the sense that an iterator accesses the items of the list in the same order **in which they were entered**. The underlying software must "remember" the order and this results in **poorer performance** (speed) when applying the *List* methods. Sets and maps overcome this performance limitation. The downside is that the items are stored (and accessed) in an order according to how the software wants to do it. They are **not** stored in the order in which they were entered.

***Set interface*:**

The most common methods of the *Set* interface in *java.util.Set* are given by:

Method Signature	Action
boolean add(Object obj)	If the object equivalent is not in the set, then *obj* is added to the set and a *true* is returned … otherwise, a *false* is returned and **nothing** is added to the set. (Duplicate items are not permitted in the set.)
void clear( )	Removes all objects from the set.
boolean contains(Object obj)	Returns *true* if *obj* is in the set … otherwise, *false*.
boolean isEmpty( )	Returns *true* if the set is empty … otherwise, *false*.
Iterator iterator( )	Returns an *Iterator* object for this set.
boolean remove(Object obj)	If *obj* is in the set, it is removed and a *true* is returned, … otherwise a *false* is returned.
int size( )	Returns the number of objects currently in the set.
boolean removeAll(Collection c)	Removes from this set all of its elements that are contained in *Collection c*. Returns *true* if changes to the set are made.
boolean retainAll(Collection c)	Retains only the elements in this set that are contained in the *Collection c*. Returns *true* if changes to the set are made.

As with the *List* interface, notice that only **objects of type *Object*** are stored in the set. The *Set* interface alone won't do anything. By definition, all methods are abstract (no implementing code). What we need are some implementing classes.

Implementation:

There are **two classes** that **implement** the *Set interface*. Each has its own rules for determining the order in which objects are stored. Remember, the items will be stored in the order it wants, **not** the order in which we add them.

1. ***HashSet*** …a hash code is computed for each object and then the items are stored in the order of these hash codes. We will not concern ourselves with these hash codes except to say that when an object is added to a *HashSet*, the method *hashCode( )* inside the *Object* class is called. (*Set s = new HashSet( )* will create a new *HashSet* object.)

2. ***TreeSet*** … items are stored in a tree structure that result in an iterator encountering the items in a natural order (alphabetical, etc.). (Instantiate with *Set s = new TreeSet( ).*)

Generics (type parameters):

While on the subject of instantiating *Set* objects it should be mentioned that Java 5.0 now allows type parameters (generics). For example, consider the following in which a *TreeSet* object is created, and to which only wrapper class integers may be added:

```
TreeSet<Integer>s = new TreeSet<Integer>( );
```

This insures "type safety" and would result in a compile time error if we ever tried to add some other type object to *s*. This concept is similar to templates in c++. Type parameters ordinarily remove the burden of casting retrieved *Object* type objects back to their original type. However, with a set, objects can only be retrieved with an iterator, and, unfortunately, must still be cast unless the iterator also uses type parameters (see page 44-3).

Accessing items in the set:

How do we access the items in our set? We use an *Iterator*. Notice that one of the methods above allows us to create an *Iterator* for our set. It is important to note that we get the *Iterator* and not a *ListIterator*. After all, a *ListIterator* would be for a ***List*** and what we have here is a ***Set*** …, duh. Therefore, we see that the items in a set are **not accessed by index** (as is done with the *ListIterator*).

Recall that an *Iterator* has only three methods:

1. *hasNext()*
2. *next()*… we are especially interested in this one since it returns the *Object* following the current position of the *Iterator*.
3. *remove()*

Printing a set:

Use *System.out.println(s);* to print *Set s*. Its *toString* method typically yields something like "[a, b, c, d]" where *a, b, c,*… represents the objects stored in *s*. Note the use of square brackets.

Exercise for Lesson 46

1. In what ways does a *Set* differ from a *List*?
2. How do you visit and print all items in a *Set*? Show code if you like.
3. Suppose you want to work with a set of integers. How would you go about adding primitive integer type variables to *Set s*?
4. What two classes implement the *Set* interface?
5. How would you go about creating an *Iterator* for a *Set* called *s*?
6. What are the three methods of an *Iterator* object?
7. Why is the performance of a *List* object fundamentally worse than that of a *Set* object?

8. What are two ways to determine if a *Set s* is empty?

9. If *Set s* has the following attempts at adding *Integer* equivalents to it, what is the value of *s.size( )*? {5,-18, 2, 5, -1, 5}

10. Show how to use the *removeAll* method to completely empty *Set s*.

Project… *HashSet*/Intersection

Consider the following two sets:

s1 = {"Bill", "Larry", "Adolph", "Regina", "Susie"}
s2 = {"Larry", "Jack", "Alice", "June", "Benny", "Susie"}

Clearly, the intersection of these two sets is {"Larry", "Susie"}. Your job is to create a class called *Hash_Set* whose *main* method finds this intersection. Make the indicated modifications in the code below to accomplish this:

```
import java.util.*;  //we need java.util.Set, java.util.HashSet, and java.util.Iterator
public class Hash_Set
{
        public static void main(String args[])
        {
                Set s1 = new HashSet( ); //Create s1
                   s1.add("Bill");
                        …
                Set s2 = new HashSet( ); //Create s2
                   s2.add("Larry");
                        …

                //Build the intersection set, s3
                Create a set, s3
                Create iter1, an Iterator for s1
                while( ??? )
                {
                        Use iter1 to cycle through all objects in s1.
                        Use s2.contains(obj) to see if a particular object from s1 is in s2
                        If it is, then add this object to s3
                }

                //Print the intersection set
                Create iter3, an Iterator for s3
                while( ??? )
                { Use iter3 to cycle thru all objects in s3 and then print them. }
        }
}
```

If all occurrences of *HashSet* above are changed to *TreeSet*, you will get exactly the same results except they will print in a different order.

Project… *HashSet*/Union

Modify the ***Intersection*** project so as to make *s3* the **Union** of *s1* and *s2*.

The code will be substantially the same except for the loop where we formerly created the intersection. We now just blindly add every object of *s1* to *s3* (which will eventually be the complete union set).

Following this loop, create another loop where we again just blindly add objects from *s2* to *s3*. No harm is done if we try to add duplicate objects that are already in *s3*. Recall that the *add* method will **not** add an object to a set if its equivalent is **already** there.

The output of your program should give the set (the order is not important):

{"Larry", "Jack", "Alice", "June", "Benny", "Susie", "Bill", "Adolph", "Regina"}

Project… Don't Make Me Take That Final!

Miss Informed has a policy of allowing her students to be exempt from her final exam if certain criteria have been met. First, a student must have made 89 or above in **all** his or her classes. Second, he or she must have had no discipline referrals to the principal's office. Shown below are the contents of a typical data file that she would need to analyze to see if students are exempt:

```
12 9
Bob English 98
Larry English 92
Alice English 96
Wilbur English 93
Bob Math 91
Larry Math 99
Alice Math 99
Wilbur Math 90
Bob History 87
Larry History 90
```

(continued)

```
Alice History 98
Wilbur History 94
Pete Jan 21
Pete Jan 22
John Feb 4
Bob Feb 19
Pete Mar 8
Jack Mar 20
Alice Mar 28
Fred April 5
Sally May 4
```

The first line of data contains two integers. The first integer, 12 in the example, indicates the number of lines of grade data that follows. The second integer, 9 in the example, indicates the number of lines of discipline data that follows the grade data. The resulting output for this data (required in alphabetical order) represents the students that are exempt:

```
Larry
Wilbur
```

Note that extraneous information is given. It is not necessary to know the course name or the date of a discipline referral. Produce the required output by using a set in your program in which you add names to the set if they have an A in a course and then remove them if a grade below 90 is encountered. Then, as you cycle through the discipline data, remove any names from the set that you encounter there. Finally, use an iterator to cycle through the set and print the names. If you use the *TreeSet* class, the names will automatically be in alphabetical order.

HashSet/TreeSet... Contest Type Problems

1. Which of the following replaces **<*1>** in the code to the right so as to determine whether *Set s1* is a subset of *Set s2*?

   A. !s2.contains(itr.next( ))
   B. s2[itr.next( )] = = false
   C. s2.contains(itr.next( ))
   D. s2.add(itr.next( ))
   E. None of these

2. Assume **<*1>** has been filled in correctly. Which of the following checks whether *Set s1* and *Set s2* contain the same elements?

   A. subset(s1, s2) && subset(s2, s1)
   B. (s1.compareTo(s2) = = 0)
   C. Both A and B
   D. subset(s1,s2) || subset(s2,s1)
   E. None of these

```
//This method is in the class that implements Set
public int compareTo(Object obj)
{
    ... Code that returns a 0 if the sets are identical,
    ... returns –1 if they are not identical.
}

//This method is in some other class
public static boolean subset(Set s1, Set s2)
{
    Iterator itr = s1.iterator( );
    while( itr.hasNext( ) )
    {
        if (<*1>)
            return false;
    }
    return true;
}
```

3. What replaces **<*1>** in the code to the right so that an object implementing the *Set* interface is created?

   A. new HashSet( )
   B. new TreeSet( )
   C. new BinaryTreeSet( )
   D. new SetTree( )
   E. More than one of these

4. Assume that **<*1>** has been filled in correctly. If *List lst* contains the wrapper class equivalents of the elements below, what is returned by the *static* method call *total(lst)*?

   {18 97 5 3 22}

   A. 8 B. 7 C. 6 D. 5

   E. None of these

```
public static int total(List theList)
{
    Set st = <*1>;
    Iterator iter = theList.iterator( );
    while( iter.hasNext( ) )
    {
        st.add( iter.next( ) );
    }
    st.add(new Integer(3));
    st.add(new Integer(18));
    int tot = st.size( );
    return tot;
}
```

5. Which *Object* class method is called when the *HashSet add( )* method is called?

   A. compareTo( ) B. new hashCode( ) C. hashCode( )

   D. new Hash( ) E. None of these

6. Which of the following types is capable of producing an object that could be used to "step through" the members of a *Set*, one element at a time?

A. *List* B. *Iterator* C. *String* D. *Map* E. None of these

7. Which of the following is a valid declaration of a data member of a *Store* class? This data member is to hold an arbitrarily large number of *Inventory* objects.

A. private Set merchandise = new Set;
B. private Set merchandise = TreeSet(Inventory);
C. private Set merchandise = new HashSet( );
D. private Inventory[] = new Inventory[];
E. More than one of these

```
public class Inventory
{
    public Inventory(double price, String item)
    {
        this.price = (price>0)?value : .01;
        this.item = item;
    }

    public double getPrice( )
    {
        return price;
    }

    public String getItem( )
    {
        return item;
    }

    private double price;
    private String item;
}
```

Lesson 47….. *HashMap/TreeMap*

The nature of a map:

A map is like a mathematical function, i.e., a set of points { (x1, y1), (x2, y2), …}. With a map we call the *x* numbers the "keys" and the *y* numbers the "values". However, with a map we must use **objects** instead of primitive numbers for both keys and values.

Consider the following map arrangement (people and their favorite colors) of keys and values:

Keys	Values
Romeo-------------- >	red
Adam--------------- >	green
Eve------------------->	blue
Juliet----------------->	blue

Just as with a mathematical function, each key may only associate with **one** value; however, each value may associate with **several** keys. In plain English, that means that in our example above, each person can have only one favorite color. However, notice that blue is the favorite color of two different people. In even "plainer" English, keys can't be repeated, values can.

Different names:

A map goes by several different names including the following:

1. Keyed list
2. Dictionary
3. Association list
4. Table (this one is very common)

Following is a table that illustrates the mapping of keys to values:

Key	Value
"Name"	"Alfred E. Neuman"
"Job title"	"Latrine Orderly"
"Age"	19
"Sex"	"M"
"Hourly wage"	6.14

Both keys and values are added to a map in the form of objects. Notice in the above table that three of the values are *String* objects, one must be a wrapper class *Integer* and the last must be a wrapper class *Double*.

Map interface:

The most commonly used methods of the *Map interface* are as follows:

Method Signature	Action
void clear( )	Removes all *key-value* pairs from the map
boolean containsKey(Object key)	Returns *true* if the indicated *key* is present…otherwise, *false*.
boolean containsValue(Object value)	Returns *true* if the indicated *value* is present…otherwise, *false*.
Set entrySet( )	Returns a *Set* of *Map.Entry* objects. These are *key-value* pairs, and the **only** way to obtain a reference to these

	objects is from an iterator of this set. (Note that *Entry* is an inner interface of *Map*.)
Object get(Object key)	Returns the value associated with the indicated *key* … returns *null* if *key* is not present.
boolean isEmpty( )	Returns *true* if the map is empty…otherwise, *false*.
Set keySet( )	Returns a ***Set*** of the keys in the map. An *Iterator* object can be built from this *Set*.
Object put(Object key, Object value)	If *key* is already in the map, the previous *value* is replaced with the new *value* and the previous *value* is returned… otherwise, the *key-value* pair is added to the map and *null* is returned. Notice **only objects** can be added to the map.
Object remove(Object key)	If *key* is in the map, the *key-value* pair is removed and the *value* is returned…otherwise, returns *null*.
int size( )	Returns the number of *key-value* pairs in the map.
Collection values( )	Returns a *Collection* object of the *value*s in a map.

Implementing a map:

Just as the *Set* interface has two classes that implement it, so does the *Map* interface:

1. *HashMap* …an iterator will encounter the keys in what may appear to be a random order.
2. *TreeMap* …an iterator will encounter the keys in a "natural order" (alphabetical, etc.).

Retrieving key–value pairs:

We will now illustrate code that will output the key-value pairs in a *Map* object. There are two ways to do this:

Example 1:

```
Map myMap = new HashMap( );
myMap.put("Mary", new Integer(15));  //Mary is 15 years old
//Java 5.0, myMap.put("Mary", 15);
…add more key-value pairs…

Set ks = myMap.keySet( );
Iterator iter = ks.iterator( );
while( iter.hasNext( ) )
{
        Object key = iter.next( );
        Object value = myMap.get(key);
        System.out.println(key + "------>" + value);
}
```

Example 2:

```
Map myMap = new TreeMap( );
myMap.put("Mary", 15);
myMap.put("Bob", 20);

Set es = myMap.entrySet( );
Iterator it = es.iterator( );
while(it.hasNext( ))
```

```
{
        Map.Entry entry = (Map.Entry)it.next( );
        System.out.println(entry);
                //Instead of the above two lines we could just have,
                //System.out.println( it.next( ) );
}
```

This resulting printout is as follows:

```
Bob=20
Mary=15
```

Generics (type parameters):

It should be noted that *Map* objects can make use of type parameters (generics) since the release of Java 5.0. This is somewhat similar to the concept of templates in c++ and is illustrated by the following:

```
Map<String, Integer>myMap = new TreeMap<String, Integer>( );
```

This forces only *String*s to be used as keys and *Integer*s to be used as values, and thus insures "type safety". A compile time error would result if any attempt was made to store any object other than a *String* as a key or any object other than an *Integer* as a value.

Type parameters also remove the burden of casting *Object* type objects retrieved from a map back to their original type. Unfortunately objects retrieved from a map using an iterator must still be cast unless the iterator also uses generics (see page 44-3).

Username-password pairs are perfect candidates for map applications. This is because each username must be unique and generally we do not care what the passwords are. Possibly, in your school you have a local area network (LAN) in which logon usernames and passwords are required. For some enrichment activities with a LAN, see Appendix U.

Exercise A for Lesson 47

1. Write code that will create a *TreeMap* object, and add the key-value pair "Sally" –"blue".

2. What classes implement the *Map* interface?

3. Write code that will create an *Iterator* for the keys of a *Map* object called *mp*.

4. Write a line of code that will create a *Map* object called *hoover* using the *HashMap* implementation.

5. How do maps differ from sets?

6. What happens when a key is used for inserting a value in a map and that key is already present?

7. Is it possible for a map to exist with the following key-value arrangement? If not, why not?

Key	Value
23	18
19	-17
46	9
19	-19
2	180

8. How would you determine the number of key-value pairs in a map?

9. Suppose you have a *Map* object called *tiny* and you know that it has a key of type *Object* called *obj*. Write code that will print the corresponding value.

Exercise B for Lesson 47 (advanced exercise)

Consider an automated drilling machine that automatically changes its own drill bits. This machine can hold up to 16 different sizes of drill bits. The various sizes are held in a "tool holder" in which the "tool positions" are labeled "T1", "T2", …"T16". For each unique job, these tool locations are loaded with specific sizes specified for that particular job. In the *ToolControl* class below, *Map toolLocationMap* correlates each tool position with a specific drill size. The permitted drill sizes are *Integer*s 1 through 76.

Also, in the *ToolControl* class is *Map drillInfoMap* that correlates each drill size to a specific *DrillInfo* object. The *DrillInfo* objects specify diameter, rpm, and feed rate as shown by the following class:

```
public class DrillInfo
{
        //Constructor
        public DrillInfo(double dia, int revPerMin, double fr)
        {
                diameter = dia;
                rpm = revPerMin;
                feedRate = fr;
        }
        …other methods not shown…

        public double diameter;
        public int rpm;
        public double feedRate;
}
```

Next is our *ToolControl* class. In it, *drillInfoMap* will use *Integer* drill sizes 1 through 76 as the keys and their corresponding *DrillInfo* objects as the values. *Map toolLocationMap* will use *String* tool location designators "T1" – "T16" as keys and the *Integer* drill sizes at those locations as values.

```
public class ToolControl
{
        public ToolControl( ) //Constructor
        {
                //Populate map with all 76 drill sizes & corresponding DrillInfo objects.
                drillInfoMap.put(new Integer(1), new DrillInfo(.251, 4000, 1.6));
                // Java 5.0, drillInfoMap.put(1, new DrillInfo(.251, 4000, 1.6));
                . . .
                drillInfoMap.put(new Integer(76), new DrillInfo(.006, 70000, 4.55));
        }

        ... Create methods for this class in problems 1 - 5...

        public Map drillInfoMap = new TreeMap( );
        public Map toolLocationMap = new TreeMap( );
}
```

1. Create the *setToolLocation* method. It receives a tool location (example, "T2") and drill size, and uses them to create a new entry in *Map toolLocationMap*. This method should return *false* if a drill already occupies this tool position; otherwise, create the map entry and return *true*.
   ```
   public boolean setToolLocation(String position, int drillSize)
   {                                   }
   ```

2. Create the *deleteToolLocation* method. It receives a tool location (example, "T2") and deletes the corresponding entry from *Map toolLocationMap*.
   ```
   public void deleteToolLocation(String position)
   {                                   }
   ```

3. Create the *getToolRpm* method. It receives a tool location (example, "T2") and returns the *rpm* setting (an integer) for this tool. If there is no drill bit installed at this tool position, return –1.
   ```
   public int getToolRpm(String position)
   {                                   }
   ```

4. Create the *getPosition* method. It receives an *int* drill size (1 – 76) and returns the tool holder position (example, "T2") at which the drill bit of this size is located. If the drill size is not found, return "X".
   ```
   public String getPosition(int toolSize)
   {                                   }
   ```

5. Create the *getFeedRate* method. It receives an *int* drill size (1 – 76) and returns the feed rate for a drill of this size.
   ```
   public double getFeedRate(int drillSize)
   {                                   }
   ```

HashMap/TreeMap… Contest Type Problems

```
public class Restaurant
{
    // methods and constructors not shown

    private String name;
    private boolean fourStar;
    private int seatingCapacity;
}

public class Menu
{
    boolean isENTREE( )
    {
        return category = = ENTREE;
    }

    //other methods and constructors not shown

    private String item;
    private int category;

    <*1> DESSERT = 0;
    <*1> ENTREE = 1;
    <*1> APPETIZER = 2;
    <*1> DRINK = 3;
}
```

1. Which of the following replaces each instance of **<*1>** in the code to the right to declare class constants that are accessible everywhere?

   A. private static final int
   B. static final int
   C. public static final int
   D. final public int
   E. More than one of these

2. Which of the following builds a *Map* named *mp* which can be used to map from restaurants to menus?

   A. Map mp = new Map( );
   B. Map mp = new Map(Restaurant, Menu);
   C. Map mp = new HashMap(Menu, Restaurant);
   D. Map mp = new TreeMap(Restaurant,Menu);
   E. None of these

3. Assume that *Map mp* has been built correctly, and that *Restaurant fojos* and *Menu chinese* have been built correctly. Which of these adds to *Map mp* the key *fojos* with value *chinese*?

   A. mp.put(fojos.name, chinese.category);
   B. mp[fojos] = chinese;
   C. mp.put[Chinese] = fojos;
   D. mp.put(fojos, chinese);
   E. None of these

4. Which of the following can be run outside class *Menu* to check whether the menu associated with *Restaurant papas* in *Map mp* is an entrée?

   A. mp.get(papas).isENTREE( )
   B. mp.get(papas).category = = Menu.ENTREE
   C. ((Menu)mp.get(papas)).isENTREE( )
   D. ((Menu)mp.get(papas)).category = = ENTREE
   E. None of these

5. Suppose that *StudentRecord* is a user-defined class that holds personal information about students. Which of the following built-in classes can be used to make a student directory, matching each student's name (stored as a *String*) with their information?

   A. *ArrayList* B. *TreeMap* C. *TreeSet* D. *HashSet* E. More than one of these

Project… Mapping Bank Accounts

In this project we will modify the *BankAccount* class. It might be easiest for you if you simply paste in code from the *BankAccount* class in the "Sorting BankAccount Objects Projects" in Lesson 45. Modify that class as shown below.

```
public class BankAccount implements Comparable
{
        public BankAccount(String nm, double amt)
        {
                name = nm;
                balance = amt;
                accountCounter++;
                accountID = accountCounter;
        }

        public int compareTo(Object otherObject)
        {
                BankAccount otherAccount = (BankAccount)otherObject;

                int retValue;
                if(balance < otherAccount.balance)
                {
                   retValue = -1;
                }
                else
                {
                   if(balance > otherAccount.balance)
                   {
                      retValue = 1;
                   }
                   else
                   {
                      retValue = 0;
                   }
                }
                return retValue;
        }

        public void deposit(double dp)
        {
             balance = balance + dp;
        }

        public void withdraw(double wd)
        {
             balance = balance - wd;
        }

        public String name;
        public double balance;
        private static int accountCounter = 0;
        public int accountID;
}
```

Notice that the necessary modifications are shown in bold above. It is significant that the *private* instance field *accountCounter* is *static*. This insures that as new accounts are created, each gets a **unique** account ID. This is important since we will use *accountID*'s as the keys in a map. The name of the individuals owning the accounts should not be used as keys since several different people could have the same name. It is a requirement of maps that the keys be unique.

Your primary job is to create a *Tester* class as follows. Again, you will have a big head start on this if you paste in code from the *Tester* class of the project in Lesson 45.

```
import java.io.*;
import java.util.*;
import java.text.*; //for NumberFormat
public class Tester
{
   public static void main(String args[])
   {
      NumberFormat formatter = NumberFormat.getNumberInstance( );
      formatter.setMinimumFractionDigits(2);
      formatter.setMaximumFractionDigits(2);

      String name;
      int j;
      BankAccount ba;
      Use HashMap to create a Map object called accounts
      Scanner kbReader = new Scanner(System.in);
      for(j =0; j < 4; j++) //provides for inputting 4 accounts
      {
         System.out.print("Please enter the name to whom the account belongs. ");
         name = kbReader.nextLine( );

         System.out.print("Please enter the amount of the deposit. ");
         double amount = kbReader.nextDouble( );
         System.out.println(" "); //gives an eye pleasing blank line between accounts

         ba = new BankAccount(name, amount);
         Use the put method to place a key-value pair in accounts. The key should be an object
          version of ba.accountID. The value should be ba.
      }

      //Print all the accounts in the map
      Create a Set object called accountsSet using the keySet method of accounts
      Create an Iterator object called iter from the accountsSet object.
      while(  loop through all the Iterator's objects   )
      {
         Use the next method of iter to create an Object called key.
          Use the get method of accounts to retrieve the associated value and cast as BankAccount
          object called ba.
          Print accountID, name, and balance in this format   3 >>> Bob Jones >>> 138.72
      }
      System.out.println(" ");

      //Ask for keyboard input...for an accountID
      System.out.print("Please enter the ID for the account that you wish to view. ");
      int id = kbReader.nextInt( );
```

```
        //Print info on that account
        Convert the primitive int type id into a wrapper class version called idw.
        Use idw with the get method of accounts to retrieve the desired account...store in ba.
        Print accountID, name, and balance in this format   3 >>> Bob Jones >>> 138.72
    }
}
```

A typical run is shown below:

```
Please enter the name to whom the account belongs. Elvis
Please enter the amount of the deposit. 473.83

Please enter the name to whom the account belongs. Frank Sinatra
Please enter the amount of the deposit. 82.38

Please enter the name to whom the account belongs. Dan Blocker
Please enter the amount of the deposit. 3922.92

Please enter the name to whom the account belongs. Lacy Bertran
Please enter the amount of the deposit. 4882.03

2 >>> Frank Sinatra >>> 82.38
4 >>> Lacy Bertran >>> 4,882.03
1 >>> Elvis >>> 473.83
3 >>> Dan Blocker >>> 3,922.92

Please enter the ID for the account that you wish to view. 2
2 >>> Frank Sinatra >>> 82.38
```

Project… Code Talker

Consider a file called Data.txt with the following content:

```
13
beaver=swim
hello=fierce
spank=like
freedom=wrench
yellow=can't
whale=for
ketchup=pickles
yes=me
meter=I
foreign=state
staple=but
wood=sandwich
hand=could
meter always spank ketchup staple meter yellow beaver
```

The first line gives a number that specifies how many dictionary items we have. Following is that number of pairs of words separated by an equal sign. The word to the left of the equal sign is the "coded" word and to the right is its real meaning. Following the dictionary is a single line of text that is to be decoded. If a coded word is in the dictionary then prints its real meaning according to the dictionary. If a coded word is not found, then just print that word.

The output should be:

```
I always like pickles but I can't swim
```

Use a *Map* object to store a pair of *Strings*. Let the **key** be the coded word and the **value** be its real meaning.

Project... Histogram

Suppose we have the following **single line** of text in a file called Words.txt:

> hello, mud, yellow, book, mud, car, bank, mud, hello, book, book, ruby, yellow, cow, toenail, bank

Write a program that will count the number of occurrences of each word and present them in alphabetical order as follows:

```
bank,2
book,3
car,1
cow,1
hello,2
mud,3
ruby,1
toenail,1
yellow,2
```

In writing this program it is suggested that *split* be used to produce an array of all the individual words in the line of text. Create a *TreeMap* object and while cycling through each word in this array, add it to the *TreeMap* object (The word itself will be the Key and the corresponding Value will be a running count of how many times that words is used.) If a word is not found in the *Map*, then add it and set a count Value of 1. If it's already there, then increment the count Value.

> By using a *TreeMap* instead of a *HashMap* the Keys stored in the *Map* will automatically be encountered in alphabetical order as we iterate through the *KeySet* object produced from the *Map*. This means you will need to create a *KeySet* object and from it create an *Iterator* that you will use to step through the objects.

****

Finally, modify the program using *printf* so that the output is in histogram form and is formatted as follows:

```
Words              Frequency
bank                      **
book                     ***
car                        *
```

```
cow                     *
hello                  **
mud                   ***
ruby                    *
toenail                 *
yellow                 **
```

Project… Student Classification

Consider the following data file called *StudentData.txt*:

```
Sophomore Julie
Freshman Fred
Senior Bill
Senior Agnes
Junior Betty
Senior Jezebel
Sophomore Ahab
Junior David
Sophomore Solomon
Senior Boaz
Junior Ruth
```

Using a *Map* object, create a program that will process the file so as to produce the following output:

```
Freshman(Fred)
Junior(Betty, David, Ruth)
Senior(Agnes, Bill, Boaz, Jezebel)
Sophomore(Ahab, Julie, Solomon)
```

The keys for the *Map* object should be Freshman, Sophomore, etc. (notice alphabetical order) and the associated value for each should be a *Set* containing the alphabetized names of the individuals belonging to that classification.

Lesson 48….. Flow Charts & Optimizing for Speed

A logical flow:

The following drawing is called a flow chart and is used when the program is rather complex. It allows us to design the logical flow of a program without first getting into the details of specific code. The flow chart below is for the purpose of inputting a number from the keyboard (call it *n*) and then printing all of the numbers that divide evenly into *n*. For example, if we input *6* for *n*, the printout would be *1, 2, 3, 6*.

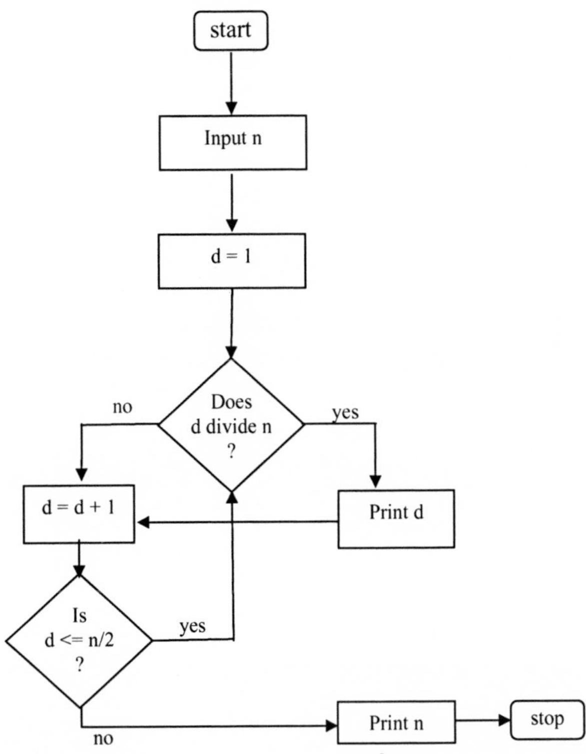

Write the code:

We will now begin writing code for this flow chart. One of the basic structures is the following *do–while* loop with an *if* inside it.

```
...
do
{
        if( n % d = = 0 ) //test for divisibility by d
        {
                ...
        }
        ...
}while( d <= n / 2 );
...
```

Project... Divisors of a Number

Complete the code for the flow chart on the previous page. A typical screen output is as follows:

```
What is the number? 6
1   2   3   6
```

Be sure to test your program with 2,000,000,000 (two billion, a two followed by nine zeros) and time how long it takes to run (author's test run took 105 seconds on a very old computer).

Here is how you can make the computer calculate the time that it takes to run this algorithm. In your code just before the algorithm begins, place this line of code:

```
long startTime = System.currentTimeMillis( );
```

This gives the time that has elapsed in milliseconds since midnight, Jan1, 1970 UTC up until when this command was issued. Then, at the end of your algorithm, place these lines of code:

```
long endTime = System.currentTimeMillis( );
long elaspedTime = endTime – startTime;
System.out.println("Your algorithm took " + (elaspedTime)/1000.0 + " to run.");
```

While on the subject of timing, it should be mentioned that Java 5.0 provides an additional timing command as illustrated by the following:

```
long myTime = System.nanoTime( );
```

This provides the precision (plenty of digits) for nanosecond timing but not necessarily the accuracy (the times its returns may be incorrect to varying degrees). Presumably, Sun Microsystems included this in the new release of Java in anticipation of incredibly fast computers in the future and operating systems with very fine granularity.

****

Optimizing performance:

We are going to do some things now to optimize the time performance of this program. Let's look at the *boolean* associated with *while*. Notice that every time through the loop (1 billion times) we repeatedly ask the computer to divide *n* by *2*. We can realize a little improvement in the running time by taking this calculation (that never changes) **outside** the loop.

Project... Optimized Code for Divisors of a Number

Make the necessary modifications to move the calculation of *n/2* outside the loop. Again, test with two billion. This time the author's time was 100 sec, a very small and not very dramatic improvement.

****

An audacious claim:

Now we are going to do something **really dramatic**; we are going to make this code run much faster. What if we told you it would run twice as fast? Pretty impressive, huh? Now, suppose we said it would run ten times as fast. What about 1000 times as fast? At this point you are probably very suspicious and are thinking, "No way! Not possible." Well, here is the real truth. **We are going to make it run 44,000 times faster**. You can take the old run time, divide by 44,000 and see that the new run time will be only a fraction of a second.

How is this possible? Here is how we will do it. Let's suppose we are testing for all the divisors of 100. First test 1 and of course it divides, so we print it. But wait! When we divide by 1, let's also look at its "partner," 100 (1 divides into 100, 100 times). Let's just go ahead and print its partner right now.

Now test 2 to see if it divides into 100. It does, and it has 50 as its "partner," so print both of them. Continuing this way we also get the following pairs; 4 & 25, 5 & 20, and 10 & 10. We need not go beyond 10 (which is the square root of 100). Figure 48-1 below illustrates this partnering, factor-pair relationship.

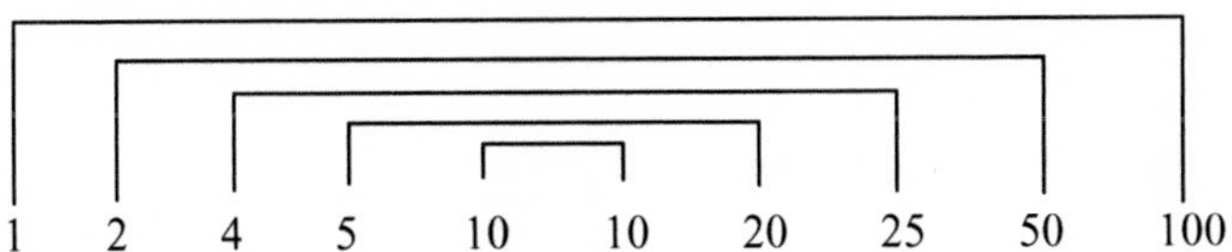

Figure 48-1 Factor-pairs for 100

Project... Super Optimized Code for Divisors of a Number

Modify your code to take advantage of these short cuts. Notice that the square root of 2 billion is close to 44,721, which is close to the audacious claim of 44,000 above. In reality your code will take a little longer than one second to run because of the overhead associated with printing a large number of divisors on the screen. The actual calculations have, however, been speeded up exactly as claimed.

Lesson 49….. Singly Linked List

An example of a linked list:

A linked list is by its very nature an **ordered** list. The order is the sequence in which we encounter the list items as we traverse the list from its head (the start of the list) all the way to the end. As an example of objects that have such a natural order, let's think of the nodes of a pipeline as it zigzags its way across the landscape. Each node will have the following data associated with it.

- A position in feet from some starting point
- A descriptive name

In Fig 49-1 below we see such a pipeline and in Fig 49-2 its corresponding data structure implemented as a linked list.

Fig. 49-1 A three "node" pipeline.

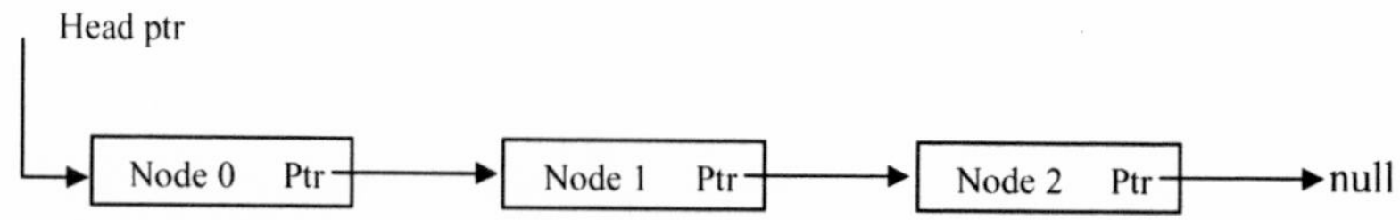

Fig. 49-2 Linked list using only forward pointing pointers (singly linked).

The fundamental parts:

As we see from this example a linked list is a **chain** of objects in which each object (node) has two fundamental parts:

- The various data members of the object… These contain the primary data associated with each node of the linked list, and for our example will be a position in feet (from some starting point) of our node and a description such as "Pump station", etc.

- A pointer field that indicates the next item in the chain. Actually, this data member is a **reference** to the next object in the list.

The linked list example above is a **singly** linked list. If we begin traversing the list from node 0, then we just follow the pointer to the next node, and from there to the next one, etc. We could not, however, work our way backwards because there are no backwards pointing pointers. That type of linked list **does** exist. It's called a doubly linked list and will be addressed in the next lesson.

Creation of the node objects:

Let's now turn our attention to the creation of the node objects for our pipeline example. We will use the following class to produce these objects:

```
public class PipelineNode
{
        public PipelineNode(int pos, String descr, PipelineNode ptr)  //Constructor
        {
                position = pos;
                description = descr;
                nextNode = ptr;
        }

        public int position;
        public String description;
        public PipelineNode nextNode;
}
```

Next, we need a class with a *main* method in which we will call an *append* method that will in turn create node objects and link them together.

```
public class Tester
{
        public static void main(String args[])
        {
          //Creation of the nodes
          append(0, "Pump station");
          append(3050, "Hwy 35");
          append(4573, "Tank farm");   // 3050 + 1523 = 4573
        }

        //append a new node to the end of the list and adjust pointers
        public static void append(int pos, String descr)
        {
                PipelineNode newNode = new PipelineNode(pos, descr, null);
                if(headNode = = null) //There are no nodes yet so the node we
                {                         //"append" will be both the head and the tail
                    headNode = newNode;
                }
                else
                {
                    tailNode.nextNode = newNode;  //update the old tailNode
                }
                tailNode = newNode; //specify a new tailNode
        }

         private static PipelineNode headNode = null;
         private static PipelineNode tailNode = null;
}
```

This *Tester* class doesn't really do anything except create and link the nodes. Let's add to the *Tester* class by causing it to print the data along each node as we traverse the list from start to finish. We will call this method *traverseAndPrint*.

```
public static void traverseAndPrint( )
{
    PipelineNode currentNode = headNode;
    int nodeNum = -1;
    do
    {
            nodeNum++;
            System.out.println("Node number: " + nodeNum);
            System.out.println("Position: " + currentNode.position);
            System.out.println("Description: " + currentNode.description);
            System.out.println(""); //gives a blank line between nodes

            currentNode = currentNode.nextNode;
    }while(currentNode != null); //We don't need to know ahead of time how many
}                                //nodes there are.
```

Notice that traversing the loop is general in that it does not assume knowledge of how many nodes there are. Modify the *main* method as follows in order to test this new method:

```
public static void main( String args[] )
{
    //Creation of the nodes
    append(0, "Pump station");
    append(3050, "Hwy 35");
    append(4573, "Tank farm");

    traverseAndPrint ( );
}
```

The resulting printout is as follows:

```
Node number: 0
Position: 0
Description: Pump station

Node number: 1
Position: 3050
Description: Hwy 35

Node number: 2
Position: 4573
Description: Tank farm
```

Something startling:

If we analyze what's just happened, there is something really startling. How does the code in *traverseAndPrint* know what the node objects are? Except for the instance fields *headNode* and *tailNode*, the node objects aren't instance fields and are, in fact, not even named. Yet, in the *traverseAndPrint* method we are obviously accessing these node objects and printing their attributes. We could still access them even if there were hundreds of nodes.

The reason that we have access to these nodes is that they are "chained" together via the *nextNode* instance field of the *PipelineNode* class and hence all its objects. If we have access to the *headNode* in any method (and we do since *headNode* is an instance field) then, via the chain, we have access to all the nodes.

Adding a node:

Now, let's suppose we wish to add another node as shown in Fig 49-3. Notice this new node will have index 2 and falls between **old** nodes 1 and 2. The project below gives suggestion on how to do this.

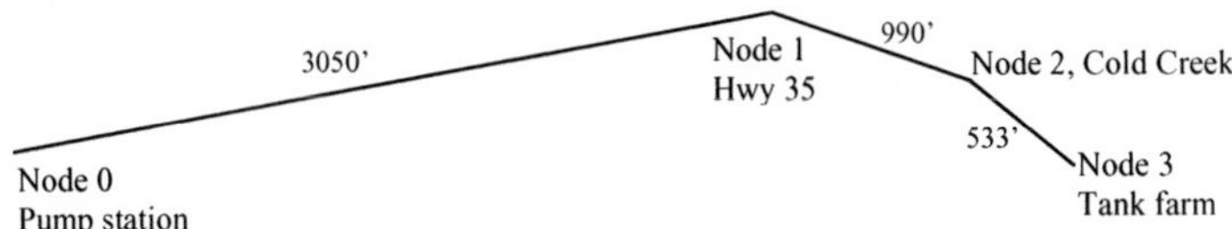

Fig. 49-3 A four "node" pipeline. The new node will be node 2, and the old node 2 becomes node 3.

Project... *insert* Method for Singly Linked List

Create a method with the following signature:

```
public static void insert(int pos, String descr, int indx)
```

This method will insert a new node into the interior of our singly linked list. The parameter *pos* is the position in feet of the new node along the pipeline. The parameter *descr* is the word description of the new node. The parameter *indx* is the index number of the existing node before which the new node will be inserted. For example, if *indx* is 32, then the new node will now be at index 32 and the old node 32 will now be at index 33.

The code in this method need not address the issue of putting the new node at the very end of the list. We already have a method for that, the *append* method. Your code should, however, address the possibility of *indx* being equal to 0, which would mean that the new node is to become the new head of the list.

In all cases your code should adjust the pointer of the node object immediately preceding the new, inserted node object. Adjust the *main* method of the *Tester* class in the following way to test *insert*.

```
public static void main( String args[] )
{
   //Creation of the nodes
   append(0, "Pump station");
   append(3050, "Hwy 35");
   append(4573, "Tank farm");  //3050 + 990 + 553 = 4573

   traverseAndPrint( );
   System.out.println("*******  now insert a node before old node 2  ******\n");
   insert(4040, "Cold Creek", 2); // 3050 + 990 = 4040
   traverseAndPrint( );
}
```

The resulting printout will be as follows:

```
Node number: 0
Position: 0
Description: Pump station

Node number: 1
Position: 3050
Description: Hwy 35

Node number: 2
Position: 4573
Description: Tank farm

*******  now insert a node before old node 2  *******

Node number: 0
Position: 0
Description: Pump station

Node number: 1
Position: 3050
Description: Hwy 35

Node number: 2
Position: 4040
Description: Cold Creek

Node number: 3
Position: 4573
Description: Tank farm
```

Students should not get the idea that applications of the singly linked list are limited to situations having a geometric aspect, as does our pipeline example. For example, we could maintain an alphabetized list of names (and associated data) using a singly linked list. The names would simply be linked in alphabetical order.

Why use a linked list?

Finally, we examine the question of why we would ever want to use a linked list as opposed to an ordinary array. Ordinary arrays nearly always provide better runtime performance; however, when it comes to efficient memory usage there is a situation in which the linked list is superior. That situation is when we are unable to predict the list's maximum size. In that case, the array may suffer from either of the following problems:

- If the array is dimensioned too small, we might run out of space.
- If we dimension too large, then we will waste a large portion of memory.

The way we overcome this problem is by using a linked list in which pointers (and the object of which they are a part) only come into existence, as they are needed. Thus, it is the dynamic creation and elimination of objects (in dynamic memory) and their associated pointers that give a memory advantage for linked list.

Singly Linked List… Contest Type Problems

```
public class Node
{
        public Node(int i, String s, Node n)
        {
                v1 = i;
                s1 = s;
                next = n;
        }

        public int v1;
        public String s1;
        public Node next;
}
```

1. Given *ns* as an object of the class to the right, how would you print data member *s1* of the *Node* object that follows *ns* in a singly linked chain of *Node* objects?

A. System.out.println(ns.s1);
B. System.out.println((ns.next).s1);
C. System.out.println(s1);
D. System.out.println((Node)ns.next.s1);
E. None of these

2. Given *ns* as an object of the class to the right, what would you use to determine if *ns* is the last object in a linked list?

A. if(ns = = null)
B. if(next = = null)
C. if(ns.next = = null)
D. if((ns.next).next = = null)
E. None of these

3. Which of the following would be a proper way to instantiate a *Node* object if that object were to be the last in the linked list "chain"?

A. Node nn = new Node(4, "Yes", null);
B. Node nn = new Node("Yes", 4, null);
C. Node nn = new Node(null, null, null);
D. Node nn = new Node(1, "Zero", new Node( ));
E. None of these

4. What is true concerning the traversing of a singly linked list?

A. It can only be traversed in one direction.
B. In doing a traversal while searching for a particular element, you might be unlucky and have to traverse the entire list.
C. In doing a traversal while searching for a particular element, you might be lucky and only need to inspect the first item.
D. All of the above
E. None of these

5. Suppose a singly linked list of *Cow* objects has a reference to the first object called *headCow*. Which of the following is *headCow*?

A. A *Cow* object
B. The integer 0
C. A *String* that gives the value of the first *String* field of the first object in the chain
D. A *String* reference
E. None of these

Lesson 50…. The *LinkedList* Class (doubly linked) and Stacks

In Lesson 49 we investigated a singly linked list. Here, we turn our attention to a doubly linked list. Fig. 50-1 illustrates such linkage between the nodes of a list.

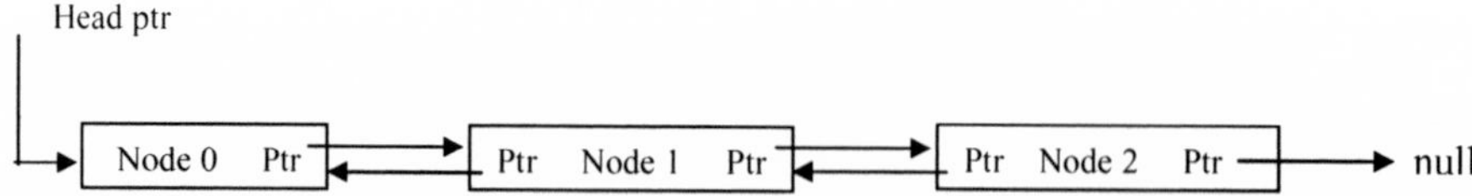

Fig. 50-2 Linked list using both forward and backward pointing pointers (doubly linked).

In this doubly linked list we can traverse the list in either direction. This adds some convenience and makes some operations faster.

Rather than develop our own doubly linked list class, we will use a class that exists as part of Java. It is called the *LinkedList* class, is doubly linked, and requires the following import:

```
import java.util.LinkedList;
```

The *LinkedList* class implements the *List* interface (see Lesson 42) and adds some additional methods of its own. Following are the most important *LinkedList* methods:

Method Signature	Description
void add(int index, Object o)	Inserts *Object o* at the position specified by *index*.
void add(Object o)	Appends *o* to the end of the list.
void addFirst(Object o)	Inserts *o* at the beginning of the list.
void addLast(Object o)	Appends *o* to the end of the list.
void clear( )	Remove all elements from the list.
boolean contains(Object o)	Returns true if the list contains *o*.
Object get(int index)	Returns the object at the position specified by *index*.
Object getFirst( )	Returns the object at the head of the list.
Object getLast( )	Returns the object at the end of the list.
int indexOf(Object o)	Returns the index of the first occurrence of *Object o*, searching from left to right. Returns –1 if the object is not found.
boolean isEmpty( )	Returns *true* if list is empty, *false* otherwise.
int lastIndexOf(Object o)	Returns the index of the first occurrence of *Object o*, searching from right to left. Returns –1 if the object is not found.
ListIterator listIterator(int index)	Returns a *ListIterator* object for this list.
Object remove(int index)	Remove the object at the position specified by *index* and returns the object.
boolean remove(Object o)	Remove the first occurrence of *o*, searching from left to right.
Object removeFirst( )	Remove the object at the head of the list and return the object.
Object removeLast( )	Remove the object at the end of the list and return the object.
Object set(int index, Object o)	Replaces the object at the position specified by *index* with *o*, then returns the old object.
int size( )	Returns the number of elements in the list.
Object[ ] toArray( )	Returns an array containing all of the elements in the list in the correct order.

Creating a stack class:

We are going to use the *LinkedList* class to implement yet another class, a stack class. First, we must discuss what a stack is. To understand a software stack, think of a stack of trays in a cafeteria. As trays are washed, they are put on top of the stack. As new customers come through the line, they remove a tray from the top of the stack. A software stack is similar. We put data on **top** of the stack (***push***), and we also remove data from the **top** of the stack (***pop***, sometimes called *pull*). A data structures like this in which the last datum in, is the first to be taken out, is called a LIFO (last in, first out). **A stack is a classic example of a LIFO**.

There is also a totally different data structure in which the first datum in, is the first to be taken out (FIFO). **The queue structure is a classic example of a FIFO** (see Lesson 53). An example of a queue is a line of people waiting to buy tickets at a box office. The first one in the line will be the first one to buy tickets and to get out of the line. Queues can also be implemented with a linked list as the underlying structure.

In the following, we illustrate a sequence of *push* and *pop* operations on a stack.

Operation	**Resulting stack after operation**	**Comments**
push 157.3	157.3	
push 22	22 157.3	new data is added to the top of the stack
push -18	-18 22 157.3	
pop	22 157.3	pop returns –18 and removes from stack
pop	157.3	pop returns 22 and removes from stack
push 500	500 157.3	

Do it with an *interface*:

The way we are going to specify the design of our stack class is via an *interface*. The following *interface* gives the methods of our stack class.

```
public interface StackIntrfc
{
        void push(double d); //place d on top of the stack
        double pop( ); //return top item in the stack and then remove from stack
        double peek( ); //return the top item in the stack and leave the stack intact
        int size( ); //returns the size (depth) of the stack
        void clear( ); //remove all items from the stack
}
```

Project... *StackLL* Class

Create a stack class called *StackLL* that *implements* the *StackIntrfc interface* above (You must enter the *interface*; it's not part of Java). Use a *LinkedList* object as the underlying data structure. **The head of the list will correspond to the top of the stack**. As you may have noted in the *interface*, the stack will contain only *doubles*, and since *LinkedList* stores only **objects,** you must use the *Double* wrapper class.

Use the following *Tester* class to test *StackLL* (the rems show what should be printed):

```
public class Tester
{
    public static void main( String args[] )
    {
        StackLL stck = new StackLL( );
        System.out.println( stck.size( ) ); //0
        stck.push(157.3);
        stck.push(22);
        stck.push(-18);
        double j = stck.pop( );
        System.out.println(j); // -18.0
        System.out.println( stck.peek( ) ); //22.0
        System.out.println( stck.pop( ) ); //22.0
        System.out.println( stck.size( ) ); //1
        stck.clear( );
        System.out.println( stck.size( ) ); //0
    }
}
```

The output will appear as follows:

```
0
-18.0
22.0
22.0
1
0
```

Practical Applications:

Now that we have produced a *Stack* class, let's look at some practical applications. We will describe only two; however, there are many others.

1. A stack is used in computer languages to keep track of method calls. Suppose we are at point A in a program at which we call *method1* that in turn calls *method2*. Ultimately, we will return back up this "calling chain" to the original position, point A. The way this is all accomplished in software is that when the first call to *method1* is initiated, the return address (the address of point A) is pushed on the Call Stack along with all the variables in scope at that time. When the point is reached in *method1* (point B) at which there is a call to *method2*, all the variables of *method1* and the return address of point B are pushed on the Call Stack. *method2* executes, and when finished, all the variables and the return address for *method2* are popped off the stack, and *method1* continues until it is finished. Then the remaining information on the stack (the return address of point A and the associated variables) are popped and code execution follows from point A.

Very succinctly, we may conclude that a **Call Stack supports operations in a "chain" of method calls.**

2. Many software applications have undo operations. Suppose we are using a graphics editor in which we are editing a picture to which we have made several modifications. When we access undo (typically with Ctrl Z) we expect the last modification we made to be "undone". If we undo again we expect the next-to-the-last thing we did to be undone, etc. This is a description of a LIFO in which multiple undo's are implemented with a stack. Because of the complexity of software development of such a stack, some software applications limit the user to only a single undo.

3. A stack is used in web browsers to keep a list of sites visited. When you click on the Back button in a browser it pops the URL Stack, and you return to the site immediately preceding the current site.

A stack based calculator:

For our next project we are going to implement a stack-based calculator. What exactly is a stack-based calculator? Hewlett-Packard produced these type calculators at one time and are the preferred type for calculator contests, or wherever speed is important. They use Reverse Polish Notation (RPN).

A stack-based calculator will seem very awkward if you have never used one before, but they actually make the entry of complex expression much easier than with traditional calculators. Let's consider the following arithmetic expression whose answer is 2:

(10 + 2) / (9 – 3)

With a traditional calculator we would enter the following sequence in **infix** form (with the operator **between** the two operands):

(, 10, +, 2,), /, (, 9, - 2,), =

Notice that we are forced to enter two pairs of parenthesis in order to group the numerator and denominator. If we don't use the parenthesis it is even more awkward. With an RPN calculator we would, instead, enter the following sequence in **postfix** form (with the operator **following** the two operands):

10, 2, +, 9, 3, -, /

When finished, the top of the stack would contain 2, the answer. This all seems very strange, but it does produce the answer. Here are the rules behind this peculiar sequence:

- If a number is entered it is pushed on the stack.
- If a math operation symbol is entered, the stack is popped twice and those numbers are used as the operands for that math operation. The math operation is performed and the answer is pushed back on the stack.
- At the end of all operations the answer is at the top of the stack.

How it works:

Let's analyze step by step what happens as we enter this sequence *10, 2, +, 9, 3, -, /* :

Entry	Resulting Stack	Comment
10	10	Push 10 on the stack.
2	2 10	Push 2 on the stack.
+	12	2 and 10 are popped, 10+2 is calculated, and the answer (12) is pushed back on the stack.
9	9 12	Push 9 on the stack.
3	3 9 12	Push 3 on the stack.
-	6 12	3 and 9 are popped, 9-3 is calculated, and the answer (6) is pushed back on the stack.
/	2	6 and 12 are popped, 12 / 6 is calculated, and the answer (2) is pushed back on the stack.

There, remaining at the top of the stack, and, in fact, the only item on the stack, is the answer (2).

Project… Stack Calculator

Create a *Tester* class that allows keyboard entry of double precision numbers and the math operators +, -, /, and *. Use the *StackLL* class developed in the last project. Test your finished code with the sequence keyboard 10, 2, +, 9, 3, -, / which, of course, represents the problem

$$(10 + 2) / (9 - 3)$$

After entering the sequence, pop the stack (by entering Q to quit) and print the answer. It should be 2. The output screen should appear as follows:

```
Enter number, math operation(+,-,*, or /), or Q to quit: 10
Enter number, math operation(+,-,*, or /), or Q to quit: 2
Enter number, math operation(+,-,*, or /), or Q to quit: +
Enter number, math operation(+,-,*, or /), or Q to quit: 9
Enter number, math operation(+,-,*, or /), or Q to quit: 3
Enter number, math operation(+,-,*, or /), or Q to quit: -
Enter number, math operation(+,-,*, or /), or Q to quit: /
Enter number, math operation(+,-,*, or /), or Q to quit: Q
The answer is 2.0
```

Try some other problems on your "stack calculator". For example, try *3, 2, 5, +, ** which is the problem *3(2 + 5)*.

Miscellaneous *Stack* facts:

At this point it should be mentioned that Java **does** have a *Stack* class requiring an import of *import java.util.Stack;*. Of course, in this lesson we wrote our own stack class as an excuse to use the *LinkedList* class; however, Java's own *Stack* class also uses all the methods that were introduced in this lesson (*push*, *pop*, *peek*, *size*, and *clear*), and stores *Object* type objects.

In addition to the methods presented here there is also a *toString* method that returns a *String* similar to "[A, B, C]" where C is the top of the stack.

LinkedList and Stacks…. Contest Type Problems

1. Consider a waitress handing off orders to a short-order cook, and the processing of those orders. This is an example of which of the following?

A. LIFO B. FIFO C. Stack D. Queue E. More than one of these

2. What code should replace **<#1>** in the code to the right?

A. lkdList = new LinkedList( );
B. LinkedList lkdList = new LinkedList( );
C. lkdList.clear( );
D. lkdLst = new LinkedList;
E. None of these

3. Assuming that **<#1>** above has been filled in correctly in the code to the right, what code would replace **<#2>** in order to implement a *push* operation on the stack?

A. lkdList.push(x);
B. lkdList.addFirst(x);
C. lkdList.addFirst(new Integer(x));
D. lkdList.addLast(new Integer(x));
E. None of these

4. Assuming that **<#1>** and **<#2>** above have been filled in correctly in the code to the right, what code would replace **<#3>** in order to implement a pop operation on the stack?

A. return lkdList.getLast( );
B. return lkdList.removeFirst( );
C. lkdList.getLast( );
D. lkdList.removeFirst( );
E. None of these

5. Assuming **<#1>** and **<#3>** have been filled in correctly in the code to the right, which of the following would be a correct usage of the *pop* method? (Assume this code is in the *main* method of some other class and that the *BigStack* object, *bs*, already exists.)

A. bs.pop( );
B. System.out.println(bs.pop( ));
C. int pk = bs.pop( );
D. All of the above
E. None of these

```
// BigStack is a stack class using a LinkedList
//object as the underlying data structure. It
//maintains a stack of Integer objects. The head
//of the list is considered the top of the stack.
public class BigStack {
    public BigStack  {
        <#1>
    }

    public void push(int x)  {
        <#2>
    }

    public int pop( )  {
        <#3>
    }

    private LinkedList lkdList;
}
```

6. What code should replace **<#1>** in the code to the right in order to correctly implement the *peek* method?

A. return Integer.intValue(myList.getFirst( ));
B. return myList.getFirst( );
C. return Integer.intValue((Integer)myList.getLast( ));
D. return (Integer)myList.getLast( );
E. None of these

```
/*peek method returns the top item (int
equivalent) of a stack without removing it. The
underlying data structure is a LinkedList
object, myList. The end of the list is considered
the top of the stack.*/
public int peek( )
{
    <#1>
}
```

7. Suppose we wish to store several items of data in a particular sequence and then retrieve them in reverse sequence. Which of the following would be best suited to this job?

A. Queue B. Stack C. Stack and queue would work equally well D. Tree E. None of these

8. Which of the following statements is true?

A. Linked lists always have better runtime performance than arrays.
B. When working with an array that is dimensioned too small, and the amount of data is unpredictable, there is a danger of running out of space.
C. If we are unable to predict a list's maximum size, then a linked list may be the most efficient usage of memory.
D. Both A and B
E. Both B and C

9. Which of the following package names will import the *LinkedList* class?

A. java.io B. java.util C. java.lang D. java.awt E. None of these

10. Which of the following will store in *String pugh* the result of popping a stack object called *theStack* which stores *String*s as *Object* type objects? (Assume that generics were not used in the creation of *theStack*.)

A. pugh = theStack.pop( ); B. pugh = ((String)theStack).pop( ); C. pugh = (String)theStack.pop( );
D. pugh = new theStack.pop( ); E. pugh = theStack.pop(new String s);

11. Suppose that *Strings* "One", "Two", and "Three" are successively pushed onto *Stack st1*. All are popped off, and as each *String* is popped of it is immediately pushed onto *Stack st2*. What is returned by the *toString* method of *st2* ?

A. "[Three, Two, One]" B. "[One, Two, Three]" C. "(Three, Two, One)"
D. "(One, Two, Three)" E. None of these

12. What is printed by the code to the right?

A. Black Beard the pirate
B. pirate the Beard Black
C. thepirate the Beard Black
D. BeardPirate the Beard Black
E. None of these

```
Stack st = new Stack( );
st.push("Black");
st.push("Beard");
String str1 = (String)st.peek( );
st.push("the");
st.push(str1);
String str2 = (String)st.pop( );
st.push("Pirate");
System.out.println(str2);
while(!st.isEmpty)
{
   System.out.print((String)st.pop( ) + " ");
}
```

Lesson 51….. Binary Search

Consider the following array of ordered integers. It is very important that they **be in order** so that the techniques we are to discuss will work.

Index	0	1	2	3	4	5	6	7	8	9	10	11	12	13
Value	-7	15	21	22	43	49	51	67	78	81	84	89	95	97

Fig 51-1 An ordered array of integers.

Our task is to examine this array and see if 22 is present, and if it is, report its index. If it is not present, report an "index" of –1. Of course, we can instantly tell at a glance that 22 is, indeed, present, and that its index is 3. That's easy for us as humans, but is it this straightforward for a computer program? (Actually, it's not easy for humans either if the size of the array is several thousand or, perish the thought, in the millions.)

The binary search technique looks at a range of index numbers that is determined by a lower bound (*lb*) and an upper bound (*ub*), subdivides that range in halves, and then continues the search in the appropriate half. We illustrate this by initially setting *lb* = 0 and *ub* =13 and realizing that the number we seek lies somewhere on or between them (the shaded region).

	lb													ub
Index	0	1	2	3	4	5	6	7	8	9	10	11	12	13
Value	-7	15	21	22	43	49	51	67	78	81	84	89	95	97

Fig 51-2 *lb* and *ub* are initially set.

Find the midpoint *m* using integer arithmetic, 6 = (lb + ub)/2. This position is illustrated below.

	lb						m							ub
Index	0	1	2	3	4	5	6	7	8	9	10	11	12	13
Value	-7	15	21	22	43	49	51	67	78	81	84	89	95	97

Fig 51-3 Midpoint *m* is determined.

Next, we ask if the number we seek (22) is at position *m*. In this case it is not, so we next ask if 22 is less than or greater than the value at position *m*. 22 is, of course, less that 51 so we indicate the new search area by the shaded area below and redefine *ub* = 5.

	lb					ub								
Index	0	1	2	3	4	5	6	7	8	9	10	11	12	13
Value	-7	15	21	22	43	49	51	67	78	81	84	89	95	97

Fig 51-4 A new *ub* and search region are defined.

Again, we calculate m = (lb + ub) / 2 using integer arithmetic and get 2. This new *m* value is shown in Fig. 51-5.

	lb		m			ub								
Index	0	1	2	3	4	5	6	7	8	9	10	11	12	13
Value	-7	15	21	22	43	49	51	67	78	81	84	89	95	97

Fig 51-5 A new *m* value of 2 has been determined as the midpoint.

Repeat what we have done before by determining if the number we seek (22) is equal to the value at position *m* (21). It is not, so as before, we ask if 22 is less than or greater than 21. Of course, it's greater than 21, so we now redefine *lb* = 3 and have the new search area shown in Fig 51-6.

				lb		ub								
Index	0	1	2	3	4	5	6	7	8	9	10	11	12	13
Value	-7	15	21	22	43	49	51	67	78	81	84	89	95	97

Fig 51-6 A new, smaller search area defined by *lb* and *ub*.

Are you beginning to see a pattern here? We are cutting our search area in half each time. At this rate we could examine an array of over a million integers with only 20 iterations of this process.

Let's average *lb* and *ub* as before, and this time *m* is 4. The result is shown in Fig 51-7 below.

				lb	m	ub								
Index	0	1	2	3	4	5	6	7	8	9	10	11	12	13
Value	-7	15	21	22	43	49	51	67	78	81	84	89	95	97

Fig 51-7 Ready to test if the value stored at index 4 is what we seek.

Ask if the 22 (the value we seek) is stored at index *m* = 4. It is not, so now ask if 22 is less than or greater than 43. It's less than 43 so we redefine *ub* as 3. Notice now that *lb* and *ub* are the same and we have just about "squeezed" the search area down to nothing. The redefined boundaries and the resulting recalculation of *m* are shown below. If we don't find the number we seek in this single cell that's left, the number is not in the array, and we would have to report a "failure" value of –1 as a result of our search.

				lb = m = ub										
Index	0	1	2	3	4	5	6	7	8	9	10	11	12	13
Value	-7	15	21	22	43	49	51	67	78	81	84	89	95	97

Fig 51-8 The lower bound, upper bound and the midpoint all coincide.

Now, when we ask if 22 (the number we seek) is at index 3, the answer is, "yes", so we exit this process and report index 3 as the answer.

Ending the process:

We will code this entire process shortly, however, there is something worth noticing here. As we squeezed down to ever-smaller ranges, the indices *lb* and *ub* move closer to each other. If the number we seek is not in the array, we will find that the algorithm actually moves these two value "right past each other". Therefore we can use the condition *ub* < *lb* as a condition to exit the loop, or… *ub* >= *lb* to stay in the loop.

Implementing our own binary search:

Our first illustration of code implementing the binary search will be to search the integer array {-7, 15, 21, 22, 43, 49, 51, 67, 78, 81, 84, 89, 95, 97}. Notice that this is the array used in the example above. We will continue the tradition of using the variables *lb* and *ub*; however, instead of *m* we will use *mid*. The student should be aware that when looking at binary searches written by other programmers, other variables are often used in the place of our *lb* and *ub*. Popular choices are *left* & *right*, *front* & *back*, or *start* & *end*.

The following class provides a *main* method for testing and a *binarySearch* method where the search is actually done.

```
public class Tester
{
   public static void main(String args[])
   {
          int i[] ={-7, 15, 21, 22, 43, 49, 51, 67, 78, 81, 84, 89, 95, 97};
          System.out.println(binarySearch(i, 22));    //prints 3
          System.out.println(binarySearch(i, 89));    //prints 11
          System.out.println(binarySearch(i, -100)); //prints -1
          System.out.println(binarySearch(i, 72));    //prints -1
          System.out.println(binarySearch(i, 102));  //prints -1
   }

   //Look for srchVal in the a[] array and return the index of where it's found
   //Return –1 if not found
   private static int binarySearch(int a[], int srchVal)
   {
          int lb = 0;
          int ub = a.length - 1;

          while(lb <= ub)
          {
                    int mid = (lb + ub)/2;
                    if(a[mid] = = srchVal)
                    {
                              return mid;
                    }
                    else if (srchVal > a[mid])
                    {
                              lb = mid + 1;  //set a new lowerbound
                    }
                    else
                    {
                              ub = mid -1;  //set a new upper bound
                    }
          }
          return -1;  //srchVal not found
   }
}
```

Project…Binary Search, Reverse Order

Modify the above class so that the exact same *i[ ]* array in the *main* method is ordered in **descending** order. Then modify the *binarySearch* method so it will search this new array properly.

Project… Binary Search with Objects

Modify the binary search listed on the previous page so as to accommodate objects. First, we must adjust the *main* method so that the *int* array is converted into an *Integer* array. The *int* values of 22, 89, -100, 72, and 102 for which we formerly searched, must now also be *Integer* objects. These modifications are detailed below:

```
public class Tester
{
        public static void main(String args[])
        {
                int i[] = {-7, 15, 21, 22, 43, 49, 51, 67, 78, 81, 84, 89, 95, 97};
                Integer iw[] = new Integer[14];
                for(int k = 0; k < 14; k++)
                {
                   iw[k] = new Integer(i[k]); //Java 5.0, iw[k] = ik];
                }

                System.out.println(binarySearch(iw, new Integer(22))); //3
                        //Java 5.0, System.out.println(binarySearch(iw, 22));
                System.out.println(binarySearch(iw, new Integer(89))); //11
                System.out.println(binarySearch(iw, new Integer(-100))); //-1
                System.out.println(binarySearch(iw, new Integer(72))); //-1
                System.out.println(binarySearch(iw, new Integer(102))); //-1
        }

        private static int binarySearch(Object a[], Object srchVal)
        {
             … students supply this code …
        }
}
```

Notice that the *binarySearch* method now receives *Object* type objects so as to be as general as possible. Wrapper class *Integer* objects implement the *Comparable* interface (and therefore have a *compareTo* method); however, if you use this method to do a binary search on an ordered array of **other** objects, you must insure that those objects implement the *Comparable* interface.

Supply the code for the *binarySearch* method remembering that the parameters it receives are *Object* type objects, and if either is used to call the *compareTo* method, it must first be cast as a *Comparable* or original object type.

****

Recursive Binary Search:

We offer one last way to do a binary search. The class at the top of the next page uses recursion to implement a binary search. Notice that the *binarySearch* method uses four parameters.

```
public class Tester
{
        public static void main(String args[])
        {
                int i[] ={-7, 15, 21, 22, 43, 49, 51, 67, 78, 81, 84, 89, 95, 97};
                int lb = 0;
                int ub = i.length -1;
                System.out.println(binarySearch(i, 22, lb, ub));   //prints 3
                System.out.println(binarySearch(i, 89, lb, ub));   //prints 11
                System.out.println(binarySearch(i, -100, lb, ub)); //prints -1
                System.out.println(binarySearch(i, 72, lb, ub));   //prints -1
                System.out.println(binarySearch(i, 102, lb, ub));  //prints -1
        }

        private static int binarySearch(int a[], int srchVal, int lb, int ub)  //recursive
        {
                if(lb > ub)
                {
                        return -1;
                }
                else
                {
                        int mid = (lb + ub)/2;
                        if(a[mid] = = srchVal)
                        {
                                return mid;
                        }
                        else if (srchVal > a[mid])
                        {
                                return binarySearch(a, srchVal, mid + 1, ub);
                        }
                        else
                        {
                                return binarySearch(a, srchVal, lb, mid -1);
                        }
                }
        }
}
```

****

Pros and cons:

Quite often we have to ask ourselves if a binary search is really worthwhile, especially when compared to doing a linear search. (A linear search is typically done on an **unordered** array.)

A linear search is done by starting at index 0 of an array and just marching all the way to the end asking at each index, "Is this the value?" With good luck we will get a match on the first index we try, but on the other hand, with bad luck, it will be the very last possible index. Therefore, the Big O value for a linear search is O(n) and it is not very efficient.

Since a binary search is much, much faster on the average than a linear search, we have to ask ourselves if sorting the array (as required before doing a binary search) is worthwhile. If the array is to be searched only once, then a linear search would probably save time in the long run. However, if several searches are to be done, then the time investment in sorting the array would probably pay off, and the binary search would be preferred.

It's all in the *Arrays* class:

We would be remiss if it was not mentioned that the *Arrays* class in the *java.util* package has *sort* and *binarySearch* methods. These have already been discussed in <u>Lesson 19</u>; however, here is a summary of that information:

a. **Sort** the array in ascending order.
   public static void sort(int a[]) //**Signature**

   Example:
   ```
   int b[] = {14, 2, 109, . . . 23, 5, 199};
   Arrays.sort(b); //the b array is now in ascending order
   ```

b. Perform a **binary search** of an array for a particular value (this assumes the array has already been sorted in ascending order). This method returns the index of the <u>last</u> array element containing the value of *key*. If *key* is not found, a negative number is returned… *–k –1* where *k* is the index before which the key would be inserted.
   public int binarySearch(int a[], int key)   //**Signature**

   Example:
   ```
   //Assume array b[] already exists and has been sorted in ascending order.
   //Suppose the b array now reads {2,17, 36, 203, 289, 567, 1000}.
   int indx = Arrays.binarySearch(b, 203); //search for 203 in the array
   System.out.println(indx); //3
   ```

Unfortunately, *Arrays.binarySearch* does not work on any objects other than *String* and *Comparable* object arrays. It *does* work on all the primitive data type arrays.

****

Some miscellaneous facts:

Finally, here are a few random facts about binary searches (on an array of *n* elements).

1. Array must already be sorted.

2. Big O value is O(log n) for both iterative and recursive types.

3. $\log_2 n$ is the worst case number of times we must "halve" the list.

4. The largest size array that can be searched while comparing at most *n* elements is 2^n-1.

Exercise on Lesson 51

1. If we have an array of 32 numbers, what is the maximum number of times we will need to halve the array in a binary search for a particular number?

2. If we are doing a binary search for the value *104* in the array below, what will be the **next** values for *m*, *lb*, and *ub* assuming their current values are *lb=0, m=6, & ub=13* as shown?

	lb						m							ub
Index	0	1	2	3	4	5	6	7	8	9	10	11	12	13
Value	-54	11	14	59	61	65	72	88	89	92	104	105	106	111

lb = ?
ub = ?
m = ?

3. What must be required of an array of numbers before a binary search can be done?

4. In the following binary search of an array already sorted in ascending order, fill in the code for **<#1>** and **<#2>** so that the search is done properly.

```
private static int binarySearch(int a[], int srchVal)
{
        int left = 0;
        int right = a.length - 1;

        while(right >= left)
        {
                int middle = (left + right)/2;
                if(a[middle] = = srchVal)
                {
                        return middle;
                }
                else if (srchVal < a[middle])
                {
                        <#1>
                }
                else
                {
                        <#2>
                }
        }
        return -1;
}
```

5. Suppose you have the following array of *doubles* called *dd[ ]*.

   {82.92, 56.1, 77.02, … 150.23 , .0231}

   Show how you would convert this array into a corresponding array of wrapper class *Doubles* called *dw[ ]*.

6. Suppose *obj1* and *obj2* are objects of type *Object* that implement the *Comparable* interface. What is wrong with the following code and how would you fix it?
   int c = obj2.compareTo(obj1);

7. What is the Big O value for a binary search?

8. What is the Big O value for a linear search?

9. Is it possible for a linear search to be faster than a binary search if they search the same array?

10. What is the smallest number of comparisons a linear search might have to make when searching an array of length *n*?

11. What is the largest number of comparisons a linear search might have to make when searching an array of length *n*?

12. Which is generally more efficient, a linear or a binary search if the array is already ordered?

13. If you only have to search a large unsorted array one time, which would be the most efficient, a linear or binary search? Why?

14. Assume you have an unsorted *double* array called *dd[ ]*. Use the *Arrays* class to show how to do a binary search for 107.3. Print "Hubba hubba" if it's found.

15. Suppose *Arrays.binarySearch(a, 18)* returns a value of –17. Between what two indices in array *a* does 18 fall?

16. Will the *Arrays.binarySearch* method work on an array of *String* objects?

Binary Search… Contest Type Problems

1. Call the *binSrch* method shown to the right with *binSrch(str, 0, str.length, "eplison")*. How many times is the *compareTo* method called if the *str* array is as follows?

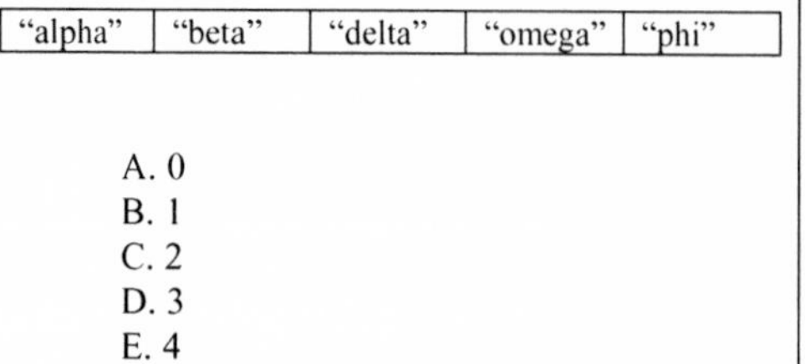

"alpha"	"beta"	"delta"	"omega"	"phi"

A. 0
B. 1
C. 2
D. 3
E. 4

```
public static boolean binSrch(Comparable p[], int
                              start, int end, Comparable thing)
{
    if(start > end)
        return false;
    int m = (start + end)/2;
    if (p[m].equals(thing))
        return true;
    else if(p[m].compareTo(thing)<0)
        return binSrch(p, m + 1, end, thing)
    else
        return binSrch(p, start, m-1, thing)
}
```

2. What figure of merit does a time complexity analysis of the code to the right yield?

A. O(n)
B. $O(n^2)$
C. O(log n)
D. $O(2^n)$
E. None of these

3. What must be required of an array upon which a binary sort is to be done?

A. Must be sorted in ascending order B. Must be sorted in descending order C. Either A or B

D. Can only be of a primitive type, no objects allowed E. None of these

4. What replaces **<#1>** in the code to the right so that a binary search is correctly done?

A. left/2 + right/2
B. (left + right)/2
C. .5 * (right + left)
D. Both A and B
E. None of these

5. What replaces **<#2>** in the code to the right so that a binary search is correctly done?

A. cmp = = 0
B. cmp < 0
C. cmp > 0
D. cmp <=0
E. None of the these

```
public static boolean binarySearch(Comparable
                                   x[], Object srchVal)
{
    int left = 0, right = x.length-1;
    do
    {
        int m= <#1>;
        int cmp = x[m].compareTo(srchVal);
        if(<#2>)
        {
            return true;
        }
        else if(cmp > 0)
        {
            right = m – 1;
        }
        else
        {
            left = m + 1;
        }

    }while(right>=left);
    return false;
}
```

6. Which of the following would replace **<#1>** in the code to the right so that a binary search is correctly done?

A. init >= fini
B. init > fini
C. init < fini
D. init <= fini
E. None of these

```
//binary search
public static boolean seek(Comparable p[], int
                init, int fini, Comparable lookFor)
{
     if(<#1>)
        return false;
     int m = (init + fini)/2;
     if (p[m].equals(lookFor))
         return true;
     else if(p[m].compareTo(lookFor)<0)
         return seek(p, m + 1, fini, lookFor)
     else
         return seek(p, init, m-1, lookFor)
}
```

7. Which of the following is a legitimate way to search an unsorted integer array called *bj* for the value stored in *int i*, and print *true* if it's found and *false* if not found.

A. `System.out.println( Arrays.binarySearch(bj, i) );`

B. `Arrays.sort(bj);`
   `System.out.println( Arrays.binarySearch(bj, i) >= 0 );`

C. `System.out.println( Arrays.binarySearch(i, bj) );`

D. `Arrays.sort(bj);`
   `System.out.println( Arrays.binarySearch(bj, i) );`

E. None of these

Lesson 52….. Binary Search Tree

We will begin by showing how a binary search tree is constructed. We will construct our tree from the following sequence of integers; 50, 56, 52, 25, 74, and 54. Each number will result in a "node" being constructed. The nodes in the series of figures below are depicted with circles, and the sequence of figures shows the sequence in which the nodes are added.

The rules:

As can be observed from the drawings, a new integer (*n*) is added by starting at the root node (top level node) as the first "comparison node" and then using the following rules:

1. If the number we are to insert (*n*) is greater than the "comparison node", move down the tree and to the right; the first node encountered is the new "comparison node".
2. If the number we are to insert (*n*) is less than or equal to the "comparison node", move down the tree and to the left; the first node encountered is the new "comparison node".
3. If, after comparing at a node position, a node does not exist in the direction in which we try to move, then insert a new node containing the integer *n* at that position.

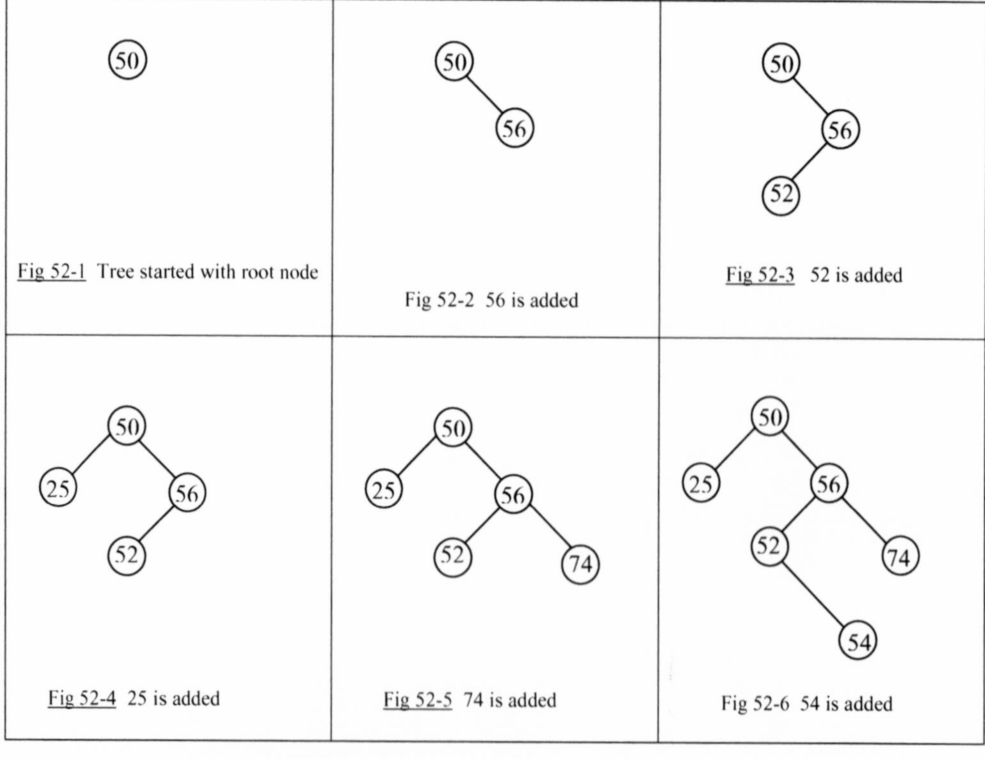

Fig 52-1 Tree started with root node

Fig 52-2 56 is added

Fig 52-3 52 is added

Fig 52-4 25 is added

Fig 52-5 74 is added

Fig 52-6 54 is added

Creation of the *BSTNode* class:

We will now create a class call *BST* (binary search tree) that will allow us to add nodes in the fashion described above. However, we must first have a class that creates the nodes themselves. What information must a node contain? For storing integers in the nodes, as we are doing in this example, each node should contain the following:

1. The actual data (an integer for the example above)
2. A reference to the right-hand node immediately beneath this node (*null* if it doesn't exist)
3. A reference to the left-hand node immediately beneath this node (*null* if it doesn't exist)

We are going to call this node-creating class, *BstNode*. Its implementation is shown below.

```
public class BstNode
{
        public BstNode(int i)  //Constructor
        {
                leftNode = null;
                rightNode = null;
                intData = i;
        }

        public int intData;
        public BstNode leftNode;
        public BstNode rightNode;
}
```

Notice that the three state variables in this class correspond to the three numbered requirements mentioned earlier. Also, notice that the *leftNode* and *rightNode* fields are set to *null* since when a node is constructed, there are no other nodes "hanging off it" yet.

The *BST* class:

Next, we turn our attention to the *BST* class itself. In the constructor, we simply create the root node (the highest level node).

> The reader is strongly urged to look over Appendix W (Tree Definitions). There, you will get a firm grounding in the tree-terms we have already used here and new ones we will be using soon.

The constructor and state variables are as follows for the *BST* class:

```
public class BST
{
        public BST(int i) //constructor
        {    // Root node is instantiated at the time of creation of the tree object.
               rootNode = new BstNode(i);    //create a node with the above class
        }
        ...more code to come...

        BstNode rootNode;
}
```

The *addNode* method:

Now comes the most important (and most complex) method of the *BST* class, the *addNode* method in which decisions are made as to the correct position for each new node to be added. Here are the rules for inserting a new node after first setting the root node as the *currentNode*.

1. If the number we are to insert (*n*) is greater than the *currentNode*, move down the tree and to the right; the first node encountered is the new *currentNode*.
2. If the number we are to insert (*n*) is less than or equal to the *currentNode*, move down the tree and to the left; the first node encountered is the new *currentNode*.
3. Continuing in this same fashion, move down the tree. If, after comparing at a node position, a node does not exist in the direction in which we try to move, then insert a new node containing the integer *n* at that position.

If these rules seem familiar, they are essentially the same as those at the top of page 52-1. Here, in this latest rendition, we become more specific with regard to the variable names to be used in the method that implements the rules. The complete class (including the *addNode* method) now reads:

```
public class BST
{
   public BST(int i)  //constructor: Root node added at the time of creation of the tree
   {
         rootNode = new BstNode(i);
   }

   public void addNode(int i)
   {
      BstNode currentNode = rootNode;
      boolean finished = false;
      do
      {
         BstNode curLeftNode = currentNode.leftNode;
         BstNode curRightNode = currentNode.rightNode;
         int curIntData = currentNode.intData;

         if(i > curIntData)  //look down the right branch
         {
                  if(curRightNode == null)
                  {  //create a new node  referenced with currentNode.rightNode
                        currentNode.rightNode = new BstNode(i);
                         finished = true;
                  }
                  else //keep looking by assigning a new current node one level down
                  {   currentNode = currentNode.rightNode;  }
         }
         else  //look down the left branch
         {
                  if(curLeftNode == null)
                  {  //create a new node referenced with currentNode.leftNode
                        currentNode.leftNode = new BstNode(i);
                        finished = true;
                  }
                  else
                  {  //keep looking by assigning a new current node one level down
```

```
                    currentNode = currentNode.leftNode;
                }
            }
        }while(!finished);
    }
    BstNode rootNode;
}
```

It is left to the reader to examine the code in the *addNode* method and to convince himself that the three numbered rules are being implemented.

A class for testing:

To test the *BST* class, use the following *Tester* class:

```
public class Tester
{
        public static void main(String args[])
        {
                //the first integer in the tree is used to create the object
                BST bstObj = new BST(50);
                bstObj.addNode(56);
                bstObj.addNode(52);
                bstObj.addNode(25);
                bstObj.addNode(74);
                bstObj.addNode(54);
        }
}
```

Prove that it really works:

The integers mentioned in the example at the beginning of this lesson are added to the tree with this test code. But how do we really know that it is working? What we need is some type of printout. If we add the following *traverseAndPrint* method to the *BST* class we will see that our class does, indeed, perform as advertised.

```
public void traverseAndPrint(BstNode currentNode )
{
        System.out.print("data = " + currentNode.intData);
                //To aid in your understanding, you may want to just ignore this
                //indented portion and just print the integer. In that case, change the
                //line above to a println instead of a print.
                if(currentNode.leftNode == null)
                {    System.out.print("   left = null");    }
                else
                {    System.out.print("   left = " + (currentNode.leftNode).intData);  }

                if(currentNode.rightNode == null)
                {    System.out.print("   right = null");  }
                else
                {    System.out.print("   right = " + (currentNode.rightNode).intData);}
                System.out.println("");

        if(currentNode.leftNode != null)
            traverseAndPrint(currentNode.leftNode);
```

```
        if(currentNode.rightNode != null)
            traverseAndPrint(currentNode.rightNode);
}
```

This method has recursive calls to itself and will print every node in the tree. In addition to the data stored in each node (an integer), it also prints the contents of the two nodes "hanging off" this node.

Test this new method by adding the following code at the bottom of the *main* method in the *Tester* class.

```
//print all the nodes
bstObj.traverseAndPrint(bstObj.rootNode);
```

For the data suggested in the examples on page 52-1 the output will appear as shown below when the *main* method in the *Tester* class is executed:

```
data = 50     left = 25     right = 56
data = 25     left = null   right = null
data = 56     left = 52     right = 74
data = 52     left = null   right = 54
data = 54     left = null   right = null
data = 74     left = null   right = null
```

****

Project... *BST find* Method

Now we come to what a binary search tree is all about, the search. You are to create a method of the *BST* class called *find*. Its signature is as follows:

```
public boolean find(int i)
```

It returns a *true* if *i* is found in the binary tree and *false* if it's not found. This method will use essentially the same rules as those for the *addNode* method except when we come to the place where we formerly added a node; we will exit the method and say that the search was unsuccessful. Likewise, there is more to the comparisons. We can no longer just test to see if the data we are searching for is greater than or less than that of the *currentNode*. We must now also test for equality.

To test the *find* method, add the following code to the bottom of the *main* method in *Tester*.

```
System.out.println(bstObj.find(74));  //This is one it will find...prints a true
System.out.println(bstObj.find(13));  //This is one it won't find...prints a false
```

Why use a Binary Search Tree?

What can searching a Binary Search Tree (BST) do that we could not accomplish searching a linear array? The BST can do it faster, much faster. The Big O value for a reasonably balanced BST is O(log n). For an unordered array it's O(n); however, for an ordered array, a binary search is also of the order O(log n). So, what are the advantages of a binary search tree over searching an ordered array (using a binary search) since their Big O values are the same? The advantages are:

1. With an ordered array, ordering is necessary after the insertion of each new element. An alternative to this is inserting the new element in the correct position. In either case, the time required to do this is typically considerably more than the time required to insert a new node in a *BST*.

2. In an array, we must pre-dimension the array.
   a. If we dimension to small, we run the risk of running out of space if more nodes need to be added than were originally anticipated.
   b. If we dimension to large, we waste memory and may degrade the performance of the computer.

   With the *BST* object, we dynamically create nodes as we need them in dynamic memory. There is no need to know ahead of time how many there will eventually be.

Anonymous objects:

Have you noticed that with the *BST* class, the **node objects that contain our data are not named** (except for the root node)? We have to traverse the tree and each node we encounter gives references to the two nodes "hanging off" it with *leftNode* and *rightNode*. Recall that we had a similar situation in <u>Lesson 49</u> with the singly linked list in which we had a "chain" of nodes, each with a reference to the next. Here, each node has references to **two** nodes that follow it.

Balanced Tree:

Above it was mentioned that the Big O value for searching a Binary Search Tree was O(log n) if the tree was reasonably balanced. What do we mean by a balanced tree? Refer back to <u>Fig 52-6</u> and it can be seen that this tree is not balanced. There are more nodes to the right of the root (50) than to the left. An extreme case of this is shown below.

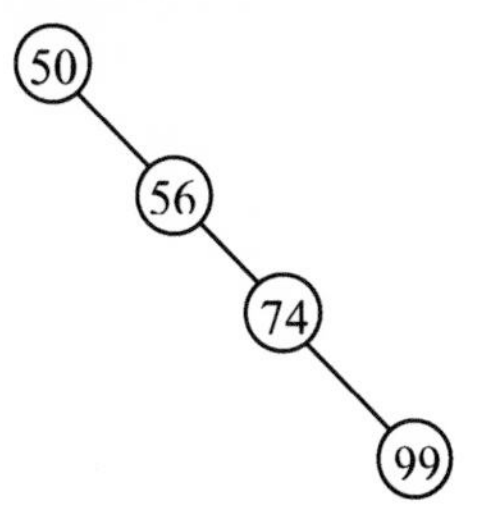

<u>Fig 52-7</u> A totally unbalanced "tree"

Consider the following sequence of numbers to be added to a binary tree.

{50, 56, 74, 99}

The resulting "tree" to the left is totally unbalanced. Every new node to be added lies to the right of the previous node. In this case (which is clearly the worst case) the Big O value for searching the tree is O(n). If there are *n* items we might very well have to do *n* comparisons before finding the desired one.

If we are **very** unlucky, just such a tree **might** result when we add our nodes. With random data, it is not very likely to be as bad as <u>Fig 52-7</u>; however, what is more likely, is that that tree be somewhat out of balance which would, of course, reduce the efficiency of the search. What can we do to prevent this unbalance? It is beyond the scope of this book, however, there are algorithms that can detect this and "rebalance the tree". Nothing comes free, and this rebalancing adds complexity to the code as well as additional processing time.

Generalizing, Using Objects for Data:

It is possible to modify our class so that instead of just storing primitive integers we could store objects. To do this we would replace the code everywhere we pass an *int* variable as an argument, with *Comparable obj* .

The only catch is that the *obj* object that we pass in, **must implement the *compareTo* method**. The other requirement is that the former state variable, *int intData* be replaced with *Comparable data.* Rather than modify the *BST* class that we have already done, we are going to present another class that adds *Comparable* type objects to nodes in a Binary Search Tree. This class is just about the ultimate as far as brevity of code is concerned; however it is more difficult to understand because it uses recursion.

```
public class BsTree
{
   public BsTree(Comparable d)
   {
            theData = d;
            leftNode = null;    //This and next line could be omitted,
            rightNode = null;  //they are automatically null.
   }

   public BsTree addNode(Comparable d)
   {
            if(d.compareTo(theData) > 0)
            {   //d should be inserted somewhere in the branch to the right
                 if(rightNode != null)
                        //right node exists, go down that branch, look for place to put it
                         rightNode.addNode(d);
                 else
                        rightNode = new BsTree(d);  //Create new rightNode, store d in it
            }
            else
            {   //d should be inserted somewhere in the branch to the left
                 if(leftNode != null)
                        //left node exists, go down that branch, look for place to put it
                        leftNode.addNode(d);
                 else
                        leftNode = new BsTree(d);  //Create a new leftNode, store d in it
            }
            return this;
   }
   private Comparable theData;
   private BsTree leftNode, rightNode;
}
```

It is left to the reader to create a *find* method comparable to those of the *BST* class earlier in this lesson. We also need a *traverseAndPrint* method for this class. Three different versions of *traverseAndPrint* will be offered below as the various types of traversals are discussed.

Traversal types:
There are four traversal types. They are preorder, inorder, postorder, and level order traversals. Each visits **all** of the nodes in the tree, but each in a different order.

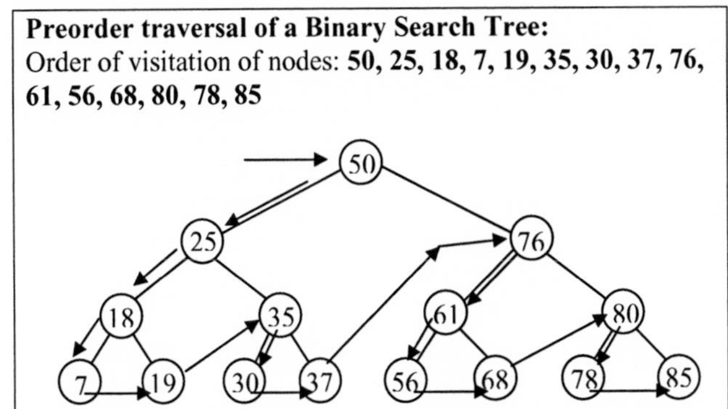

Fig. 52-8
Preorder traversal follows the sequence of arrows. **Rule: A node is visited before its descendants.**

The following code implements a preorder traversal of a tree as depicted in Fig. 52-8. An easy way to remember this code is to note the printing for this preorder traversal comes before the two recursive calls.

```
public void traverseAndPrint( ) //Use with BsTree class on previous page.
{
        System.out.println(theData);
        if( leftNode != null )  leftNode.traverseAndPrint( );
        if( rightNode != null )  rightNode.traverseAndPrint( );
}
```

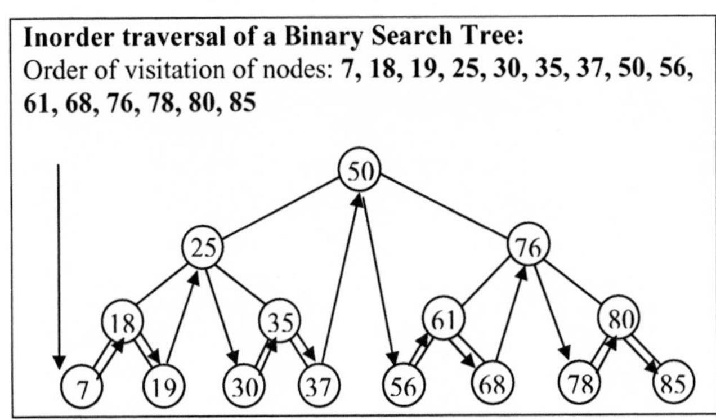

Fig. 52-9
Inorder traversal follows the sequence of arrows. The order is the ascending order of a sorted list. **Rule: A node is visited after its left subtree and before its right subtree.**

The following code implements an inorder traversal of a tree as depicted in Fig. 52-9. This technique is important since it **visits the nodes in a "sorted order."** An easy way to remember this code is to note the printing for this inorder traversal comes in-between the two recursive calls.

```
public void traverseAndPrint( )
{
```

```
        if( leftNode != null ) leftNode.traverseAndPrint( );
        System.out.println(theData);
        if( rightNode != null ) rightNode.traverseAndPrint( );
}
```

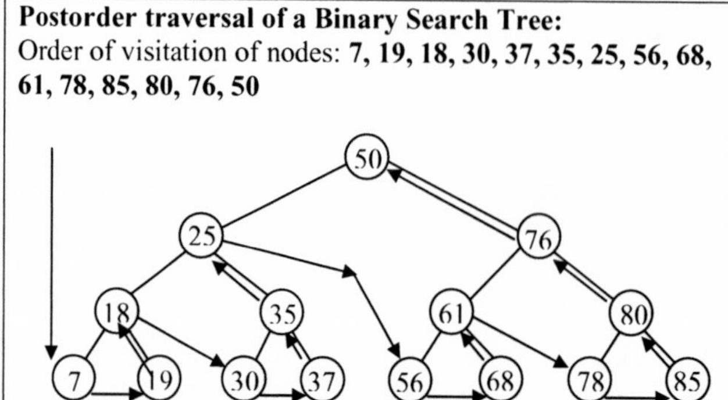

Fig. 52-10
Postorder traversal follows the sequence of arrows. **Rule: A node is visited after its descendants.**

The following code implements a postorder traversal of a tree as depicted in Fig. 52-10. An easy way to remember this code is to note the printing for this postorder traversal comes after the two recursive calls.

```
public void traverseAndPrint( )
{
        if( leftNode != null ) leftNode.traverseAndPrint( );
        if( rightNode != null ) rightNode.traverseAndPrint( );
        System.out.println(theData);
}
```

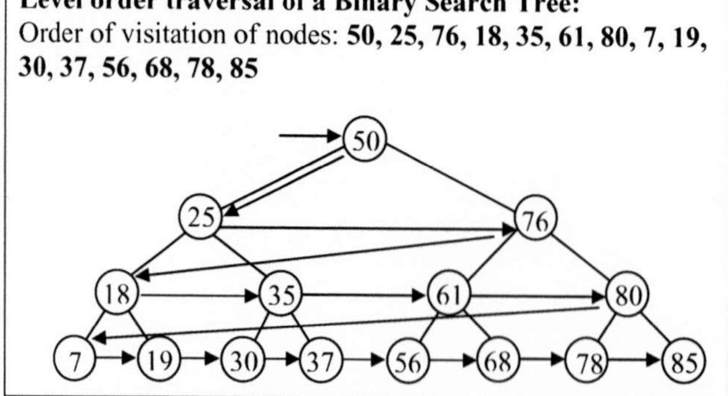

Fig. 52-11
Level order traversal follows the sequence of arrows.

The code that would implement this is a bit more involved than the others. One way to do it is to have counters that keep up with how deep we are in the tree.

An Application of Binary Trees… Binary Expression Trees

Consider the infix expressions (6 + 8) * 2 and 5 + (3 * 4). The expression trees to the right are a result of parsing these expressions. As can be inferred from the drawings, the following rules apply for an expression tree:

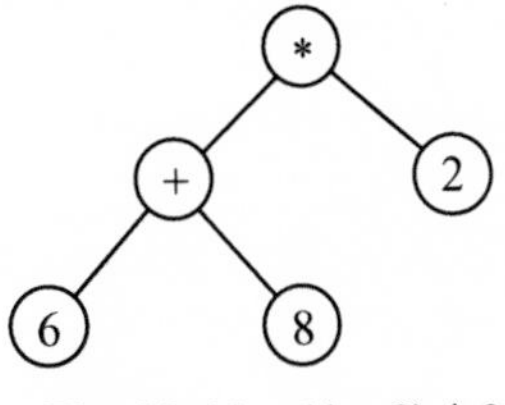

Fig. 52-12 (6 + 8) * 2

- Each leaf node contains a single operand.
- Each interior node contains an operator.
- The left and right subtrees of an operator node represent subexpressions that must be evaluated **before** applying the operator at the operator node.
    - The levels of the nodes in the tree indicate their relative precedence of evaluation.
    - Operations at the lower levels must be done **before** those above them.
    - The operation at the root of the tree will be the last to be done.

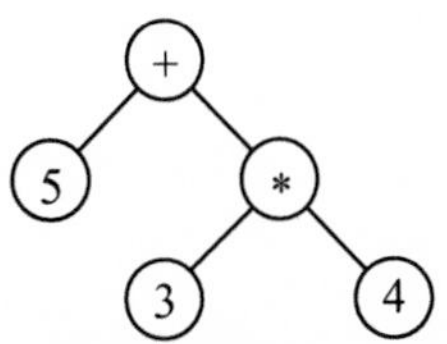

Fig 52-13 5 + (3 * 4)

We will now look at a larger expression tree and see how the inorder, preorder, and postorder traversals of the tree have special meanings with regard to the mathematics of an expression.

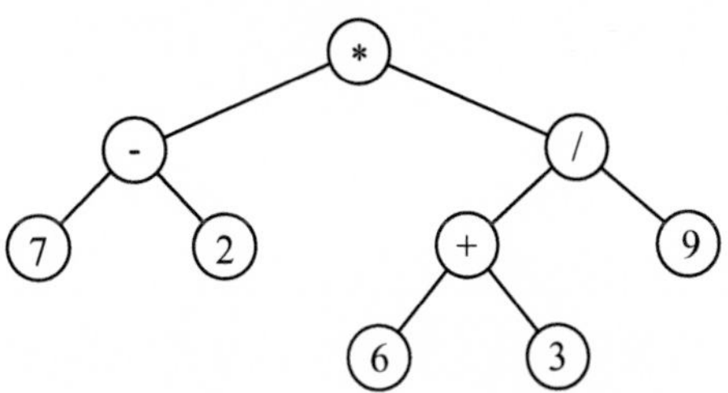

Fig. 52-14 A binary expression tree for the infix expression (7 - 2) * ((6+3) / 9)

An **Inorder Traversal** of the above expression tree yields the **infix** form: (7 - 2) * ((6+3) / 9)

A **Preorder Traversal** of the above expression tree yields the **prefix** form: * - 7 2 / + 6 3 9

A **Postfix Traversal** of the above expression tree yields the **postfix** form: 7 2 - 6 3 + 9 / *
Notice that the postfix form is Reverse Polish Notation (RPN), the form that was used for the stack calculator of Lesson 50.

Binary Search Tree… Contest Type Problems

1. Which of the following replaces **<*1>** in the code to the right to make the *traverseAndPrint* method visit and print every node in a "Postorder" fashion?

A.
```
if(leftNd != null)  leftNd.traverseAndPrnt( );
System.out.print(info);
if(rightNd!=null) rightNd.traverseAndPrnt( );
```

B.
```
if(leftNd != null)  leftNd.traverseAndPrnt( );
if(rightNd!=null) rightNd.traverseAndPrnt( );
System.out.print(info);
```

C.
```
System.out.print(info);
if(leftNd != null)  leftNd.traverseAndPrnt( );
if(rightNd!=null)rightNd.traverseAndPrnt( );
```

D.
```
leftNd.traverseAndPrnt( );
rightNd.traverseandPrnt( );
```

E. None of these

2. Assume **<*1>** has been filled in correctly. Which of the following creates a *Bst* object *obj* and adds 55 as a wrapper class Integer?

A.
```
Integer J;
J = 55;
Bst obj = new Bst(J);
```

B.
```
Bst obj = new Bst( new Integer(55) );
```

C.
```
Bst obj;
obj.add(55);
```

D.
```
Bst obj;
obj.add( new Integer(55) );
```

E. None of these

3. Assume **<*1>** has been filled in correctly and that *n* objects are added to an object of type *Bst* in order from largest to smallest. What is the Big O value for searching this tree?

A. O(n log n)
B. O(log n)
C. O(n)
D. O(n^2)
E. None of these

```
//Binary Search Tree
public class Bst
{
    public Bst(Comparable addValue)
    {
        info = addValue;
    }

    public Bst addNd(Comparable addValue)
    {
        int cmp = info.compareTo(addValue);

        if(cmp<0)
        {
            if(rightNd!=null)
                rightNd.addNd(addValue);
            else
                rightNd=new Bst(addValue);
        }
        else if(cmp>0)
        {
            if(leftNd!=null)
                leftNd.addNd(addValue);
            else
                leftNd=new Bst(addValue);
        }
        return this;
    }

    public void transverseAndPrnt( )
    {
        <*1>
    }

    private Comparable info;
    private Bst leftNd;
    private Bst rightNd;
}
```

4. When a *Bst* object is constructed, to what value will *leftNd* and *rightNd* be initialized?

A. this
B. 0
C. null
D. Bst object
E. None of these

5. After executing the code below, what does the resulting tree look like?

```
Bst obj = new Bst(new Integer(11));
obj.add(new Integer(6))
obj.add(new Integer(13));
```

A. ArithmeticException

B.
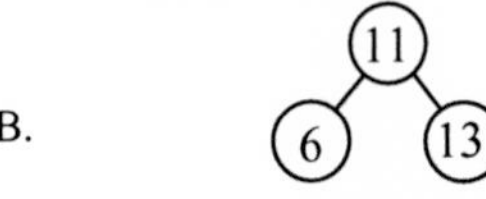

C.
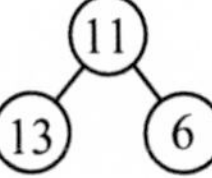

D.
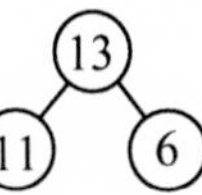

E. None of these

6. What replaces **<*1>** in the code to the right so that a "Preorder" traversal is done?

A.
```
if(leftNd != null)  leftNd.traverseAndPrnt( );
System.out.print(info);
if(rightNd!=null)rightNd.traverseAndPrnt();
```

B.
```
if(leftNd != null)  leftNd.traverseAndPrnt( );
if(rightNd!=null)rightNd.traverseAndPrnt();
System.out.print(info);
```

C.
```
System.out.print(info);
if(leftNd != null)  leftNd.traverseAndPrnt( );
if(rightNd!=null)rightNd.traverseAndPrnt();
```

D.
```
leftNd.traverseAndPrnt( );
rightNd.traverseandPrnt( );
```

E. None of these

```
//Binary Search Tree
public class Bst
{
    public Bst(Comparable addValue)
    {
        info = addValue;
    }

    public Bst addNd(Comparable addValue)
    {
        int cmp = info.compareTo(addValue);

        if(cmp<0)
        {
            if(rightNd!=null)
                rightNd.addNd(addValue);
            else
                rightNd=new Bst(addValue);
        }
        else if(cmp>0)
        {
            if(leftNd!=null)
                leftNd.addNd(addValue);
            else
                leftNd=new Bst(addValue);
        }
        return this;
    }

    public void transverseAndPrnt( )
    {
        <*1>
    }

    private Comparable info;
    private Bst leftNd;
    private Bst rightNd;
}
```

7. What is a disadvantage of an unbalanced Binary Search Tree?

A. No disadvantage B. Uses excessive memory C. Limited accuracy
D. Reduced search efficiency E. None of these

8. Average case search time for a Binary Search Tree that is reasonably balanced is of what order?

A. O(n log n) B. $O(n^2)$ C. O(n) D. O(1) E. None of these

9. What positive thing(s) can be said about a completely unbalanced tree that results from adding the following integers to a tree in the sequence shown?

{ 5, 6, 7, ... 999, 1000}

A. The items are automatically in numerical order along the long sequential strand.
B. The smallest number is automatically the root node. C. The largest number is the root node.
D. Both A and B E. Both A and C

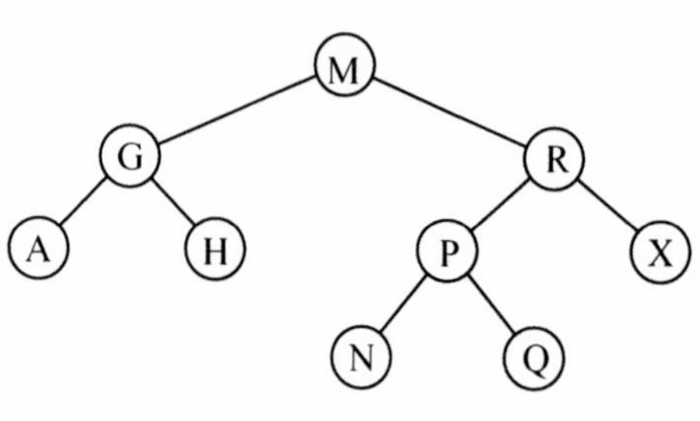

10. In what order are the nodes visited in the tree to the left if a preorder traversal is done?

A. A, G, H, M, N, P, Q, R, X
B. M, G, A, H, R, P, N, Q, X
C. A, H, G, N, Q, P, X, R, M
D. M, G, R, A, D, P, X, N, Q
E. None of these

11. In what order are the nodes visited in the tree to the left if a postorder traversal is done?

A. A, G, H, M, N, P, Q, R, X
B. M, G, A, H, R, P, N, Q, X
C. A, H, G, N, Q, P, X, R, M
D. M, G, R, A, H, P, X, N, Q
E. None of these

12. In what order are the nodes visited in the tree to the left if an inorder traversal is done?

A. A, G, H, M, N, P, Q, R, X
B. M, G, A, H, R, P, N, Q, X
C. A, H, G, N, Q, P, X, R, M
D. M, G, R, A, H, P, X, N, Q
E. None of these

13. For the tree above, which of the following is a possible order in which the nodes were originally added to the binary search tree?

A. M, G, R, A, H, X, P, N, Q
B. M, G, R, A, H, Q, N, P, X
C. M, R, A, G, H, X, P, N, Q
D. A, G, H, M, N, P, Q, R, X
E. None of these

14. What mathematical infix expression is represented by the binary expression tree to the right?

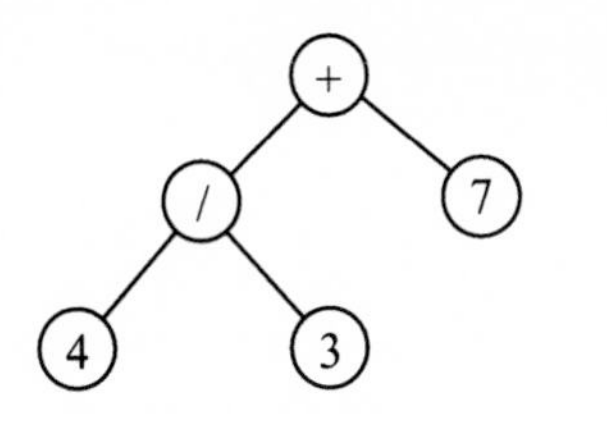

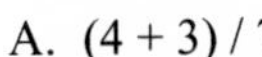

A. (4 + 3) / 7
B. 4 / (3 + 7)
C. 7 / 4 / 3 + 7
D. (4 / 3) + 7
E. None of these

15. What mathematical infix expression is represented by the binary expression tree to the right?

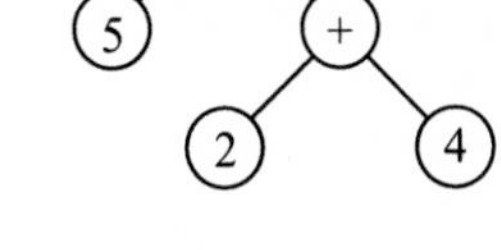

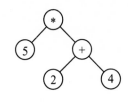

A. 5 * 2 + 4
B. 5 * (2 + 4)
C. (2 * 4) + 5
D. 5 * 2 * (+4)
E. None of these

16. Which of the following is a postfix version of the following mathematical expression?

(37 - 59) * ((4 + 1) / 6)

A. * - 37 59 / + 4 1 6
B. (37 - 59) * ((4 + 1) / 6)
C. 37 59 - 4 1 + 6 / *
D. 37 - 59 * 4 + 1 / 6
E. None of these

17. What is the minimum number of levels for a binary tree with 20 nodes?

A. 20 B. 7 C. 6 D. 5 E. None of these

18. What is the maximum number of levels for a binary tree with 20 nodes?

A. 20 B. 7 C. 6 D. 5 E. None of these

Lesson 53… Queues

Standing in line:

When you stand in a line to buy tickets at a movie box office, you are standing in a queue. This is a classic example of a First-In-First-Out (FIFO) data structure. The first person in the movie line is the first one to leave the line (after buying tickets), and a new person entering the line always enters at the **end** of the line.

Our own interface:

Is there an existing *interface* that's a standard part of Java that could help us design a queue? No, unfortunately there isn't one, so we must design our own. An *interface* with all the essentials for a queue is given below.

```
public interface Queue
{
        boolean isEmpty( );  //returns true if nothing in the queue
        void enqueue(Object obj );  //places object obj at the back of the queue
        Object dequeue( );  //removes and returns object at front of the list
        Object peekFront( );  //returns object at the front of the list
}
```

An underlying data structure:

As we think of implementing this in software, we first need to consider what underlying data structure to use. A natural choice is the *LinkedList* class. Below, we review just a few of the methods of the *LinkedList* class and how we might use them to implement the *Queue* interface in a class that we will call *LinkedListQueue*.

```
void addLast(Object obj) … use for enqueue
Object removeFirst( ) … use for dequeue
boolean isEmpty( ) … use for isEmpty
Object getFirst( ) … use for peekFront
```

The implementation:

Here is the full implementation of the *Queue* interface in our new *LinkedListQueue* class.

```
import java.util.*;  //necessary for LinkedList class
public class LinkedListQueue implements Queue
{
        public LinkedListQueue( )  //constructor
        {       lst = new LinkedList( );       }

        public void enqueue(Object obj)
        {       lst.addLast(obj);              }

        public Object dequeue( )
        {       return lst.removeFirst( );     }

        public Object peekFront( )
        {       return lst.getFirst( );        }
```

```
        public boolean isEmpty( )
        {       return lst.isEmpty( );          }

        private LinkedList lst;  // state variable
}
```

Some miscellaneous facts concerning queues:

The ***front*** of a queue, as it is most commonly called, is sometimes called *first*, *start*, or *beginning*. The ***back*** of a queue, as it is commonly called, is sometimes called *rear* or *end*.

The *enqueue* and *dequeue* methods for the *LinkedList* and *ArrayList* implementations of the *Queue* interface both have a Big O value of O(1).

If a queue class is implemented using ordinary arrays, the *dequeue* method will typically have a Big O value of O(n), where *n* is the size of the queue. This is due to the necessity of "compacting" the array after removal of the item at index 0. Typically, the other methods will have a value of O(1).

Exercise on Lesson 53

1. What is the meaning of the acronym FIFO?

2. What is the meaning of the acronym LIFO?

3. Of which type is a queue, a LIFO or a FIFO?

4. Identify each of the following as a FIFO or LIFO:
   a. Cars lined up at a toll both.
   b. Students turn in tests to a teacher and place them on top of a stack. The teacher grades the papers by selecting the next paper to grade from the **bottom** of the stack.
   c. Students turn in tests to a teacher and place them on top of a stack. The teacher grades the papers by selecting the next paper to grade from the **top** of the stack.
   d. A dishwasher in a cafeteria places newly washed trays on top of a stack and patrons take their tray from the top of that stack.
   e. Characters entered from a keyboard into a character buffer in a computer.

5. What is the difference between the *peekFront* and *dequeue* methods?

6. In the *LinkedList* implementation of the *Queue* interface, which *LinkedList* method is responsible for implementing the *enqueue* method?

7. In the *LinkedList* implementation of the *Queue* interface, which *LinkedList* method is responsible for implementing the *dequeue* method?

8. In the *LinkedList* implementation of the *Queue* interface, which *LinkedList* method is responsible for implementing the *peekFront* method?

9. Is the *Queue* interface a standard part of Java and if so, in what package is it found?

10. What is output by the following, assuming an empty queue object *q* already exists?

```
q.enqueue("Hello");
q.enqueue("Hello again");
q.enqueue("Good bye");
System.out.print(q.dequeue( ));
System.out.print(q.peekFront( ));
System.out.println(q.dequeue( ));
```

11. What is output by the following code?

```
LinkedListQueue q = new LinkedListQueue( );
for(int j = 0; j < 5; j++)
{
        q.enqueue(new Integer(j)); //Java 5.0, q.enqueue(j);
}

for(int j = 4; j >= 0; j--)
{
        System.out.print( ((Integer)q.dequeue( )).intValue( ) );
        // Java 5.0, System.out.print( (Integer)q.dequeue( ));
}
```

12. What is output by the following code?

```
LinkedListQueue q = new LinkedListQueue( );
int x = 1;
Integer iw = new Integer(37); //Java 5.0, Integer iw = 37;
do
{
        x++;
        q.enqueue(new Integer(x)); //Java 5.0, q.enqueue(x);
        iw = q.dequeue( );
}while(x < 4);
System.out.println(iw.intValue( )); //Java 5.0, System.out.println(iw);
```

Use the following class for problems 13 and 14:

```
public class TheIntQueue {
        public TheIntQueue(int maxSize) {
                intArray = new int[maxSize];
                size = 0;
        }

        public void enqueue( int x) {
                intArray[size] = x;
                size++;
        }
        ...other methods not shown...

        private int[] intArray;
        private int size;
}
```

13. What is the greatest number of integers that could be stored if this class is instantiated with *TheIntQueue iq= new TheIntQueue(59);* ?

14. After just one call of the *enqueue* method, what is the value of *size*?

Project …Who's Next?

Ye Olde Computer Co. has two service reps that take phone calls and help customers with software problems. These customers are placed in a phone queue to await their turn for help. Naturally, customers have to wait in the queue until all those waiting before them have begun their help session and when one of the service reps is finally available.

Our task here is to determine how much time each customer must wait and add all the wait-times together for a grand total of wait-time. The wait-time for a customer is defined as the time elapsed from when he arrives in the phone queue until he is "dequeued" and his help begins. Assume that as a service rep finishes helping a customer, he is immediately available to help the next customer at the head of the phone queue.

The following data will make up a text file call Customers.dat:

```
5 20
7 10
10 40
15 30
20 10
25 32
35 50
43 26
```

In this file each line represents a customer. The first integer represents his arrival time (in minutes from some arbitrary starting time) in the phone queue and the second is the time (in minutes) required to solve his problem. It is assumed that no two customers arrive at the same time. For this data the answer is 160 minutes of accumulated waiting time, and the output is just:

Create a project called *WhosNext* and enter the *interface Queue* and the class *LinkedListQueue* (both on p 53-1). The class with the *main* method will also be called *WhosNext* and will consist of the *BaseClass* code from Lesson 27 and the following additional code.

```
LinkedListQueue q = new LinkedListQueue( );
...place customer data in q...

//Initialize some variables
 int TotalWaitTime = 0;
Scanner sc = new Scanner((String)q.peekFront( ));
 int firstCustArrivalTime = sc.nextInt( );
        int nextAvailTimeA= firstCustArrivalTime;
        int nextAvailTimeB= firstCustArrivalTime;

//dequeue each customer and calculate his wait-time.
 while(...determine if queue is not empty...)
{
        //Get customer data
        ...dequeue next item in q and use a Scanner object to produce the
           following two variables... custArrivalTime and custHelpTime...

         //Get time this customer's help begins (the time he is dequeued)
         int dequeueTime = 0;
        if(nextAvailTimeA <= nextAvailTimeB) //decide which rep to use
        {
                ...calculate dequeueTime for this customer...
                (Note: This is not necessarily nextAvailTimeA because the queue may
                be empty and the next customer hasn't arrived yet.)

                ...calculate nextAvailTimeA based on dequeueTime and
                   custHelpTime...
        }
        else
        {
                ...calculate dequeueTime for this customer...
                (Note: This is not necessarily nextAvailTimeB because the queue may
                be empty and the next customer hasn't arrived yet.)

                ...calculate nextAvailTimeB based on dequeueTime and
                   custHelpTime...
        }

        ...calculate thisWaitTime based on dequeueTime and
           custArrivalTime...

        TotalWaitTime = TotalWaitTime + thisWaitTime;
}
...print TotalWaitTime...
```

Project …Shifting Marquee

Create a marquee that is a circular left-shifting text message that consists of stock market prices. Use the following file (Marquee.dat) as the input data:

```
7
DELL 29.85  VIGN 14.82  MOT 26.27  JDSU 1.95  PAGE .94  MCLL .32
22
VSSL 22.80  CCC 18.22  IBM 12.66  COK 11.86  AL 22.00
12
UUJ 11.01  HP 23.27  CSCO 19.86  ZW 12.75  BTDF 22.96
```

There are three sets of data above consisting of two lines each. The first line of each set contains an integer that indicates how many times our test program is to shift the display to the left. The second line is the data to be shifted. Notice that the data consists of one space between the company and the price. That is followed by **two** spaces and then the next company and price are given. (These spacing rules are also followed during shifting.)

The display will only show the 40 leftmost characters (all shift lines are at least 40 characters in length). After the indicated amount of shifting for each line, the output will appear as follows:

```
.85  VIGN 14.82  MOT 26.27  JDSU 1.95  P
 IBM 12.66  COK 11.86  AL 22.00  VSSL 22
P 23.27  CSCO 19.86  ZW 12.75  BTDF 22.9
```

To accomplish this use a *LinkedList* object as the basic structure for a queue. **Do not use the *LinkedLinkQueue* class** from page 53-1. Rather, use the *LinkedList* object directly to simulate a queue and when you need to *enqueue*, use the *addLast* method. For *dequeue* operations use *removeFirst*, etc. This simulation is a "quick and dirty" way to produce a queue and has the virtue of being faster to write than taking the time to create the *LinkListQueue* class.

The basic premise of this program is to create a queue with **each individual character** of a shift line as a *String* object in the queue. Shift left by *dequeue*ing a *String* (actually, a single character) from the front of the queue and then immediately *enqueue*ing it to the end of the queue. This is what creates "circular" queueing.

One possible way to produce the final output is to use the *toString* method of the queue (actually, a *LinkedList* object). That result will be enclosed in a set of square brackets and will have ", " between each element, all of which will need to be eliminated from the final printout.

Queues… Contest Type Problems

1. What code should replace **<#1>** in the code to the right in order that the *dequeue* method be properly implemented?

```
A. for(int j=0; j<size-1; j++)
        intValues[j] = intValues[j+1];
B. for(int j=0;j<size-1;j++)
        intValues[j+1] = intValues[j];
C. for(int j=0; j<size/2;j++)
        intValues[j] = intValues[j+1];
D. for(int j=0; j<size/2;j++)
        intValues[j] = intValues[j-1];
E. None of these
```

2. What code should replace **<#2>** in the code to the right in order that the *peekFront* method be properly implemented?

    A. return intValues[1];
    B. return intValues[0];
    C. return intValues[size];
    D. return intValues[size-1];
    E. None of these

3. Assuming that **<#1>** and **<#2>** have been properly filled in, what is output by the code below?

```
IntQueue q = new IntQueue(100);
q.enqueue(36);
q.enqueue(21);
q.enqueue(7);
System.out.println(q.peekFront( ) +
                        q.dequeue( ));
```

    A. 72
    B. 3621
    C. 2136
    D. 28
    E. None of these

4. Assuming that **<#1>** and **<#2>** have been properly filled in, what is the running time for a *dequeue* method call if a total of *n* objects have previously been enqueued and nothing has yet been dequeued?

    A. O(1)   B. $O(n^2)$ C. O(log n)
    D. O(n)   E. None of these

5. Assuming that **<#1>** and **<#2>** have been properly filled in, what is output by the following code?

```
IntQueue q = new IntQueue(20);
q.enqueue(3);
q.enqueue(q.dequeue( ));
Sysetm.out.println(q.size);
```

    A. 0   B. 1   C. 2
    D. throws exception   E. None of these

```
//int array based queue. Index 0 is front of queue
public class IntQueue
{
    public IntQueue(int max)
    {
        intValues = new int[max];
    }

    public void enqueue(int val)
    {
        intValues[size] = val;
        size++;
    }

    public int dequeue( )
    {
        int retVal = intValues[0];
        <#1>
        size--;
        return retVal;
    }

    public int peekFront( )
    {
        <#2>
    }

    public int size = 0;
    private int[] intValues;
}
```

6. In the class to the right, which default constructor could be added to the class that would automatically enqueue the *String* "Santa Claus" when an object is created with this constructor?

A. public default StringQueue( );
   { enqueue("Santa Claus"); }
B. Illegal, can't have two constructors
C. public StringQueue( )
   { enqueue("Santa Claus"); }
D. public StringQueue("Santa Claus")
   { enqueue(this); }
E. None of these

```
public class StringQueue
{
    public StringQueue(String str)
    {
        enqueue(str);
    }

    public void enqueue(String s) { ... }
    public String dequeue( ) { ... }
    public String peekFront( ) { ... }
    public Boolean isEmpty( ) { ... }

    ... state variables and not shown ...
}
```

7. Assuming the correct default constructor from problem 6 is properly added to the class to the right, which of the following would be an appropriate way to create a *StringQueue* object?

A. StringQueue q = new StringQueue("gesundheit");
B. StringQueue q = new StringQueue( );
C. StringQueue q = new StringQueue;
D. More than one of these
E. None of these

8. Assume the *DblQ* class queues *double* precision numbers via the *enqueue* method and returns *doubles* via the *dequeue* method. What is output by the code to the right?

A. 5.015.025.03
B. throws exception
C. 5.035.025.01
D. 15.06
E. None of these

```
DblQ dq = new DblQ( );

dq.enqueue(5.01);
dq.enqueue(5.02);
dq.enqueue(5.03);

System.out.print( dq.dequeue( )
                       + dq.dequeue( ) );
System.out.println( dq.dequeue( ) );
```

9. Which of the following is true of both stacks and queues?

A. The items are stored in a definite sequence.
B. Items in the middle of the sequence of items are directly and immediately accessible.
C. Items can be removed from only one end of the sequence of items stored.
D. More than one of these
E. None of these

10. *Qclass* is a class implementing an *ArrayList* based queue. What will be the output of the code to the right?

A. throws exception
B. null
C. foggy nights
D. Nothing
E. None of these

```
Qclass qq = new Qclass( );

System.out.println( qq.dequeue( ) );
qq.enqueue("foggy nights");
System.out.println( qq.dequeue( ) );
```

Lesson 54… Inner Classes

Inner classes are classes inside other classes. The class in which an inner class resides is known as the **outer class**. Inner classes are typically only used when the class is very specialized and not likely to be of any use other than in the outer class in which it resides.

Inside a method:

There are two distinct ways to apply an inner class. The first is when the inner class is **inside a method**. This case is illustrated below:

```
public class OuterClass
{
   public static void main(String args[])
   {
            class InnerClass
            {
                     InnerClass(int val)  //constructor
                     {
                           icDataMember = val;
                     }

                     int icMethod( )
                     {
                           return (icDataMember + ocMethod( ) + ocDataMember);
                     }

                     int icDataMember;
            }
            int a = 2;
            InnerClass obj = new InnerClass(100);
            System.out.println(obj.icMethod( ));

   }

   private static int ocMethod( )
   {      return 10;    }

   public static int ocDataMember = 3;
}
```

Five important rules:

- The class signature *class InnerClass* cannot be prefaced by *private* or *public*.
- The code of the method in which the inner class resides must come **after** the inner class.
- All code in the inner class has access to all methods and state variables of the outer class.
- Local variables in the method in which this class is placed are not accessible to the inner class.
- The inner class is only accessible from **inside** the method in which it resides.

Project… Inner Class Inside a Method

Create a new project called *InnerClassInMethod*. Create a class inside that project as shown on the previous page. Pay special attention to the test code in bold print. Its output should be 113.

The return statement of *icMethod* sums three values.

- Which demonstrates accessibility to outer class state variables?
- Which demonstrates accessibility to outer class methods?
- Which demonstrates accessibility to the inner class state variables?

Modify the return statement of the icMethod method to read:

```
return (icDataMember + ocMethod( ) + ocDataMember + a);
```

What is the result when you try to compile? Why?

Create a new method within the outer class as follows:

```
public static void ocMethod1( )
{
   InnerClass obj = new InnerClass(50);
}
```

Compile and state any conclusions to which it brings you.

****

Inside an outer class:

Another way to create an inner class is to place it directly **inside an outer class** (but not inside a method) as follows:

```
public class OuterClass
{
        public void test( )
        {
            int a = 2;
            InnerClass obj = new InnerClass(100);
            System.out.println(obj.icMethod( ));
        }

        private static int ocMethod( )
        {
            return 10;
        }

        public static int ocDataMember = 3;
```

```
//************************************************
class InnerClass
{
        InnerClass(int val)  //constructor
        {
                icDataMember = val;
        }

        int icMethod( )
        {
                return (icDataMember + ocMethod( ) + ocDataMember);
        }

        int icDataMember;
}
//************************************************
}
```

Several important rules:

- The class signature, *class InnerClass*, can be prefaced by *public* or *private*; however they have no effect.
- The inner class may be placed at any position (relative to the remaining code) within the outer class.
- The methods and state variables of the inner class are accessible from any of the methods of the outer class via objects instantiated from the inner class.
- All methods and state variables of the outer class are accessible to methods of the inner class.

These rules are demonstrated with the following project.

Project… Inner Class Inside an Outer Class

Create a new project called *InnerClassInOuter*. Create a class inside that project as shown on the previous page. Pay special attention to the test code in bold print. It will also be necessary to create a *Tester* class as follows:

```
public class Tester
{
        public static void main(String args[])
        {
                OuterClass oc = new OuterClass( );
                oc.test( );
        }
}
```

Execute this *main* method and the output should be 113 as before.

Add the following line of code to the *main* method above, compile, and execute.

```
InnerClass ic1 = new InnerClass(14);
```

To what conclusions does this lead you?

Exercise for Lesson 54

1. What's wrong, if anything, with the following code?

```
public class Apple
{
        public void hal( )
        {
                System.out.println("Hello");
                x ++;

                class Orange
                {
                        …
                }
        }

        public int x = 2;
}
```

2. In the code for problem 1, which class is the outer class?

3. In the code for problem 1, which class is the inner class?

Use the following code for questions 4-7.

```
public class RayVac
{
   public static void main(String args[])
   {
            class Calcs
            {
                    Calcs(int val)
                    {       data = val;     }

                    int inMethod( )
                    {
                            return (data + methodOc( ) + dataOc);
                    }

                    int data;
            }
            int b = 2;
            Calcs obj = new Calcs(50);
            System.out.println(obj.inMethod( ));

   }
```

```
    private static int methodOc( )
    {
        return 1;
    }

    public static int dataOc = 3;
}
```

4. What is output when the *main* method runs?

5. Comment on the legality of replacing the single line of code in *methodOc* with the following.

```
Calcs ob = new Calcs(44);
int j = ob.inMethod( );
```

6. What is the signature of the constructor of the inner class?

7. If the keyword *public* in *public static int dataOc = 3;* was changed to *private*, would the data member *dataOc* still be accessible from within the inner class?

8. Is it legal to place an inner class inside an outer class without it being inside a method of the outer class? If so, does it matter at what position it is placed (as long as it's not inside a method)?

9. Is an inner class ever accessible from outside the outer class?

Lesson 55… Heaps

Special binary tree:

A special type of binary tree, a heap, has two types, a min heap and a max heap. Fig 55-1 below illustrates a min heap, the type primarily discussed in this lesson. From this point on, if mention is made of a heap in general, it may be assumed that it is a **min heap**.

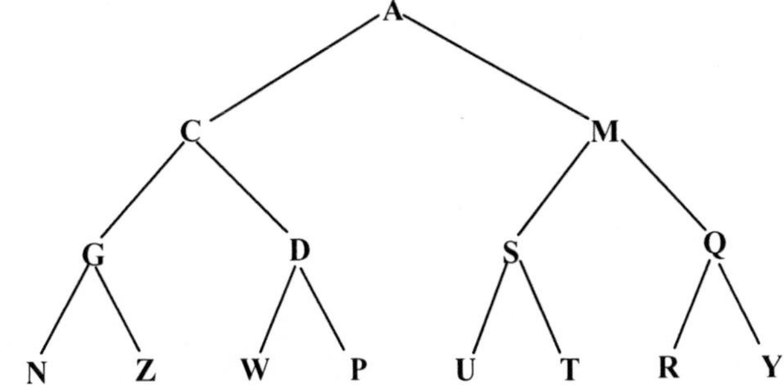

Fig. 55-1 Min type heap characterized by each parent node being smaller than its children.

Parent node always smallest:

Notice that each parent node in the above min heap is less than either of its child nodes. In a max heap, just the opposite is true. Do not look for any relationship between the two child nodes. There is none. Looking at the example above, we observe that the node containing ***G*** has ***N*** as its left child node and ***Z*** as its right child node. There would be no problem at all with interchanging ***N*** and ***Z***. Notice that they would still meet the requirement of being larger than their parent node.

Complete tree:

In addition to the requirement that every node be smaller than any node in its subtree, it is also required that the tree be **complete**. A complete binary tree is one in which any missing leaf nodes are confined to the bottom level and on the far right.

Fig. 55-2 A complete binary tree. Missing nodes must be leaf nodes on the bottom level, far right.

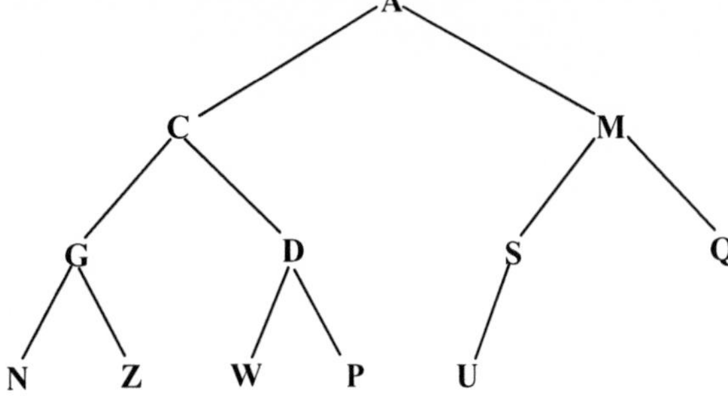

Full tree:

Leaves need not be missing from a complete tree, and in that event, it is also called a **full tree** (all leaves present on the bottom level). The binary tree in Fig. 55-1 is an example of a full tree.

Two rules for a heap:

In summary, the two requirements that a binary tree qualify as a heap are:

1. The tree must be complete.

2. Each node is smaller than any value in its subtree. Of course, this means each subtree is also a heap.

(Unlike a binary search tree, heaps are permitted to have two nodes of the same value.)

Indices of a heap:

For convenience the nodes in a binary tree are indexed starting with 1 on the root node. Proceed down one layer, and then number from left to right. This is illustrated in Fig. 55-3.

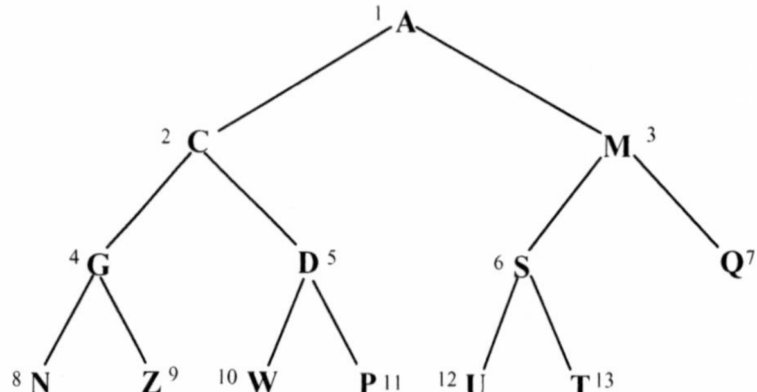

Fig. 55-3 A heap with properly indexed nodes. Note that indexing does **not** start with 0 as is usually the case in Java.

Adding a node:

Suppose we wanted to add a node with value ***J*** to the heap above (Fig. 55-3). Clearly, we cannot permanently attach it as a child node to ***Q*** since that would violate the rule of the parent being of a smaller value than the child. Somehow we must add the new node in a way that the tree remains complete and the new node finds a position so that it is less than all values in its subtree. Here is the way to accomplish this. First, add ***J*** as a new leaf for ***Q*** so that the tree remains complete. This is shown in Fig. 55-4 below.

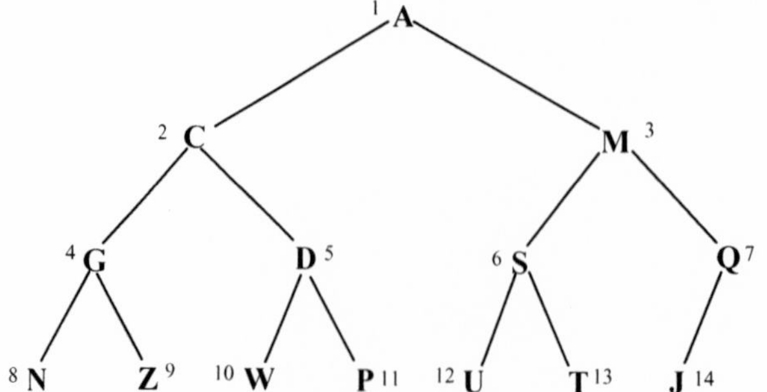

Fig. 55-4 ***J*** has been added as a new node.

We note that ***Q*** is larger than ***J*** so they need to be swapped. This is shown in Fig 55-5 below.

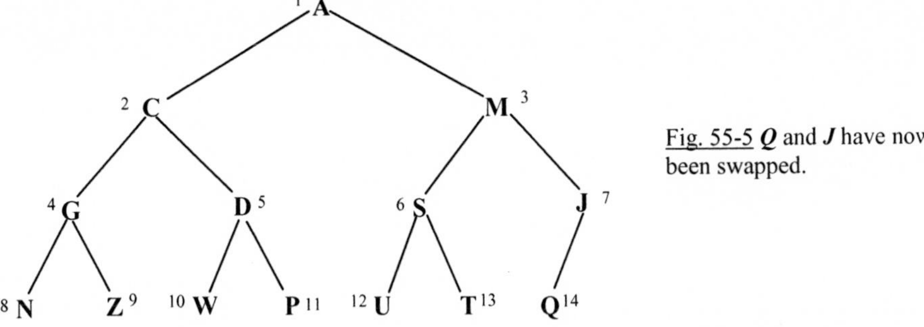

Fig. 55-5 ***Q*** and ***J*** have now been swapped.

Next, we notice that ***M*** and ***J*** are out of order, so swap them as shown in Fig.55-6 below.

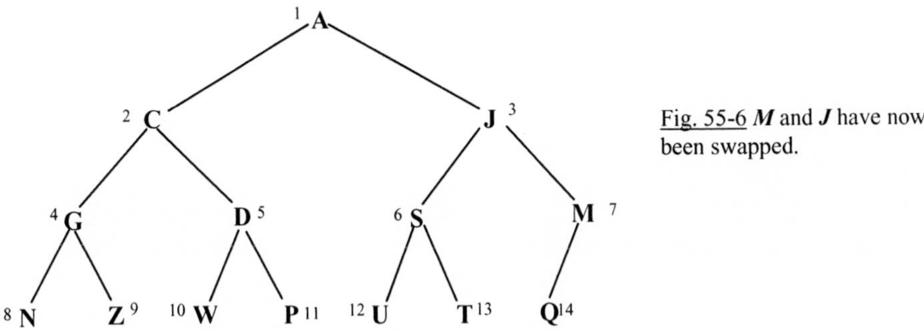

Fig. 55-6 ***M*** and ***J*** have now been swapped.

J has now fallen into its correct position, so this **reheap-up** process is finished. In a heap with *n* items the maximum number of reheap comparisons would be $\log_2(n)$ (Big O(log n)).

Removal of a node from a heap:

We will only demonstrate how to remove the root node since that is by far the most common node to remove. This will be an important operation in the next lesson on priority queues. Consider the following tree in which the root node has been removed.

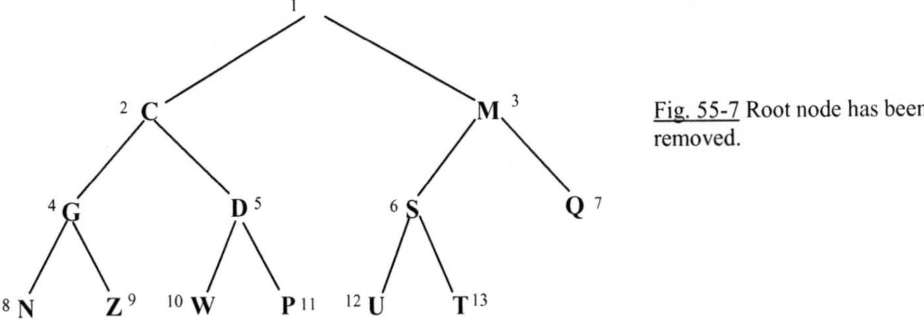

Fig. 55-7 Root node has been removed.

The next step is to cut off the last leaf, ***T***, and place it in the root node position. This is shown in Fig. 55-8 below.

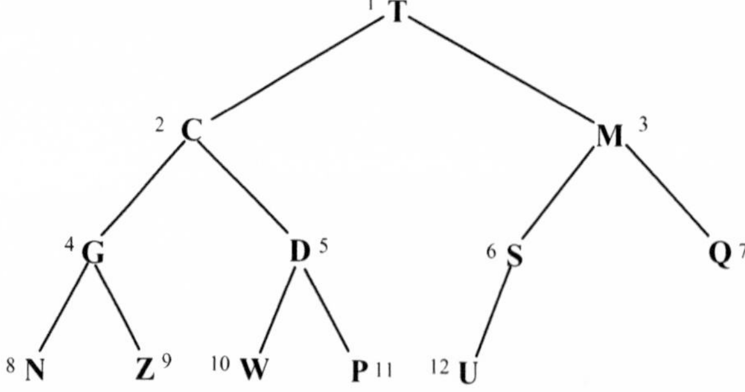

Fig. 55-8 The *T* leaf has been cut off and placed in the root.

T is now illegally larger than both of its children, *C* and *M*. The procedure now is to **reheap-down** by swapping *T* with its smaller child. Therefore, we will swap *T* and *C* as follows.

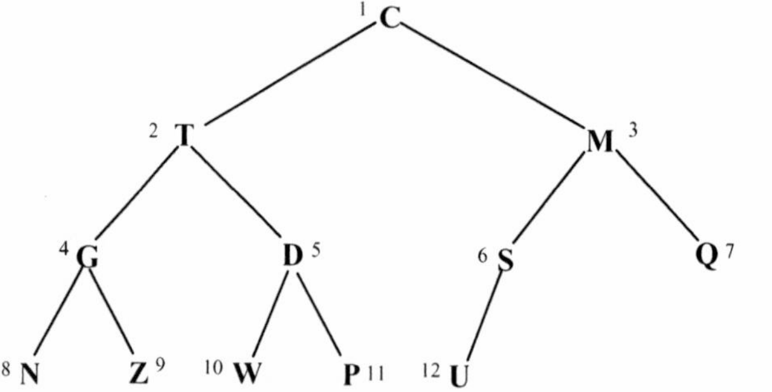

Fig. 55-9 *T* and *C* have been swapped.

T is still not in its correct position since it is larger than its two children, *G* and *D*. Swap *T* with its smaller child, *D*.

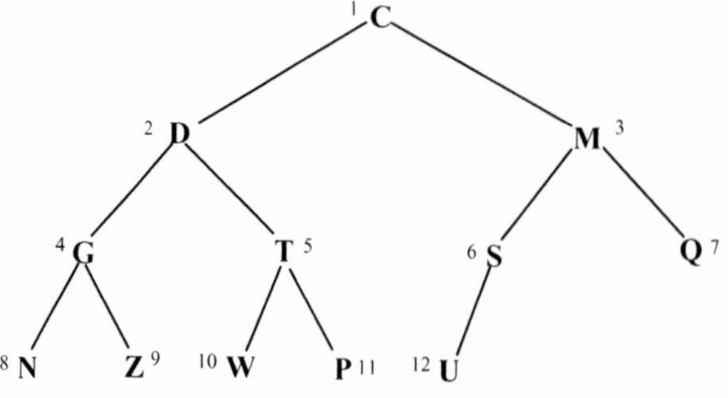

Fig. 55-10 *D* and *T* have been swapped.

Still, no cigar! *T* and *P* must now be swapped to complete the **reheap-down** process. In a heap with *n* items, the maximum number of reheap comparisons would be $\log_2(n)$ (Big O(log n)).

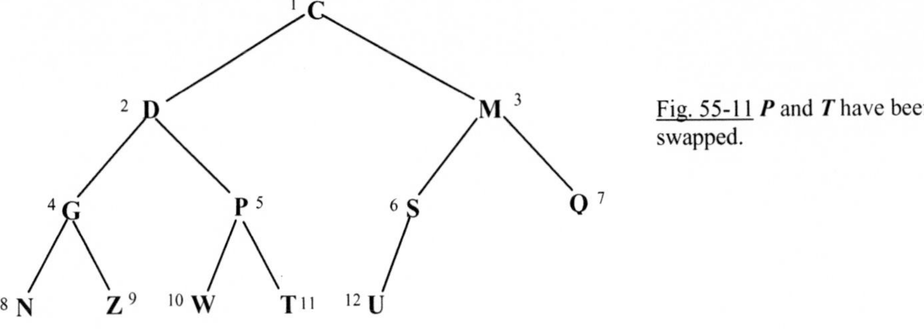

Fig. 55-11 ***P*** and ***T*** have been swapped.

The heap is now correct with ***T*** in its correct position.

Exercise on Lesson 55

Unless stated otherwise, all references to heaps in these questions are assumed to be min heaps.

1. What are the two requirements of a binary tree in order that it qualifies as a heap?

2. What is a full tree?

3. What is a complete tree?

4. What is the difference in a min heap and a max heap?

5. Suppose some heap node values and their corresponding indices are as follows:

   B,1 D,2 N,3 H,4 E,5 T,6 R,7 O,8 Y,9

   Draw the heap that corresponds to this data.

6. Does the root of a heap always contain the smallest value?

7. Describe the process for removing the root node.

8. Can we always depend on the largest value of a heap to be one of the leaves?

9. Does every node in a heap have to have a child?

10. Describe the process of adding a node to a heap.

11. Remove the root node from the following tree and draw the resulting new tree after the reheap-down procedure has finished.

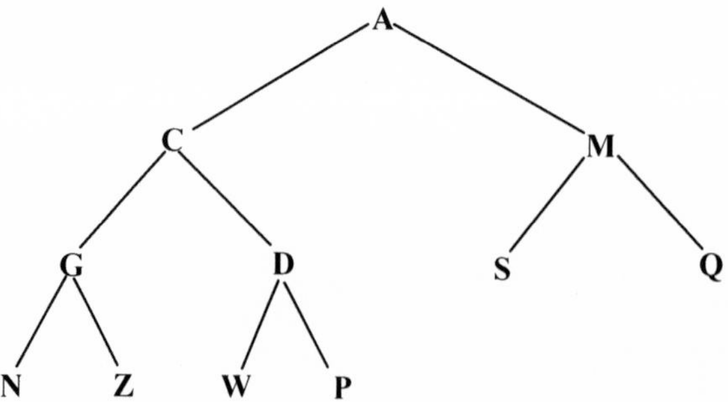

12. Are two nodes permitted to have the same value in a heap?

13. Are all heaps binary trees?

14. Are all binary trees heaps?

15. What is the most common node to remove in a heap?

16. What type of heap requires the value of each node to be greater than any value in its subtree?

17. Add a node with value ***H*** to the tree below. Draw the resulting new heap after the reheap-up process.

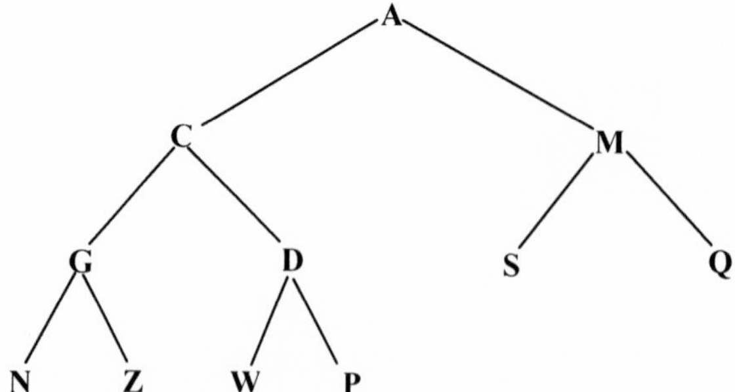

18. What is the maximum Big O value for the insertion of a new node into a heap?

19. What is the maximum Big O value for the removal of the root node from a heap?

Project… Printing a Heap

The purpose of this project will be to print a heap. The reason this is important is that in the next lesson we will implement a priority queue based on an array heap. During development and debugging it is important to be able to test the heap at intermediate points by viewing a printout of the heap.

Create a text file called *HeapData.in* with the following content.

```
A
C
M
G
D
S
Q
N
Z
W
P
U
T
```

Notice that the sequence of these items is in the index sequence of nodes in the heap in Fig. 55-3. Create a project called *PrintTree* with class *Tester* that will input the letters from the *HeapData.in* text file and print the heap in the following fashion.

```
A
C M
G D S Q
N Z W P U T
```

It is suggested that each letter be put into an array starting with index 1 as is conventional with heaps (index 0 in the array will be unused). The only real challenge here is in determining when to start a new line. Notice a new line is started after the character with index **1** is printed, after the character with index **3** is printed, after the character with index **7** is printed, after the character with index **15** is printed…. These indices form the following pattern:

$$2^1\text{-}1,\ 2^2\text{-}1,\ 2^3\text{-}1,\ 2^4\text{-}1, \ldots$$

Use an *if* statement to detect when these character are printed and then start a new line.

Project… A Heap of Trouble (advanced)

The printout produced by the previous project is just barely better than no printout at all. What we need is a printout that looks closer to the real thing,…like the following:

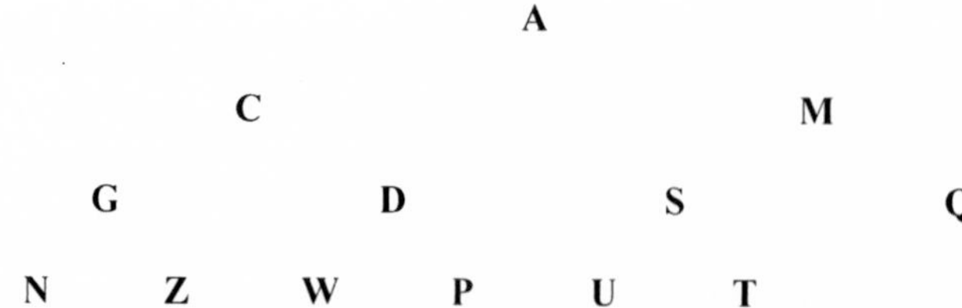

Fig. 55-12 A more desirable printout. Even though there are no connecting lines we can still tell what a parent node's children are.

To produce this printout we need to notice several things about the horizontal spacing. In order to see some patterns our first step will be to place the printed characters in a grid as in Fig. 55-13.

← 7 spaces→							A						
← 3 sp→			C	← 7 spaces→							M		
1sp	G	← 3 sp→			D	← 3 sp→			S	← 3 sp→			Q
N	1sp	Z	1sp	W	1sp	P	1sp	U	1sp	T			

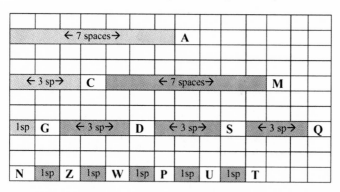

Fig. 55-13 Detail of desired horizontal spacing. As we move from row to row the number of spaces form a predictable pattern.

The spacing in the grid above falls into two different distinct patterns.

1. As we proceed down the rows the **leading spaces** (lighter shading above) form the following pattern where *n* (4 for this example) is the number of levels of the tree.

   $7 = 2^{n-1}-1$ level 1
   $3 = 2^{n-2}-1$ level 2
   $1 = 2^{n-3}-1$ level 3
   $0 = 2^{n-4}-1$ level 4

2. As we proceed down the rows the **inner spaces** (darker shading above) form the following pattern where *n* (4 for this example) is the number of levels of the tree.

   inner spaces do not apply to the first level
   $7 = 2^{n-1}-1$ level 2
   $3 = 2^{n-2}-1$ level 3
   $1 = 2^{n-3}-1$ level 4

The code you write for the *Tester* class in this project, *HeapOfTrouble*, should detect which row we are on as was suggested in the previous project and apply the appropriate formulas to generate the desired number of spaces. We should mention at this point that we are assuming that the console output of your IDE uses monospaced fonts. Most do. If your IDE lets you select fonts, choose one of the Courier fonts. They are monospaced which means each character takes up the same amount of horizontal space when printed. See Appendix AB for more on monospaced fonts.

Another critical aspect of this project is the ability to determine from the number of items to be printed just how many levels (*n*) there will be for the tree. We will use a logarithm base 2 to accomplish this. The following chart shows the relationships involved.

Index (i)	$Log_2(i)$	Value	(int) $Log_2(i)$	Tree Level (n)
1	$Log_2 1$	0.0	0	1
2	$Log_2 2$	1.0	1	2
3	$Log_2 3$	1.5849624872207642	1	2
4	$Log_2 4$	2.0	2	3
5	$Log_2 5$	2.321928024291992	2	3
6	$Log_2 6$	2.5849626064300537	2	3
7	$Log_2 7$	2.8073549270629883	2	3
8	$Log_2 8$	3.0	3	4
9	$Log_2 9$	3.1699249744415283	3	4
10	$Log_2 10$	3.321928024291992	3	4
11	$Log_2 11$	3.4594316482543945	3	4
12	$Log_2 12$	3.5849626064300537	3	4
13	$Log_2 13$	3.700439691543579	3	4
14	$Log_2 14$	3.8073549270629883	3	4
15	$Log_2 15$	3.906890630722046	3	4
16	$Log_2 16$	4.0	4	5
…	…	…	…	…

Table 55-1

Math.log(x) is given for base *e*, so to calculate log base *2* of *x* we must use the following standard formula for converting log bases:

```
Math.log(x) / Math.log(2)
```

Finally, the number of tree levels (*n*) required for *x* items is given by:

```
int n = (int)( Math.log(x) / Math.log(2) ) + 1;
```

Use portions of the last project to produce a new project, *HeapOfTrouble*, in which we have two classes, *Tester* and *HeapPrinter*. The *HeapPrinter* class will have a *static* method called *printHeap*. By putting this *static* method in a class by itself we will easily be able to use this class for testing our implementation of an array heap in the next lesson.

Use the *Tester* class to input the *HeapData.in* file from the last project. In *main* of *Tester* be sure to pack the incoming data into an array in which the first element of the file has index *1*. In the *printHeap* method determine the number of levels and the number of spaces needed as discussed above. Use these ideas to print the heap so as to look like Fig. 55-12.

Admittedly, the heap printer from this project is very simplistic in that it assumes that each node of the heap prints as just a single character. What if the nodes to be printed consist of differing numbers of characters? At first this might seem like a difficult task to tackle; however, all we need to do is determine the maximum number of digits to be printed and then set up print "fields" that always print this same width. When printing any *String* representing a node having a smaller number of characters than this maximum field width, we simply "pack" both sides of the *String* with the appropriate number of characters so as center the characters in the field.

Lesson 56… Priority Queues

Not like an "ordinary" queue:

In Lesson 53 we learned about queues behaving in a FIFO fashion. However, in this lesson we learn that if our queue is a priority queue, it will behave in an entirely different way. The first item inserted will not necessarily be the first item out. Rather, we assign a priority to the items and they are removed from the queue (dequeued) with the **highest priority item removed first**.

Examples of priority queues:

We will offer three examples of real life situations that use priority queues. In these example you will find items waiting in a queue to be processed in an order corresponding to their priority:

1. An AWACS Air Force plane is flying in the vicinity of a theater of war operations. It collects information electronically from hundreds or even thousands of sources from the various battlefields and places them in a priority queue while awaiting processing. Suppose one item in the queue is information about a flight of enemy aircraft approaching one of our aircraft carriers. Another piece of information waiting in the queue might be an intelligence report about movement of a small enemy truck convoy many miles from the main battle. Clearly, the enemy aircraft approaching our carrier will have the highest priority in the queue and should be processed immediately in order to protect the carrier.

2. A print server is a computer to which a printer is attached. Other "client" computers on the network send print jobs to the server where they are cached (temporarily stored) while waiting their turn to print. The printer attached to the print server can only print one job at a time. It is the job of the print server to put the waiting jobs in a queue (a priority queue) and assign a priority to each job. Suppose there are ten small jobs waiting to print where each is only a page or so. Also, suppose there is one very large job (a 500 page pdf file) waiting to print. A reasonable way to setup the print server would be to give the lowest priority to the large job. Thus, the small jobs would print first and the ten people sending those jobs would be kept happy. Likely, the person sending the large job would not expect to get his printout very quickly anyway.

3. Microprocessors have provisions for "interrupts" of both the hardware and software type. An interrupt does just what it sounds like it might do. The processor suspends what it is doing, takes on another task, and when finished, returns to the first task. It is even possible for one interrupt to interrupt the task of a previous interrupt.

   To understand interrupts, think of an executive sitting at a desk writing a report when the phone rings. Work is suspended on the report while the phone is answered. During the phone conversation a secretary slips a piece of paper in front of the executive for a signature. Signing the paper is only a momentary distraction after which the phone conversation is continued. After hanging up the phone, work is resumed on the report, and so it is with interrupts. One task interrupts another, and when completed, the original task continues.

Now think of a computer system monitoring several processes in a chemical plant. Suppose one possible interrupt from the monitoring would involve the processing of an impending overflow of an acid tank. Another might be an interrupt resulting from the temperature rising a little too high in a storage room. Clearly, the overflow of the acid tank must be handled immediately and would be elevated to the highest priority in the priority queue thus enabling it to be handled first.

Selecting a data structure:

Now we turn our attention to actually creating a priority queue in software. First, we must select a data structure with which to implement our priority queue. The simplest would be an array; however, in order to enqueue a new object we would need to scan the array for proper positioning in the array. An alternative would be to order the array, and then adjust the order as new objects are enqueued. If the number of items in the array is very large, these operations can be quite time consuming. *ArrayList*s and *LinkedList*s would suffer the same performance penalties.

Finally, we settle on a heap as ideal data structure for our priority queue. The heap we studied in the previous chapter is tailor-made for service as a priority queue since "dequeuing" would simply be done by removing the root node. This is because the value of the root node is always guaranteed to be smaller than the value of any other node in the min heap. Since small node values are at the top of the heap, we must require **higher priority items in our priority queue to have the lowest node values**. This is easily handled mathematically by devising a scheme in which we would consider "high" priority to yield a low "score" that would be assigned as a node value.

The *PriorityQueue interface*:

What we need first is a priority queue *interface*. We will devise our own since one is not provided as a standard part of Java. The interface presented below is "standard" in that it is the one used by most programmers implementing a heap based priority queue.

```
public interface PriorityQueue
{
        void enqueue(Object obj);  // sometimes called add
        Object dequeue( );   // sometimes called removeRoot o removeMin
        Object peek( );
        boolean isEmpty( );
}
```

Array is the winner after all:

When selecting an underlying data structure for the heap, strangely enough, the simple array rejected earlier resurfaces as the most efficient candidate. This is especially true if we number the nodes (the indices of the array) as shown in Fig.55-3 of the last lesson.

Project… Who Has Highest Priority?

Notice in the implementation of the *PriorityQueue interface* on the following page (put it all in a new project called *HighestPriority*), there is missing code that must be supplied in the implementing class. Supply the necessary code for both the *peek*, *isEmpty*, *enqueue* and *dequeue* methods: the code is quite simple. The most complex methods of the class, *reheap_up* and *reheap_down* have already been presented in Lesson 55. Don't forget to create the *interface* first, or the class won't compile. For your convenience in testing your new *HeapPriorityQueue* class, a *Tester* class is supplied as follows.

```
public class Tester
{
   public static void main(String args[])
   {
            HeapPriorityQueue hpq = new HeapPriorityQueue( );
            Integer iw;

            iw = new Integer(8);  //Java 5.0, iw = 8;
               hpq.enqueue(iw);

            iw = new Integer(2);  //Java 5.0, iw = 2;
               hpq.enqueue(iw);

            iw = new Integer(1);  //Java 5.0, iw = 1;
               hpq.enqueue(iw);

            iw = new Integer(9);  //Java 5.0, iw = 9;
               hpq.enqueue(iw);

            iw = new Integer(5);  //Java 5.0, iw = 5;
               hpq.enqueue(iw);

            iw = new Integer(4);  //Java 5.0, iw = 4;
               hpq.enqueue(iw);

            while(!hpq.isEmpty( ))
            {
                 System.out.println(hpq.dequeue( ));  //Prints in sequence 1, 2, 4, 5, 8, 9
            }
   }
}
```

Notice from the *PriorityQueue interface* that our priority queue (heap) contains objects. In the following implementation it is assumed that those objects implement the *Comparable interface*. Supply the missing code as described in the project above.

```
public class HeapPriorityQueue implements PriorityQueue
{
        public HeapPriorityQueue( ) //constructor
        {
            obj = new Object[100];
        }

        public boolean isEmpty( )
        {
            …
        }

        public Object peek( )
        {
            …
        }

        public void enqueue(Object ob)
        {
                //Add the new node as the last leaf and then reheap up
                …
        }

        public Object dequeue( )
        {
                //Cut off last leaf and place in root, decrement numObjects, and then
                //reheap down. Then return the original root.
                …
        }

        private void reheap_down( )
        {
                //The value in the root moves down the heap until it falls into its
            proper place
                //At each step as it moves down, it is swapped with its smaller child.
                Object root = obj[1];
                int parentIndx = 1;
                int childIndx = 2;
                while(childIndx <= numObjects)
                {
                        if( (childIndx < numObjects) &&

                          (((Comparable)obj[childIndx+1]).compareTo(obj[childIndx])<0) )
                        {
                                childIndx++;
                        }

                        if( !(((Comparable)obj[childIndx]).compareTo(root)<0) )
                        {       break;    }
```

```
                  obj[parentIndx] = obj[childIndx];
                  parentIndx = childIndx;
                  childIndx = parentIndx * 2;
            }
            obj[parentIndx] = root;
      }

      private void reheap_up( )
      {
            //The new node moves up the tree swapping places with its parent
            //until it falls into place.
            Object lastLeaf = obj[numObjects];
            int childIndx = numObjects, parentIndx = childIndx / 2;
            while( (parentIndx >= 1) &&
                 (((Comparable)lastLeaf).compareTo(obj[parentIndx])< 0) )
            {
                  obj[childIndx] = obj[parentIndx];
                  childIndx = parentIndx;
                  parentIndx = childIndx / 2;
            }
            obj[childIndx] = lastLeaf;
      }

      private Object obj[];
      private int numObjects = 0;
}
```

Project… Smile for the Camera

In a new project called *SnapShot* (a modification of the *HighestPriority* project) we will further refine the use of the *HeapPrinter* class from Lesson 55 so as to print a "snapshot" of a priority heap. First, copy everything from *HighestPriority* into the new *SnapShot* project. Then paste in a copy of the *HeapPrinter* class from Lesson 55. In it the *printHeap* method is expecting an array of characters. The *HeapPriorityQueue* class maintains an array of *Object* type objects that comprise the data for the heap; that will be our starting point.

Modify the *HeapPriorityQueue* in the following ways:

- Make the data member *obj[ ]* public.
- Provide a public method *getArray* that will return this array.
- Make the data member *numObjects* public.

Now modify the *Tester* class in the following ways:

- Eliminate the loop that dequeues.
- Retrieve the *Object* array from the *HeapPriorityQueue* object.
- Retrieve the *numObjects* data member.
- Create a character array *ch[ ]* that contains the equivalent of the numbers in the *Object* array just retrieved.
- Call the *printHeap* method and pass both the *Object* array and the *numObjects* variable.

The resulting printout should look like this:

```
        1

     5     2

   9  8  4
```

****

Heapsort:

A heap based priority queue can be used for sorting an array if we do the following:

- *Enqueue* array items in any order into a heap.
- *Dequeue* all the items. The order in which they are dequeued will automatically be in ascending order. As each item is dequeued, store it back in the original array starting at index 0.

The following is a code fragment illustrating a heapsort. It is assumed that an array of objects, *SomeClass obj[]*, already exists and that the class from which they were instantiated implements the *Comparable* interface. It is also assumed that object *HeapPriorityQueue hpq* already exists.

```
...
for(int j = 0; j < obj.length; j++)
{
        hpq.enqueue(obj[j]);
}

int indx = 0;
while( !hpq.isEmpty( ) )
{
        obj[++indx] = (SomeClass)( hpq.dequeue( ) );
}
```

The *obj* array has now been sorted in ascending order. Since we used *enqueue* and *dequeue* operations (both of which are O(log n)), the heapsort algorithm also yields a time complexity analysis of O(log n).

Exercise on Lesson 56

Assume all heaps in this exercise are min type heaps.

1. How does removal of objects (dequeuing) from a priority queue differ from a regular queue?

2. Object *A* has higher priority in a heap based priority queue than object *B*. Futhermore, suppose that *val* is the variable associated with objects that is ultimately used when comparing node values. Which of the following would be a valid pair consistent with these facts?
    a. A.val = 37
       B.val = -19
    b. A.val = -5
       B.val = 0
    c. A.val = 18
       B.val = 18
    d. None of these

3. Could customers lined up at a hot-dog stand be considered a priority queue?

4. Could patients waiting in an emergency room be considered a priority queue?

5. When performing an *enqueue* operation on a priority queue, which fundamental operation is done?
    a. Remove the root node
    b. Remove last leaf
    c. Add last leaf
    d. None of these

6. When performing a *dequeue* operation on a priority queue, which fundamental operation is done?
    a. Remove the root node
    b. Remove last leaf and place it in root
    c. Add last leaf
    d. More than one of these

7. Which is the most efficient underlying data structure to use when implementing a heap used in a priority queue?
    a. Array
    b. LinkedList
    c. ArrayList
    d. Map
    e. Set

8. What is the maximum Big O value for an *enqueue* operation on a heap based priority queue?

9. What is the maximum Big O value for a *dequeue* operation on a heap based priority queue?

10. Describe the two fundamental operations in executing a heap sort on an array of objects.

Lesson 57… Lookup Tables and Hashing

Is there a faster way?

Suppose we need to lookup something in a data structure. If the structure is an array that has been sorted, we could use a binary search to quickly find the desired item. A binary search tree would also be fast to search. As fast as these techniques are, they **do** take **some** time (O(log n)) to execute, and especially so if we consider the removal of tree nodes and the onerous task of rebalancing a tree. Is there a faster way? Yes, if we use a lookup table or perhaps a hash table.

Lookup tables:

One of the benefits of using a lookup table is that we can completely avoid doing a search. If the table is properly constructed, we just specify an **index** within an array and immediately access the desired element stored there.

In lookup tables the item we wish to find is addressed with a **key**. That key corresponds to a **value** that we retrieve from the table. The key and its corresponding value in a table are very important concepts in both the simple lookup table and its cousin, the hash table.

- The **key** is initially known and is **used to access a slot in the lookup table**.
- The **value** is what we **want to retrieve from the lookup table**. The key sends us to **only one** particular slot in the table.

As an example, think of the zip code 78377 as being a **key** that yields a **value** of "Refugio, Tx" from a lookup table. Similarly, a key of 76869 would yield a value of "Pontotoc, Tx" from the same table.

In simple cases the key **is** the array index itself. In other cases the index is easily computed from the key. Both of these cases are discussed below.

The key is the index itself:

An example of this is a color palette, which is a very efficient use of memory space to store a color image. In this scheme, every pixel in the image is examined and of the billions of possible colors, only 256 colors are decided on that could best be used to represent the entire picture. Then, each pixel in the image is assigned a number between 0 and 255 representing one of these colors. When we receive one of these "palletized" images, all we get is a series of bytes, each holding one of the color numbers ranging from 0 to 255. Each byte represents the color of an individual pixel. This information would be useless unless there was a way to "decode" what these numbers mean. For example, suppose one of these bytes stores the number 187. How is the computer that is to render the picture to know what color to produce for this particular pixel? Fortunately, each palletized image also comes with three "decoding" tables. These tables are the red, green, and blue tables that give the intensity needed for each of the color guns in the display monitor. Thus, for a palletized image, three lookup tables are involved in displaying the correct color for any particular index. The 256 color intensities for these tables are arranged as a simple array addressed with indices ranging from 0 to 255. Each of these indices, of course, corresponds to one of the original 256 colors selected for our image.

Suppose a pixel has a color palette number of 187. To produce this color on the screen, we access index 187 in the following three tables:

Index	red[] array
0	192
1	17
…	
187	**67**
…	
255	201

Table 57-1

Index	green[] array
0	119
1	238
…	
187	**108**
…	
255	249

Table 57-2

Index	blue[] array
0	14
1	4
	…
187	**198**
	…
255	82

Table 57-3

The RGB value of color 187 would be set for display on a monitor with a method similar to *rgb(red[187], green[187], blue[187])* which is equivalent to *rgb(67, 108, 198)*. In this example the **key** (the index itself) is 187 and the three tables yield the **values** of red=67, green=108, and blue=198. It is the combination of these colors that will produce the color desired for palette value 187.

The index is easily computed from the key:

Suppose we have the function $f = sin^2(.001x+3) + ln(x^4+1) + 2x$ that needs to be computed many times in a program where we know that *x* is restricted to 0 and positive multiples of 5 up to a maximum value of 10,000 (0, 5, 10, 15,…9995, 10000). Furthermore, let's assume that the performance of this program is critical and that the code must execute as quickly as possible.

We could pre-compute all values for the *f* formula and store in an array with indices from 0 to 10,000. When a value for *f* is needed for a particular *x*, we would simply access it as *f[x]*. This scheme, however, would be very wasteful of memory space since not all 10,000 indices are used. A more practical approach would be to first divide *x* by five and have the array organized as shown in Table 57-4 below.

Key value (x)	Index (i = x / 5)	f Value using x
0	0	f[0] = 0.019914880394935608
5	1	f[1] = 16.45789337158203
10	2	f[2] = 29.227657318115234
…	…	…
9,995	1999	f[1999] = 20027.01171875
10,000	2000	f[2000] = 20037.017578125

Table 57-4

This scheme would use one fifth the memory and only suffers a small time penalty (the time required to divide by 5).

The two examples above illustrate the following three reasons **why we would want to use a lookup table**:

1. **Disorganized or nonsensical data can be organized into a table** for easy lookup if the key to finding the data can be used as an index or an index can be easily computed from it. The color palette discussed above is an example.

2. Notice that with the color palette scheme, **memory is saved** since the image in the example above only occupies about one third the memory that it would have if we had allocated three bytes to each pixel (one byte for each color).

   The reader should be aware that this palletized scheme for images is seldom used anymore. It original advantage was that it **saved memory**. Today, memory is so abundant and inexpensive that palletized images are rarely used (rather, 3 bytes or more are used per pixel). While the scheme does save memory, the quality of the images suffers since many images require considerably more than just 256 different colors. However, the point is made that the scheme does save memory and could be used in applications other than images.

3. When **performance** is an issue, using a lookup table of precomputed values is often faster than computing the formula in real time each time it is needed.

When lookup tables are <u>not</u> easily implemented:

In summary, lookup tables are only practical if the key is directly the same as the index or, at least is easily converted to an index. Not all organizations of data meet these criteria. There are two distinct cases in which the organization of data into a lookup table is impossible or at least not easily implemented.

The method of converting a key into an index is not immediately obvious:

Consider a registry of guests staying at a hotel. <u>Table 57-5</u> shows a mapping of guest's names to room numbers (other information about the guest could also be part of the value).

<u>Key</u>, Guest Name	Index	<u>Value</u>, Room number
	0	
…	…	…
Clinton, Bill	16	1102
Bush, George	39	204
Washington, George	139	1486
…	…	…
Lincoln, Abraham	147	159
…		
	179	

<u>Table 57-5</u>

It is not at all obvious how the *String* "Clinton, Bill" produces the index 16. The technique that accomplishes this is referred to as *hashing*. Somehow the hashing code must take names and convert them into an even distribution of indices from 0 to 179 (there are 180 hotels rooms, and thus a need for 180 indices). A little later we will look at a specific technique that will hash these names.

Inefficient use of memory space:

Keys can be converted into indices; however, in some cases, keys that would otherwise be easily converted to indices, tend to form clusters or bunches that results in an unacceptable excess of wasted memory. Consider the mapping of keys to values in Table 57-6 below in which dates are paired with battles from American History. The battles are from the Revolutionary War, the War of 1812, and the Civil War, and therefore, form three distinct date clusters. If we use the indices in the column labeled Index 1, the waste is absolutely dreadful. The indices run from 0 to 18,631,023. This is clearly unacceptable. In the column labeled Index 2, things are a little better where we just subtract 17,761,103 from the indices of the Index 1 column. This is an improvement, but still not good enough. In the Index 2 column, the indices go all the way to 869, 920, which is still far too wasteful.

The clustering is also a concern. Even if we could get the indices in a cluster to pack tightly together, we would still have all the wasted indices between clusters. Is there a way to generate the indices so that the indices are evenly distributed over the range, say, 0 to 75? The way to do this is again, of course, hashing.

Key, Date	Index 1	Index 2	Value, Battle
	0		
…			
1776 11 03	17761103	0	Battle A
…			
1776 12 15	17761215	112	Battle B
…			
1777 03 21	17770321	9218	Battle C
…			
…			
…			
1812 05 18	18120518	359415	Battle D
…			
1812 07 25	18120725	359622	Battle E
…			
…			
…			
1861 04 22	18610422	849319	Battle F
…			
1862 01 24	18620124	859021	Battle G
…			
1863 10 23	18631023	869920	Battle H

Table 57-6

Hashing techniques:

Now that we have clearly defined a need for this thing called hashing, how do we do it? Let's begin by recognizing that it is an extension of the lookup table concept. The differences are:

- A **hash function** (method) uses the keys to create the indices.

- There is no longer a one-to-one correspondence between keys and indices. Several keys could map to the same index.
- The table is now called a **hash table**.
- The hash table will now store the keys as well as the associated values.

Basic hash function requirements:

Here are the requirements of a hash function that will determine the indices for the array that is the basic structure for the table:

- The **range of needed indices** should be clearly defined. The hash function will produce indices strictly in this range.
- The hash code needs to create a reasonably **even distribution** of indices within the specified range.
- There must be some **algorithm** that generates indices from the expected keys and yet adheres to the above two requirements.
- The algorithm must execute reasonably fast or we might as well just use an ordered array or a binary search tree as the basic structure for our data.
- The generated indices must minimize "**collisions**". See the following discussion for more on collisions.

Collisions:

The phenomenon of collisions is one of the major differences between lookup and hash tables. In a lookup table, every key **maps to just one** index: in fact, in many cases the key **is** the index. In hash tables it is possible for the hashing function to **map several keys to the same index**. This is known as a collision and is clearly undesirable, but at the same time, unavoidable. There are several ways to handle collisions:

- **Chaining** In this approach every element in the hash table is referred to as a **bucket** and is implemented as a structure that can hold multiple values. This structure could be an array, *ArrayList*, *LinkedList*, or perhaps a binary search tree.
- **Probing** A probing function converts the current index at the point of collision into a new, unused index where the value can be stored. The probing function keeps trying until it finds a vacant slot into which to store the value. There are many different ways to do probing. Two of the simpler ones are linear probing and quadratic probing.
    - **Linear Probing** Continue moving away from the current index a set number of slots (usually one) until a vacant slot is found. This could be implemented by moving in just one direction or in both directions. While simple, this method does suffer from more clustering.
    - **Quadratic probing** For less clustering, instead of moving just one slot at a time, use this sequence of slot-moves: 1, 4, 9, 16, …

A figure of merit:

The **load factor** for a hash table is defined to be the ratio of the items stored in the table to the total number of available buckets. To minimize collisions the ratio should be low. However, a low load factor is wasteful of memory, so like most things, a compromise must be struck.

Implementing a hash function:

Suppose that we have two parallel arrays that will serve as the repository for a hash table. Let's assume that keys are encoded dates from the date-battle example of Table 57-6.

Using an integer representation of those dates, pass them to the following hash function and observe the returned indices. Notice the method assumes there are 75 table slots and uses the modulus operator to calculate the returned index.

```
public static int hashCode(int key)
{
        final int TABLE_SIZE = 75;
        return key % TABLE_SIZE;
}
```

The *hashCode* method makes no attempt to resolve collisions; it just creates a "suggested" index. It is up to the code that receives this index to resolve any collisions that might occur.

Project… A Taste of Hash

Create a project called *HashTest*, and in the *main* method of a *Tester* class printout the indices returned by the *hashCode* method above. For test data, use the values in the Index 1 column of Table 57-6. Notice the distribution of returned indices over the permitted range of 0 to 74.

You printout should appear as follows where the distribution from 0 to 74 looks reasonable:

```
17761103>>>53
17761215>>>15
17770321>>>46
18120518>>>68
18120725>>>50
18610422>>>72
18620124>>>24
18631023>>>48
```

Project… Hashing Abraham Lincoln

Create a project called *HashingAbe* with a *main* method inside a *Tester* class. The project should also have a *static* method called *hashCode* to which you can pass a key (a *String*) as a parameter. As usual, the method should return an index of type *int*. Use the following "rule" for hashing the *String*.

Create *int keyInt* consisting of the following calculations:

- The ASCII code of the first character of *key* times 1000, plus
- the ASCII code of the second character of *key* times 100, plus
- the ASCII code of the next to last character of *key* times 10, plus
- the ASCII code of the last character of *key*.

The *hashCode* method should assume a table size of 180. The returned *int* type that is to be used for the index of a hash table will be *keyInt % TABLE_SIZE*.

In the *main* method test the four names from Table 57-5. The resulting printout from *main* should be as follows:

```
Bush, George>>>39
Clinton, Bill>>>16
Lincoln, Abraham>>>147
Washington, George>>>139
```

****

The *Object* class *hashCode* method:

If the key for your hash table is an object, recall that it inherits the *Object* class (the cosmic superclass) and thus inherits four important methods:

Signature	Description
String toString( )	Returns a *String* representation of the object. For example, for a *BankAccount* object we get something like *BankAccount@1a28362.*
boolean equals(Object obj)	Tests for the equality of objects. This tests to see if two variables are references to the same object. It does not test the contents of the two objects.
Object clone( )	Produces a copy of an object. This method is not simple to use and there are several pitfalls.
int hashCode( )	Returns an integer from the entire integer range.

Table 57-7

This last method is of particular interest to us here. Since the *int i* it produces can lie anywhere in the range *Integer.MIN_VALUE <= i <= Integer.MAX_VALUE* you will still need to calculate modulo *TABLE_SIZE* to produce an integer suitable as an index for your hash table. Many programmers do not consider this *hashCode* method of the *Object* class to be a very good hash function since it bases its returned integer on the position in memory at which the object resides. Many programmers prefer to override the cosmic superclass *hashCode* method with one of their own that is more closely tuned to the requirements of the particular class it represents.

Miscellaneous facts about hash tables:

- Big O value for data storage or retrieval is O(1).
- Hash tables are relatively difficult and slow to traverse in order with respect to the keys or values.
- The *HashSet* and *HashMap* classes both use hash tables. Objects stored in these structures are not required to be *Comparable* or have a *Comparator*. Rather, many programmers like to provide custom *hashCode* functions for their classes instead of using the one inherited from *Object*.
- The *String*, *Double*, and *Integer* classes all have their own *hashCode* methods that are considered quite good.

Exercise for Lesson 57

1. In either a lookup or hash table a key is used to lookup a what?

2. A very complicated mathematical function of *x* needs to be computed for integer values of *x* ranging from 0 to 100. Would this problem be a better candidate for a lookup table or a hash table?

3. If we have a choice which is better to use, a lookup table or a hash table? Why?

4. Define "load factor" as it is used with regard to hash tables.

5. If plenty of memory is available, which is most desirable, a small load factor or a large load factor?

6. What is a disadvantage of a small load factor?

7. What is the largest possible value for a load factor?

8. If the *hashCode* method inherited from the cosmic superclass is used, what range of integers does it generate?

9. Suppose *int j* represents a range of integers from 173 to 5847. Write a simple *hashCode* function (method) that will receive *j*, convert it into a range of indices suitable for addressing an array of length 75, and then return this value.

10. With regard to hashing, what is a collision?

11. What are the two general ways of handling collisions?

12. What are the two types of probing discussed in this lesson? Which is more prone to clustering?

13. Is clustering good or bad in a hash table?

14. What is the term we use to measure the quality (with regard to the possibility of collisions) of hash table?

15. In a lookup table is it possible for several keys to map to one index?

16. In a hash table is it possible for several keys to map to one index?

17. What do we call the condition of a key mapping to more than one index?

For problems 18-20 consider the following distribution of indices generated by a hash function. The permitted range of indices is 0–100 and each index in the list was generated by a different key.

{1, 6, 18, 18, 19, 36, 38, 39, 40, 41, 41, 42, 59, 61}

18. Do you see evidence of any clustering and if so, where?

19. Other than some possible clustering, does the distribution seem fairly even?

20. Do you see evidence of any collisions and if so, where?

21. In both lookup and hash tables, which of the following is true?
    a. Keys are used to locate values
    b. Values are used to locate keys

22. What are some chaining data structures that could be used?

23. An array of length *len* is used to store a hash table. How many buckets are there in this hash table?

24. What is the Big O value for storage of data in a hash table if there are no collisions?

25. Is it easy to traverse a hash table in ascending order of the keys?

Lookup and Hash Tables… Contest Type Problems

1. What code replaces **<#1>** in the hash code method to the right?

   A. *int*
   B. *long*
   C. *double*
   D. *String*
   E. None of these

```
public static <# 1> hashCode(String key, int table_len)
{
        keyInt = 0;
        for(int j = 0; j<=2; j++)
        {
                keyInt = 10*keyInt + key.charAt[j];
        }
        return <#2>;
}
```

2. Assuming that **<#1>** has been filled in properly in the code to the right, which of the following would be an appropriate replacement code for **<#2>**?

   A. key % table_len
   B. table_len % key
   C. keyInt % table_len
   D. table_len % keyInt
   E. None of these

3. Assuming that **<#1>** and **<#2>** have been filled in correctly and if the method to the right is called with the following code, what is returned?

   ilds = hashCode("AB");

   A. throws an exception
   B. 816
   C. 7227
   D. "AB"
   E. None of these

4. Assuming that **<#1>** and **<#2>** have been filled in correctly and if the method to the right is called with the following code, what is returned?

   ilds = hashCode("ABC");

   A. throws an exception
   B. 816
   C. 7227
   D. "ABC"
   E. None of these

5. If the code to the right is part of a probing function used for resolving collisions in a hash table, which type of probing is most likely being done?

A. Bucket
B. Chaining
C. Linear
D. Quadratic
E. None of these

```
indxSeed = 1;
boolean foundIt = true;
while(foundIt)
{
        indx = indxSeed * indxSeed;
        indxSeed++;
        if(key = = keyArray[indx])
        {
                foundIt = false;
        }
}
```

6. Suppose a hash function is observed to be very slow. Which of the following might be a cause of this?

A. A low load factor B. A high load factor C. A slow method of chaining
D. The hash function doesn't produce an even distribution E. More than one of these

7. Which of the following is true about hash tables?

A. Makes efficient use of memory
B. Is fast in the storage and retrieval of data
C. Makes ordered traversals of the data easy
D. Is useful in sorting
E. None of these

8. The function $g = 3^x$ (where x is restricted to the values 4, 5, 6, 7, and 8) would be a most appropriate candidate for use in which of the following?

A. Hash table B. Lookup table C. *LinkedList* D. *ArrayList* E. None of these

Case Study

Distance to a Meandering Trail

Case Study… Distance to a Meandering Trail

Consider the following trail that is the result of connecting a sequence of twelve trail-points. **It is our job to determine the nearest distances from some arbitrary test-points to the trail**. Four such test-points are shown; they are labeled A, B, C, and D. The dashed lines indicate the nearest distance from each of these points over to the trail.

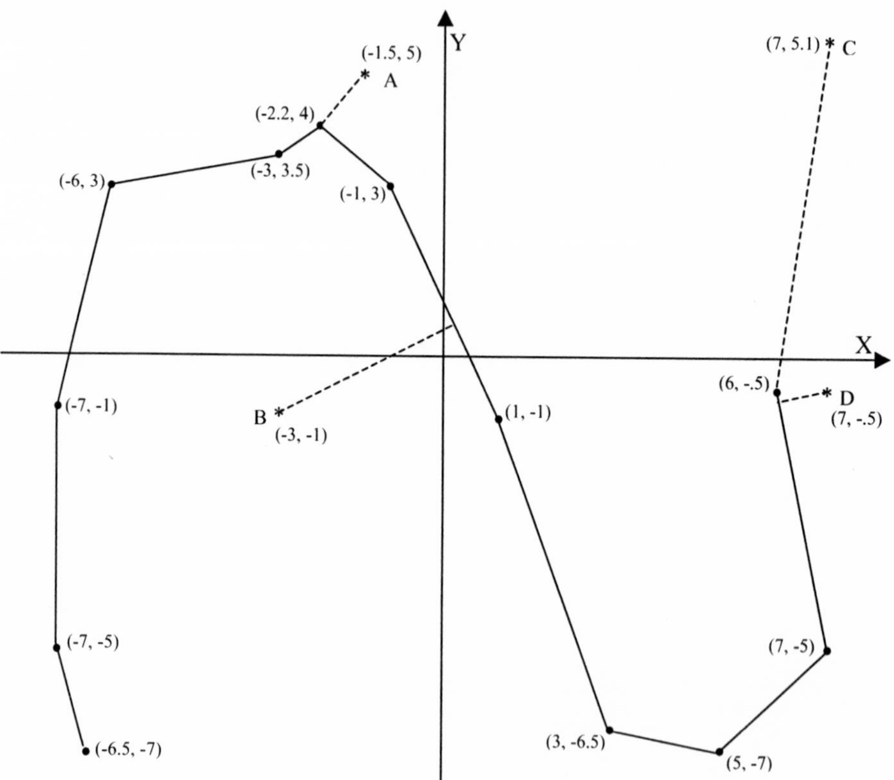

Fig. CS1-1

We will begin by creating two text files. The first file will be named *TrailData.in* and will contain the sequence of 12 points as follows. (Be sure to enter parenthesis and commas.)

(-6.5, -7)
(-7, -5)
(-7, -1)
(-6, 3)
(-3, 3.5)
(-2.2, 4)
(-1, 3)
(1, -1)
(3, -6.5)
(5, -7)
(7, -5)
(6, -.5)

The second text file will be called *TestData.in* and will contain data exactly as shown by the following (notice a space following the letters):

```
A (-1.5, 5)
B (-3, -1)
C (7, 5.1)
D (7, -.5)
```

The final output of this program will be:

```
Test point A distance to trail >>> 1.2206555604934692
Test point B distance to trail >>> 3.5777087211608887
Test point C distance to trail >>> 5.68858528137207
Test point D distance to trail >>> 0.9761870503425598
```

****

This is a fairly long, sophisticated project and the secret to success is not to bite off too much at once. Do a small, fundamental part of the code, test it, and revise as necessary. Then do a little more, test, and get that part working too. This will be our approach here.

The first thing we must do is create a project. Let's call our project *DistToTrail* and have it include a class called *Tester*. To make things go a little faster, we will paste in the contents of the *BaseClass* class developed in Lesson 27 and use that code to input the *TrailData.in* file. After creating two arrays, *double trailX[ ]* and *trailY[ ]* (both dimensioned to a length of 12), strip off the parenthesis and commas and store the *x* coordinates in *trailX[ ]*. Similarly, store the *y* coordinates in *trailY[ ]*. Use the following temporary code for testing:

```
for(int j = 0; j < 12; j++)
{
        System.out.print(trailX[j] + ", " + trailY[j] + "    ");
}
System.out.println("");
```

The output of this test should look like this:

```
-6.5, -7.0
-7.0, -5.0
-7.0, -3.0
-6.0, 3.0
-3.0, 3.5
-2.2, 4.0
-1.0, 3.0
1.0, -1.0
3.0, -6.5
5.0, -7.0
7.0, -5.0
6.0, -0.5
```

The code for the project up to this point (and including the above test) can be found in the Blue Pelican Java Answer Book in the Case Study section titled "**Part 1**".

****

So far, so good. Next, we will bring in the *TestData.in* file and store its parts in three different arrays. Remove the previous test code and add new code to *main* that will create the following arrays with each dimensioned to a length of 4: *char testLetter[ ], double testX[ ], double testY[ ].*

Now write code that will bring in this file and separate the parts of each line of text and store each in one of the new arrays just created. Use the following test code to verify that this section of the code is working:

```
for(int j = 0; j < 4; j++)
{
        System.out.print(testLetter[j] + "   " + testX[j] + ", " + testY[j]);
}
System.out.println("");
```

The output of this test should appear as follows:

```
A   -1.5, 5.0
B   -3.0, -1.0
C   7.0, 5.1
D   7.0, -0.5
```

The code for the project up to this point (including the test just above) can be found in the Blue Pelican Java Answer Book in the section titled "**Part 2**".

****

Now we come to the major part of the code for this project. This code will go in another class called *LineStuff*. Briefly, the *LineStuff* class can be described by the following list. At this point, do not try to implement any of this. Just scan the list and become somewhat familiar with the methods and state variables. Implementation will come later, step-by-step.

1. A constructor receives four *double* parameters that represent the coordinates of the two **end points of a line segment.**
    a. These four parameters are assigned to the *double* state variables *segX1*, seg*Y1*, *segX2*, and *segY2*.
    b. Use the coordinates of the end points of the line segment to determine the equation of the line in Ax + By + C = 0 form.
        i. Be sure to handle the special case in which the line is vertical.
        ii. Store *A*, *B*, and *C* in state variables of the same name.
2. Method *public double distToLine(double tpX, double tpY)*

a. The parameters *tpX* and *tpY* represent the coordinates of a **test-point** not necessarily on our line.
b. Return the distance from the point *(tpX, tpY)* to the line described by Ax + By + C = 0. This involves the use of a formula from Analytic Geometry that will be presented a little later.

3. Method *public boolean onSegment(double tpX, double tpY)*
   a. This method tests to see if the perpendicular projection of (*tpX*, tpY) onto line Ax + By + C = 0 falls on the segment defined by *(segX1, segY1), (segX2, segY2).*
   b. Returns *true* if on the segment.
   c. Returns *false* if not on the segment.

   This analysis is somewhat complicated and will be explored later.

4. Create the following *public double* state variables:
   segX1, segY1, segX2, segY2, A, B, C

Constructor and State Variables
Ok, time to get busy and start building the *LineStuff* class. In your project, create the skeleton of the *LineStuff* class.

Create the *double* state variables *segX1, segY1, segX2, segY2, A, B, and C.*

Next, create part of the constructor and assign the parameters to the state variables *segX1*, *segY1*, *segX2*, and *segY2*.

In the Answer Book this code is labeled as "**Part 3**".

****

Your next task is to finish the constructor by using the parameters to generate the equation of the line, thus producing *A*, *B*, and *C*. Be very careful here. You should not immediately calculate the slope of the line because it may be infinite. Instead, find out first if it is infinite by testing the denominator of the slope formula (m = (y2 - y1)/(x2 - x1)). This test is:

```
if( (x2 – x1) = = 0 )
```

In fact, we can get in trouble if the difference between *x1* and *x2* is very, very small, but still nonzero. It is suggested that you use the following test instead:

```
if( Math.abs(x2-x1) < .000000001 )
```

Some IDE's like BlueJ will let your directly test your class without having to create test code in *main* of the *Tester* class. The table below shows the final values of *A*, *B*, and *C* after passing the test parameters *x1*, *y1*, *x2*, and *y2* to the constructor. If your IDE does not permit such testing, you will need to hard code these tests into *main* of the *Tester* class.

Test Values				Results		
x1	**y1**	**x2**	**y2**	**A**	**B**	**C**
8	-7.2	8	19.5	1	0.0	-8.0
-2.44	4.902	16.3	-187.511	10.267502…	1.0	20.1507091…
-42	-19.1	17.03	-19.1	0.0	1.0	19.1000003…

Table CS1-1

The full code for the constructor and state variables for *LineStuff* is labeled as "**Part 4**" in the Answer Book.

***distToLine* method**

Implement the *distToLine* method as previously described. Use the following formula to determine the distance from the test-point *(tpX, tpY)* to the line Ax + By + C = 0:

$$\text{Dist} = |A(tpX) + B(tpY) + C| \div \sqrt{A^2 + B^2}$$

Fig. CS1-2 Distance from a point to a line

Test the *distToLine* method by creating a *LineStuff* object. Send the arguments below to the constructor and verify that you get the expected results back from the *distToLine* method.

Arguments Sent to Constructor				Test-Point		*distToLine*
Point #1		Point #2				
x	y	x	y	x	y	double
-1	3	1	-1	-3	-1	3.57708721…
7	-5	6	-.5	7	5.1	2.19099736…
-7	-5	-7	-1	-3	-1	4.0

Table CS1-2

In the Answer Book the full implementation of this method is labeled "**Part 5**".

***onSegment* method**

When projecting a test-point over to a line, there are two distinct cases. First, consider the scenario to the right in which a test-point projects over to a line and falls in the **interior** of the segment originally defining the line. In this case, the point of projection is **on** the segment and the *onSegment* method should return a *true*.

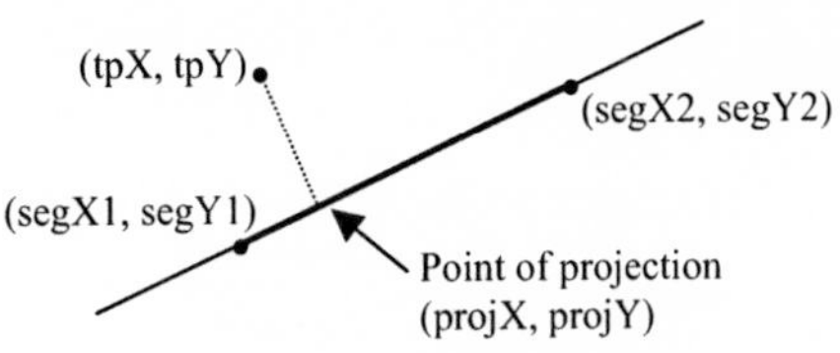

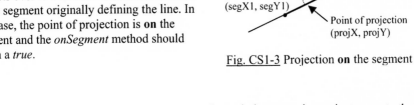

Fig. CS1-3 Projection **on** the segment

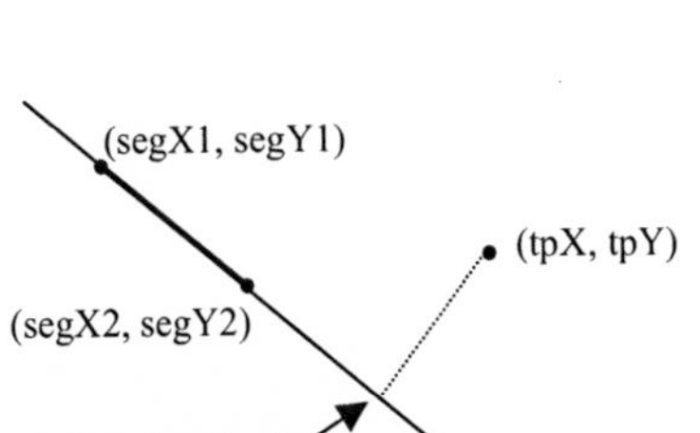

Fig. CS1-4 Projection **not** on the line

Second, the test-point projects over to the line so as to fall **outside** the line segment originally defining the line. An example of this scenario is found in the drawing to the left. The *onSegment* method should return a *false*.

How can we distinguish between these two situations? This is accomplished by **comparing the three distances** between the three points on the line.

Let's examine these distances for the case when the point of projection falls **on** the line segment. Fig CS1-5 shows three distances. The relative sizes of these distances will be used to verify that the point of projection does, indeed, fall on the line segment.

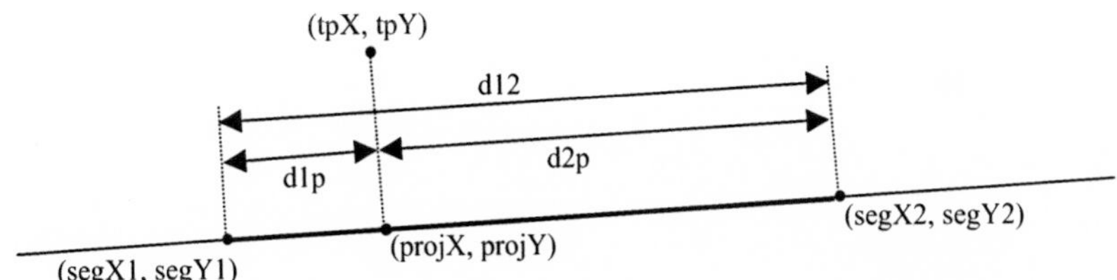

Fig. CS1-5 Point of projection falls in the **interior** of the line segment.

From Fig. CS1-5 we see that the condition for the point of projection to fall in the **interior** of a line segment is for *d1p* **and** *d2p* to **both** be less than or equal to *d12*. This would result in the *onSegment* method returning a *true*.

You will need to calculate the distances *d1p*, *d2p*, and *d12*. Use the following distance formula to calculate, for example, the distance between (x_1, y_1) and (x_2, y_2).

$$\text{dist} = \sqrt{(x_2 - x_1)^2 + (y_2 - y_1)^2}$$

Now lets examine the case when the point of projection falls **outside** the line segment originally defining the line.

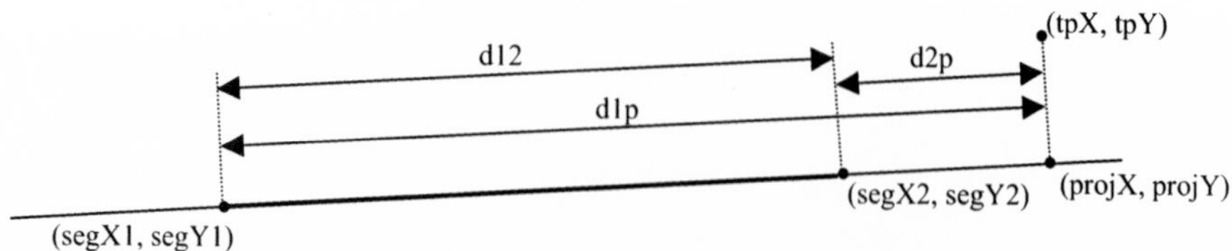

Fig CS1-6 Point of projection falls on the **exterior** of the line segment.

From Fig. CS1-6 we see that the condition for the point of projection to fall on the **exterior** of the line segment is for **either** *d1p* **or** *d2p* to be greater than *d12*. This would result in the *onSegment* method returning a *false*.

This is all well and good; however, there is still one major obstacle. How do we find the point of projection *(projX, projY)*? Very succinctly, here is how it's done. In Fig CS1-7 we note that the two lines labeled *line1* and *line2* are perpendicular (their slopes are negative reciprocals of each other). That will help us obtain the equation of *line1*. The equation for *line2* is already known; using the state variables *A*, *B*, and *C,* it is $Ax + By + C = 0$.

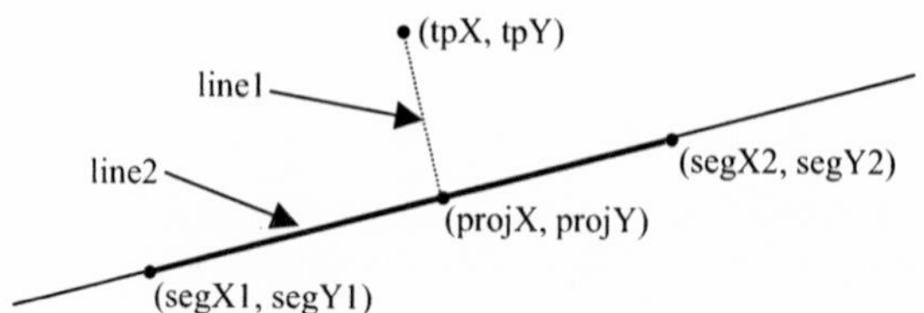

Fig CS1-7 *line1* and *line2* are solved simultaneously to find the point of projection

After finding the equation of *line1*, solve the two lines simultaneously as follows to find the desired intersection point *(projX, projY)*:

Assuming that the equation of *line1* is of the form $(A1)x + (B1)y + C1 = 0$, the solutions are:

$$\Delta = A1(B) - A(B1)$$
$$x = [\ -C1(B) + B1(C)\ ] / \Delta$$
$$y = [\ -C(A1) + A(C1)\ ] / \Delta$$

The solution here, *(x, y)*, is the desired intersection point *(projX, projY)*.

Following is a flow chart that should prove useful in putting all these ideas together.

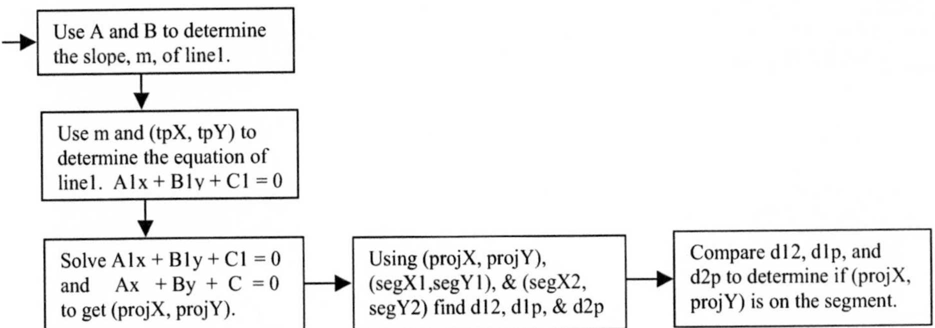

Fig. CS1-8 *onSegment* flowchart

Test the *onSegment* method by creating a *LineStuff* object. Send the arguments below to the constructor and verify that you get the expected result back from the *onSegment* method.

Arguments Sent to Constructor				Test-Point		*onSegment*
Point #1		Point #2				
x	**y**	**x**	**y**	**x**	**y**	**boolean**
-1	3	1	-1	-3	-1	true
7	-5	6	-.5	7	5.1	false
-7	-5	-7	-1	-3	-1	true

Table CS1-3

In the Answer Book the full implementation of the *onSegment* method is labeled "**Part6**".

****

After having accomplished all of the above, the *LineStuff* class is complete. Next, we turn our attention to the *Tester* class. The additional code to be placed there looks at each test-point and determines the nearest point on the trail. The nearest point may **either** be the distance of a perpendicular projection onto the trail **or** the distance to a trail-point. In Fig CS1-1 test-point A is nearest a trail-point while test-point B is nearest a perpendicular projection onto the trail. For each test-point, both types of distances must be considered. Use the following to assist you in writing the code that determines the nearest place on the trail for each test-point.

1. A loop will cycle through the four test-points. The remaining items listed below will **all** be placed inside this loop.

2. Cycle through all eleven line segments (determined by the twelve trail-points) and determine the point of projection of the test-point onto each line defined by these segments.

3. Determine if the point of projection is on the segment (use *onSegment*). If it is, then get the distance to the line using *distToLine* and store the returned distance in the *double dist[ ]* array. Increment an integer counter, *distArrayCounter*, as each new distance is stored there. In the end it will finally become the length of this array.

4. Cycle through all twelve trail-points and determine the distance from the test-point to each. Store each of these distances in the *dist[ ]* array and increment *distArrayCounter* each time.

5. Sort the *dist[ ]* array.

6. The first item in the array is the desired shortest distance.

7. Produce output for each iteration of the loop described by item 1 above. The final output should appear as follows:

```
Test point A distance to trail >>> 1.2206555604934692
Test point B distance to trail >>> 3.5777087211608887
Test point C distance to trail >>> 5.68858528137207
Test point D distance to trail >>> 0.9761870503425598
```

The implementation of the code for the above seven steps is labeled in the Answer Book as "**Part 7**". Following that is the complete code for the *Tester* class.

On the next page is a flow chart that is the equivalent of the above seven steps:

****

Following is a practical application of a project such as this:

> In GIS (Geographical Information System) software there might be a trail of points representing a road or perhaps a pipeline. As a mouse pointer is moved across a map containing such a trail, we could repeatedly call a method implementing the ideas of this project to continuously show the distance from the mouse pointer to the trail.

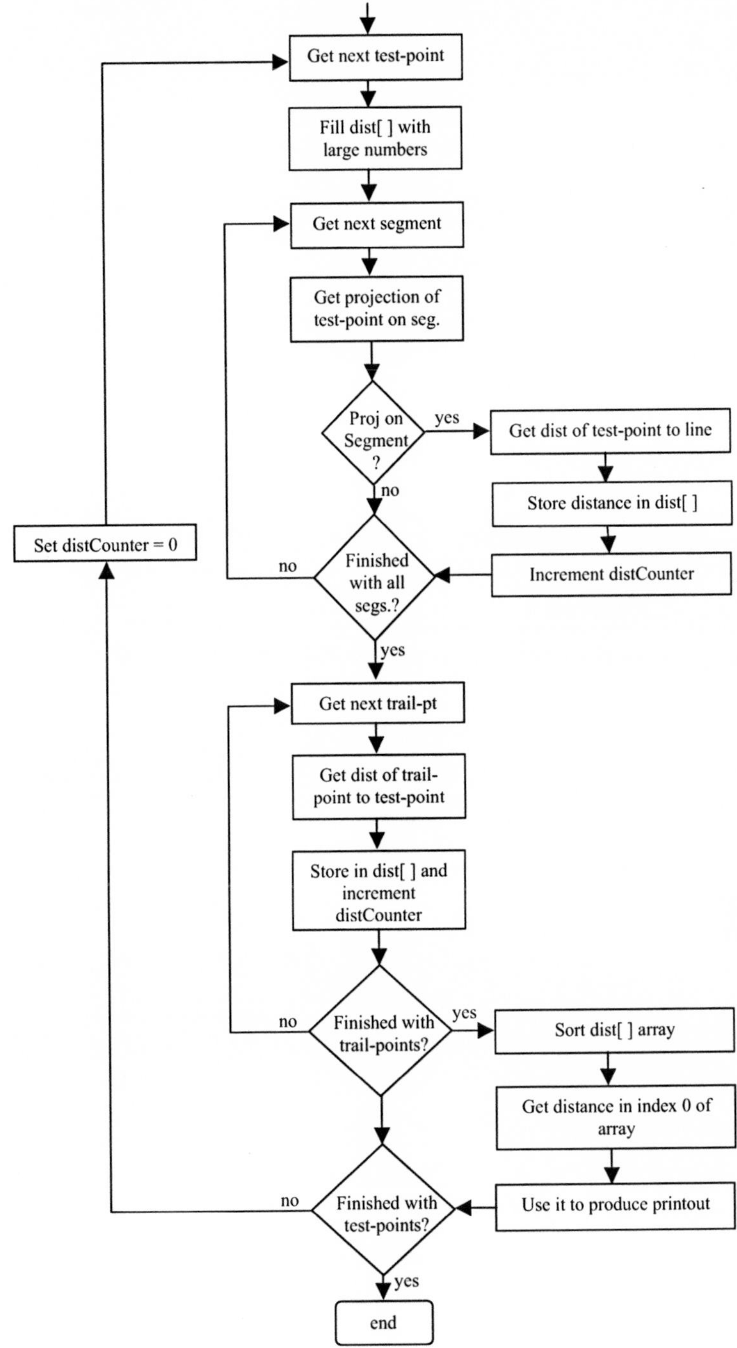

Fig. CS1-9 Flow chart for determining nearest point.

Golden Nuggets of Wisdom

(Short Learning Activities)

Study one of these each day (followed by a quiz on the following day) during the six weeks preceding a contest to help sharpen your Java skills.

Golden Nugget of Wisdom # 1

In each problem below, state what's printed.

1.
```
for(int j = 0; j < 5; j++)
{
        ...
}
System.out.println(j); //???
```
Won't compile. The scope of *j* is confined to the loop. It's not recognized outside the loop.

2.
```
int j = 19;
for(j = 0; j < 5; j++)
{
        ...
}
System.out.println(j); //???
```
Prints 5. On the last iteration of the loop j is incremented to 5 but this doesn't satisfy the loop condition, j < 5, so the loop is exited…however, j is still 5 and that's what's printed.

3.
```
for(int j = 0; j < 5; j++)
{
        int k = 10;
}
System.out.println(k); //???
```
Won't compile. The scope of k is limited to the loop; therefore, k is not recognized outside the loop.

4. What are two other names for instance fields?

   State Variables and Data Members

Golden Nugget of Wisdom # 2

```
public class Bystander
{
    public void method1(int x){          }
    public void macho(int x, String s){          }
    public void macho(int x, int y){          }
}


public class Parent
{
    public void method2( ){.......}
}


public class Child extends Parent
{
    public void method1(int x){          }
    public void method2( ){.......}
}
```

****

1. Name two methods that represent overriding.
   ***method2...*in both the *Parent* and *Child* classes. Objects made with the *Child* class will use its *method2* in preference to *method2* in the *Parent* class.**

2. Name two methods that represent overloading.
   The two *macho* methods in the *Bystander* class

3. Name two methods that represent polymorphism.
   ***method1...*in both the *Bystander* and *Child* classes. They have nothing to do with each other...totally unrelated.**

Golden Nuggets of Wisdom # 3

1. What does it mean when it is said that some class **realizes** an interface?

   Answer: It simply means that this particular class **implements** the interface.

2. Consider the following usage of the *split* method:

```
String s = "abcd123efgh456";
String sp[] = s.split("\\d+");
System.out.println(sp.length + sp[1]); //2efgh
```

   Note that while "\\d+" is a regular expression indicating one or more digits there is a different meaning to "\\D+". It is left to the reader to explore this and other similar regular expression in Appendix AC.

   In the example above there are only two elements of *sp*. They are:

   sp[0] = "abcd"   and   sp[1] = "efgh"

3. System.out.println(18 ^ 10); // **Prints 24...exclusive oring**

```
18 = 1 0 0 1 0
10 =   1 0 1 0
     ---------
     1 1 0 0 0 = 24
```

Golden Nugget of Wisdom # 4

1. String s = "Hello";
   System.out.println(s.substring(4,5));

   H e l l o
   0 1 2 3 4

   Notice the highest index is 4, yet we have an index of 5 in the code above! Actually, this is legal because the meaning of the second parameter (5 in this case) is to "pull back" one notch for the last character of the *substring*. So, the *println* above would legally print an "o".

   It would be easier to pick-off the last character of *s* using the one parameter form of substring, *s.substring(4)*;.

   There is a more straight forward way to pick up the last character of a *String* using *charAt( )*. If you know the last character's index, use, for example, *s.charAt(4)*. If you don't know how long the *String* is, use *s.charAt(s.length( ) - 1)*;.

2. String s = "Hello";
   String ss = s.substring(3,3)
   System.out.println(ss); //**prints nothing**
   System.out.println(ss.length( )); //**0**
   ss = s.substring(3,2); // **StringIndexOutOfBoundsException**

3. Returning an array from a method:

   The following method will return an int array.

   ```
   public int [] myMethod( )
   {
           int ss[] = {1,2,3,4};
           return ss;
   }
   ```

   Call this method as follows:

   ```
   int bb[] = myMethod( );
   ```

Golden Nugget of Wisdom # 5

Masking:

Consider the integer 93. In binary it is written as:

93_{dec} = 1 0 1 1 1 0 1
bit "positions" 6 5 4 3 2 1 0

Now, suppose we are interested in bit position number 3. What is it? From above we see that it's 1. Similarly, bit position 5 is a 0. How can we programmatically determine the value of various bit positions? We do this by **masking**.

93_{dec} = 1 0 1 1 1 0 1
mask = 0 0 0 1 0 0 0 = $8_{dec} = 2^3$ ...all except bit position 3 are **masked**.
0 0 0 1 0 0 0 result of bitwise AND

Notice with the bitwise **AND** with this particular mask that we are guaranteed all 0's in the answer except in bit position 3. In that position the bit will be the same as that of the number with which the mask is bitwise **AND**-ed.

The following code will identify the bit values in any desired position:

```
import java.io.*;
import java.util.*;
public class Masking
{
   public static void main(String [] args)
   {
         Scanner reader = new Scanner(System.in);

         System.out.print("Enter an integer value? ");
         int x = reader.nextInt( );

         System.out.print("What bit position in the integer entered above do you wish
                                                                        to read? ");
         int p = reader.nextInt( );

         int m = (int)Math.round(Math.pow(2, p));  //create the mask
         int a = x & m;
         if(a= =0)
         {
            System.out.println("Bit position " + p + " is a 0.");
         }
         else
         {
            System.out.println("Bit position " + p + " is a 1.");
         }
   }
}
```

In the line of code above, where we create the mask we can't trust *Math.pow( )* alone because of round-off errors. This is why we use the *round( )* method. Since it returns a *double*, we must cast the entire thing to an *int* type.

Golden Nugget of Wisdom # 6

1. **Illegal method calls:**

```
public interface Country
{
        int method1(double d);
}

public class State implements Country
{
        public int method1(double d)
        {
                … some code …
        }

        public void method2(int x )
        {
        … some code …
        }
}
```

```
Country obj1 = new State( ); // Notice Country is the interface and State is the
                             // implementing class

obj1.method1(38.2);  //Legal because obj1 is a Country object and method1 is a
                     //method specified in Country

obj1.method2(3);  //Illegal because obj1 is a Country object and method2 is not
                  //a method specified in Country
```

2. **Converting a decimal number to a binary, hex or octal string:**

```
int j = 17;
System.out.println(Integer.toBinaryString( j ));  // 10001
System.out.println(Integer.toHexString( j ));  // 11
System.out.println(Integer.toOctalString( j ));  // 21
```

The last three lines of code could, instead, be done this way:

```
System.out.println(Integer.toString(j, 2));
System.out.println(Integer.toString(j, 16));
System.out.println(Integer.toString(j, 8));
```

Golden Nuggets of Wisdom # 7

1. StringBuffer s = new StringBuffer("Groovy Dude");
   s.insert(3, "YES");
   System.out.println(s); //**prints GroYESovy Dude**
   // Notice it inserts just <u>before</u> index 3

2. String s1 = "A";
   String s2 = "a";
   System.out.println(s1.compareTo(s2));. //**prints a negative number**

   Notice that "A" alphabetically precedes "a." Alphabetical sequence is determined by the ASCII codes. ASCII code for "A" is 65 and it's 97 for "a." Since 65 < 97, that is why "A" < "a" in an "alphabetical" sense.

3. String s1 = "B";
   String s2 = "a";
   System.out.println(s1.compareTo(s2));.
   //**prints a negative number since "B" alphabetically precedes "a". ("B"'s**
   //ASCII code is 66 and "a"'s is 97; hence "B" < "a".

4. int x = 8;
   double y = 2.3
   String s = "hello";
   System.out.println(x + y + s + x + y); // **prints 10.3hello82.3**
   Moving from left to right, we encounter regular addition so we get 10.3. Next, we encounter a *String*, so we go into the concatenation mode and get "10.3hello". We are now in a *String* mode, so the remaining "+"'s are concatenations… and we get "10.3hello82.3".

Golden Nuggets of Wisdom # 8

1. **Escape characters: \” \\ \n \’ \t**
   System.out.println("Path:\tC:\\NerdStuff\nFile:\t\"nerd.doc\"\nH\'e\'llo");
   Prints the following:

   Path: C:\NerdStuff
   File: "nerd.doc"
   H'e'llo

2. **Use of null:**
   Suppose *acc* is some object that has **not yet been initialized**. Is the following parenthesis *true* or *false*?
   if(acc = = null) **true**
   {

   }

3. **Use of continue:**
```
while( …some condition … )
{
        …some code…
        continue;
        … some more code …
          ← jumps to here and we continue to loop
}
```

4. **An unusual use of <u>break</u>:**

```
YourDogsName: //this is a label that designates the outer loop…notice the colon
while ( …outer loop condition… )
{
        while ( …inner loop condition… )
        {
                if ( …something really bad happens… )
                {
                        break YourDogsName; // Just as a plain “break” would
                                            //break out of the inner loop. This
                                            //breaks out of the outer loop.
                }
        }
}
```

Golden Nuggets of Wisdom # 9

1. m = (...some Boolean expression...) ? (...set m to this if true...) **:** (...set m to this if false...);

   ```
   if(...some Boolean expression...) // The above can be rewritten like this
   {
           m = something;
   }
   else
   {
           m = something else;
   }
   ```

2. **Bitwise not**.... ~13 gives a weird negative number

   $13_{decimal}$ = 0 0 ....0 0 1 1 0 1 $_{binary}$
   |
   sign bit, 0 means its positive

   $\sim 13_{decimal}$ = 1 1 ....1 1 0 0 1 1 $_{binary}$
   |
   sign bit, 1 means its negative

3. **Shifting**

   12 << 3 ....gives 96...12 * 2^3 .....sign is preserved
   -12 << 3 ....gives -96...12 * 2^3 .....sign is preserved
   16 >> 3 ....gives 2.....16 / 2^3 .....sign is preserved
   -16 >> 3 ....gives -2.....16 / 2^3 .....sign is preserved
   -16 >>> 3 ....gives 536870910 .....sign is **not** preserved

4. **Modulus with fractions**
   5.1%3 **returns a 2.1**...3 divides into 5.1, one time. Then subtract 5.1 – 3 and get 2.1.

Golden Nuggets of Wisdom # 10

1. Constants….. (**final**)

```
public class BankAccount
{
   public BankAccount( )
   {
        balance = 5;  //Ok to initialize it here in the constructor
   }

   public void aMethod( )
   {
        balance = 5; //Not legal
   }

   public final int balance;  //Notice the constant is not initialized here as we
                              //would normally do.
}
```

2. System.**arraycopy**(a, aStartIndex, b, bStartIndex, howManyToCopy);
   a is an array…….*b* is an array
   "From me to you" ….copies from *a* to *b*.

3. **Calling one constructor from another**:

```
public class BankAccount
{
        public BankAccount(double bal)
        {
                balance = bal;
        }

        public BankAccount( )
        {
                this(4.18);  //calls the top constructor
        }
}
```

Golden Nuggets of Wisdom # 11

1. **Bitwise OR-ing** and **AND-ing** symbols can be used with *boolean* values. They give **exactly** the same answers that regular **AND-ing** and **Or-ing** do. This is somewhat strange and the only reason for using them is to effectively Boolean **AND** or **OR** while circumventing short-circuiting…see Nugget 15, items 1 and 2.

   boolean a = true, b = false, c = true, d = false;

   (a && c) returns *true*…….(a & c) returns *true*

   (a && b) returns *false*…….(a & b) returns *false*

   (a || c) returns *true*…….(a | c) returns *true*

   (a || b) returns *true*…….(a | b) returns *true*

   etc.…

2. x * =y + z;
   …means x = x * (y+z); //y+z **must** be in parenthesis.

3. int x = -5;
   int y = 9;
   System.out.println(x % y);
   -5

   What about when the signs are mixed? -5 % (-9)   -5 %9   5 % (-9)
   For the problem *a%b*, the sign of the answer will always be the sign of *a*. The sign of *b* is totally ignored.

4. **FIFO**…..first-in-first-out….classic example is a **queue** of people waiting to buy tickets in front of a box-office. The first person in line **(First In)** will be the first one to buy tickets and get out **(First Out)**.

   LIFO…….last-in-first-out……classic example is a **stack**. The last thing we push on the stack **(Last In)** will be the first thing we pop (sometimes called pull) off the stack **(First Out)**.

Golden Nuggets of Wisdom # 12

1. int x = 5;
   int y = 2;
   double d = (double)(x/y);
   System.out.println(d); // **prints 2.0**
   The parenthesis around *x/y* creates a little "world of its own" and since *x* and *y* are both integers, integer arithmetic is done giving 2.0 (not 2.5). This answer is then cast into a *double*.

2. int x = 5;
   int y = 2;
   double d = (double)x/y;
   System.out.println(d); // **prints 2.5**
   Only the *x* is cast as a *double*. *x/y* is now done with *double* arithmetic since *x* has been cast as a *double*.

3. Integer X = new Integer(5); //Java 5.0, Integer X = 5;
   BankAccount myAccount = new BankAccount(5);
   if (X = = myAccount)
   {

   }
   Is the parenthesis *true* or *false*, or will this not even compile?
   It won't compile because these two objects are incompatible for comparison.

4. Access Control....also called Access Control Modifier. These specify the accessibility of state variables, methods, and classes:

   a. public ...accessible from anywhere.
   b. private ...accessible from just within its own class.
   c. Package ...all methods of classes in the same package can access the feature. This is the **default** access control if none is specified. It is illegal to actually write Package; however, in the absence of an Access Control Modifier, Package is assumed.
   d. protected ...access is permitted by methods of the same class, subclasses, and classes in the same package.

Golden Nuggets of Wisdom # 13

1. Consider the running time (Big O) for the following code:

```
for (int j = 0; j < p; j+=20)  //O(p / 20)...drop the constant factor to get O(p)
{
        for(int k = 0; k < q; k*=4) //O(log4q)... drop the base 4 to get O(log q)
        {
                ...
        }
}
```

Since one loop is nested in the other, we multiply...**O(p log(q))**. Notice that we drop the base 4 on the log and just call it log. This is because the log of any base is directly proportional to the log of any other base.

2. Is there any difference in the following expressions?

   5 / 3 * 4.1 and 5 * 4.1 / 3

   With **pencil & paper** there is **no** difference.

   On the computer however, if 5 / 3 is done first (as in the left example above), both are integers, so the answer to that part is obtained with integer arithmetic and will be 1....this corrupts everything else after that. On the other hand, if 5 * 4.1 is done first (as in the right-hand example above), then the compiler sees the 4.1 and does *double* arithmetic. Of course, the rest of the calculation will be as it would be with pencil and paper.

3. How do we declare an array of objects? Let's consider the *BankAccount* class.

```
BankAccount theAccounts[] = new BankAccount[500];  //Creates 500 objects;
                                                   //however, they are each null

theAccounts[17] = new BankAccount(205); //Initializes 17th account to have $205
```

Likewise, each of the remaining 499 accounts must be initialized separately.

Golden Nuggets of Wisdom # 14

1. All objects inherit the cosmic superclass *equals* method. With this method, variables are compared to see if they reference the same object. Some standard classes (like *String* and the wrapper classes) override *equals* and implement their own so as to compare **object contents**. (If you create objects from your own class, and if you want the *equals* method, you will have to specifically put it in your class.)

```
Integer i = new Integer(23);  //Java 5.0, Integer i = 23;
Integer j = new Integer(23);  //Java 5.0, Integer j = 23;
Integer k = j;
System.out.println(i.equals(j));  //true
System.out.println(i = = j);  //false,... they are different objects.
System.out.println(k = = j);  //true,.... they are references to the same object.
```

```
Integer i = new Integer(23);  //Java 5.0, Integer i = 23;
Double j = new Double(23); //java 5.0, Double j = 23;
System.out.println(i.equals(j));  //false
```

Please note that for *i.equals(j)* to be *true*, both *i* and *j* must be of the <u>same object type</u>....and furthermore must have the <u>same values</u>.

```
System.out.println(i.equals(j));  //will compile as long as i and j are both objects
                                  //If they are different object types it will still
                                  //compile but will be false.
```

2. Consider the relationships between decimal, hex, and binary

Dec	0	1	2	3	4	5	6	7	8	9	10	11	12	13	14	15
Hex	0	1	2	3	4	5	6	7	8	9	A	B	C	D	E	F
Bin	0	1	10	11	100	101	110	111	1000	1001	1010	1011	1100	1101	1110	1111

Now let's think of the **<u>exclusive or</u>** problem 0x4BA ^ 0x132

Let's break up each into its binary form.

0x4BA = <u>0100</u> <u>1011</u> <u>1010</u> (4 B A)　　　　0x132 = <u>0001</u> <u>0011</u> <u>0010</u> (1 3 2)

Stack them and do an **<u>exclusive or</u>** remembering that two 1's yields a 0.

```
0x4BA= 0100  1011  1010
0x132 = 0001  0011  0010
        0101  1000  1000  =  0x588, the answer
          5     8     8
```

Golden Nuggets of Wisdom # 15

1. ```
   int j = 3;
   int k = 5;
   int count = 0;
   if ( (j = = k) && (count++ < 59))
   {    . . .    }
   System.out.println(count);
   ```

   Prints 0…Since (j = = k) evaluates false, the entire "if( )" is doomed to come out false, regardless of whether (count++ < 59) is *true* or *false*. "Short circuiting" just skips the second parenthesis to save time; therefore, the increment on *count* **is never done.**

2. Here's a case in which short-circuiting **does not** take place. Back in Nugget 11, item 1 we explored using bitwise **AND-ing** and **OR-ing** symbols with *boolean* quantities. Suppose as in #1 above we similarly have:

   ```
   int j = 3;
   int k = 5;
   int count = 0;
   if ( (j = = k) & (count++ < 59))
   {    . . .    }
   System.out.println(count); //Prints 1 since there is no short circuiting using &.
   ```

3. How do we convert a *double* or an *int* type variable into a *String*?

   ```
   String m = String.valueOf(15.302);  //Works on doubles.
   String n = String.valueOf(18);  //Works on integers.
   String p = "" + 15.302; //Concatenation is probably the simplest way.
   ```

4. Use *extends* when we wish one class to inherit another. Use *implements* when we wish one class to have all the methods listed in an *interface*. The following example illustrates the *School* class inheriting the *District* superclass. *School* also implements both the *TextBook* and *LunchRoom* interfaces. Notice the order. The keyword *extends* comes first, followed by *implements*.

   ```
   public class School extends District implements TextBook, LunchRoom
   {
           . . .
   }
   ```

   Only one class can be extended; however, several interfaces can be implemented.
   ```

Golden Nuggets of Wisdom # 16

1. What's wrong with the following method signature?

   public boolean static hoover(int x)

   The order should be...... *public static boolean hoover(int x)*. Notice, the type specifier (*boolean* in this case) should <u>immediately</u> precede the method name.

2. String s = "Zorro";
   s = s.replace('r', 'x');
   System.out.println(s); // **Zoxxo ... notice it replaces <u>ALL</u> occurrences of r**

3. What is the meaning of *String [ ] args* in

   public static void main(String [ ] args) ?

   If we write it as, *String args[]*, we know that *args* is a *String* array. Furthermore, the array is of length *args.length*...which means this is the number of command line arguments.

   See page 19-4 to review DOS prompt usage of command line arguments.

4. Using an enhanced *for*-loop, write code that will find the product of all the integers in array *x* (assume *x* is of type *int*).

   ```
   int product = 1;
   for(int val:x)
           product *= val;
   ```

5. What is printed by the following?

   ```
   double []d = {20.0, 20.1, 20.2, 20.3}
   for( double valD: d)
           valD = valD + 1.0;
           //The line just above compiles and runs but doesn't affect the d array.
           //This is because enhanced for-loops are "read-only".

   for(double w : d)
           System.out.print(w + ", ")
           20.0, 20.1, 20.2, 20.3
   ```

Golden Nugget of Wisdom # 17

1. Consider the overloaded *String* method *indexOf*. Following are the **signatures** of the several versions:
    a. int indexOf(String s)
    b. int indexOf(String s, int startingIndex)
    c. int indexOf(int ch) //ch is the ASCII code of a desired character
    d. int indexOf(int ch, startingIndex)
    e. int indexOf(char ch)
    f. int indexOf(char ch, startingIndex)

    There is a "last" version of each of the above that searches from right to left, for example:
    ```
    int j = myString.lastIndexOf("Hello");
    ```

2. Different references to the **same** array:
    Because arrays are objects, two or more variables can refer to the same array as in the following example:

    ```
    int []frst, sec;  // same as int frst[], sec[];
    frst = {1, 2, 3, 4, 5};

    sec = frst;
    sec[2] = 99;
    System.out.println(frst[2]);  //notice that even though we changed only
                                  //sec[2] to 99, frst[2] also changes to 99.
    ```

3. It is possible to erase an array from memory so that it takes up almost no memory space. To do this, simply set the array name equal to ***null*** as follows:
    ```
    int myArray = new int[500];  //occupies 500 * 4 bytes of memory
    . . .
    myArray = null;  //occupies almost no memory now
    myArray[45] = 2003;  //generates a "null pointer exception"
    ```

    A major lesson here is that you can set any object equal to *null*.

4. Boolean operators have the following order of precedence that should be **memorized**:

    & ^ | && ||

    Example:
    (false && true || false) yields *false*.

    Example:
    (true && true ^ true) yields *false*.

Golden Nugget of Wisdom # 18

1. Suppose we have two classes, *Big* and *Little*. *Little* is a subclass of *Big*. Both have a *void* method called *xray*; however, the *xray* method in *Little* is different and **overrides** the version of *xray* in *Big*.

```
Big x = new Little( );
x.xray( ); //Which version of xray does it use?
```

   The version in *Little*

2. What we call **methods** in this book, some other texts call **functions** or **subroutines**.

3. What we call **signatures** in this book, some other texts call **headers**.

4. Determining object type, legal methods, and where the methods are implemented. (See Lesson 38.)

<class, superclass, or interface name> objectName = new **<class or subclass name( )>**;

↑ This specifies the object type and what methods the object can use.

↑ This tells us where the methods are implemented that we are to use (including the constructor(s)).

5. The *boolean* quantity *anObject instanceof ClassOrInterface* returns *true* if the *anObject* object was derived from either the *class* or *interface* represented by *ClassOrInterface*. (See Lesson 38.)

6. The code in the left-hand panel below will produce the stack shown in the right-hand panel at the completion of *stck.push("C");*. The *toString* method of the *Stack* class is invoked to produce the resulting printouts:

Stack stck = new Stack( );	C ← top of stack
stck.push("A");	B
stck.push("B");	A
stck.push("C");	
System.out.println(stck);	[A, B, C] ← printout (notice top of stack is to the far right)
String s = (String)stck.pop( );	
String ss = (String)stck.peek( );	
System.out.println(s + ss + stck);	CB[A, B]

Golden Nugget of Wisdom # 19

It is possible to have multiple constructors in the same class as is illustrated below:

```
public class DemoClass
{
        public DemoClass( )  //This one with no parameters is called the default
        {                     //constructor.
                …
        }

        public DemoClass(int i)
        {
                …
        }

        public DemoClass(int i, String s)
        {
                …
        }

        … remainder of class not shown…
}
```

1. All of the following instantiations are legal, and each will seek out the appropriate constructor.
    a. DemoClass obj1 = new DemoClass( );
    b. DemoClass obj2 = new DemoClass(36);
    c. DemoClass obj3 = new DemoClass(12, "Yes");

2. It is possible to make one constructor call another using the *this* keyword. For example, suppose we instantiate an object *obj* using the default constructor as follows:

    ```
    DemoClass obj = new DemoClass( );
    ```

    Futhermore, suppose we want the default constructor to call the two-parameter constructor and **always** pass an *int* value of 22 and a *String* value of "Sierra". To accomplish this, modify the default constructor as follows:

    ```
    public DemoClass( )
    {
            this(22, "Sierra");
            …
    }
    ```

Golden Nugget of Wisdom # 20

1. Initialization blocks are blocks of code embedded within a class that run only once when the class is loaded. As the name implies, they are mostly used to initialize variables. **Multiple** initialization blocks are possible as is shown in the sample class below:

```
public class DemoClass
{
        //Non-static Initialization block
        {   stateVar1 = 50;   }

        //Static Initialization block
        static //To manipulate static variables, use a static initialization block
        {   stateVar2 = 20;   }

        public DemoClass( ) //constructor
        {
                stateVar1++;
                stateVar2--;
        }

        ... Methods and other state variables...

        public int stateVar1; //If initialization blocks exist above don't do any
        public static int stateVar2;                        //initializing here.
}
```

2. Rules for initialization blocks:

- Blocks only run once when the class is initially loaded.
- Blocks are executed in the order in which they occur.
- Regardless of placement, during the **one time of execution**, code in the blocks executes **before** code in a constructor.

3. Sample usage:

```
DemoClass demo1 = new DemoClass( );
System.out.println( demo1.stateVar1 + "    " + demo1.stateVar2); //51   19
DemoClass demo2 = new DemoClass( );
System.out.println( demo2.stateVar1 + "    " + demo2.stateVar2); //51   18
```

Initialization blocks are rarely used and there really is no point in using them as in the two sample blocks above. It would be more straightforward to just initialize these two state variables on the bottom two lines where they are declared. So, what is the real purpose of initialization blocks? Suppose we have a program that absolutely must run as fast as possible; however, it has loops that require the laborious, time-consuming calculation of something like *Math.tan(Math.log(Math.sqrt(1- x* x)))* for values of *x* ranging from 1 to 360 in increments of 1. In this case it would wise to iterate 360 times through a loop in an initialization block and precalculate all these values and store in a state variable array such as *double val[ ]*. Then in the actual program, when needed, quickly access the desired value with *val[x]*.

Golden Nugget of Wisdom # 21

Consider the following two classes:

```
public class Tester
{
        public static void main(String args[])
        {
                int j;
                //System.out.println(j);  //This line will not compile because j has
                                            //not been initialized.

                MyClass mc = new MyClass( );
                System.out.println(mc.q);  //prints 0
        }
}


public class MyClass
{
        public MyClass( )
        {
                System.out.println(q);  //  prints 0
        }

        …other methods and state variables

        public int q;  //q is automatically initialized to 0
}
```

Notice that numeric state variables are automatically initialized to zero unless initialized otherwise; however, ordinary (local) numeric variables (e.g. *j* above) **must be initialized before being used**.

****

In the **absence** of specific initialization, we can say the following about declarations:

1. When only declared, local variables are **not** automatically initialized to anything.

2. When only declared, objects are initialized to ***null*** (for an exception, see 4 below).

3. When declared, numeric arrays are initialized to **zero**.

4. When declared, a state variable is initialized to 0 (if it's a numeric) or to "" (empty *String*) if it's a *String*.

Golden Nugget of Wisdom # 22

1. Prototype:
The term prototype is extensively used in the c++ language. In Java, a method **prototype** is basically the signature of an abstract method (has a trailing semicolon and no following code). Following are examples:

```
void delStat(int pdq, String s);
String conCatBunch( );
double[][] burnTime(double d, int i);
```

Suppose an object, *obj*, has *Object* type objects stored in it. The following would be the **prototype** of the *getStuff( )* method such that *obj.getStuff( )* would return a two dimensional array of *Object* type objects:

```
Object [][] getStuff( );
```

2. Short-Circuiting:
Consider the following two questions that involve short-circuiting.

A. When Boolean **And-ing** two *boolean* expressions, when is only one expression evaluated?

   a. When the left expression is *false* **a**
   b. When the right expression is *false*
   c. When the left expression is *true*
   d. When the right expression is *true*

B. When Boolean **OR-ing** two *boolean* expressions, when is only one expression evaluated?

   a. When the left expression is *false*
   b. When the right expression is *false*
   c. When the left expression is *true* **c**
   d. When the right expression is *true*

3. *isLetter, isDigit, isLetterOrDigit, isWhitespace, isLowerCase, isUpperCase*
In order to determine if the character at index *j* of *String ss* is a letter, for example, which of the following would be an appropriate way to evaluate the *boolean* that is returned?

a. ss.isLetter(j)
b. ss.charAt(j).isLetter
c. Character.isLetter(ss.charAt(j))
d. ss.charAt(is.Letter( ))
e. Character.ss.isLetter(j)

Answer is c. The method *isLetter( )* method is a *static* method in the *Character* class and we must begin with *Character* (unless it's imported).

Golden Nugget of Wisdom # 23

1. ***char* and *int*:**
One of these can be directly stored into the other; however, the opposite can only be done with a cast. See items 2 and 3 on page 13-1 for details.

```
char ch = 'x';
int j = 3;
ch = j;  //illegal
ch = (char)j;  //legal
j = ch; //legal
```

2. ASCII codes:

Character	ASCII	Character	ASCII	Character	ASCII
0	48	A	65	a	97
1	49	B	66	b	98
2	50	C	67	c	99
. . .	. . .	. . .	. . .	. . .	. . .
8	56	Y	89	y	121
9	57	Z	90	z	122

3. Casting *Object*s back to their original form:
Suppose we have a *Queue* class that stores *Object* type objects. Futhermore, suppose that we are storing *String* objects there (they are automatically converted to the *Object* type). How do we get the *Object* type object **returned** by the *dequeue* method converted back to a *String* type object. Assume that we have a *Queue* object called *q*.

1. (String)(q.dequeue( ))
   This is the best way since it clearly shows we are casting what is returned by *dequeue*.

2. (String)q.dequeue( )
   On the surface this looks like we are incorrectly casting just the *q* instead of what *q.dequeue( )* returns; however, it actually **means the same** as number 1 above.

4. XOR
XOR means bitwise exclusive-or. Its operator symbol is ^.

Golden Nugget of Wisdom # 24

The following facts about Boolean Algebra were presented in Lesson 32. Examples are presented here in different forms, yet are still applicable to the theorems. Study the examples and convince yourself that they are really representations of the original theorems. (Remember that addition here represents **Or**-ing and multiplication represents **AND**-ing.)

1. Subtle Theorem:
This is subtle and not very obvious. It can be easily confirmed with a truth table.

a + b = a + (!a)*(b) ...same as a || b = a || (!a) && (b)

Example1: !c + d = !c + c * d
Example 2: a + !b = a + (!a) * (!b)

2. Law of Absorption:
In these theorems, the value of *boolean b* **does not matter** (it could just take a hike).

a = a * (a + b) ...same as a = a && (a || b)
a = a + (a * b) ...same as a = a || (a && b)

Example 3: !k = !k * (!k + !h)
Example 4: !k = !k * (!k + h)
Example 5: !k = !k + (!k * !h)
Example 6: !k = !k + (!k * h)

****

3. A two-dimensional *int* array is created and printed as follows:

```
int ary[][] = {   {1, 2, 3, 4},
                  {5, 6, 7, 8},
                  {9, 0, 1, 2}   };

for(int row = 0; row < ary.length; row++)
{
        for(int col = 0; col < ary[row].length; col++)
        {
                System.out.print(ary[row][col] + " ");
        }
        System.out.println("");
}
        printout →    1 2 3 4
                      5 6 7 8
                      9 0 1 2
```

Golden Nugget of Wisdom # 25

Random Numbers: The following facts/examples are extracted from Lesson 30.

```
Random r = new Random( ); //create a random object.
int i = r.nextInt( ); // This yields a randomly selected integer in the range
                      // Integer.MIN_VALUE to Integer.MAX_VALUE.
                      //(-2,147,843,648 to 2,147,843,647 as specified in Appendix C)
int j = r.nextInt(7); // Yields an integer in the range 0 ←→ 6
double d = r.nextDouble( ); // Yields a double in the range 0 (inclusive) ←→ 1
                            //(exclusive)
```

1. Print 20 integers in the range from 7 ←→ 19.

```
for(int j = 0; j < 20; j++)
    System.out.println( 7 + r.nextInt(13) ); // 13 = 19 – 7 + 1
```

2. Print 3005 floating point numbers in the range from 127.19 ←→ 156.225.

```
for (int j = 0; j < 3005; j++)
    System.out.println( 127.19 + 29.035 * r.nextDouble( ) );
    // 29.035 = 156.225 – 127.19
```

Maps, Sets, keySet: (See Lesson 46 and Lesson 47)

1. Items in a set can't be repeated.
2. The key values in a map can't be repeated, the values can.
3. Write code that will create an *Iterator* object from *Map m*. Use it to print the key-value pairs in *m*. Assume that only *String* objects are stored as the objects in the map.

```
Set keySet = m.keySet( ); //produces a Set object of the keys in m
Iterator itr = keySet.iterator( ); //produces a Iterator for Set keySet
while( itr.hasNext( ) ) //loop through the objects in the set
{
    String key = (String)itr.next( );
    String value = (String)m.get(key);
    System.out.println("key = " + key + "-----> value = " + value );
}
```

Golden Nugget of Wisdom # 26

Recursion: See Lesson 40 for more examples.

1. What is printed by the following? // **54 ...(0 + 6 + 24 + 24)**
System.out.println(recur1(0));

```
public static int recur1(int n)
{
        if (n > 10)
                return n - 2;
        else
        {
                n = n * 3;
                return n + recur1(n + 2);
        }
}
```

2. What is displayed by *mayo(20);* ? **0<2<6<20**

```
public static void mayo(int n)
{
        if (n < 2)
                System.out.print(n);
        else
        {
                mayo(n / 3);
                System.out.print("<" + n);
        }
}
```

Notice on this method we pass in these values of *n*.
20 6 2 0
Nothing is printed until the last time when we are down to a 0. Then we start coming back up the calling chain and printing.

3. What is returned by *horseFly(4);* ? **70**

```
public static int horseFly(int n)
{
        if (n = = 0)
                return 2;
        else if (n = = 1)
                return 5;
        else
                return 2* horseFly(n - 1) +  horseFly(n - 2);

}
```

The way we approach this is to just build the sequence from the rules we see expressed in the code. Term 0 has a value of 2 and term 1 has a value of 5.

Term number	→0	1	2	3	4
Value	→2	5			

How will we get term 2? Well, the rule in the code says it's twice the previous term plus the term before that. That gives us 2*5 + 2 = 12. Continue this to obtain the other terms.

Term number	→0	1	2	3	4
Value	→2	5	12	29	**70**

4. What is printed by the *h(3)*? **]]]M[[[**

```
public void h(int z)
{
    if(z = = 0)
        System.out.print("M");
    else
    {
        System.out.print("]");
        h(z-1);
        System.out.print("[");
    }
}
```

Let's begin analyzing this by observing the output of *h(0)*. It simply prints an "M".

Term number	→0	1	2	3
Value	→M			

Now, what about *h(1)*? It first prints a "]" followed by *h(z-1)*. But *h(z-1)* is simply the previous term, and we already know that it's an "M". A "[" follows. So our 2nd term is "]M[".

Term number	→0	1	2	3
Value	→M	]M[		

Similarly, each subsequent term is the previous term sandwiched in between "]" and "[" and so we have:

Term number	→0	1	2	3
Value	→M	]M[	]]M[[	]]]M[[[

So, if we are asked for *h(3)* the answer is **]]]M[[[.**

Golden Nugget of Wisdom # 27

Big O: The Big O value for an algorithm is roughly proportional to the time it takes the algorithm to run. (See Lesson 39.)

- When asked for the **smallest** Big O value, this is equivalent to asking for the smallest run time (**best case**).
- When asked for the **largest** Big O value, this is equivalent to asking for the largest run time (**worst case**).

1. The run time for the following code is proportional to $(n + 80)30n = 30n^2 + 240n$. Following the practice of dropping the coefficients and using only the largest power, we are led to the Big O value of $O(n^2)$.

```
for(int j = 0; j < n + 80; j++)
{
        for(int k = 0; k < 30*n; k++)
        { ...some code... }
}
```

2. Big O for the following code is O(log n). Time is proportional to $\log_2 n$.

```
for(int j = 0; j < n; j*=2)
{ ...some code... }
```

3. If *ob* is an *ArrayList* object, then Big O for *ob.add(index, obj)* is O(n) since this insertion of a new object at *index* will require some fractional number of the preexisting *n* elements to be moved forward one slot. A similar argument can be made for *ob.remove(index)* also being O(n).

4. Review the chart on page 41-15.

****

floor, ceil, and round methods **methods**: (See Lesson 6).

1. Math.ceil(-156.72) returns –156.0

2. Math.floor(-156.72) returns –157.0

3. Math.ceil(156.72) returns 157.0

4. Math.floor(156.72) returns 156.0

5. Math.round(156.72) returns 157.0

6. Math.round(-156.42) returns -156.0

7. Math.round(-156.88) returns -157.0

Golden Nugget of Wisdom # 28

The *split* method and regular expressions: (See Lesson 17 and Appendix AC)

String s = "Weird things"; //Use for problems 1 – 7.

1. String sp[] = s.split("i"); **//sp[0] = "We", sp[1] = "rd th" , sp[2] = "ngs"**

2. sp = s.split("\\s"); // **"\\s" means white space, sp[0] = "Weird", sp[1] = "things"**

3. sp = s.split("ei"); // **sp[0] = "W", sp[1] = "rd things"**

4. sp = s.split("m"); // **sp[0] = "Weird things"**

5. sp = s.split("r|h"); // **"r|h" means either 'r' or 'h', sp[0] = "Wei", sp[1] = "d t"**
   // sp[2] = "ings"

6. sp = s.split("[hi]"); // **"[hi]" means h or i (same as "h|i") sp[0] = "We"**
   // sp[1] = "rd t" sp[2] = "" sp[3] = "ngs"
   //(notice the element of zero length)

7. sp = s.split("ir|in"); // **"|" means OR, sp[0] = "We", sp[1] = "d th", sp[2] = "gs"**

String s = "Three spaces \t3"; //Use for problem 8.

8. sp = s.split("\\s+"); **//The + indicates multiple white space characters**
   //sp[0] = "Three" sp[1] = "spaces" sp[2] = "3"

String s = "abc239 xyz9304amnop"; //Use for problems 9.

9. sp = s.split("[0-9]+a"); **//"9304a" is a delimiter sp[0] = "abc239 xyz"**
   //sp[1] = "mnop"

10. "\\." Escape sequence for a literal period.

String s = "WaW7423WV is my password"; //Use for problem 11.

11. String sp[] = s.split("W[1-8]*|[^\\w]");
    The delimiters are a W followed by zero or more digits between 1 and 8
    or
    <u>not</u> a word character.
    sp[0] = ""
    sp[1] = "a"
    sp[2] = ""
    sp[3] = "V"
    sp[4] = "is"
    sp[5] = "my"
    sp[6] = "password"

Golden Nugget of Wisdom # 29

1. The *Iterator* interface is much simpler than the *ListIterator* interface. The three methods of the *Iterator* interface are: (see Lesson 44)

Iterator method signature	Action
boolean hasNext( )	Returns *true* if there are any items following the current position.
Object next( )	Returns item following current position and then advances the position… providing there is at least one item after the current position.
void remove( )	Removes the item returned by last successful *next( )* …providing there were no other intervening remove operation.

2. We **must handle** checked exceptions with one of two choices. Notice that with checked exceptions, doing nothing is **not** a choice, it won't even compile unless you do one of the following: (see Lesson 37)

   A. Handle the exception with ***try, catch, finally***.

```
try{ ...some code that might generate a checked exception...   }

catch(<Exception Class Name>  objectName)
{
        ...code here only runs if an exception was thrown in the try block...
}

finally{  ... this code always executes...}
```

   B. Put a *throws IOException* (or some other appropriate checked exception) tag on the method signature as in the following example:

```
public void readTheDisk( ) throws IOException
{
... code that uses a file reader...might encounter a corrupt or missing
    file...
}
```

3. Application of *abstract* and *final* to a class (see Lesson 36):
   a. *abstract*… can't instantiate objects from the class. If the class has any *abstract* methods, the class **must** also be *abstract*.
   b. *final* …can't inherit this class.

4. Application of *abstract* and *final* to a method (see Lesson 36):
   a. *abstract*… the method has no code. Code must be implemented in an inheriting class. Method signature ends in a semicolon.
   b. *final*… this method can't be overridden in an inheriting class.

Golden Nugget of Wisdom # 30

1. **Static methods and variables** (see Lesson 20)
Static variables (also called **class variables**) are declared with the *static* keyword.
    public int statVar = 30; //just an ordinary data member
    public static int statVar1 = 30; //a static data member

    There are two ways to access a *static* data member or *static* method. For the sake of the following examples, assume that the class name is *MyClass* and that it has *static* method *method1* and *static* instance field *statVar1*.
    a. Instantiate an object of the class (call it *obj*) and use it to access the variable or the method… *obj.statVar1… obj.method1( ).*

    b. Without an object, use the class name directly …*MyClass.statVar1 … MyClass.method1( ).*

    Static data members retain their previous values as new objects are created and are available to all objects. They present the same value to all objects.

2. **NumberFormat class** (see Lesson 27 and Appendix Z)
    //An object is not made with "new", rather it is returned by a *static* method.
    NumberFormat fmt = NumberFormat.getNumberInstance( );
    fmt.setMaximumFractionDigits(4); //guaranteed to show no more than 4 places
    fmt.setMinimumFractionDigits(3); //guaranteed to show at least 3 places
    String s = fmt.format(5.0); // s = "5.000"
    String s = fmt.format(3.22058); // s = "3.2206"

3. **The ListIterator interface** (see Lesson 44)
The *ListIterator* interface has the methods of the *Iterator* interface (*hasNext*, *next*, and *remove*) plus the following (notice *remove* has been modified):

ListIterator method signature	Action
void remove( )	Removes the item returned by last successful *next()* or *previous()* …providing there were no intervening *add* or *remove* operations.
boolean hasPrevious( )	Returns *true* if there are any items preceding the current position.
Object previous( )	Returns the item preceding the current position and moves the position back.
int nextIndex( )	Returns index of next item (-1 if none). In effect this is the current position of the *ListIterator*.
int previousIndex( )	Returns index of previous item (-1 if none).
void add(o)	Insert object o just left of the current position.
void set(o)	Replaces the last item returned by last successful *next()* or *previous()* with object o …providing there were no intervening *add* or *remove* operations.

Appendices

Appendix A ...Key Words

The following key-words must be used in the proper context. They should not be used as class, primitive variable, or object names.

abstract	double	import	private	throws
boolean	else	inner	protected	transient
break	extends	instanceof	public	try
byte	final	int	rest	var
case	finally	interface	return	void
catch	float	long	short	volatile
char	for	native	static	while
class	future	new	super	
const	generic	null	switch	
continue	goto	operator	synchronizer	
default	if	outer	this	
do	implements	package	throw	

Appendix B ...Escape Sequences

If you want to print any of the characters in the left column below, you can't just insert them into the sequence of other characters to be printed. For example, the apostrophe (sometimes called a single quote) would not print properly in the statement below:

System.out.println("It's a good thing."); //won't print correctly

Desired Character	Escape Sequence	Meaning
	\b	backspace
	\t	tab
	\n	new line (also called line break)
	\r	carriage-return
	\f	form feed
"	\"	double quotation mark
'	\'	single quotation mark
\	\\	backslash

System.out.println("It\'s a good thing."); //correct way to do it

Appendix C ...Primitive Data Types

Type	Storage	Range of Values
Numeric Types:		
byte	1 byte	-128 to 127 *
short	2 bytes	-32,768 to 32,767
int	4 bytes	-2,147,483,648 to 2,147,483,647 **
long	8 bytes	-9,223,372,036,854,775,808L to -9,223,372,036,854,775,807L
float	4 bytes	-3.40282347E+38f to -3.40282347E+38f ***
double	8 bytes	-1.79769313486231570E+308 to 1.79769313486231570E+308
Miscellaneous types:		
char	2 bytes	0 to 65,536
boolean	1 **bit**	true, false

Both *float* and *double* types are considered to be "floating point" numbers.

The types *byte*, *short*, *int*, and *long* are all integers.

* It is interesting to see what happens when an integer that exceeds the range of a *byte* is cast as a *byte*. Consider the following:

```
byte x = (byte)128;
```

The value of *x* is –128, and here's why:

128_{dec} in binary is written as an eight bit *byte* as: 1 0 0 0 0 0 0 0
This *byte* has its most significant bit set to a 1 so this is interpreted as a **negative** number (see Appendix G). What is the value of this negative number? As explained in Appendix G, invert all 8 bits and add one as follows:

0 1 1 1 1 1 1 1 (inverted form)
1 (add 1)
1 0 0 0 0 0 0 0 (notice we "carried" to get the final 1 on the left)
This is equivalent to 128_{dec}, so our final answer is –128.

** The *Integer* class has two data member constants that give these two values:

- Integer.MIN_VALUE = -2,147,483,648
- Integer.MAX_VALUE = 2,147,483,647

*** Any time we wish to store a literal number in a *float* variable, append an *f*; otherwise, the compiler will see the number as a *double*:

```
float x = 123.76f;
```

Appendix D…..ASCII Codes

Dec	Hex	Oct	Binary	Html	Character	Comments/Description
0	0	000	000 0000		**NUL**	Null **(Shaded region, unprintable characters)**
1	1	001	000 0001		**SOH**	Start of heading
2	2	002	000 0010		**STX**	Start of text
3	3	003	000 0011		**ETX**	End of text
4	4	004	000 0100		**EOT**	End of transmission
5	5	005	000 0101		**ENQ**	Enquiry
6	6	006	000 0110		**ACK**	Acknowledge
7	7	007	000 0111		**BEL**	Bell, beep, etc
8	8	010	000 1000		**BS**	Backspace
9	9	011	000 1001		**TAB**	Horizontal tab
10	A	012	000 1010		**LF**	Line feed; also called NL (new line)
11	B	013	000 1011		**VT**	Vertical tab
12	C	014	000 1100		**FF**	Form feed; also called NP (new page)
13	D	015	000 1101		**CR**	Carriage return
14	E	016	000 1110		**SO**	Shift out
15	F	017	000 1111		**SI**	Shift in
16	10	020	001 0000		**DLE**	Data link escape
17	11	021	001 0001		**DC1**	Device control 1
18	12	022	001 0010		**DC2**	Device control 2
19	13	023	001 0011		**DC3**	Device control 3
20	14	024	001 0100		**DC4**	Device control 4
21	15	025	001 0101		**NAK**	Negative acknowledge
22	16	026	001 0110		**SYN**	Synchronous idle
23	17	027	001 0111		**ETB**	End of transmission block
24	18	030	001 1000		**CAN**	Cancel
25	19	031	001 1001		**EM**	End of medium
26	1A	032	001 1010		**SUB**	Substitute
27	1B	033	001 1011		**ESC**	Escape (the Esc key on the keyboard)
28	1C	034	001 1100		**FS**	File separator
29	1D	035	001 1101		**GS**	Group separator
30	1E	036	001 1110		**RS**	Record separator
31	1F	037	001 1111		**US**	Unit separator
32	20	040	010 0000			Space
33	21	041	010 0001	!	**!**	Exclamation mark
34	22	042	010 0010	"	**“**	Double quote
35	23	043	010 0011	#	**#**	Pound sign
36	24	044	010 0100	$	**$**	Dollar sign
37	25	045	010 0101	%	**%**	Percent sign
38	26	046	010 0110	&	**&**	Ampersand
39	27	047	010 0111	'	**‘**	Apostrophe
40	28	050	010 1000	(	**(**	Left parenthesis
41	29	051	010 1001	)	**)**	Right parenthesis

Dec	Hex	Oct	Binary	Html	Character	Comments/Description
42	2A	052	010 1010	*	*	Asterisk
43	2B	053	010 1011	+	+	Plus sign
44	2B	054	010 1100	,	,	Comma
45	2D	055	010 1101	-	-	Dash (also used as a minus sign)
46	2E	056	010 1110	.	.	Period
47	2F	057	010 1111	/	/	Forward slash
48	30	060	011 0000	0	**0**	Digits
49	31	061	011 0001	1	**1**	
50	32	062	011 0010	2	**2**	
51	33	063	011 0011	3	**3**	
52	34	064	011 0100	4	**4**	
53	35	065	011 0101	5	**5**	
54	36	066	011 0110	6	**6**	
55	37	067	011 0111	7	**7**	
56	38	070	011 1000	8	**8**	
57	39	071	011 1001	9	**9**	
58	3A	072	011 1010	:	**:**	Colon
59	3B	073	011 1011	;	**;**	Semicolon
60	3C	074	011 1100	<	<	Less than symbol
61	3D	075	011 1101	=	=	Equal sign
62	3E	076	011 1110	>	>	Greater than symbol
63	3F	077	011 1111	?	**?**	Question mark
64	40	100	100 0000	@	@	"at" sign
65	41	101	100 0001	A	**A**	Upper case (capital) letters
66	42	102	100 0010	B	**B**	
67	43	103	100 0011	C	**C**	
68	44	104	100 0100	D	**D**	
69	45	105	100 0101	E	**E**	
70	46	106	100 0110	F	**F**	
71	47	107	100 0111	G	**G**	
72	48	110	100 1000	H	**H**	
73	49	111	100 1001	I	**I**	
74	4A	112	100 1010	J	**J**	
75	4B	113	100 1011	K	**K**	
76	4C	114	100 1100	L	**L**	
77	4D	115	100 1101	M	**M**	
78	4E	116	100 1110	N	**N**	
79	4F	117	100 1111	O	**O**	
80	50	120	101 0000	P	**P**	
81	51	121	101 0001	Q	**Q**	
82	52	122	101 0010	R	**R**	
83	53	123	101 0011	S	**S**	
84	54	124	101 0100	T	**T**	
85	55	125	101 0101	U	**U**	
86	56	126	101 0110	V	**V**	
87	57	127	101 0111	W	**W**	

Dec	Hex	Oct	Binary	Html	Character	Comments/Description
88	58	130	101 1000	X	**X**	
89	59	131	101 1001	Y	**Y**	
90	5A	132	101 1010	Z	**Z**	
91	5B	133	101 1011	[	**[**	Left square bracket
92	5C	134	101 1100	\	\	Backslash
93	5D	135	101 1101	]	**]**	Right square bracket
94	5E	136	101 1110	^	^	
95	5F	137	101 1111	_	_	Underscore
96	60	140	110 0000	`	`	
97	61	141	110 0001	a	**a**	
98	62	142	110 0010	b	**b**	
99	63	143	110 0011	c	**c**	
100	64	144	110 0100	d	**d**	
101	65	145	110 0101	e	**e**	
102	66	146	110 0110	f	**f**	
103	67	147	110 0111	g	**g**	
104	68	150	110 1000	h	**h**	
105	69	151	110 1001	i	**i**	
106	6A	152	110 1010	j	**j**	
107	6B	153	110 1011	k	**k**	
108	6C	154	110 1100	l	**l**	
109	6D	155	110 1101	m	**m**	Lower case (small) letters
110	6E	156	110 1110	n	**n**	
111	6F	157	110 1111	o	**o**	
112	70	160	111 0000	p	**p**	
113	71	161	111 0001	q	**q**	
114	72	162	111 0010	r	**r**	
115	73	163	111 0011	s	**s**	
116	74	164	111 0100	t	**t**	
117	75	165	111 0101	u	**u**	
118	76	166	111 0110	v	**v**	
119	77	167	111 0111	w	**w**	
120	78	170	111 1000	x	**x**	
121	79	171	111 1001	y	**y**	
122	7A	172	111 1010	z	**z**	
123	7B	173	111 1011	{	{	Left curly brace
124	7C	174	111 1100			|	"pipe" symbol
125	7D	175	111 1101	}	}	Right curly brace
126	7E	176	111 1110	~	**~**	Tilde
127	7F	177	111 1111		**DEL**	Delete **(unprintable character)**

ASCII is an acronym for "American Standard Code for Information Interchange" and was originated by visionary, Robert Bemer, in the early 1950's. This computer science pioneer made numerous contributions when, in the early days of computing, instead of concentrating on hardware (as most were doing), he specialized in software.

Appendix E…..Saving Text Files

Before we learn to make text files (see Appendix F for a better understanding of text files), we need to adjust how files display in Windows Explorer. We need to be able to see file extensions, etc. so as to verify the file names and locations that we create. The following settings are suggested:

First, right-click on Start in the lower left corner of the desktop. Then click on Explore. This launches Windows Explorer.

In Windows Explorer click on the drop-down on this icon and then select Details.

Fig. E-1

Click on the Tools Menu item and then select Folder Options.

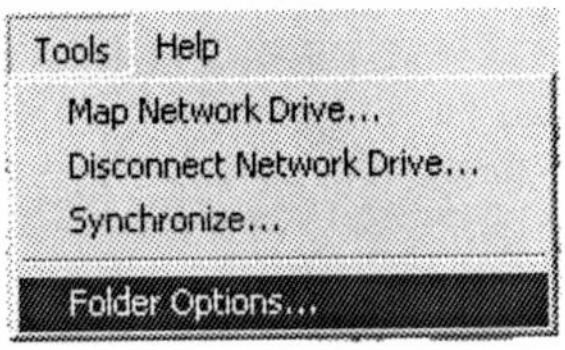

Fig.E-2

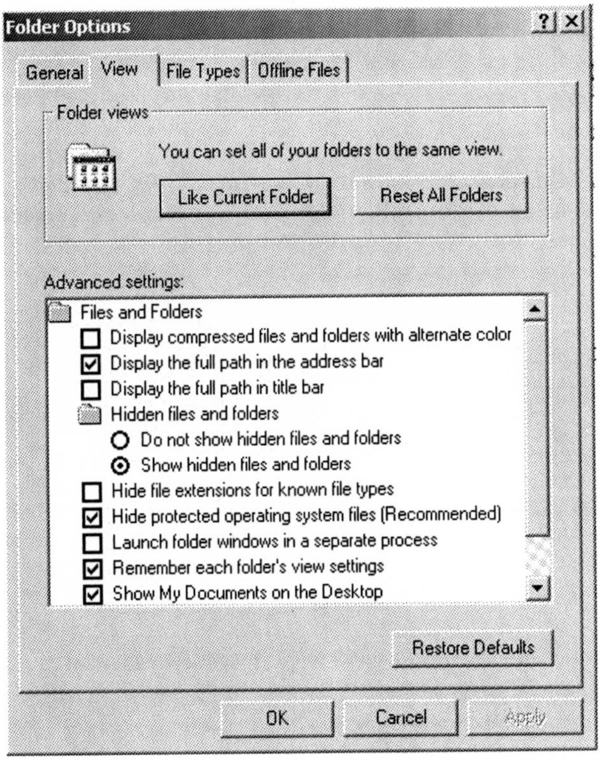

On the Folder Options dialog, select the View tab.

Make the settings shown here.

Click the Apply button.

Click the Like Current Folder button. You will be asked to confirm this last operation. Just answer "Yes".

Click OK.

Fig. E-3

In creating text files (sometimes called ASCII coded text files) for this course, we recommend Microsoft Notepad. To access Notepad use the following menu sequence:

Start | Programs | Accessories | Notepad

The most important thing to remember is to set the Save as type box in the Save as dialog correctly. There are two possible settings:

1. **Text Documents**
   This saves a text file with the extension ".txt". Students will often choose this setting and type in a file name something like, "Data36.in", expecting that to be the full file name. If the settings on the previous page have not been done, the file viewed either in Windows Explorer or under the My Computer icon on the desktop will hide the extension and show the file as "Data36.in" ...when, in fact, the **full** file name is "Data36.in.txt".

   a. The number one thing to remember about the Text Documents setting is that **a final extension of ".txt" is appended** to whatever name you type in the File name box. With the proper setting from the previous page, the file name will be viewed as "Data36.in.txt" and you would see the error of your ways.

   b. If ".txt" is the desired file extension, then don't try to enter an extension in the File name box. Just enter something like "Data36" and the ".txt" extension will automatically be added to it to produce "Data36.txt".

2. **All Files (*.*)**
   This setting also produces text files. However, **no** extension is automatically added when you save the file. So, if you type "Data36.in" in the File name box, that's the final file name.

If you are using Windows 98, regardless of the setting in the Save as type box it will always append a ".txt" to the end of the file name. If necessary use Windows Explorer to change the name of the file and thus amend the extension as needed. (When renaming, Windows may tell you that this could make the file unstable. Don't worry about this; just go ahead and click OK.)

You can also use Microsoft WordPad (a very simple word processor) to create text files. To access WordPad, use the following menu sequence:

Start | Programs | Accessories | WordPad

When you save, choose Text Document from the Save as type box. This is the **only** way to save as a text document. Unfortunately, it also appends a ".txt" to whatever you type in the File name box. If you desire a different extension, your only recourse will be to go into Windows Explorer, right-click on the file and then rename it.

Regardless of how you create your text file, you should **verify its existence and location** by using either Windows Explorer or the desktop icon, My Computer. If the settings on the previous page were made correctly, you should be able to view the full name and extension of your file.

Appendix F....Text and Binary Files Explained

There are two fundamental ways to store files…text and binary. We will show how to store the number 12345 in both formats:

1. **Text**

   It takes 5 bytes to store 12345, one byte for each character. Below are the contents of each byte:

49_{dec}	50_{dec}	51_{dec}	52_{dec}	53_{dec}
$011\ 0001_{bin}$	$011\ 0010_{bin}$	$011\ 0011_{bin}$	$011\ 0100_{bin}$	$011\ 0101_{bin}$

   Look in Appendix D and you will see, for example, that 49_{dec} is the ASCII code for 1_{dec} 50_{dec} is the ASCII code for 2_{dec}, etc.

2. **Binary**

   It takes four bytes (because it's an integer, see Appendix C) to store the number 12345 as follows.

   $0000\ 0000 \quad 0000\ 0000 \quad 011\ 0000_{bin} \quad 011\ 1001_{bin}$

   "Jammed" together we have

   $00000000000000001100000111001_{bin} = 12345_{dec}$

Appendix G .....Two's Complement Notation

The two's complement notation is the protocol used to store **negative numbers**. Let's consider the integer (4 bytes) 13 in its binary form:

$00000000\ 00000000\ 00000000\ 00001101_{bin} = 13_{dec}$

What could we do to make this a negative number? The way we approach this is to think about negative 13 in this way:

13 + (negative 13) = 0

So, our requirement will be that negative 13 be represented in such a way that when added to 13 it will give a result of 0.

We will begin by adding the original binary form of 13 to the ones' complement (invert, 1's changed to 0's and vice versa) of 13.

```
 00000000 00000000 00000000 00001101
 11111111 11111111 11111111 11110010
 -----------------------------------
 11111111 11111111 11111111 11111111
```

This is **not** what we want. We want all zeros; however, notice if we add 1 to this answer a carry will "ripple" all the way through, and if we just ignore the last carry on the end, we have our answer of 0.

```
 11111111 11111111 11111111 11111111
                                   1
 -----------------------------------
100000000 00000000 00000000 00000000
|
Ignore this last carry
```

So, the way to get –13 is to invert 13 and add 1.

```
00000000 00000000 00000000 00001101 (13 in binary)

11111111 11111111 11111111 11110010 (13 inverted)
                                  1 (add 1)
-----------------------------------
11111111 11111111 11111111 11110011 (two's complement form of –13)
```

Rules/Observations:

1. To produce the negative of a number (two's complement form), perform the following three steps.
   a. Express the number in binary form
   b. Invert the number (change 1's to 0's and vice versa)
   c. Add 1
2. Negative numbers will always have a most significant bit (msb) value of 1.
3. Positive numbers will always have an msb value of 0.

4. This msb is known as the **sign bit** and does **not** have a positional value as do the other bits.

As an interesting exercise, you might try the following code.

```
int x = ???; // enter any number you like for ???
System.out.println( x + (~x + 1) ); //prints 0 for any value of x
                                     //Notice you are inverting x and adding 1 to produce
                                     //the negative of x.
```

****

We are now going to take a completely different approach to ten's complement and see that when extending this idea to the binary system, we would have the two's complement.

Consider an old-fashioned car mileage indicator (odometer). If the register rotates forward, it performs addition one mile at a time. If the register rotates backward, it performs subtraction one mile at a time. Below is a five-digit register rotating backwards:

00004
00003
00002
00001
00000
99999
99998
99997

What we have done here is to work the problem 4 – 7, because we started with 4 and then rotated backwards 7 places. The answer is, of course, –3. However, the 99997 we got is what we call the ten's compliment of 3. In other words, 99997 is one way to represent –3. To see that 99997 really corresponds to –3, let's work the problem 4 + (-3) and see if we get +1.

 00004
 99997 (This corresponds to –3)
100001 (This is the answer if we ignore the "left-most" carry.)

Similarly, a backwards rotating "binary" odometer would look like this:

0100
0011
0010
0001
0000
1111
1110
1101

Again, what we are doing here is working the problem 4 – 7, because we start with 4 and rotate backwards 7 places. The answer is –3 and the 1101_{bin} we get is what we call the two's complement of 3. To see if this really works, let's do the problem 4 + (-3) and see if we get 1.

$$
\begin{array}{rl}
0100_{\ bin} = & 4_{\ dec} \\
\underline{1101}_{\ bin} = & -3_{\ dec} \\
10001_{\ bin} = & 1 \text{ (ignoring the “left-most” carry)}
\end{array}
$$

Notice that the two's compliment representation of $-3_{\ dec}$ ($1101_{\ bin}$) is exactly what we would get from the previous discussion where we would have inverted and added 1.

Appendix H ….Operator Precedence

Suppose there was a need to evaluate this expression:

((int)(3 *a)) ^ p | 3 & q | ~b

What part would you do first? You would need a chart specifying the order in which operations are done.

As a matter of good programming, you should never write such a statement because it is difficult to maintain. Instead, break this up into a sequence of several lines of code in which the sequence determines the order you intend. Below is the order in which operations are done.

Operator	Function
( )	Parenthesis
[ ]	Array subscript
.	Object member selection
++	Increment
--	Decrement
+	Unary plus sign. Unary operators accept only one operand.
-	Unary minus sign. (for example, -2 means negative two)
!	boolean NOT
~	Bitwise NOT
(type)	Type cast, example: (int)
Arithmetic Operators	
*	Multiplication
/	Division
%	Modulus
+	Addition or concatenation
-	Subtraction
<<	Bitwise shift left
>>	Bitwise shift right
>>>	Bitwise shift right, preserve sign
Comparison Operators	
<	Less than
<=	Less than or equal to
>	Greater than
>=	Greater than or equal to
instanceOf	Class membership
= =	Equal to
!=	Not equal to
Boolean Operators	
&	boolean AND without short-circuit if boolean arguments
&	Bitwise And
^	boolean exclusive OR without short-circuit if boolean arguments

<table>
<tr><th>Operator</th><th>Function</th></tr>
<tr><td>^</td><td>Bitwise exclusive OR</td></tr>
<tr><td>|</td><td>boolean OR without short-circuit if boolean arguments</td></tr>
<tr><td>|</td><td>Bitwise OR</td></tr>
<tr><td>&&</td><td>boolean AND with short-circuit</td></tr>
<tr><td>||</td><td>boolean OR with short-circuit</td></tr>
<tr><td></td><td></td></tr>
<tr><td>?:</td><td>Ternary conditional</td></tr>
<tr><td>=</td><td>Assignment</td></tr>
<tr><td>+=</td><td>Addion and assignignment</td></tr>
<tr><td>-=</td><td>Subtraction and assignment</td></tr>
<tr><td>*=</td><td>Multiplication and assignment</td></tr>
<tr><td>/=</td><td>Division and assignment</td></tr>
<tr><td>%=</td><td>Modulo and assignment</td></tr>
<tr><td><<=</td><td>Shift left(preserve sign) and assign</td></tr>
<tr><td>>>=</td><td>Shift right(preserve sign) and assign</td></tr>
<tr><td>>>>=</td><td>Shift right(do not preserve sign) and assign</td></tr>
<tr><td>&=</td><td>boolean or bitwise AND and assignment</td></tr>
<tr><td>|=</td><td>boolean or bitwise OR and assignment</td></tr>
<tr><td>^=</td><td>boolean or bitwise exclusive OR and assignment</td></tr>
</table>

Appendix I ....Creating Packages and Importing Classes

Java has several classes supplied with the language that you must "import" before you can make objects from them and/or access their methods. Let's suppose your class is called *MyClass* and you wish to import the *Random* class (for the purpose of creating random numbers inside the methods of your class).

First, you must know the "package" name. For the *Random* class the package name is **java.util** . There are **several** classes in this package. To bring in the Random class only, place the following command at the top of your class as follows:

```
import java.util.Random;
//Use multiple lines here if there is a need to import other classes
public class MyClass
{
        ...methods and state variables...
}
```

It is very common to import **all** of the classes in a package using the wildcard character "*".

```
import java.util.*;
```

Below we list just a few packages and some useful classes in them.

java.util	Random, Arrays, StringTokenizer, Interface, ListIterator, Set
java.text	NumberFormat
java.io	File, FileWriter, PrintWriter, IOException

****

(Before proceeding, the reader might want to first read Appendix X concerning the compiling and execution of classes from a command line prompt. That knowledge is assumed in much of the following discussion.)

Why we have packages:
Now we come to the task of understanding what "packages" really are and how to create them. Packages serve two basic needs:

1. Packages are a convenient way to organize classes. Simply put, this means we can put **related** classes in the same package. When it is realized that there are thousands of classes, this is not only a convenience, it's a necessity.

2. Packages help us avoid naming conflicts. As new classes are created, it is inevitable that there will be conflicts with some of the thousands of existing classes. Such conflicts are avoided by using the package name as a prefix to the class name (for example, *java.util.Arrays.sort();*, where *java.util* is the package name and *Arrays* is a class inside it.)

Creating a package:
Let's now look at the six steps needed to create a package. For each step, two examples will be given.

1. Choose a **base folder path** under which the package will be stored.

   Example 1: C:\MyBaseFolder

   Example 2: C:\MyStuff\Libraries

2. Create a package name. You want your package name to be unique so that your package/class names will not conflict with others. Simple names may not conflict on your development computer; however, if you distribute your class to the outside world where you have no control, there might be a conflict.

   Example 1: mypackage

   Example 2: cleveland.maplest.smith.bill (Notice multiple parts are separated by dots.)

3. Create a sub folder(s) under the base folder path that matches the package name.

   Example 1: C:\MyBaseFolder\mypackage

   Example 2: C:\MyStuff\Libraries\cleveland\maplest\smith\bill

4. Create your source files and include as the very first noncomment line, a *package* statement. Be sure these files are saved with the *.java* extension.

   Example 1:
   ```
   package mypackage;
   public class Tester
   {  … some code …  }
   ```

   Example 2:
   ```
   package cleveland.maplest.smith.bill;
   public class Test
   {  … some code …  }
   ```

   Source files in which there is no *package* designator are said to be stored in the *default package.*

5. Copy your source file (the text file with extension *.java*) into the package subfolder.

   Example 1: C:\MyBaseFolder\mypackage\Tester.java

   Example 2: C:\MyStuff\Libraries\cleveland\maplest\smith\bill\Test.java

6. Change to the **base folder** and from that position compile the class so as to produce a corresponding *.class* file. The following assumes you are in the "command line prompt" screen via the sequence *Start | Run | cmd* and that the *Path* variable points to the *bin* folder of your Java SDK as described in Appendix X.

Example 1: cd C:\MyBaseFolder (make the base folder the current folder)
javac mypackage\Tester.java (compile)

Example 2: cd C:\MyStuff\Libraries
javac cleveland\maplest\smith\bill\Test.java

How Java finds Classes:
We should now have a package; however, it's useless unless we know how to use it. First, we need to understand how Java finds the classes its needs. The compiler uses a special object called the *class loader* to sequentially locate the classes it needs.

1. The *class loader* first searches for standard Java classes that are a fundamental part of the language.

   Optional packages are sought in the following ways.

2. Next, an extension mechanism is used to look for *.jar* files (bundling several classes) in the *...jre\lib\ext* subfolder of the Java SDK installation. **This is where you should put extra or nonstandard jar files so that your IDE can recognize them.**

3. Finally, if the desired class is not found inside a *.jar* file in the *ext* folder, then the *class loader* searches the *classpath*. The discussion that follows shows how to create a *classpath* so the compiler and JVM (Java Virtual Machine needed at runtime) can locate and use classes within packages we create or otherwise bring in from the outside world.

Creating and using *classpath*:
The *classpath* variable simply does what its name suggests. It provides a path for Java indicating where we are storing our extra classes. There are three ways to use *classpath*:

For each "Example 1" below we will assume that we are trying to compile a class file Called *MyClass1.java* and that it has references to the *Tester* class in the *mypackage* package. Likewise, for each "Example 2" below we will assume that we are trying to compile a class file called *MyClass2.java* and that it has references to the *Test* class in the *cleveland.maplest.smith.bill* package. Also assume that *MyClass1.java* and *MyClass2.java* are in the same folder and that that folder is the current folder.

- Use *-classpath* as a command line option when compiling.

  Example 1: javac –classpath .;C:\MyBaseFolder MyClass1.java

  Example 2: javac –classpath .;C:\MyStuff\Libraries MyClass2.java

  In using the *–classpath* option notice that it is immediately followed by the paths at which the **base folder** of our package is located. Separate the various paths with semicolons. Notice for each example that we are specifying two paths. One is simply a "dot". This indicates the current directory and if not used, the compiler will not see *MyClass1.java* or *MyClass2.java* in the current directory. **Always use the dot**.

- The above technique of using the *–classpath* option can become tedious if used very often during a session in the DOS prompt window. There is a way to enter the class path **just once** and have it persist during the current "command line" session. At the command line prompt, enter the following:

  Example 1: set classpath = **.**;C:\MyBaseFolder

  Example 2: set classpath = **.**;C:\MyStuff\Libraries

  When compiling, all you now have to enter is *javac MyClass1.java* etc.

- Setting *classpath* as just described has the drawback of being only a temporary Environment Variable. It evaporates and is lost as soon as we close the command line window. In Windows 2K and XP there is a way to make it persist even after the computer is turned off and/or restarted. To do this, use the following sequence:

  Start | Settings(skip this step for XP) | Control Panel | System | Advanced Tab | Environment Variables

  Create a new User Variable for <your logon name> called *classpath* with contents equivalent to the **base folder** path:

  Example 1: **.**;C:\MyBaseFolder

  Example 2: **.**;C:\MyStuff\Libraries

  Typically, this takes effect without the necessity of a reboot, but if things don't work immediately, try restarting the computer. If you want this new *classpath* to affect **all users** and if your logon name has Administrative permission, instead, create a new *classpath* variable in the System Variable section with the same contents as above.

  If you created a System Variable, restart the computer. The *classpath* variable should now be in effect and permanent.

Accessing your own packages from within an IDE:
Unfortunately, none of the above techniques allows you to access your own class packages from within an IDE. It will be necessary to make setting from within the IDE to access these outside classes. Look for a Settings, Preference, etc. menu and then usually for a Libraries submenu. Many times the IDE will not call it a *classpath*. All you will need to do is specify the **base folder path** of where your package resides. It is a common mistake to give the full path right down to the class itself. Part of that path is, of course, the package name itself. Just remember to give **only** the base folder path. For our two examples it would be:

Example1: C:\MyBaseFolder

Example 2: C:\MyStuff\Libraries

Notice that this IDE setting typically does not require the "dot" as does the *classpath* variable.

After all this talk about packages you way have wondered where important classes like, for example, those given by java.util.* are located. Search your hard disk for a folder or sub folder matching this package name, and you won't find it. The class must be there somewhere because we use it all the time, but where? It's tucked away along with the bulk of the standard runtime classes in a jar file. Its location is typically:

C:\Program Files\Java\jdk1.5.0_04\jre\lib\rt.jar

If you have Winzip on your computer you can examine the classes inside this or any other jar file.

In summary, a student of Java should be able to look at an import statement such as the following and be able to tell which is the name of the class and which is the name of the package.

```
import java.util.StringTokenizer;
```

For this example, *java.util* is the name of the package and *StringTokenizer* is the name of the class.

Appendix J .....Typical Contest Classes and Interfaces

class java.lang.object

- boolean equals(Object other)
- String toString( )
- int hashCode( )

interface java.lang.Comparable

- int compareTo(Object other)
  //return value < 0 if *this* is less than *other*
  //return value = 0 if *this* is equal to *other*
  //return value > 0 if *this* is greater than *other*

class java.lang.Integer implements java.lang.Comparable

- Integer(int value) //constructor
- intValue( )
- boolean equals(Object other)
- static String toString(int i)
- static String toString(int i, int base)
- int compareTo(Object other) //specified by java.lang.Comparable
- static int parseInt(String s) //Parses the string argument as a signed decimal integer
- static int parseInt(String s, int base) //returns a decimal int (s is expressed in base b)

class java.lang.Double implements java.lang.Comparable

- Double(double value) //constructor
- double doubleValue( )
- boolean equals(Object other)
- String toString( )
- int compareTo(Object other) //specified by java.lang.Comparable
- static double parseDouble(String s)

class java.lang.String implements java.lang.Comparable

- int compareTo(Object other) //specidied by java.lang.Comparable
- boolean equals(Object other)
- int length( )
- String substring(int from, int to) //returns the substring at *from* and ending at *to-1*
- String substring(int from) //returns *substring(from, length( ))*
- int indexOf(String s) //returns the index of the first occurrence of s; -1 if not found
- int indexOf(String str, int fromindex) //returns the index of the first occurrence of of *str*
  // starting at index *fromindex*
- char charAt(int index) //returns the character at the specified index
- int indexOf(int ch) //returns the index of the first occurrence of of thecharacter *ch*
- int indexOf(int ch, int fromindex) // returns the index of the first occurrence of the
  //character *ch* starting at index *fromindex*
- String toLowerCase( ) //converts all characters to lower case
- String toUpperCase( ) //converts all characters to upper case
- String [] split(String regex) //splits String into elements of a String array around matches
  //to the "regular expression" regex

- String replaceAll(String regex, String replacement) //replace all matches to the regular // expression regex with replacement
- String replaceFirst(String regex, String replacement) //replace first matche to the regular // expression regex with replacement

class java.lang.Character

- static boolean isDigit(char ch)
- static boolean isLetter(char ch)
- static boolean isLetterOrDigit(ch)
- static boolean isLowerCase( )
- static boolean isUpperCase( )
- static char toUpperCase(char ch)
- static char toLowerCase(char ch)

class java.lang.Math

- static int abs(int x)
- static double abs(double x)
- static double pow(double base, double exponent)
- static double sqrt(double x)
- static double ceil(double a)
- static double floor(double a)
- static double min(double a, double b)
- static double max(double a, double b)
- static long round(double a)

class java.util.Random

- int nextInt( ) //returns Integer.MIN_Value ≤ int value ≤ Integer.MAX_Value
- int nextInt(int i) //returns 0 ≤ int value ≤ i-1
- double nextDouble( )

interface java.util.List<E>

- boolean add(E x)
- int size( )
- Iterator<E> iterator( )
- ListIterator<E> listIterator( )

class java.util.ArrayList<E> implements java.util.List<E>

(methods in addition to the List methods)

- E get(int index)
- E set(int index, E x) //replace the element at index with *x* and returns old one
- void add(int index, E x) //inserts *x* at position *index* sliding elements right of *index* //forward one position. Adjusts *size.*
- E remove(int index) //removes element from position *index*, sliding elements at //position *index* + *1* and higher to the left. Adjusts *size.*

class java.util.LinkedList<E> implements java.util.List<E>

(methods in addition to the List methods)

- void addFirst(E x)
- void addLast(E x)

- E getFirst( )
- E getLast( )
- E removeFirst( )
- E removeLast( )

interface java.util.Set<E>

- boolean add(E x)
- boolean contains(Object x)
- boolean remove(Object x)
- int size( )
- Iterator<E > iterator( )

class java.util.HashSet<E> implements java.util.Set<E>
class java.util.TreeSet<E> implements java.util.Set<E>

interface java.util.Map<K, V>

- boolean containsKey(Object key)
- Set <Map.Entry<K, V>> entrySet( ) //Returns a set of Map.Entry objects (only //referenced with an iterator)
- V get(Object key)
- Set <K> keySet( )
- Object put(K key, V value)
- int size( )

class java.util.HashMap implements java.util.Map<K, V>
class java.util.TreeMap implements java.util.Map<K, V>

interface java.util.Map.Entry<K, V>

- K getKey( )
- V getValue( )
- V setValue(V value)

interface java.util.Iterator<E>

- boolean hasNext( )
- E next( )
- void remove( )

interface java.util.ListIterator extends java.util.Iterator<E>
(methods in addition to the Iterator methods)

- void add(E x)
- void set(E x)

class **java.lang.StringBuffer**

- StringBuffer append(char c)
- StringBuffer append(string str)
- StringBuffer append(StringBuffer sb)
- int capacity( )
- char charAt(int index)
- StringBuffer delete(int start, int end) //character at index *end* is not deleted

- StringBuffer deleteCharAt(int index)
- StringBuffer insert(int offset, char c) //insert just before index *offset*
- StringBuffer insert(int offset, String s) //insert just before index *offset*
- StringBuffer replace(int start, int end, String replacementString)
  // the substring starting at index *start* and ending with index *end –1* is replaced with
  //*replacementString*
- StringBuffer reverse( ) //for example, changes "Hello" into "olleH"
- int length( )
- void setCharAt(int index, char ch)
- String substring(int start)
- String substring(int start, int end)
- String toString( )

class **java.lang.StringTokenizer**

- StringTokenizer(String(String str)
  /* Constructs a string tokenizer for the specified string. The tokenizer uses the default delimeter set, which is " \t\n\r\f": the space character, the tab character, the newline character, the carriage return character, and the form-feed character. Delimiter characters themselves will not be treated as tokens.*/
- StringTokenizer(string str, String delim)
  /* Constructs a string tokenizer for the specified string. The characters in the *delim* argument are the delimiters for separating tokens. Delimiter characters themselves will not be treated as tokens.*/
- int CountTokens( )
- boolean hasMoreTokens( )
- String nextToken( )
- String nextToken(String delim)
  /* Returns the next string in this string tokenizer's string. First, the set of characters considered to be delimiters by this StringTokenizer object is changed to be the characters in the String *delim*. Then the next token in the string after the current position is returned. The current position is advanced beyond the recognized token. The new delimiter set remains the default after this call. */

class **java.util.Scanner**

- Scanner(InputStream source) //source is normally System.in
- Scanner(File inputFilePathAndName)
- Scanner(String s) //Total of three constructors
- String next( ) //Returns the next String from the current position up to the next delimiter
- String nextLine( ) //Returns the String from the current position to the end of the line.
- double nextDouble
- int nextInt( )
- Scanner useDelimiter(String regex)
- String findInLine(String regex) //Advances position and returns the String found or null.
- boolean hasNext(String regex)
- boolean hasNext( )
- boolean hasNextDouble( )
- boolean hasNextInt( )
- Scanner skip(String regex)
- Sting findWithinHorizon(String regex, int x) //search limited to next x characters

Appendix K .....Exception Classes

Following is a list of some of the exception classes found in java.lang. The indentations are an indication of inheritance with the leftmost of an adjacent pair being the superclass. Beside some of the exception classes are uses and some (but not all) conditions that would cause that exception.

- Exception
  - RuntimeException

    (all below this point are **unchecked** exceptions)
    - ArithmeticException ...division by 0, etc.
    - IllegalArgumentException ...can be used to enforce method preconditions
      - NumberFormatException...illegal conversion of String to numeric
    - IllegalStateException...can be used to enforce method preconditions
    - IndexOutOfBoundsException
      - StringIndexOutOfBoundsException ... index<0 or index>=String length
      - ArrayIndexOutOfBoundsException ... index<0 or index>=array length
    - NullPointerException ...trying to use a variable not referencing an object
    - UnsupportedOperationException

If you are not sure of which of these exception to use, you can always use *RuntimeException* as in the following code:

```
if( ...something bad happens... )
{
        RuntimeException e = new RuntimeException("Your own error message goes
                                                                        here.")
        throw e;
}
```

****

Some subclasses of *IOException* are *EOFException* ... end of file,
FileNotFoundException,
MalformedURLException,
UnknownHostException

All of these are **checked** exceptions.

Appendix L .....An Essay on Interfaces

Students often question the usefulness of Interfaces. This essay presents an interesting point of view and, hopefully, shows their true utility.

What is the physical interface to the various systems of an aircraft that a pilot sees when he sits in the cockpit?

The interface consists of all the instruments, dials, gauges, and controls that a pilot sees in front of him. For example, he doesn't deal directly with the elevator at the rear of the plane…rather the yoke (part of the interface) control circuitry that, in turn, moves the elevator and thus makes the plane go up or down.

Now suppose we are the aircraft manufacturer and we have a number of models that we produce. When a pilot sits in the cockpit of **any** of our models, we want him to see essentially the same interface. In other words, we want the same color scheme, things to be essentially in the same position, and the controls to work basically the same…**we want standardization**. Thus a pilot who has flown one of our models could feel fairly comfortable when moving to another model he has never flown.

How do we make sure all our models have this common interface? We send the specification for what the layout of the cockpit is to our design engineers so they will work this basic design into new models they create.

…. And so it is with software interfaces. We tell the software engineers who create classes for us, the signatures of the methods we want. (We do this by giving them an *interface*.) All we have to do is look at the first line of their class and see if it says *implements*. We need not look further. We are assured that they have implemented every method of the interface we specified… otherwise, their class won't compile.

Thus we see that the *interface* does four things for us:

1. It lets us specify the exact method signatures we want in a class that someone else will design for us… without us having to implement the code.
2. It promotes uniformity if several classes implement this same *interface*… just as the airplane cockpit will be uniform between the various models.
3. We can look at the first line of a class and if it says *implements*, we know the author has implemented **everything** we specified… we have no need to look further in the code to be assured of this.
4. Someone who wants to know how to use a class need not look through what might be thousands of lines of code that make up the class. It would be much easier to look at the *interface* to see how to use the class. Let's say that another way. It's **much** easier to look at the *interface* document to see how we **interface** to the class.

Appendix M .....Input from the Keyboard

From Lesson 7 we learned that the *Scanner* class makes it easy to obtain input from the keyboard. For versions of Java preceding 1.5, use the following somewhat more complicated technique (requires importing *java.io.**).

```
BufferedReader reader = new BufferedReader(new InputStreamReader(System.in));
String s = reader.readLine( );  //Reads in a line of text
```

This code is capable of throwing the checked exception *IOException* so, either handle with *try-catch* or append *throws IOException* to the method signature. The *InputStreamReader* class inputs one byte at a time from the keyboard. *BufferedReader* allows many bytes to be handled as a line of text.

****

For versions of Java preceding 1.5 there is an easier class to use for keyboard input, *TerminalIO*, however, it is not one of the standard Java classes. Below is a website from which *TerminalIO* can be downloaded:

http://www.bluepelicanjava.com/Download_jar.htm (that's an underscore between d and j)

Put this *jar* files in the appropriate folder similar to the following:

C:\Program Files\Java\jdk1.5.0_04\jre\lib\ext

Two popular programming environments, BlueJ and JCreator will both recognize classes within *jar* files placed in this folder. **Do not** place your *jar* file into *C:\Program Files\Java\jdk1.5.0_04\lib\ext*. This is a different, although similarly named folder.

After importing *TerminalIO*, use as follows:

```
KeyboardReader reader = new KeyboardReader( );
int i = reader.readInt( );  //reads in an integer
double d = reader.readDouble( );  //reads in a double
String s = reader.readLine( );  // reads in an entire line of text
```

Appendix N .....Using the BlueJ Programming Environment

The BlueJ IDE (integrated development environment) is a free download at http://www.bluej.org/download/download.html. The following sequence of steps details how to create a BlueJ project and then classes within that project.

Run BlueJ. From the Project menu item choose New Project.

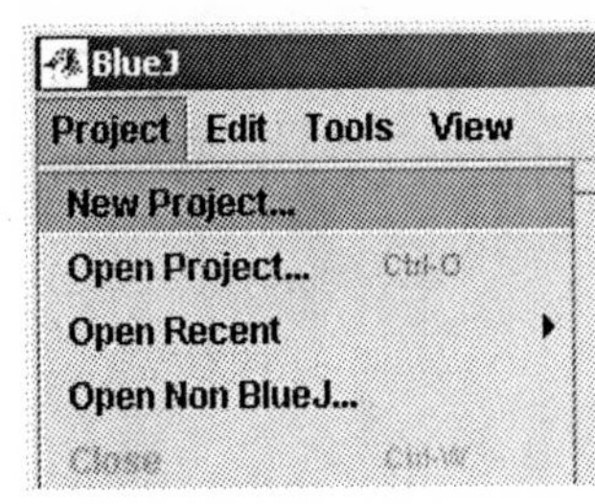

Fig. N-1

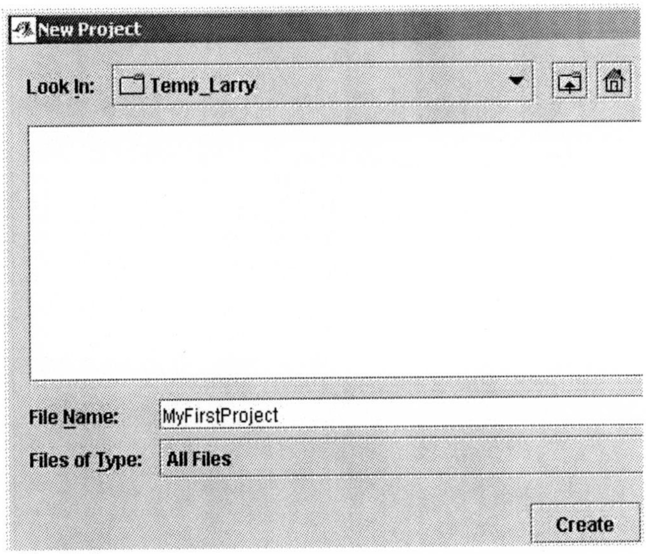

Fig. N-2

Use the Look In control to navigate to the desired location of your project. For this example we chose the folder, *Temp_Larry*.

In the File Name control enter the name of your project. The name in this example is *MyFirstProject*.

Click the Create button.

Your project now exists. You need to add at least one class to the project. To add a class click the New Class button.

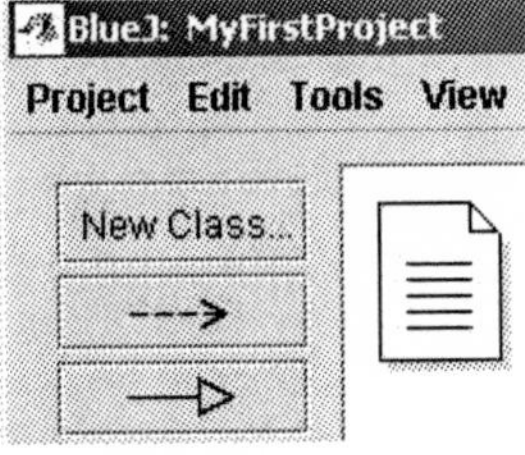

Fig. N-3

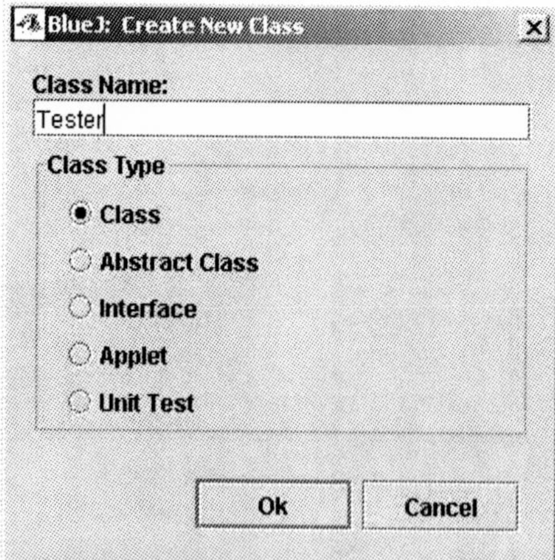

Fig. N-4

Give your class a name in the Class Name control. The name in this example is *Tester*.

Choose any one of the Class Type buttons (typically class). It really doesn't matter which one since your instructor will probably have you wipe out any code it produces so that you can practice entering it yourself.

Click OK.

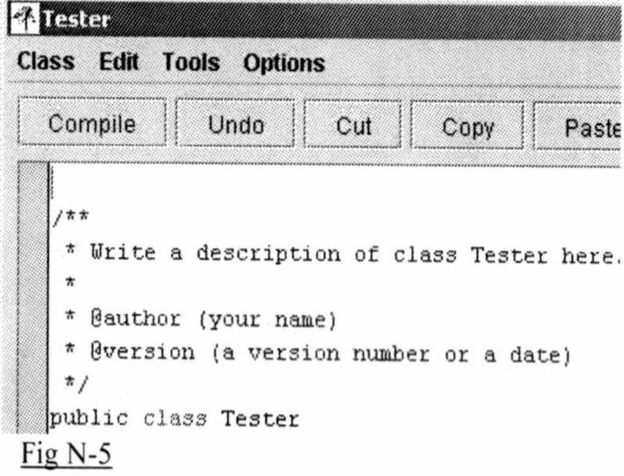

Fig N-5

Enter your code here. (Most instructors will have you delete the preexisting code.)

Click on the Compile button when you have finished entering the code. Any errors you might have made will be detailed at the bottom of this screen.

If you exit the screen just above without a successful compile, the icon for this class will have stripes as shown to the right.

Fig. N-6

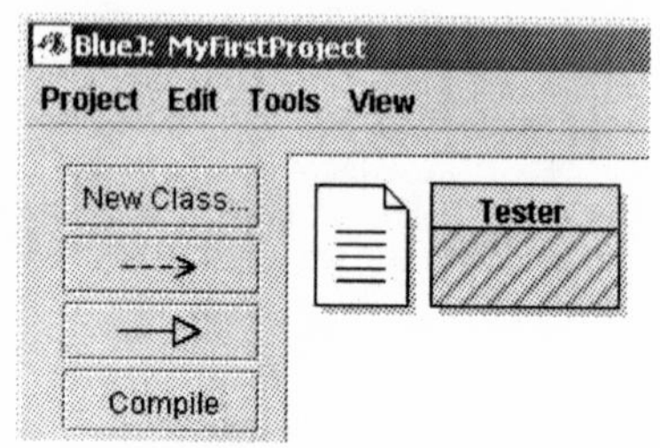

This class icon indicates that it has been compiled successfully (no stripes). To run your program, right-click on this class icon (Tester for this example).

Fig. N-7

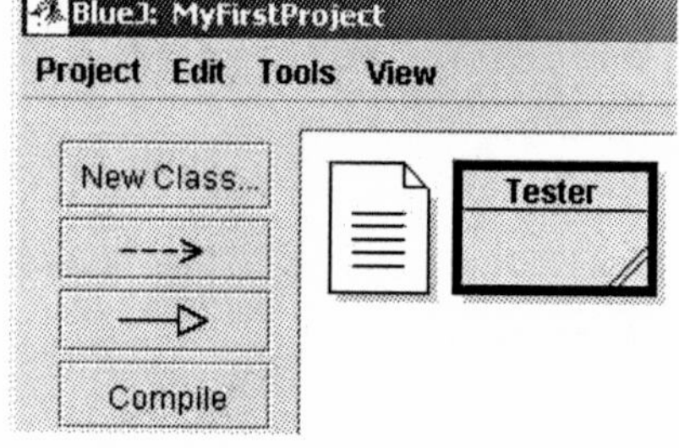

Click on void main(args).

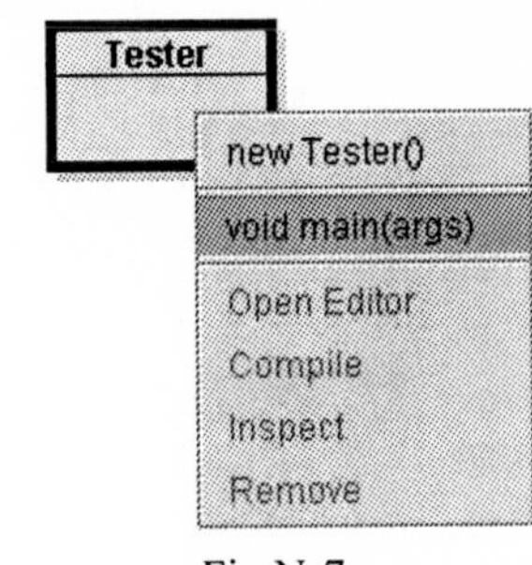

Fig.N-7

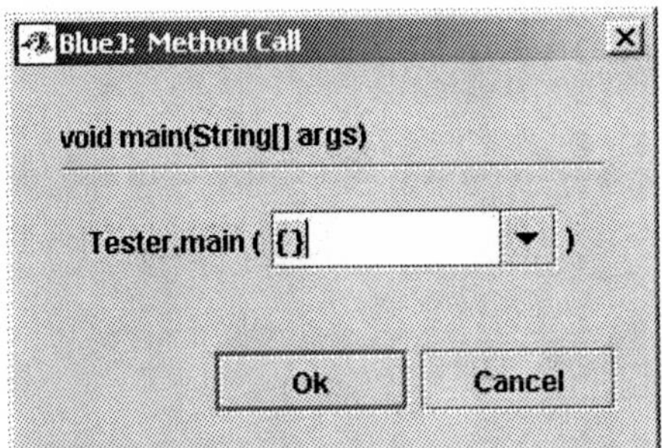

Fig. N-8

Yet another dialog opens. Click on Ok and your program will run.

The Terminal Window pops up to display any output that your program produces. If desired you can close this window after viewing.

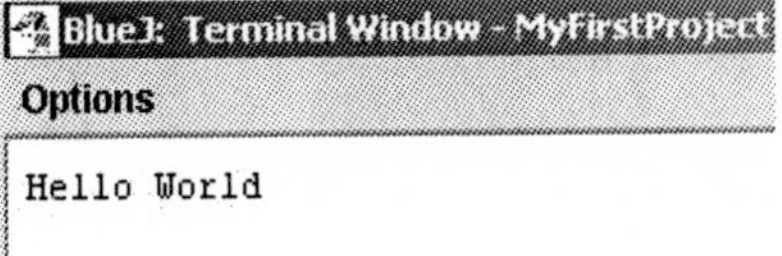

Fig. N-9

See Appendix M for how to make jar files available to BlueJ.

Appendix O .....Using the JCreator Programming Environment

The JCreator IDE (integrated development environment) is a free download at http://www.jcreator.com/download.htm. The following sequence of steps details how to create a JCreator project and then classes within that project.

Run JCreator. From the Project menu item choose New Project....

Fig. O-1

Choose Empty Project and click the Next button.

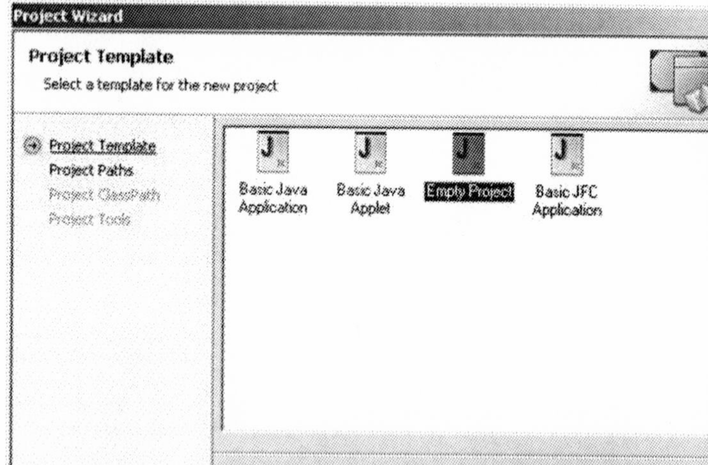

Fig. O-2

In the Name control, enter the desired name of your project. Here, we have chosen the name *MyBigProject*. The **default** values for Location, Source Path, and Output Path are the normal ones you will choose. In this example we have changed these so that everything gets stored in *C:\Temp_Larry*.

Click the Finish button.

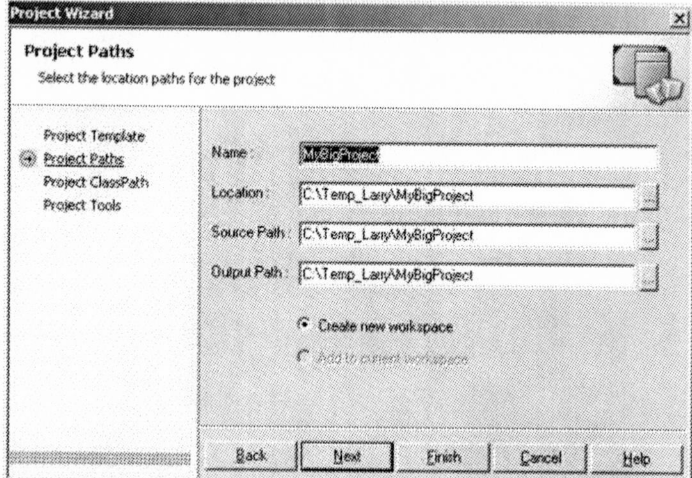

Fig. O-3

Create a new class within your project with Project | New Class. The dialog to the right will pop up.

In the Name control, enter the desired name of your class.

Most instructors will ask that you leave the six check boxes unchecked so that you can later enter the code yourself.

Click the Finish button.

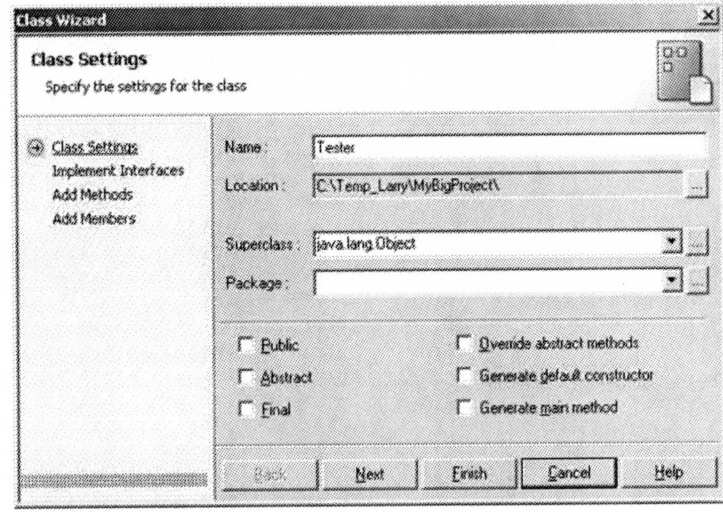

Fig. O-4

In the large area to the far right you can enter your code for this class.

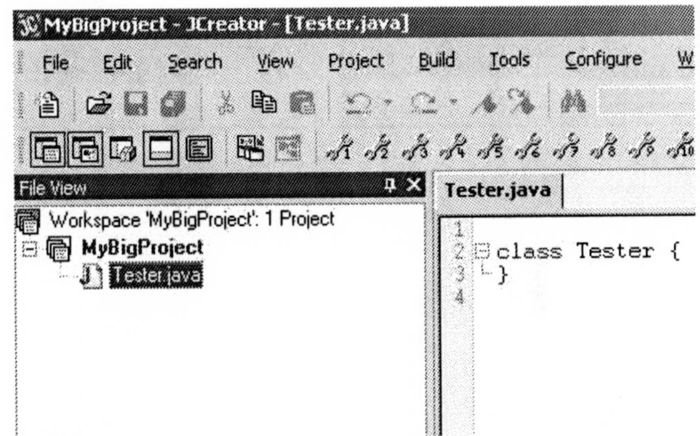

Fig O-5

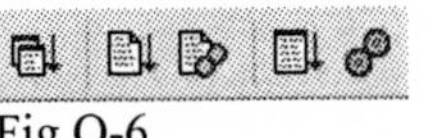

Fig O-6

Use these tools to compile your project and then to execute the code. There are 5 tools here and for reference we will number them from left to right (1 – 5).

1. Batch compile
2. Compile current file(class)
3. Execute the *main* method of the current class
4. Compile all classes in a project
5. Execute project…automatically seeks out the *main* method.

See Appendix M for how to make jar files available to JCreator.

Appendix P ….. Time Allocation for Lessons and Tests

Lesson	Time	Comments
"First day" activities	1 day	Pass out books, demonstrate how to log-on, create project folder, learn how to launch and configure programming environment.
Lesson 1	1 day	Enter the "Hello World" program into the computer and execute.
Lesson 2	1 day	Illustrate each point of Lesson 2 by modifying the code of the "Hello World" program of Lesson 1. Assign the exercise on Lesson 2 as homework. There should be some time to work on this towards the end of the period and time to check answers.
Lesson 3	2 days	Illustrate each point of Lesson 3 by running code. Assign Exercise on Lesson 3. Grade assignment at end of 2nd day.
Test through Lesson 3	1 day	Allow the students to work on the test, take it up at the end of the class, and let them know when them come back the next day they can make any corrections they look up that night. Keep beginning students from becoming discouraged from the start by making this an open-book test.
Lesson 4	2 days	Have the students run many of the code examples in their IDE (integrated development environment) Some of the problems on the exercise must be finished as homework in order to fit this lesson into one day.
Lesson 5	1 day	Run several of the code examples.
Lesson 6	1 day	Run several of the code examples.
Lesson 7	1 day	Do the first project together in class and assign the "Full Name" project as a written assignment. Typical grades range from 92 to 51. Problems 5, 9, 11, 12, 2, and 25 were those most often missed. On the day after the test go over these specific problems.
Test through Lesson 7	1 day	At this point still let the students use the book for the test… try to build up their confidence.
Lesson 8	2 days	Many of the code example need to be run on the computer as they are discussed.
Lesson 9	2 days	Be sure to actually run the first two code examples.
Lesson 10	3 days	Definitely run the code "menu" example.
Test through Lesson 10	1 day	This test may be difficult for some. On the day before the test let the students look over a copy of the test for about 10 minutes so there will be no surprises on the day of the test.
Lesson 11	3 days	This is the most important lesson so far. Be sure to run several of the code examples. This is where we begin to acclimate the students to "contest type problems".
Lesson 12	3 days	Again, run many of the code examples… very important concepts here. After the 14 regular exercise problems are completed, give the 5 "contest type" problems as a quiz.
Lesson 13	2 days	Emphasize the techniques for storing a char into a *String* and vice versa. Have students memorize the ranges of ASCII codes.
Lesson 14	2 days	Use chalk board for demo of conversion techniques.
Test through Lesson 14	2 days	This will be a lengthy test and it is suggested that it not be an open-book test. Many students will need two days. Let the first day be an eye-opener for them so they will study overnight and continue the next day.
Make-up test through Lesson 14 (**Alternate Test through Lesson 14**)	2 days	In order not to discourage students who do poorly on the original test, you might possibly want to give this 16-question re-take. Spend one day correcting the mistakes from the original and then one day taking this new test… The questions on this test are mostly what is likely to have been missed on the original test.
Lesson 15	3 days	Spend time on this lesson! This is the most important lesson so far. Have students enter and test the code for the *Circle* class. There are 20 questions on the exercise for this lesson. If the students do poorly on the exercise there is a "redemptive" quiz that could be given.
Lesson 16	3 days	This is a follow up to lesson 15…very important concepts here.

Test through Lesson 16	1 day	This is primarily a test on objects and classes (lesson 15 and 16).
Lesson 17	3 days	Students will find this much easier than the previous lessons on objects.
Lesson 18	3 days	Let students know that arrays will be used in nearly all future lessons.
Lesson 19	4 days	Be sure to do the programming projects.
Test through Lesson 19	2 days	It is suggested that this test be split across two days. Overnight they can study what they saw on the test and didn't understand.
Lesson 20	2 days	
Lesson 21	1 day	
Lesson 22	1 day	
Test through Lesson 22	2 days	This is a difficult test. Let the students work on it for 30 minutes or so the first day, take it up, let them study overnight, and then finish the second day.
Lesson 23	4 days	Plan to spend 1 day going over the material in the textbook. The second day can be devoted to doing and explaining the exercises. The programming project will also take a complete period if the students are forced to do most of it themselves. The contest type problems will require a day. Some of those problems are tricky and will require some explanation.
Lesson 24	3 days	Many lesson from this point on depend on inputting data from a file. Make sure the students get a good foundation.
Test through Lesson 24	1 day	This test is considerably shorter than the others and probably easier.
Lesson 25	3 days	Honing skills with file input.
Lesson 26	1 day	Actually this lesson can be done in half a period.
Lesson 27	2 days	Be sure students keep the *BaseClass* class. They will paste code from it into many of their future projects.
Test through Lesson 27	1 day	
Lesson 28	3 days	The project in this lesson will take an entire day for most students.
Lesson 29	2 days	
Test through 29	1 day	
Lesson 30	3 days	Be sure to do the Monte Carlo project.
Lesson 31	1 day	Stress the *append* and *toString* methods.
Lesson 32	3 days	DeMorgan's theorem is very important.
Lesson 33	1 day	
Test through 33	1 day	
Lesson 34	2 days	Some important concepts are here.
Lesson 35	3 days	
Test through 35	1 day	
Lesson 36	3 days	This can be done in three days; however, this is such an important lesson that it might be more desirable to allocate 4 days.
Test through 36	1 day	This test focuses strictly on Lesson 36, the inheritance lesson.
Lesson 37	2 days	
Lesson 38	2 days	
Test through 38	1 day	
Lesson 39	2 days	
Lesson 40	3 days	This lesson on recursion is especially important.
Test through 40	1 day	
Lesson 41	6 days	Spend one day for each sorting type.
Test on Lesson 41	1 day	
Lesson 42	1 day	
Lesson 43	3 days	ArrayList. Spend at least one day on the project.
Lesson 44	4 days	Iterators
Test on Lesson 44	1 day	
Lesson 45	3 days	These concepts are very important. Be sure to do all three projects.
Test on Lesson 45	1 day	
Lesson 46	2 days	
Lesson 47	3 days	
Test on Lesson 47	1 day	
Lesson 48	2 days	
Lesson 49	3 days	

Lesson 50	2 days	
Test on Lesson 50	1 day	
Lesson 51	3 days	
Lesson 52	3 days	
Test on Lesson 52	1 day	
Lesson 53	2 days	
Lesson 54	2 days	
Test on Lesson 54	1 day	
Lesson 55	3 days	
Lesson 56	3 days	
Lesson 57	3 days	
Test on Lesson 57	1 day	

See http://www.bluepelicanjava.com/LessonPlans.htm for eventual posting of detailed lesson plans.

Appendix Q ….. AP (A & AB) Correlation

Items on the A and AB Exam	Page numbers
int, double	2-1
+, -,*, /, ++, --, %	4-2
= =, !=, >, <, >=, <=	8-1, 9-1
&&, ||, !	8-1
Casting (int), (double)	5-1
String concatenation	3-1
Escape sequences \”, \\, \n	3-1, C-1
System.out.print( ) and System.out.println( )	1-1, 1-2
One-dimensional arrays	18-1—19-1
Two-dimensional arrays	35-1
if, if/else	9-1
while, do/while	12-1
for	11-1
Design new and modify existing classes	15-1—16-7
return types	15-1
public classes, private instance variables, public and private methods	15-1—16-7
final local variables	5-1
final class, final methods	36-2, 3
static methods	19-3, 20-1
null	Nugs-17
this	36-3, 36-11__36-15, 46-6
super	36-1, 3,7, 36-12—36-15
Constructors	15-1
static variables	20-2
Inheritance hierarchies	36-1—36-15
Modifying and creating subclasses	36-1—36-15
Modifying, creating, and implementing interfaces	38-1—38-8
abstract classes and abstract interfaces	38-1
equals method for objects	9-1, 16-2
= = and != for objects	16-2
Comparison of objects with Comparable.compareTo	45-1
Conversion to supertypes and subtype casts	36-4, 45-3—45-4
Package concepts, creating, importing	7-1, 19-3, I-1, M-1
Exceptions concepts; checked and unchecked	37-1—37-11
String	2-1, 3-1
Math class	6-1
Random class	30-1
Object	36-4
ArrayList	43-1
Wrapper Classes; Double, Integer	21-1
Sorting methods	19-3, 41-1—41-17
List interface	42-1
Set interface	46-1
Map interface	47-1

Appendix R… Texas TEKS Correlation, Computer Science I

Texas TEKS (Knowledge and Skills)	Student Expectations	Page(s)
01. Foundations. The student demonstrates knowledge and appropriate use of hardware components, software programs, and their connections.	A. Demonstrate knowledge and appropriate use of operating systems, software applications, and communication and networking components.	S-4, U-1
01. Foundations. The student demonstrates knowledge and appropriate use of hardware components, software programs, and their connections.	B. Compare, contrast, and appropriately use the various input, processing, output, and primary/secondary storage devices.	S-5
01. Foundations. The student demonstrates knowledge and appropriate use of hardware components, software programs, and their connections.	C. Make decisions regarding the selection, acquisition, and use of software taking under consideration its quality, appropriateness, effectiveness, and efficiency.	14-4, U-1
01. Foundations. The student demonstrates knowledge and appropriate use of hardware components, software programs, and their connections.	D. Delineate and make necessary adjustments regarding compatibility issues including, but not limited to, digital file formats and cross platform connectivity.	E-2, T-2
01. Foundations. The student demonstrates knowledge and appropriate use of hardware components, software programs, and their connections.	E. Differentiate current programming languages, discuss the use of the languages in other fields of study, and demonstrate knowledge of specific programming terminology and concepts.	V-1, V-2
01. Foundations. The student demonstrates knowledge and appropriate use of hardware components, software programs, and their connections.	F. Differentiate among the levels of programming languages including machine, assembly, high-level compiled and interpreted languages.	V-1, V-2
01. Foundations. The student demonstrates knowledge and appropriate use of hardware components, software programs, and their connections.	G. Demonstrate coding proficiency in a contemporary programming language.	Lessons 1 - 48
02. Foundations. The student uses data input skills appropriate to the task.	A. Demonstrate proficiency in the use of a variety of input devices such as keyboard, scanner, voice/sound recorder, mouse, touch screen, or digital video by appropriately incorporating such components into the product.	7-1, 45-5, U-1
02. Foundations. The student uses data input skills appropriate to the task.	B. Use digital keyboarding standards for the input of data.	1-1, 7-1
03. Foundations. The student complies with the laws and examines the issues regarding the use of technology in society.	A. Discuss copyright laws/issues and model ethical acquisition and use of digital information, citing sources using established methods.	T-2
03. Foundations. The student complies with the laws and examines the issues regarding the use of technology in society.	B. Demonstrate proper etiquette and knowledge of acceptable use policies when using networks, especially resources on the Internet and intranet.	T-2
03. Foundations. The student complies with the laws and examines the issues regarding the use of technology in society.	C. Investigate measures, such as passwords or virus detection/prevention, to protect computer systems and databases from unauthorized use and tampering.	47-2, T-2
03. Foundations. The student complies with the laws and examines the issues regarding the use of technology in society.	D. Discuss the impact of computer programming on the World Wide Web (WWW) community.	36-5, V-1
04. Information acquisition. The student uses a variety of strategies to acquire information from electronic resources, with appropriate supervision.	A. Use local area networks (LANs) and wide area networks (WANs), including the Internet and intranet, in research and resource sharing.	U-1
04. Information acquisition. The student uses a variety of strategies to acquire information from electronic resources, with appropriate supervision.	B. Construct appropriate electronic search strategies in the acquisition of information including keyword and Boolean search strategies.	8-1, 8-3
05. Information acquisition. The student acquires electronic information in a variety of formats, with appropriate supervision.	A. Acquire information in and knowledge about electronic formats including text, audio, video, and graphics.	14-4, E-1, E-2, E-3

05. Information acquisition. The student acquires electronic information in a variety of formats, with appropriate supervision.	B. Use a variety of resources, including foundation and enrichment curricula, together with various productivity tools to gather authentic data as a basis for individual and group programming projects.	14-4, U-1
05. Information acquisition. The student acquires electronic information in a variety of formats, with appropriate supervision.	C. Design and document sequential search algorithms for digital information storage and retrieval.	39-3, 41-2, 47-1
06. Information acquisition. The student evaluates the acquired electronic information.	A. Determine and employ methods to evaluate the design and functionality of the process using effective coding, design, and test data.	7-3, 11-5, 15-8, 16-6, 17-6, 23-5, 24-5
06. Information acquisition. The student evaluates the acquired electronic information.	B. Implement methods for the evaluation of the information using defined rubrics.	U-1
07. Solving problems. The student uses appropriate computer-based productivity tools to create and modify solutions to problems.	A. Apply problem-solving strategies such as design specifications, modular top-down design, step-wise refinement, or algorithm development.	27-3, 27-4, L-1, 25-6, 30-6
07. Solving problems. The student uses appropriate computer-based productivity tools to create and modify solutions to problems.	B. Use visual organizers to design solutions such as flowcharts or schematic drawings.	48-1, 48-2
07. Solving problems. The student uses appropriate computer-based productivity tools to create and modify solutions to problems.	C. Develop sequential and iterative algorithms and code programs in prevailing computer languages to solve practical problems modeled from school and community.	25-6, 26-2, 27-4, 38-7
07. Solving problems. The student uses appropriate computer-based productivity tools to create and modify solutions to problems.	D. Code using various data types.	2-1, 8-1, 10-1, 18-1, D-1
07. Solving problems. The student uses appropriate computer-based productivity tools to create and modify solutions to problems.	E. Demonstrate effective use of predefined input and output procedures for lists of computer instructions including procedures to protect from invalid input.	37-1, 38-1, 42-1
07. Solving problems. The student uses appropriate computer-based productivity tools to create and modify solutions to problems.	F. Develop coding with correct and efficient use of expressions and assignment statements including the use of standard/user-defined functions, data structures, operators/proper operator precedence, and sequential/conditional/repetitive control structure.	4-1, 6-1, 8-1, 9-1, 10-1, 12-1, H-1
07. Solving problems. The student uses appropriate computer-based productivity tools to create and modify solutions to problems.	G. Create and use libraries of generic modular code to be used for efficient programming.	6-1, 19-3, 21-1, 23-1, 31-1, 37-1, 46-1, 47-1
07. Solving problems. The student uses appropriate computer-based productivity tools to create and modify solutions to problems.	H. Identify actual and formal parameters and use value and reference parameters.	15-2, 15-3, 34-1
07. Solving problems. The student uses appropriate computer-based productivity tools to create and modify solutions to problems.	I. Use control structures such as conditional statements and iterated, pretest, and posttest loops.	9-1, 10-1, 11-1, 12-1
07. Solving problems. The student uses appropriate computer-based productivity tools to create and modify solutions to problems.	J. Use sequential, conditional, selection, and repetition execution control structures such as menu-driven programs that branch and allow user input.	9-1, 7-1, 10-1,
07. Solving problems. The student uses appropriate computer-based productivity tools to create and modify solutions to problems.	K. Identify and use structured data types of one-dimensional arrays, records, and text files.	18-1, 19-1, 24-1, F-1
08. Solving problems. The student uses research skills and electronic communication, with appropriate supervision, to create new knowledge.	A. Participate with electronic communities as a learner, initiator, contributor, and teacher/mentor.	36-5, U-1
08. Solving problems. The student uses research skills and electronic communication, with appropriate supervision, to create new knowledge.	B. Demonstrate proficiency in, appropriate use of, and navigation of LANs and WANs for research and for sharing of resources.	47-2, T-2, U-1

08. Solving problems. The student uses research skills and electronic communication, with appropriate supervision, to create new knowledge.	C. Extend the learning environment beyond the school walls with digital products created to increase teaching and learning in the foundation and enrichment curricula.	14-4, U-1
08. Solving Problems. The student uses research skills and electronic communication, with appropriate supervision, to create new knowledge.	D. Participate in relevant, meaningful activities in the larger community and society to create electronic projects.	36-5, U-1
09. Solving problems. The student uses technology applications to facilitate evaluation of work, both process and product.	A. Design and implement procedures to track trends, set timelines, and review/evaluate progress for continual improvement in process and product.	39-1, 41-2, 41-4, 41-6, 41-9
09. Solving problems. The student uses technology applications to facilitate evaluation of work, both process and product.	B. Use correct programming style to enhance the readability and functionality of the code such as spacing, descriptive identifiers, comments, or documentation.	1-2, 2-2, 15-1
09. Solving problems. The student uses technology applications to facilitate evaluation of work, both process and product.	C. Seek and respond to advice from peers and professionals in delineating technological tasks.	36-5, U-1
09. Solving problems. The student uses technology applications to facilitate evaluation of work, both process and product.	D. Resolve information conflicts and validate information through accessing, researching, and comparing data.	45-1, 45-5, U-1
09. Solving Problems. The student uses technology applications to facilitate evaluation of work, both process and product.	E. Create technology specifications for tasks/evaluation rubrics and demonstrate that products/product quality can be evaluated against established criteria.	14-4, U-1
10. Communication. The student formats digital information for appropriate and effective communication.	A. Annotate coding properly with comments, indentation, and formatting.	1-2, 2-2, 27-3
10. Communication. The student formats digital information for appropriate and effective communication.	B. Create interactive documents using modeling, simulation, and hypertext.	9-3, 11-5
11. Communication. The student delivers the product electronically in a variety of media, with appropriate supervision.	A. Publish information in a variety of ways including, but not limited to, printed copy and monitor displays.	14-4, U-1
12. Communication. The student uses technology applications to facilitate evaluation of communication, both process and product.	B. Seek and respond to advice from peers and professionals in evaluating the product.	36-5, U-1
12. Communication. The student uses technology applications to facilitate evaluation of communication, both process and product.	C. Debug and solve problems using reference materials and effective strategies.	14-4, A-1 – U-1

Appendix S ..... A History of Computers

What was the first computer and who built it? Depending on who you ask, you will likely get a variety of answers. Frenchman Blaise Pascal built a gear-driven counting machine in 1642 when he was only eighteen years old. His machine could only add and subtract; however, it was revolutionary for its time. Pascal went on to make numerous contributions to the field of mathematics.

In the early 1820's Charles Babbage, an Englishman, began his "Difference Engine" and worked on it for ten years before abandoning it for a much better design, the "Analytical Engine". Due to a lack of funding and the inability of the technology of the times to produce parts to exacting tolerances, neither of these mechanical machines was ever completely finished. It is widely acknowledged today that they would have worked.

Fig S-1. Part of Babbage's Difference Engine.

Babbage enlisted the help of Ada Lovelace, daughter of English poet Lord Byron, to devise ways to program this first general-purpose (although non-existent) computer. Actually, her role was mostly in the generation of publicity for his projects. There is a computer language named ADA in honor of this first programmer. The language was originally mandated for use in U.S. military equipment, but never received widespread acceptance by the general programming community.

Fig S-2.The ENIAC in operation. This photo shows about half of the machine.

During World War II the U.S. military was in dire need of a better and faster way of creating "trajectory tables" for its various big guns. These tables, each calculated by hand, required many hours of tedious work by teams of mathematicians. The calculations took into account the angle of the gun, wind speed and direction, temperature, barometric pressure, humidity, and type of shell. With an increasing number of new types of guns and shells being produced, those human "computers" as they were called, were simply overwhelmed. A newer, faster method was badly needed.

Out of this necessity was born the first electronic digital computer, the ENIAC. It was finally finished in 1946 (the war was over by then) and was a monster consisting of 19,000 vacuum tubes and 1,500 relays. It completely occupied a large room, weighed several tons, and consumed enough electricity to power a small town. Unfortunately, because of the unreliability of vacuum tubes, it was in constant need of repair. In spite of this, it was still one of the most valuable assets of the U.S. in the early days of the cold war with the Soviet Union.

Few people today would recognize the ENIAC as a computer. It had no "keyboard" and no "screen" and was programmed by rewiring ("hard-wiring" as evidenced by the patch cords in Fig. S-2) the machine and flipping large arrays of switches. This was a time consuming, tedious task that resulted in many "programming" errors.

It was John von Neuman who suggested that hard wiring be abandoned and for the computer's program to be stored in memory along with the data. This was a radical idea for its day, but the technique is still used in modern computers. Von Neuman was considered by many colleagues to be the "smartest man" of the twentieth century and there are many anecdotes of his amazing mental abilities to support that belief.

At the time the ENIAC was being developed, a young Navy Lieutenant, Grace Hopper, became involved with the ENIAC and related projects. She was one of the first to program electronic digital computers. In fact, she coined the phrase "computer bug." It seems that her group's computer malfunctioned and a moth was discovered with its wing blocking the contacts of a relay. After that, whenever a program did something unexpected she would quip, "Must be a bug in the machine," and the term stuck.

Fig. S-3. Grace Hopper was the oldest person in the Navy at her time of retirement in 1986 near the age of 80. She was a frequent guest on TV shows where she handed our her trademark "nanoseconds".

Grace Hopper was a national treasure and recognizing this, the Navy allowed her to stay on active duty well past the mandatory retirement age of 65. She was 80 when she retired in 1986. She had appeared on many TV shows, including two appearances on CBS's 60 Minutes. She always responded to a greeting from hosts with, "Here, have a nanosecond" (a nanosecond is one billionth of a second) while handing them a piece of wire just a little shorter than a foot. That was her trademark and was her way of introducing a discussion of computer technology. She would explain that the speed of electrical devices is inherently limited since electrical signals take approximately a nanosecond to travel the length of the wire. She would point out that that's one of the reasons for miniaturization.

"Amazin Gracie" (as she was reverently referred to) always spoke her mind and never avoided controversy. She was slightly abrasive, a chain smoker, and most memorable, a brilliant conversationalist. Her programming abilities should not be overlooked, however. In her early days she was noted for her development of one of the first compilers.

Your author had a chance encounter with "Amazin Gracie" in 1986 just shortly before her retirement. I was returning with my family from a vacation and had a lengthy 6 hour lay-over at DFW airport in Texas before catching our final flight back to Corpus Christi, Tx. Killing time by watching the throngs of people hurrying by, I noticed a diminutive elderly lady in a Navy uniform slowly trudging along carrying two heavy bags that were nearly dragging the floor. I recognized her instantly and decided to offer to help her with the bags. I approached her with, "Excuse me, ma'am, are you Grace Hopper?" She initially said nothing, set down her bags, reached into her purse, and said, "Here, have a nanosecond." Well, I nearly died right there. Before I could compose myself a number of other people recognized her and she was mobbed, all the while graciously handing out "nanoseconds". So, my encounter with Grace was cut short…or, so I thought as I watched her slowly make her way down the concourse and out of sight, but I was happy. I had my "nanosecond".

Time passed and with about an hour before the departure of our flight, we moved to the seating area of our gate. Guess who was already there waiting for the same flight? There she was smoking one cigarette after another. She invited me to sit with her and we chatted for the better part of an hour. I was privileged to hear several interesting stories about the early development of the computer. She had opinions on just about every thing including tactics of the British Navy in the recently completed Falklands war with Argentina. I mostly just listened and consider that hour as one of my favorite memories. The "nanosecond" wire was and continues to be a prized possession. It was the best vacation I ever had.

Fig S-4. Grace Hopper's "bug" preserved in the Smithsonian Institute in Washington D.C.

The first commercially available personal computer was the MITS Altair. Its heyday was from the mid to late 1970's and would not have been recognized as a computer by most people today. It had **no keyboard** and **no screen**. Input was done in a binary fashion with switches. A switch in the "up" position was considered a "1" and "down" was a "0". Output was done by manually reading a series of lights. If a light was "on", that indicated a "1", etc. The Altair was initially available only as a kit and had to be assembled by the purchaser. Consequently, it was mostly only electronic enthusiasts that bought these machines.

Fig S-5. The MITS Altair

Fig. S-6. Bill Gates

Bill Gates, one of the world's richest men, arrived on the scene along with the Altair as a penniless, nerdy, college dropout when he was hired to write software for the Altair. Gates then went on to found Microsoft, a company that eventually became one of the world's largest corporations.

In the early 1980's Gates and the fledgling Microsoft company were fortuitously hired by the giant mainframe computer company, IBM, to write an operating system for the new IBM PC. The operating system was called MS-DOS and prevailed as "the" operating system until the advent of Windows in the early 1990's.

What is an "operating system"? The operating system is the underlying software that makes the computer operate. For example, when you do something as simple as type on the keyboard, some type of software must process that input, send it to the right place, and then create the appropriate response. Mouse input, network activity, screen output, and a host of other things are also fundamentally handled by the operating system. A big responsibility of the operating system is managing input and output (I/O) relative to the various disks in the computer. In fact, one of the first operating system for a PC was (MS-DOS), where DOS stands for "disk operating system". The old DOS based operating systems were "character" based with regard to their screen displays. In those systems a hardware ROM (read only memory) processed each character to be displayed and then generated the appropriate dots (pixels). It was this electronic ROM and associated circuitry that ultimately turned on and off the pixels on the screen.

Contrast this to the more modern GUI operating systems. (GUI mean graphical User Interface.) The Apple Macintosh had the first GUI system. Microsoft's version of the GUI is called Windows and has evolved from Windows 3.0, Windows 95, Windows 98, Windows Millennium, Windows NT, Windows 2000, into finally Windows XP at the time of this writing. (Stay tuned for more to come.)

The GUI is not character based, rather, it is graphics based. Software generates the "dots" (pixels) that make up absolutely everything on the screen. Every time the view on a screen changes the computer has to manage every single pixel as to its position and its color. This puts a tremendous strain on the system since for a moderately high resolution screen (1024 pixels across by 768 pixels down) there are 786,432 pixels. This is why it's desirable to have as fast a computer as possible. It should be mentioned that much of this burden is handled by specialized graphics circuitry rather than the CPU (central processing unit) itself.

In the early days of the PC (late 1970's and early 1980's) the major players were Radio Shack, Apple, and IBM. It is interesting to note that at the time of this writing, (2004) none of these companies are among the top three computer vendors. Those spots are reserved for Dell, Compact, and Gateway.

Fig S-7. Radio Shack TRS 80 III

The Radio Shack TRS 80 Model III was very popular in the early 1980's. It featured a "complete package" in that the computer, disk drives, and keyboard were all integrated into a single package. It had the limitation of not being able to "add-on". No slots were available.

Fig S-8. Apple IIe

The Apple IIe was huge seller in the 1980's and had slots into which third-party circuit boards could be inserted. This spawned an industry of third-party add-on products for this machine.

Fig S-9. Steve Wozniak (left) and Steve Jobs

The story of the Apple computer is truly a Cinderella story. Two Steve's (Steve Jobs and Steve Wozsanic) developed the first Apple in a garage on a shoe-string budget. Jobs is still at the head of Apple and had the business acumen to lead the company to success. The other Steve, "The Woz" as he is called, was an electronics genius, and in the early days, confounded the "experts" by developing a floppy disk drive that was simple and inexpensive to manufacture. This, together with the Apple's color graphics, made it an instant hit.

The awkward time of computing was between the development of ENIAC (mid to late 1940's(and the development of the modern modern PC (late 1970's to present). In the 1960's and 1970's an education in computer science involved the entry of programs via a key-punch system. This involved a machine of about the same weight as a refrigerator that punched holes in cardboard "IBM cards". Another machine, a card reader, typically the size of two refrigerators, read the holes and sent the appropriate messages to the computer. The computer itself was usually housed behind glass walls where white-coated attendants did its bidding.

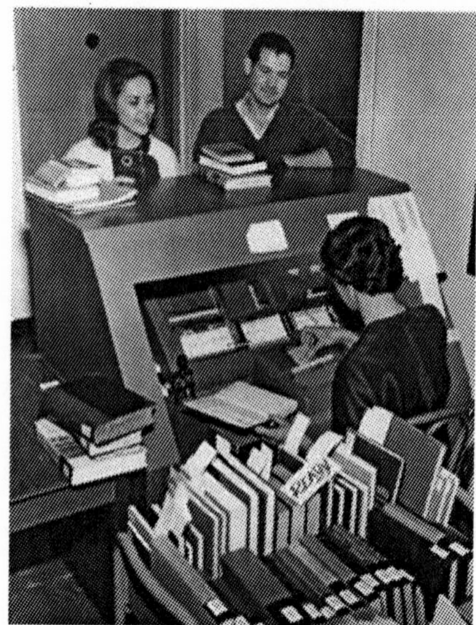

Fig S-10. A key-punch machine

What you as a Java programmer would consider one line of code was all that would go on a single card. Your "program" was then a stack of these cards. Perish the thought that you would get your stack out of order!

Jokes of that era often included the punch line, "Do not bend, spindle, fold, or mutilate." This admonition often accompanied IBM cards containing data. The card readers would often get confused if the cards were damaged in any way.

Fig S-11. A punch card (approximately 8" X 3")

Punch cards were never used with the PC. With the advent of the PC in the late 1970's, data was consistently being stored on disk. First, there were floppy disks. They went through an evolution in which a large 5.25" floppy (they were truly floppy then if you waved them around) held only 160kb (kb means kilobyte; 1,000 bytes) of memory. Floppies today are 3.5" across and hold 1.4mb (1,400,000 bytes).

Fig S-12. Old style floppy (left) and modern version

Hard disks are the main storage devices on computers and have also gone through quite an evolution. In the early 1980's a hard disk having a storage capacity of only one megabyte (10^6 bytes) cost $2000. Today, hard disks having a storage capacity of 100gb (gb means gigabyte; 10^9 bytes) cost around $150.

Appendix T ..... Viruses

Plain and simple, the act of creating a virus is an act of vandalism. It is an intentional, malicious act with the end result being the destruction of data on the target machine or the disruption of services. Since it is a crime, several hackers who have created viruses have been prosecuted and handed stiff prison sentences.

What is a virus?
A computer virus is basically a program that runs just like your own Java code. Whereas your Java code does something useful (hopefully), virus code does something destructive, or at the very least, something disruptive or annoying. All viruses have two basic features:

- They have the ability to replicate themselves, i.e. to place copies of themselves onto other disks, email, or the Internet.
- They contain a "payload", i.e. the ability to perform some harmful, disruptive, or annoying action.

What are the methods by which viruses are spread?

- Floppy disks... inserting an infected floppy into a disk drive
- Email...opening an infected email
- Internet... opening infected pages on the Internet
- Network... just having your computer connected to an unprotected network poses a risk.

What are the various categories of viruses?
At last count in 2003, there were over 80,000 known types of viruses. They break down into the following categories:

- Trojan horse viruses... This type of virus masquerades as a benign application. In the strictest sense they are not viruses since they do not replicate; however, they can be just as destructive.
- Macro viruses... These viruses use another application's programming language to replicate and do their mischief. Microsoft Word and Excel documents are popular targets for such viruses.
- Boot sector viruses... These viruses reside in the boot sector or partition table of a disk. Infection occurs when a computer is booted from a floppy having a boot sector virus.
- Internet worms... These viruses are complete, self-contained programs that are able to replicate copies of themselves to other computers. The spread of these viruses is typically done through network connections and/or email.
- File viruses...These viruses infect executable programs (typically, files with extension .com or .exe). The action of these viruses is to replicate and spread by infecting other host programs. They often overwrite a host program and destroy parts of the original code.
- Email hoax... Strictly speaking, these are not viruses but are often referred to as such. A typical email hoax message will say something like, "I may have accidentally sent you a virus in my last email. Delete such-and-such file from your hard drive to remove the virus". If you follow this advice and delete the file, you will likely do permanent damage to your operating system.

How can we protect against viruses?

- Have anti-virus software installed on your computer and/or servers in your LAN (local area network).

- To stop MS Word macro viruses, use .rtf (rich text files) instead of .doc files when using Microsoft Word. An RTF file preserves all text formatting but does not contain macros.
- To stop MS Excel macro viruses, use .csv files rather than .xls files. CSV files preserve all formatting of the spreadsheet but do not contain macros.
- Do not open suspicious emails.
- Do not allow the sending or receiving of .exe or .com files as attachments to emails. A better solution is to use ZIP software to send these files as attachments. The receiving end can use PKUNZIP to unzip the file.
- Change the boot sequence on your PC so that the hard drive boots first instead of the floppy. This prevents floppies infected with boot sector viruses from infecting the computer.
- If Windows Scripting Host (WSH) is not used, it should be turned off.

Computer ethics and etiquette:

It is unethical to produce and/or distribute computer viruses; besides, it's against the law. There are some other things that we should also be mindful of when dealing with computers, computer data, networks, and the Internet:

- Don't plagiarize other's work, whether it is data or code. Always receive permission and credit any work that originates from others.
- Don't use computer resources without permission.
- Keep your own work and data secure so as not to present a temptation to others.
- Obtain permission before using copyrighted materials.
- Don't download music without permission or compensation.
- Don't eavesdrop on the communications of others.
- When standing next to someone in the act of entering their user name and password, always look away as they make these entries.
- Recycle old computers and components that would otherwise be discarded.
- On networks with limited bandwidth, don't "hog" these resources by continually playing music from Internet "radio" stations.
- When you install software, make sure that you adhere to the license agreement.
- Do not steal someone's "identity", i.e., do not pose as someone else in any electronic or other communication.

Appendix U .....Enrichment Activities

Use of LANs and WANs

LAN stands for local area network and WAN stands for wide area network. Likely, in your school you have a LAN. Enlist the help of your instructor in setting up shared folders on various computers and for how to transfer data across the network between computers.

- Investigate the use of passwords.
- Investigate the setting of various levels of permissions.

Using a scanner and OCR software

Prepare a document using any word processor and print it. Use a scanner to produce an image file of the printed document. Then, using OCR (optical character recognition) software turn the image file back into a character based document.

- Investigate the various image formats (jpg, gif, etc) that are most suitable for this task.
- Investigate the use of exotic fonts and report on their effect on the success of the OCR process.
- Write a short essay on the difference between a text based document and an image based document even though they appear identical on the screen.

Software specifications

Pretend that you are a journalist for a technical magazine and that you have been given the assignment of reporting on the various software packages for a Binary File Editor.

- Do a search for "Binary File Editor" on the Internet.
- Prepare a chart of all such products listing the source, features, and costs.
- Prepare a summary of the relative cost-effectiveness of each product. Prepare a rubric as a means of your evaluation.
- Interview other members of your class who are also doing this project and incorporate their advice and opinions on these products into your report.

Publish information

Using the results of the Software specifications project above publish the information in a variety of ways including:

- Web pages (use MS Front Page, etc. to produce pages)
- Printed report
- Screen display
- Posters

Electronic Communities

Do an Internet search for discussion groups and Forums. Find a question-and-answer forum concerning Java. Participate in the forum by:

- asking questions
- responding to questions to which you know the answer

Prepare a report of your forum activities. (Several good java forums exist at http://www.bluepelicanjava.com/forum.htm)

Appendix V …..Computer Languages

We will examine several programming languages here and compare them to Java. First, let's look at a code fragment in Java:

```
for(int j = 0 ; j <= 20; j++)
{
        switch (a)
        {
                case 1:
                        b = 22;
                        break;
                case 4:
                        b =27/(c+1);
                        if (p > = 2)
                        {
                                System.out.println("Answer is " + b);
                        }
                        else
                        {
                                System.out.println("Answer is " + (b * c));
                        }
                        break;
                default:
                        b =19;
        }
}
```

C++

In the C++ (pronounced C plus, plus) language the equivalent code is written as:

```
for(int j = 0 ; j <= 20; j++)
{
        switch (a)
        {
                case 1:
                        b = 22;
                        break;
                case 4:
                        b =27/(c+1);
                        if (p > = 2)
                        {
                                cout << "Answer is " + b;
                        }
                        else
                        {
                                cout << "Answer is " + (b * c);
                        }
                        break;
                default:
                        b =19;
        }
}
```

For this particular example, the only difference is with how we print. To be sure, there are many other differences. In C++ there is no native *String* class; one has to be imported. None of the classes we use in Java are present in C++ although many equivalent classes are provided.

Whereas in Java we import with *import ClassName;* , in C++ the syntax is *#include<ClassName.h>* . And there are many other differences. The creation and use of classes is considered to be more straightforward in Java than in C++.

Visual Basic

Many consider Visual Basic to be the most powerful of all programming languages, as well as the easiest to use. It's only limitation in the past has been that it was strictly intended for the Windows platform. With the advent of VB.net, the distinction between development for Windows, general C++ code, and web applications has blurred. Below is the equivalent VB code corresponding to the previous Java example:

```
For j = 0 to 20
        Select Case a
                Case 1
                        b = 22
                Case 4
                        b =27/(c+1)
                        If p>=2
                                lblBox1.Text = "Answer is " + b

                        Else
                        {
                                lblBox1.Text = "Answer is " + (b * c)
                        }

                Case Else
                        b =19
        End Select
Next j
```

Visual Basic is not case sensitive and requires no semicolons or braces. Most programmers find this very liberating.

Java Script

Java Script is typically used inside web pages. JS code looks just like regular Java except where we use specific commands that relate to items displayed by a web browser. For example, in the code below we recognize it's Java script by the presence of *"JavaScript"*. Notice, that instead of methods, JS has functions. The variable *my_combo* below is a reference to a drop-down list box on a web page and the code in the function responds when a particular item in that list is clicked with a mouse.

```
<Script Language="JavaScript">
<!--
        function GoToDrive(my_combo)
        {
                var game_value=my_combo.options[my_combo.selectedIndex].value
                document.location.href = "Drives.asp?gameId=" + game_value
        }
//-->
</SCRIPT>
```

Assembly and Machine Language
Assembly language is called a low level language. It is "low level" in the sense that it is "closer" to the native language of the microprocessor itself. It is, however, much more difficult and tedious to program than one of the higher level languages like Java or Visual Basic. Following is an example of some assembly language code for the old Apple IIe that used a 6502 microprocessor. More modern assembly languages are more complex but similar.

Memory Address	Machine Code	Assembly Language
0300	A9 12	LDA #$12
0302	A9 34	LDA #$34
0304	A9 56	LDA #$56
0306	EA	NOP
0307	EA	NOP

The program above will successively load the hex values *$12*, *$34*, and *$56* into accumulator *A* and then execute two *NOP*s (no operation). Note that the machine code instruction A9 12 can be written in assembly language as *LDA #$12*. The # sign stands for "immediate mode"; that is, the machine code instruction *A9 12* means "Load accumulator *A* with the hex value *$12*." **Assembly language instructions are easier for a person to understand than the corresponding machine code. However, the microprocessor can only understand machine code.**

A single line of Java code may equate to hundreds or even thousands of lines of machine code. The act of **compiling** our Java programs **converts our code into machine code**.

Compiled versus Interpreted languages
Java is a compiled language, i.e., it is converted into machine code. Once in machine language, **then** we execute the code. To understand what an interpreted language is, let's suppose for a moment that Java is such a language. If this were true, then every time our program runs and encounters, for example, a *println*, then the interpreter would have to look up what this command means from a table of commands. Every single command would have to be "looked-up". Now, suppose we have a loop that executes one million times. Every single command in that loop is looked-up in the table on all one million iterations of the loop. Naturally, interpreted languages are typically very slow.

In the early days of the PC, nearly all languages were interpreted versions of BASIC. If compiled languages are better, why did the industry begin with interpreted ones? The answer lies in the complexity and difficulty of producing a good compiler. It takes dedication and skill far beyond that of the ordinary programmer to produce a good compiler.

Appendix W ….. Tree Definitions

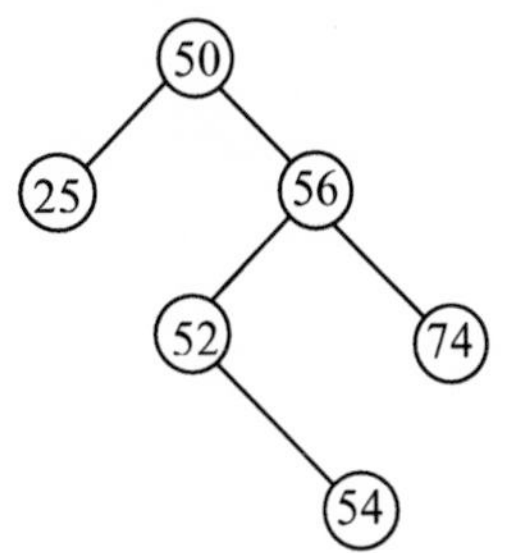

Fig W-1 Tree

If you find the terms tree, root, etc. confusing when trying to compare them to a real, physical tree, you must think of a tree as having its root at the top, and with the tree growing downward.

Such a tree is depicted to the left; in fact, it is a Binary Search Tree. We will use this example of a tree in explaining the definition of tree-terms below.

Tree Terms	Description and examples
Node	An item (data) stored in a tree….50, 25, 56, etc.
Root	Top node in a tree, level 0. It has no parent…. 50.
Parent	The parent of any node is a node one level up and connected to the node. A node has only one parent… 56 is the parent of 74, and 50 is the parent of 25.
Child	The child of a node is one level down and connected to the node… 52 is a child of 56. A node can have at most only two (**hence the term binary tree**) child nodes.
Descendents	The descendants of a node are its children, their children, etc… The descendents of 56 are 52, 74, and 54.
Ancestors	The ancestors of a node are its parent, its parent's parent, etc… the ancestors of 54 are 52, 56, and 50.
Edge/Branch	The line connecting a parent and a child.
Path	A sequence of branches connecting a child down to a descendant.
Path Length	The number of branches in a path…Path length between 50 and 54 is 3.
Depth/Level	The level of a node (depth) is equal to its path length. Thus, the root is at level 0…74 is at level 2.
Height	Height of a tree is the length of the longest path…3.
Leaf	A node that has no children… 25, 74, and 54.
Interior Node	A node that is not a leaf. It has at least one child….50, 56, 52.
Subtree	A tree that results from considering any node (and all its descendants) as a new tree.
Heap	A heap is a binary tree in which each node is greater than its two children. The sample tree above is **not** a heap.
Traversal	The traversal of a tree involves the movement between nodes and the eventual visitation of all nodes. There are four different types of traversal; preorder, inorder, postOrder, and level Order traversals.
Complete Binary Tree	A tree that has no gaps except possibly on the lowest level, and any missing leaves would be confined to the far right side.
Full Binary Tree	A full tree has the maximum number of nodes allowed for its height.

Appendix X .... Compiling and Executing Without an IDE

All of the discussion below assumes that you are using Windows 2K or XP pro. At the end of this appendix, mention is made of how you would adapt the procedures to Windows 98.

The easiest way to compile and then run your Java classes is to use an IDE such as BlueJ, JCreator, etc. It is possible, however, to create your source code, compile it, and run without having any Java IDE on your machine. You must, of course, have downloaded and installed the Java SDK (software development kit) from Sun Microsystems. For the remainder of this discussion we will assume that this has been done and it was installed at the following location on your hard drive:

C:\Program Files\Java\jdk1.5.0_04

If this is not correct for your installation of Java (perhaps as a result of the version number being different), then you will need to make the appropriate adjustments to the paths mentioned below.

Creating a source file:
First, let's create a Java source file for a simple "Hello World" class. Launch the text editor Notepad and enter the text shown below. (Navigate to Notepad via: Start | (All) Programs | Accessories | Notepad)

```
public class Hello
{
        public static void main( String args[] )
        {
                System.out.println("Hello World");
        }
}
```

Before we save this file, let's set up a folder in which to save it. For this discussion, we will assume your name is Larry and that your instructor has you put your files in the folder *C:\Temp_Larry*. Create the sub-folder *C:\Temp_Larry\HelloWorld* and save your file there as *Hello.java*. Get into Windows Explorer and confirm the location and file name. If it was accidentally saved as *Hello.java.txt*, as is often the case, you must rename it to *Hello.java*.

At this point we are going to digress and investigate the contents of the *C:\Program Files\Java\jdk1.5.0_04\bin* folder. It has a number of files in it, but four are of particular interest to us:

javac.exe....... This is a file that will compile our *Hello.java* source file and produce a corresponding class file, *Hello.class* .

java.exe........ This is the file that will "run" the *Hello.class* file and produce output to the console screen.

javaw.exe......This serves the same function as *java.exe* except that it gets rid of the console window while running a GUI application. Any print statements encountered by javaw.exe are simply ignored. (In many cases the console serves only as a debugging aid.)

javaDoc.exe...This file produces web based (html files) documentation. See Appendix AE.

The command prompt:
Now, go to a console screen using the sequence *Start | Run | cmd* . This is typically a black screen with white letters and is known by various names such as "the DOS screen", "the command prompt", "the command line screen", etc.

Change directory (cd):
At this point we are going to issue a *cd* command at the command prompt (the location of the blinking cursor) so as to change the "current folder". This will make it easy for the computer to find the files it needs if we are "parked" in the folder in which those files reside. In other words, the "current folder" is where the computer will first look for files that we enter as part of a command line. The command *cd* means "change directory" (folder). At the command prompt, issue this command:

C:\ > **cd C:\Temp_Larry\HelloWorld** — You enter the bold part. The non bold part is the on-screen prompt.

If all went well, you will see a new command prompt as follows:

C:\Temp_Larry\HelloWorld >_

This indicates that you are, indeed, "parked" in the *HelloWorld* folder where your *Hello.java* source file is located. Thus, when we issue a command that references *Hello.java* the computer will find it.

Compile:
Let's compile our file using the *javac.exe* file in the *bin* folder mentioned above. Here is the command:

C:\Temp_Larry\HelloWorld > **javac Hello.java**

Unfortunately, this won't work because the computer is unable to recognize or find *javac*. It has no idea where to find this file. The following **will** work where we explicitly give the full path to the *javac.exe* file:

C:\Temp_Larry\HelloWorld > **C:\Program Files\Java\jdk1.5.0_04\bin\javac Hello.java**

You can look in the *HelloWorld* folder and see that a new file has just been created, *Hello.class*. This is the result of the compilation. You could, of course, use Windows Explorer to look in the folder, or from the command prompt, you could issue the command *dir* and get a listing of the files. (*dir* means "directory" which is the old-fashioned term for "folder").

Setting a Path:
Entering long path names can become quite inconvenient. If we have much more activity with this session of the command prompt screen, we need a shortcut so as to avoid the necessity of entering these lengthy paths. At the command prompt, enter the *Path* that gives the location of the *javac.exe* and *java.exe* files:

C:\Temp_Larry\HelloWorld > **Path = C:\Program Files\Java\jdk1.5.0_04\bin**

We can now shorten the command necessary to compile our file:

C:\Temp_Larry\HelloWorld > **javac Hello.java**

The file *javac* is now easily found because the *Path* we set tells the computer to look in that folder for any *exe*, *com*, or *bat* files we might subsequently run from this session of the command prompt screen. Now, execute the *main* method in our compiled file by issuing the following:

C:\Temp_Larry\HelloWorld > **java Hello**

Notice in this last command line that we **don't specify the name of the class file** (which is *Hello.class*); rather, we give the **name of the class**, which is just plain *Hello*. The code will execute and any output will appear on the black DOS prompt screen, just as it would in the console window of our favorite IDE.

You should be aware that the setting of the *Path* command only persists while we are in the current session of the DOS prompt screen. If this window is closed and is then subsequently reopened, the setting will be lost.

Setting a permanent Path:
There is, however, a way to make the *Path* setting permanent via the following sequence:

Start | (Settings) | Control Panel | System | Advanced Tab | Environment Variables

Create a new User Variable for <your logon name> called *Path* with value *C:\Program Files\Java\jdk1.5.0_04\bin*. Typically, this takes effect without the necessity of a reboot, but if things don't work immediately, try restarting the computer. This *Path* setting augments the *Path* System Variable. If you want this new *Path* to affect **all users** and if your logon name has Administrative permission, instead, edit the *Path* variable in the System Variable section by appending the following to what it already has:

; C:\Program Files\Java\jdk1.5.0_04\bin

If you set the System Variable, reboot the computer. In either case you will find this new *Path* is now in effect and is permanent.

Related topics:
Two closely related subjects are the creation of packages and the setting of the *classpath* variable. See Appendix I for details on these topics.

A note concerning Windows 98:
All of the above is true with the following three exceptions:

1. Instead of using *cmd* to access the DOS prompt screen, use *command.*

2. Long path or file names (exceeding 8 characters in length) will need to be enclosed in quotes.

3. For permanent *Path* settings you will need to add the desired *Path* to the *Autoexec.bat* file since this cannot be done within the Win 98 System dialog.

Appendix Y… Bytes, Kilobytes, Megabytes, & Gigabytes

Recall from Lesson 14 that computer memory is organized into bytes and that a byte is 8 bits (for example, 10011011). The number of bytes of RAM (random access memory, a computer's main memory) is always given by powers of two. Certain powers of two have been given special names recognized throughout the industry:

Name	Abrev	Actual Number	Power of 2	Approximation
Kilobyte	kb	1,024	2^{10}	1,000 (one thousand)
Megabyte	mb	1,048,576	2^{20}	1,000,000 (one million)
Gigabyte	gb	1,073,741,824	2^{30}	1,000,000,000 (one billion)

Table Y-1

In the chart above, it is the **approximate value** that people normally think of and use most often. It is easier to remember than either the "Actual Number" or "Power of 2".

The following table shows some other common, often used megabyte values.

Name	2^x	Exact Value
16 meagbytes	2^{24}	16,777,216
32 megabytes	2^{25}	33,554,432
64 megabytes	2^{26}	67, 108,864
128 megabytes	2^{27}	134,217,728
256 megabytes	2^{28}	268,435,456
512 megabytes	2^{29}	536,870,912

Table Y-2

Appendix Z… Formatting with the DecimalFormat Class

Use the following test class to demonstrate the abilities of the *DecimalFormat* class. Note the required import.

```
import java.text.*;
public class Formatting
{
        public static void main( String args[] )
        {
                double testNum = 5847.2268;
                String pattern = "##,###.##";
                DecimalFormat df= new DecimalFormat(pattern);

                System.out.println(df.format(testNum)); //5,847.23
        }
}
```

The following table shows the output for various combinations of *String pattern* and *double testNum:*

pattern	*testNum*	**Output**
"###,###.##"	5368.8742	5,368.87
"###,###.##"	5368.876	5,368.88
"###,###.00"	38	38.00
"#,##0.##"	.9881	0.99
"$###,##0.00"	8232.6	$8,232.60
"$###,##0.##"	.9827	$0.98
"$###,##0.##"	.997	$1
"#####00.00###"	3.8749879	03.87499
"##0.##%"	.345667	34.57% (see note below)
"+"	.2245	+0
"+##"	36.889	+37
"##"	36.889	37
"##.##"	-480.0934	-480.09
"+##.##"	-480.0934	-+480.09 (blindly prints +)
"00000.00"	45.97665	00045.97

When using the percent sign, the number is **first** multiplied by 100, and **then** the pattern is applied.

Use the *applyPattern* method in the following way to apply a new formatting pattern **after** a *DecimalFormat* object has already been created.

```
DecimalFormat df = new DecimalFormat("000.##");
System.out.println(df.format(12.7391)); //012.74
df.applyPattern("0,000.00"); //applies a new pattern to the df object
System.out.println(df.format(12.7391)); //0,012.74
```

Appendix AA… Multiplication of Matrices

The use and manipulation of matrices is of great interest in computer science. It is especially useful when working with images where a very common operation is the multiplication of two matrices. In this appendix we will learn how to multiply two matrices (because it's the basis of a project in Lesson 35), but first, let's define what a matrix is:

A matrix is simply a two dimensional array of numbers. Consider the following sample matrix, A.

$$A = \begin{bmatrix} 1 & 2 & -2 & 0 \\ -3 & 4 & 7 & 2 \\ 6 & 0 & 3 & 1 \end{bmatrix}$$

The matrix sample above has dimensions 3 X 4. This means that it has 3 rows and 4 columns. It is conventional to always give the dimension of a matrix in row column (RC) order. Next, let's look at the multiplication of two matrices.

$$\begin{bmatrix} 1 & 2 & -2 & 0 \\ -3 & 4 & 7 & 2 \\ 6 & 0 & 3 & 1 \end{bmatrix} \text{X} \begin{bmatrix} -1 & 3 \\ 0 & 9 \\ 1 & -11 \\ 4 & -5 \end{bmatrix} = \begin{bmatrix} -3 & 43 \\ 18 & -60 \\ 1 & -20 \end{bmatrix}$$

How does it produce the answer matrix on the right? Below, we show how to produce the –3 in the answer:

R=0 **C=0** **R=0, C=0**

$$\begin{bmatrix} \mathbf{1} & \mathbf{2} & \mathbf{-2} & \mathbf{0} \\ -3 & 4 & 7 & 2 \\ 6 & 0 & 3 & 1 \end{bmatrix} \text{X} \begin{bmatrix} \mathbf{-1} & 3 \\ \mathbf{0} & 9 \\ \mathbf{1} & -11 \\ \mathbf{4} & -5 \end{bmatrix} = \begin{bmatrix} \mathbf{-3} & 43 \\ 18 & -60 \\ 1 & -20 \end{bmatrix}$$

Calculate 1(-1) + 2(0) – 2(1) + 0(4) = -3.

Next, we produce the 18:

R=1 **C=0** **R=1, C=0**

$$\begin{bmatrix} 1 & 2 & -2 & 0 \\ \mathbf{-3} & \mathbf{4} & \mathbf{7} & \mathbf{2} \\ 6 & 0 & 3 & 1 \end{bmatrix} \text{X} \begin{bmatrix} \mathbf{-1} & 3 \\ \mathbf{0} & 9 \\ \mathbf{1} & -11 \\ \mathbf{4} & -5 \end{bmatrix} = \begin{bmatrix} -3 & 43 \\ \mathbf{18} & -60 \\ 1 & -20 \end{bmatrix}$$

Calculate -3(-1) + 4(0) + 7(1) + 2(4) = 18.

The 1 in the answer is produced as follows:

$$\underset{R=2}{\begin{bmatrix} 1 & 2 & -2 & 0 \\ -3 & 4 & 7 & 2 \\ \mathbf{6} & \mathbf{0} & \mathbf{3} & \mathbf{1} \end{bmatrix}} \times \underset{C=0}{\begin{bmatrix} \mathbf{-1} & 3 \\ \mathbf{0} & 9 \\ \mathbf{1} & -11 \\ \mathbf{4} & -5 \end{bmatrix}} = \underset{R=2,\ C=0}{\begin{bmatrix} -3 & 43 \\ 18 & -60 \\ \mathbf{1} & -20 \end{bmatrix}}$$

Calculate 6(-1) + 0(0) + 3(1) + 1(4) = 1.

The 43 in the second column of the answer is produced as follows:

$$\underset{R=0}{\begin{bmatrix} \mathbf{1} & \mathbf{2} & \mathbf{-2} & \mathbf{0} \\ -3 & 4 & 7 & 2 \\ 6 & 0 & 3 & 1 \end{bmatrix}} \times \underset{C=1}{\begin{bmatrix} -1 & \mathbf{3} \\ 0 & \mathbf{9} \\ 1 & \mathbf{-11} \\ 4 & \mathbf{-5} \end{bmatrix}} = \underset{R=0,\ C=1}{\begin{bmatrix} -3 & \mathbf{43} \\ 18 & -60 \\ 1 & -20 \end{bmatrix}}$$

Calculate 1(3) + 2(9) –2(-11) + 0(-5) = 43.

The -60 is produced as follows:

$$\underset{R=1}{\begin{bmatrix} 1 & 2 & -2 & 0 \\ \mathbf{-3} & \mathbf{4} & \mathbf{7} & \mathbf{2} \\ 6 & 0 & 3 & 1 \end{bmatrix}} \times \underset{C=1}{\begin{bmatrix} -1 & \mathbf{3} \\ 0 & \mathbf{9} \\ 1 & \mathbf{-11} \\ 4 & \mathbf{-5} \end{bmatrix}} = \underset{R=1,\ C=1}{\begin{bmatrix} -3 & 43 \\ 18 & \mathbf{-60} \\ 1 & -20 \end{bmatrix}}$$

Calculate -3(3) + 4(9) + 7(-11) + 2(-5) = -60.

Finally, we produce –20:

$$\underset{R=2}{\begin{bmatrix} 1 & 2 & -2 & 0 \\ -3 & 4 & 7 & 2 \\ \mathbf{6} & \mathbf{0} & \mathbf{3} & \mathbf{1} \end{bmatrix}} \times \underset{C=1}{\begin{bmatrix} -1 & \mathbf{3} \\ 0 & \mathbf{9} \\ 1 & \mathbf{-11} \\ 4 & \mathbf{-5} \end{bmatrix}} = \underset{R=1,\ C=1}{\begin{bmatrix} -3 & 43 \\ 18 & -60 \\ 1 & \mathbf{-20} \end{bmatrix}}$$

Calculate 6(3) + 0(9) + 3(-11) + 1(-5) = -20.

****

Not all matrices are compatible for multiplication. The following shows the requirements for compatibility as well as a prediction for the dimensions of the product matrix.

$$A_{RC} \text{ X } B_{RC} = C_{RC}$$

C = R

Notice that the number of columns in the A matrix **must equal** the number of rows in the B matrix. The answer matrix (C) will have the same number of rows as the A matrix and the same number of columns as B.

Finally, the reader is reminded that matrices can be represented in Java as two-dimensional *int* arrays as illustrated by the following:

$$A = \begin{bmatrix} 1 & 2 & -2 & 0 \\ -3 & 4 & 7 & 2 \\ 6 & 0 & 3 & 1 \end{bmatrix}$$

In code, enter this matrix as follows:

```
int a[][] = {   {1, 2, -2, 0},
                {-3, 4, 7, 2},
                {6, 0, 3, 1 }   };
```

Appendix AB ... Monospaced Fonts

The following information about monospaced fonts is useful for the "Heap of Trouble" project in Lesson 55.

The Times New Roman font is used to print the following two lines:

....
klmnop

Next, print the same two lines using the Courier New font:

```
....
klmnop
```

Do you see the difference? Notice the space the periods occupy in the top line of each example. Each character in the Courier New font (a monospaced font) occupies **the same amount of horizontal space**. This is characteristic of a monospaced font. Most fonts are not monospaced because for normal word-processing they do not look very professional or pleasing to the eye. Consider the following paragraph in Times New Roman. The paragraph after it is done with Courier New.

> Four score and seven years ago our fathers brought forth on this continent, a new nation, conceived in liberty, and dedicated to the proposition that all men are created equal.

```
Four score and seven years ago our fathers brought forth on
this continent, a new nation, conceived in liberty, and
dedicated to the proposition that all men are created equal.
```

So if monospaced fonts are not as pleasing to the eye, why do we use them? The answer is that they are used for formatting. Suppose we wish to print the following two currency values using Times New Roman.

$147,892.88
$101,111.11

They seem to line up just fine, so what's the big deal? In this case the word processor that produced this document (Microsoft Word) is clever enough to go into a monospaced mode when writing numbers like this. However, when aligning codes as follows, we see the problem.

AIIXIULK-XXBQ
IIIXIUIB-K$%A

Each of the above two lines has the same number of characters before and after the dash. They don't line up with each other. Now, look at the same pair of codes using a monospaced font and we can observe that vertical alignment is maintained.

```
AIIXIULK-XXBQ
IIIXIUIB-K$%A
```

For a table of such codes, the monospaced version is much more pleasing to the eye. Some other monospaced fonts are:

Arial Monospace	Courier	Letter Gothic	Lucida Console
OCR-A	OCR-B	MICR	Typewriter Gothic
Typewriter Elite	Typewriter		

Appendix AC… Regular Expressions

This appendix will only present a cursory explanation of regular expressions. There is much, much more to the grammar of regular expression than will be presented here. The reason for the presentation of regular expressions in this book is for the purpose of understanding the *split* method from the *String* class. Additionally, the *replaceAll* and *replaceFirst* methods (they also use regular expressions) will be discussed here. See Lesson 18 for more on the *split* method. Certain methods of the *Scanner* class also use regular expressions.

Regular expressions describe **character patterns** that aid in the location of **matching text**. A popular program that uses regular expressions is *grep* (which stands for "generalized regular expression pattern"). *Grep* is part of UNIX, but versions do exist for Windows and MacOS.

So, how do we use regular expressions? First, we will show some examples of **general** usages of regular expressions:

Regular Expression	What it Finds
[0-9]+	Find sequences of digits like "183", "2", "19239", etc. It would **not**, for example, find 23,826 in its entirety because the comma breaks the sequence. It **would** find 23 and 826 separately. Notice that "[0-9]" denotes any digit between 0 and 9 while "[0-9]+" means "one or more" occurrence of 0 through 9.
xyz	Find occurrences of "xyz" in the text.
D[J-Zj-z]	Find occurrences of a single "D" followed by a single occurrence of a letter that falls in the range between "J" and "Z" (either upper or lower case).
[4-8][0-5][^B-M]	Find occurrences of a single digit in the range from 4 through 8 followed by another single digit in the range from 0 through 5 followed by a single letter that is **not** in the range from "B" through "M". Notice that the "^" means not.
J.[am]4	Find occurrence of a single letter "J", followed by any single character (the **period** means **any character**) followed by an "a" or an "m" followed by the digit 4.
J\\.[am]4	This means the same thing as the previous expression except \\. means we are looking for a literal period now instead of "any character".
A|b[p-z]	Find occurrences of either the letter "A" **or** the letter "b" followed by any letter in the range "p" through "z". Notice that | means OR.
Fp*[am-z]	Find occurrences of the letter "F" followed by zero or more occurrences of the letter "p" followed by the letter "a" or any letter between "m" and "z". Notice that "*" means zero or more occurrences.
C\s+	Find occurrence of "C" followed by any amount of white space.

Table AC-1 Sample regular expression usage

The following tables expose just some of the grammar used in regular expressions.

Sample Character Classes	Results, Meaning
[xyz]	A single character consisting of “x”, “y”,or “z” (simple class)
[^xyz]	Any character except “x”, “y”, or “z” (negation)
[m-yA-K]	“m” through “y” or “A” through “K”, inclusive (range)
[m-y&&[^xy]]	“m” through “y” except for “x” and “y” (subtraction)
[C-Z&&[^M-R]]	“C” through “Z”, but not “M” through “R” (subtraction)

Table AC-2 Character classes

Predefined Characters	Meaning
.	Any character
\d	A digit: [0-9]
\D	A **non**-digit: [^0-9]
\p{Name}	Matches any character in the named character class specified by *Name*. Supported names are Unicode groups and block ranges. *Name* could be something like *Digit*.
\P{Name}	Matches text **not** included in groups and block ranges specified in *Name*.
\s	A whitespace character: [\t\n\f\r\x0B]
\S	A **non**-whitespace character: [^\s]
\w	A word character: [a-zA-Z0-9]
\W	A **non**-word character: [^\w]

Table AC-3 Predefined character classes

Greedy quantifiers	Meaning
M?	“M”, once or not at all
M*	“M”, zero or more times
M+	“M”, one or more times
M{n}	“M”, exactly n times
M{n, }	“M”, at least n times
M{n,m}	“M”, at least n but not more than “m” times

Table AC-4 Greedy quantifiers

POSIX Character Classes	Results, Meaning
\p{Lower}	A lower-case alphabetic character: [a-z]
\p{Upper}	An upper-case alphabetic character: [A-Z]
\p{ASCII}	All ASCII: [x00-\x7F]
\p{Alpha}	An alphabetic character: [\p{Lower}\p{Upper}]
\p{Digit}	A decimal digit: [0-9]
\p{Alnum}	An alphanumeric character: [\p{Alpha}\p{Digit}]
\p{Punct}	Punctuation: One of !”#$%&’()*+,-./:;<=>?@[\]^_`{|}
\p{Graph}	A visible character: [\p{Alnum\p{Punct}]
\p{Print}	A printable character: [\p{Graph}]
\p{Blank}	A space or a tab: [\t]
\p{Cntrl}	A control character: [\x00-\x1F\x7F]
\p{XDigit}	A hexadecimal digit: [0-9a-fA-F]
\p{Space}	A whitespace character: [\t\n\x0B\f\r]

Table AC-5 POSIX (Portable Operating System Interface for UniX) character classes

Escape Sequence	Meaning
\\	The backslash character
\on	The character with octal value on (0<=n<=7)
\onn	The character with octal value onn (0<=n<=7)
\omnn	The character with octal value omnn (0<=m<=3, 0<=n<=7)
\xhh	The character with hexadecimal value 0xhh
\uhhhh	The character with hexadecimal value 0xhhhh
\t	The tab character ('\u0009')
\n	The new line (line feed) character ('\u000A')
\r	The carriage return character ('\u000D')
\f	The form-feed character ('\u000C')
\a	The alert (bell) character ('\u0007')
\e	The escape character ('\u001B')
\cx	The control character corresponding to "x"
\.	A literal period
\+	A literal plus sign

Table AC-5 Escape sequences used in regular expressions

Double the number of backslashes:
All of the above syntax applies when you are directly using a regular expression compiler (as with the *grep* program). When you use regular expressions in Java you must be aware that the expression will go through **two** compilers. First, the Java compiler is applied and then the regular expression compiler. Each needs its own backslash symbol for any escape sequence that might be in a regular expression. Therefore, in order to indicate, for example, whitespace (\s when used directly with the regular expression compiler) you will need to denote it as "\\s" when used inside Java. Similarly, the escape for a backslash that formerly was "\\" will now need to be "\\\\". Just remember the rule to **double the number of backslashes** in any regular expression you use with Java.

The *split* method:
Now, let's investigate how regular expressions are used with the *split* method of the *String* class. Basically, the *split* method parses a *String* into the elements of a returned array by using delimiters specified by a regular expression parameter. Following is the signature of the *split* method and some sample usage:

Signature:
public String[] split(String regex) //regular expression regex specifies the delimiters

Examples:
```
String s = "Homer Simpson is 51 years    old";
String sp[] = s.split("[0-9]+rs"); //delimiters are "51" and "rs"
        //sp[0] = "Homer Simpson is "
        //sp[1] = " yea"      sp[2] = "    old"
sp = s.split("\\s+"); //contiguous whitespace is the delimiter
        //sp[0] = "Homer"    sp[1] = "Simpson"    sp[2] = "is"    sp[3] = "51"
        //sp[4] = "years"      sp[5] = "old"
sp = s.split("m|p"); //both 'm' and 'p' are delimiters
        //sp[0] = "Ho"    sp[1] = "er Si"    sp[2] = "" (notice sp[2] is a zero length)
        //sp[3] = "son is 51 years    old"
```

sp = s.split(“j”); //sp[0] = “Homer Simpson is 51 years old”

sp = s.split([mnd]); //sp[0] = “Ho” sp[1] = “er Si” sp[2] = “pso”;
//sp[3] = “ is 51 years ol” Notice that the ‘d’ delimiter at the end
//does **not** produce a trailing empty String element.

A technique for understanding *split*:
Following is a suggested technique for recognizing the various elements into which a *String* is *split*. Assume the *String* we wish to *split* is:

s = “ChaveAAA a niceC dayCCC and coACme back sCAAoonCC”;

Here is the *split* statement itself:

String sp[] = s.split(“[AC]+”);

The delimiters will be one or more occurrences of either A or C. It could also be any combination of A and C such as ACCA. This **entire group** (ACCA) would act as a **single** delimiter.

The first thing we need to do is identify all the delimiter “groups” and strike through them as follows:

“~~C~~have~~AAA~~ a nice~~C~~ day~~CCC~~ and co~~AC~~me back s~~CAA~~oon~~CC~~”

Next, put a vertical line (the pipe symbol, |) at the **beginning** (but not the end) of the *String* and consider this a separate delimiter.
“|~~C~~have~~AAA~~ a nice~~C~~ day~~CCC~~ and co~~AC~~me back s~~CAA~~oon~~CC~~”

The separate elements of *sp* are the substrings **between** these delimiters. Notice that the only subtle one is the leading empty *String*. These elements are listed below:

“|~~C~~have~~AAA~~ a nice~~C~~ day~~CCC~~ and co~~AC~~me back s~~CAA~~oon~~CC~~”

“” “have” “ a nice” “ day” “ and co” “me back s” “oon”

A weird exception to the rule:
If multiple delimiters are “bunched” at the end of the *String*, *split* does not produce empty *Strings* between them:

Example:
String s = “Hello good buddybuddybuddy”;
String []sp = s.split(“buddy|\\s+); //sp[0] = “Hello” sp[1] = “good”

Overloaded:
The *split* method is overloaded. Its other signature is:

Signature:
public String[] split(String regex, int limit)
Here, we *split* into **at most** *limit* number of elements.

Other methods that use regular expressions:

The ***replaceAll***, ***replaceFirst***, and ***matches*** methods of the *String* class also use regular expressions:

Signature:

public String replaceAll(String regex, String replacement) //replaces all matches of regex

Example:

```
String s = "The Wright brothers were the first to fly.";
String sr = s.replaceAll("[Tt]he", "Kitty Hawk");
        //sr = "Kitty Hawk Wright brothers were Kitty Hawk first to fly."
```

Signature:

public String replaceFirst(String regex, String replacement) //replace first match to regex

Example:

```
String s = "The Wright brothers were the first to fly.";
String sr = s.replaceFirst("[Tt]he", "Kitty Hawk");
        //sr = "Kitty Hawk Wright brothers were the first to fly."
```

Signature:

public boolean matches(String regex)

Example:

```
String s = "cde code sjsk d d";
if(".*code.*")
        System.out.println("TRUE"); //Prints TRUE
```

Beware of the tricky double backslash:

Consider a problem in which we have a *String* that might look something like the following:

s = "ab?c"

Now suppose that the question mark is to act as a "wild card" in which it can stand for any alphabetical character. Futhermore, suppose that we wish to make a proper regular expression from *s*. Its proper form would be yet another *String* with "?" replaced with "\\p{Alpha}" as follows:

"ab\\p{Alpha}c"

Our task is to take *s* and programmatically change it to this new *String*. One might guess that the way to do this is:

```
s = s.replaceAll("\\?", "\\p{Alpha}");
```

Actually, this is not correct. We must remember that the \\ in the second parameter is part of a *String* and from Appendix B this is simply an escape sequence representing a **single backslash**. The correct syntax is:

```
s = s.replaceAll("\\?", "\\\\p{Alpha}");
```

Appendix AD… *Formatter* Class Specifiers and Flags

Information presented in this Appendix is applied to *Formatter* class objects and to the *printf* method. Both of these are presented in Lesson 27.

Format Specifier	**Applied to**	**Examples:** Shown here are the arguments of a *printf* command and the resulting printout.
%a	Floating point hex	(“>%a<”, 187.2209) >0x1.767119ce075f7p7<
%b	Boolean	(“>%b<”, true) >true<
%c	Character	(">%c<", 'K') >K<
%d	Decimal integer	(">%d<", 1234) >1234<
%e	Scientific notation	(">%e<", 2341.45) >2.341450e+03<
%f	Decimal floating point	(">%f<", 2341.45) >2341.450000<
%g	Uses %e or %f whichever is shorter	(">%g<", 2341.45) >2341.45<
%h	Hash code (hex equiv)	(">%h<", 3451) >d7b<
%o	Octal integer	(">%o<", 112) >160<
%n	Inserts newline char	**Does not match up to an argument**
%s	String	(">%s<", "hello") >hello<
%t	Time and date	(“>%tr<”, cal) >08:23:46 PM<
%x	Integer hexadecimal	(">%x<", 1022) >3fe<
%%	Inserts percent sign	**Does not match up to an argument**
All of these except %n and %% have upper case versions that cause the printout to be done in uppercase letters.		

Table AD-1 Format Specifiers and their meanings

Flag	**Meaning**
-	Left justification. (Default is right justification.)
#	Varies as applied to different format specifiers. %e# guarantees a decimal point. %x# causes a **0x** to be prefixed. %o# prefixes a zero.
0	Output will be padded with zeros.
space	Output will be padded with spaces (default).
+	Positive numeric output will be preceded by a plus sign.
,	Numeric values will include grouping separators (typically commas).
(	Negative numeric values will be enclosed within parentheses (minus sign is dropped). Has no effect on positive numbers. An argument of (“>%0(6.1f<” ,37.478) results in >0037.5< An argument of (“>%0(8.1f<” ,-37.478) results in >(0037.5)<

Table AD-2 Format flags and their meanings

1. These suffixes are to be appended to the %t specifier (see Table AD-1 above). For example, %tr would give the time in 12 hour hh:mm:ss AM/PM format.
2. The arguments for a %t specifier must be of type Calendar, Date, Long or long.
3. Produce a Calendar object with *Calendar cal = Calendar.getInstance();*

Suffix	**Meaning**
a	Abbreviated weekday name
A	Full weekday name
b	Abbreviated month name
B	Full month name
c	Date and time string date formatted as hh:mm:ss timeZone year
C	First two digits of year
d	Day of month (01 – 31)
D	month/day year
e	Day of month (1 – 31)
F	year-month-day
h	Abbreviated month name
H	Hour (00 – 23)
i	Day of year (001 – 366)
I	Hour (01 – 12)
k	Hour (0 – 23)
l	Hour (1 – 12)
L	Millisecond (000 – 999)
m	Month (01 to 13)
M	Minute (00 – 59)
N	Nanoseconds (000000000 – 999999999)
p	Locale equivalent of AM or PM (lowercase)
P	Locale equivalent of AM or PM (uppercase)
Q	Milliseconds from 1/1/1970
r	hh:mm:ss AM/PM (12 hour format)
R	hh:mm (24 hour format)
s	Seconds from 1/1/1970 UTC
S	Seconds (00 – 60)
T	hh:mm:ss (24 hour format)
y	Year without century (00 – 99)
Y	Year with century (0001 – 9999)
z	Offset from UTC
Z	Time zone name

Table AD-3 Time/Date suffixes

Appendix AE… javaDoc

What is javaDoc?

Generally, javaDoc is the technique used to produce standard **web-page based documentation** (html files) for Java source code using embedded rems in that source code. Specifically, *javaDoc* is an executable file that is supplied as a part of Java. It generates such documentation.

To really understand what javaDoc is all about, go to the internet and view a final product of such documentation with the following web page:

http://java.sun.com/j2se/1.5.0/docs/api/java/lang/Math.html

This is Sun's standard way of documenting a .java file. Notice all the links between the various pages and sections. Documentation for your own programs will look just like this, and it is up to you as to how much detailed information you wish to give.

So, how do we produce such documentation? The first step is to properly comment your source code as the following sample class demonstrates. We will be examining each section with regard to meaning and syntax:

```
/**This class permits the storage and retrieval of all variables necessary to describe a linear function (a line).
 * The special cases of vertical and horizontal lines are handled. For example, the method getYvalue is
 * meaningless if field vert is true. When there is the potential for such meaningless data, test the values of
 * boolean fields vert or horiz first.
 * @author Charles Cook
 * @version 2.03
 */
public class LinearFunction implements LinearFunct
{
   /**Use this constructor if the line is not vertical and if slope and y-intercept are known.
    * @param slope is the slope of the line and will be assigned to field m.
    * @param yIntc is the y intercept and will be assigned to field b.
    */
   public LinearFunction(double slope, double yIntc)
   {                    }

   //…other constructors not shown…

   /**Finds the root of the function (its x intercept).
    * @throws ArithmeticException if field horiz is true.
    * @return field b if field horiz is true. Return field xIntc if horiz is false.
    */
   public double getRoot( )
   {                    }

   // …. other methods not shown ….

   private double m; //slope
   private double b; //y-intercept
   private double xIntc;

   /**true if line is vertical, false otherwise.*/
   public boolean vert;

   /**true if line is horizontal, false otherwise. */
   public boolean horiz;
}
```

First, let's examine the following section:

```
/**This class permits the storage and retrieval of all variables necessary to describe a linear function (a line).
 * The special cases of vertical and horizontal lines are handled. For example, the method getYvalue is
 * meaningless if field vert is true. When there is the potential for such meaningless data, test the values of
 * boolean fields vert or horiz first.
 * @author Charles Cook
 * @version 2.03
 */
public class LinearFunction implements LinearFunct
```

Uses a special "bock rem":
The first thing to notice is that this is a "block rem". Typically, a block rem uses the delimiters "/*" and "*/". In order for javaDoc to recognize the block, the beginning delimiter must have **two** asterisks, "/**". The asterisks between "/**" and "*/" are not necessary; however, they are typically included as in the above vertically aligned fashion so as to give a nice, organized appearance. These block rems are always placed **immediately above** what they describe, and the beginning lines generally describe the feature being commented. Notice in this example that the class as a whole is described in a general overview.

Special tags:
Next, we notice two special **tags** that are each preceded with "@". In this case they are for the *author* and *version*. These tags are optional and can be omitted if desired.

The resulting section of the web page for the section of sample code above is:

Package **Class** Tree Index Help

PREV CLASS NEXT CLASS FRAMES NO FRAMES All Classes
SUMMARY: NESTED | FIELD | CONSTR | METHOD DETAIL: FIELD | CONSTR | METHOD

Class LinearFunction

```
java.lang.Object
  └LinearFunction
```

All Implemented Interfaces:
LinearFunct

```
public class LinearFunction
extends java.lang.Object
implements LinearFunct
```

This class permits the storage and retrieval of all variables necessary to describe a linear function (a line). The special cases of vertical and horizontal lines are handled. For example, the method getYvalue is meaningless if field vert is true. When there is the potential for such meaningless data, test the values of boolean fields vert or horiz first.

Version:
2.03

Author:
Charles Cook

Now let's take a look at the block rem just above the constructor:

```
/**Use this constructor if the line is not vertical and if slope and y-intercept are known.
 * @param slope is the slope of the line and will be assigned to field m.
 * @param yIntc is the y intercept and will be assigned to field b.
 */
public LinearFunction(double slope, double yIntc)
```

The *param* tag:
Again, the first line provides a general description, but then we notice a new tag, *param*. As before, *param* is preceded by "@" as are all tags. Each occurrence of @param describes one of the parameters passed to the method being documented. The resulting section of the web page produced by this section of sample code is:

Constructor Summary
`LinearFunction(double root)` Use this constructor if the line is vertical and x intercept is known.
`LinearFunction(double slope, double yIntc)` Use this constructor if the line is not vertical and if slope and y-intercept are known.
`LinearFunction(double x1, double y1, double x2, double y2)` Use this constructor if two different points on the line are known.

If the second link is clicked the following section of the web page is displayed:

Constructor Detail

LinearFunction

```
public LinearFunction(double slope,
                      double yIntc)
```

Use this constructor if the line is not vertical and if slope and y-intercept are known.

Parameters:
`slope` - is the slope of the line and will be assigned to field m.
`yIntc` - is the y intercept and will be assigned to field b.

Finally, we take a look at the section of code just above method *getRoot( )*:

```
/**Finds the root of the function (its x intercept).
 * @throws ArithmeticException if field horiz is true.
 * @return field b if field horiz is true. Return field xIntc if horiz is false.
 */
public double getRoot( )
```

The *throws* and *return* tags:
Notice that two new tags are used here, *throws* and *return*. They respectively document exceptions that this method might throw and what is returned by the method. If this method accepted parameters it would also have been appropriate to have included *param* tags.

The section of the web page corresponding to this latest sample code is:

Method Summary	
`double`	`getRoot()` Finds the root of the function (its x intercept).
`double`	`getSlope()` Returns the slope of the line if it exists; otherwise, return 0.
`double`	`getXvalue(double y)` If field horiz is false this method receives parameter y and substitutes it into the linear function.
`double`	`getYvalue(double x)` If field vert is false this method receives parameter x and substitutes it into the linear function.

Clicking on the top link yields the following section of the web page:

Method Detail

getRoot

```
public double getRoot()
```

Finds the root of the function (its x intercept).

Specified by:
`getRoot` in interface `LinearFunct`

Returns:
field b if field horiz is true. Return field xIntc if horiz is false.

Throws:
`java.lang.ArithmeticException` - if field horiz is true.

Notice on page AE-1 that the two public fields (state variables) are also to be documented. They also result in Summary and Detail sections in the html files.

Generating the documentation:
There are two ways to generate documentation web pages from your properly commented source code (.java files):

- From within your IDE. In BlueJ go to the *Tools* menu and then choose *Project Documentation | Regenerate*. This will both produce the web pages (html files) for all classes and interfaces in your project and then display them in a browser. The files are conveniently placed in a folder titled *doc* within the current project folder.

- Directly run the javaDoc.exe file that is included as a part of Java. Here are the steps:

- Bring up a console screen using the sequence *Start* | *Run* | *cmd* . This is typically a black screen with white letters and is known by various names such as "the DOS screen", "the command prompt", "the command line screen", etc.

  At this point we are going to issue a *cd* command at the command prompt (the location of the blinking cursor) so as to change the "current folder". This will make it possible for the computer to find the files it needs if we are "parked" in the folder in which those files reside. In other words, the "current folder" is where the computer will first look for files that we enter as part of a command line. The command *cd* means "change directory" (folder). At the command prompt, issue this command:

  ```
  C:\ > cd C:\YourFolder\YourProject Folder
  ```

  If all went well, you will see a new command prompt as follows:

  ```
  C:\ YourFolder\YourProjectFolder >_
  ```

  This indicates that you are, indeed, "parked" in the *YourProjectFolder* folder where your *YourFile.java* source file is located. Thus, when we issue a command that references *YourFile.java*, the computer will find it.

- Next issue the command:

  ```
  Path=C:\Program Files\Java\jdk1.5.0_04\bin
  ```

  This just insures that the computer will be able to find the javaDoc.exe file that is to be referenced in the next step.

- At the command prompt, issue this command:

  ```
  javaDoc –author,-version, -d docFolder *.java
  ```

  - The options *–author* and *–version* must be used;otherwise, *author* and *version* tags will be ignored.

  - The option *-d docFolder* is used in order to store the resulting html files in a different folder (in this example, a folder named *docFolder*); otherwise, the resulting html files will be stored in the current folder along with the original source files. This tends to produce undesirable clutter.

  - The *.java part indicates that **all** Java files in the current folder are to be documented. This is usually what is desired since the project may consist of several classes and interfaces, and it is desirable to have cross-links between the various html files produced. It is, however, possible to just document one source file. In that case, the syntax for this part would be something like:

    ```
    LinearFunction.java
    ```

Index

Printed in the United States
70678LV00003B/31-51